BOKO HARAM

BOKO HARAM
ISLAMISM, POLITICS, SECURITY,
& THE STATE IN NIGERIA

Marc-Antoine Pérouse de Montclos, Editor

Boko Haram: Islamism, Politics, Security, and the State in Nigeria
Copyright © 2015 by Marc-Antoine Pérouse de Montclos (Edt.). All rights reserved.

Apart from any fair dealing for the purpose of private study, research, criticism or review, as permitted under the Copyright Act, no part of this publication may be reproduced in any form, stored in a retrieval system or transmitted in any form by any means—electronic, mechanical, photocopy, recording or otherwise—without the prior permission of the publisher. Enquiries should be sent to the undermentioned address.

Tsehai books may be purchased for educational, business, or sales promotional use. For more information, please contact our special sales department.

African Academic Press
a Tsehai Publishers imprint
Loyola Marymount University
1 LMU Drive, UH 3012, Los Angeles, CA 90045

www.tsehaipublishers.com
info@tsehaipublishers.com

Paperback ISBN 10: 1-59907-097-9 | ISBN 13: 978-1-59-907097-1
Hardcover ISBN 10: 1-59907-098-7 | ISBN 13: 978-1-59-907098-8

First USA Edition: 2015 | Originally published early in 2014 under the West African Politics and Society (WAPOSO) Series by the French Institute for Research in Africa / Institut Français de Recherche en Afrique (IFRA-Nigeria), based at the University of Ibadan and at the Ahmadu Bello University, Zaria and the African Studies Centre in Leiden.

Publisher: Elias Wondimu
Typesetting: Samuel Taye; Copy Editor: Rachel Miskei
Cover Design: Endrias Zewde

Library of Congress Catalog Card Number
A catalog record for this book is available from the Library of Congress.

British Library Cataloguing in Publication Data
A catalogue record for this book is available from the British Library.

10 9 8 7 6 5 4 3 2 1

Printed in the United States of America

Los Angeles | Addis Ababa | Oxford | Johannesburg

Dedicated to all of the victims of conflict.

CONTENTS

Foreword
by Gérard Chouin. xi
Introduction
by Marc-Antoine Pérouse de Montclo. xv

PART I ▍ WHAT IS BOKO HARAM?
SOME EVIDENCE AND A LOT OF CONFUSION

1. The Message and Methods of Boko Haram
   by Kyari Mohammed   3

2. Boko Haram and its Muslim critics: Observations from Yobe State
   by Johannes Harnischfeger   33

3. Traditional Quranic Students (*almajirai*) in Nigeria:
   Fair Game for Unfair Accusations?
   by Hannah Hoechner   71

4. Christian Perceptions of Islam and Society in Relation to
   Boko Haram and Recent Events in Jos and Northern Nigeria
   by Henry Mang   97

5. Framing and Blaming: Discourse Analysis of the Boko Haram
   Uprising, July 2009
   by Portia Roelofs   127

PART II ▍ BOKO HARAM AND THE NIGERIAN STATE:
A STRATEGIC ANALYSIS

6. Boko Haram and Politics: from Insurgency to Terrorism
   by Marc-Antoine Pérouse de Montclos   155

7. Boko Haram and the Evolving Salafi Jihadist Threat in Nigeria
   by Freedom Onuoha   183

8. By the Numbers: the Nigerian State's Efforts to Counter Boko Haram
   by Rafael Serrano and Zacharias Pieri — 223

9. Body Count and Religion in the Boko Haram Crisis: Evidence from the Nigeria Watch Database
   by Gérard Chouin, Manuel Reinert, and Elodie Apard — 247

A Chronology
by Manuel Reinert and Lou Garçon — 275

ANNEXES

1: The charter of Jama'at Ansar Al Muslimin Fi Bilad al-Sudan, broadcast on Internet on 18 January 2012
   translated by Mathieu Guidère — 285

2: One of the First Videos of Ansaru, Available on 1 June 2012
   translated by Nathaniel Danjibo — 296

3: Islam and Western Education in Nigeria: Between Accommodation and Confrontation
   by Marc-Antoine Pérouse de Montclos — 303

4: Islam and Political Parties in the Sudan
   by Marc-Antoine Pérouse de Montclos — 306

Contributors Bios — 311
Index — 315

FIGURES & TABLES

FIGURES

1.1: Map of Sharia-Compliant States and the Boko Haram crisis in Nigeria
4.1: The divisions of CAN (Christian Association of Nigeria)
7.1: Hypothetical organisational structure of Boko Haram under Abubakar Shekau
7.2: Locations of Boko Haram's attacks and suicide bombings in Nigeria

TABLES

7.1: Samples of suicide bombing modes mounted by Boko Haram (June 2011–Nov 2012)
8.1: Comparison of militants and security forces killed in selected conflicts
8.2: Comparison of arrests with kills
9.1: Faith affiliation of deceased victims in the Boko Haram crisis (2009–2012)
9.2: Relative proportion of Muslims and Christians recorded during the 1952 and 1963 censuses and projected onto the 2013 administrative map of Nigeria
9.3: Low-end estimate of percentage of Muslims in selected states
9.4: Minimum and maximum estimated % of Muslims in states affected by the Boko Haram crisis
9.5: Estimation of the percentage of Muslim and Christian believers among the civilian victims labelled as "faith unknown" in the Boko Haram conflict
9.6: Estimated faith affiliation of deceased victims in the Boko Haram crisis (2009–2012)

FOREWORD

This is the first volume entirely dedicated to the analysis of a violent confrontation which has escalated in north-eastern Nigeria since the mid-2000s, between federal forces and an Islamic sectarian movement which gradually transformed into a radical jihadist armed rebellion. Commonly known as "Boko Haram", the movement was unknown to most people outside Maiduguri before 2009, when federal forces launched a military offensive against its headquarters. Extremely violent, the crackdown eventually resulted—in addition to several hundred victims hastily buried in mass graves—in the transformation of a limited in scale but well-structured Islamic sectarian movement into an underground, clandestine armed organisation with possible connections to the ever-changing jihadist scene in Africa and beyond.

Writing about Boko Haram is a difficult task, as researchers have very limited access to first-hand information. Indeed, foreign and national researchers find it almost impossible to conduct fieldwork in north-eastern Nigeria, where their security cannot be guaranteed. Recently, as the core of the conflict has seemed to be moving away from Maiduguri, capital of Borno, to the confines of Nigeria, the shores of Lake Chad and along the Cameroonian border, available information on the conflict has become even scarcer.

Such difficulties contrast with the pressing demand of the Nigerian public and the international community alike for intelligible analyses of the situation. Nigeria is the demographic and ideological centre of gravity of a very large part of West and Central Africa. The area we know today as northern Nigeria has long been a source of new ideas and knowledge that fed Islamic practice, thinking, and teaching far beyond its colonial borders. As such, the violent, poorly-managed, spiralling confrontation between the Federal Republic of Nigeria and a seemingly well-entrenched, widespread, armed Islamic movement can generate only considerable anxiety among regional stakeholders, who fear the general unrest of a large part of West and Central Africa.

The response of the academic community to such pressing demands has been largely disappointing, simply because the context is unfavourable to the production of reliable knowledge. The fear of violence and reprisals against scholars living in exposed areas, the ideological biases or political correctness which paralyse many channels of thought when dealing with Islam and terrorism, and the lack of available data— all have contributed to a relatively repetitive and shallow academic production on the Boko Haram crisis.

In this volume, edited by a leading French specialist on Nigeria, we have attempted to adopt an original standpoint in publishing a limited number of essays which, taken together, are an attempt to renovate the way we produce scholarship on such an underground movement. We have brought together a large variety of scholars, many of them related to the French Institute for Research in Africa (IFRA-Nigeria) in a one way or another, from Nigeria, France, Germany, the UK, and the US. Some immersed themselves in fieldwork a few years ago, when this was still possible, and brought back outstanding data on northern Nigeria that can no longer be collected today. Others used discourse analysis or existing data on violence in Nigeria in ways never attempted before. Some are well-known scholars in the field, while others have signed here their first scholarly publication.

Far from being an univocal assemblage of papers, the book fosters debate in constructive ways. With this book, we hope to be able to stimulate new scholarly discussions on the fast-replicating emergence across the Sahelian belt of a series of movements that cannot be satisfactorily described only in simple terms as violent, terrorist, or jihadist. For a movement such as Boko Haram to mutate from a sectarian group splitting away from the Izala movement to a full-grown rebellion threatening the integrity of the most powerful state in West Africa, you need more than religious fanatics, violent Salafist ideology, and intolerance. The ingredients that fuel the fire spreading across north-eastern Nigeria are yet to be fully described. Some are to be found within the existence of a political elite used to buying off the settlement of insurgencies and social crises and incapable of responding to a new type of threat, ideological in nature, otherwise than through the use of blunt force. Other elites among security forces also hide their own secret agendas, as sustained violence legitimates accrued budgets and assists them in securing new lucrative markets for themselves, in ways inherited from the pre-1999 era.

This book is not a cookbook. All the ingredients of the crisis are not identified, and it does not pretend to provide recipes to solve current issues. It merely offers a variety of glimpses into the Boko Haram phenomenon and fosters a better and more nuanced understanding of a crisis that threatens to destabilise a large part of Africa, and into the way we discuss it. Boko Haram has redefined the way jihadists challenge the post-colonial state in Africa. The probabilities are high that this model will soon be exported outside Nigeria. This book is timely.

Gérard Chouin
Assistant Professor of History
College of William & Mary
Virginia, USA

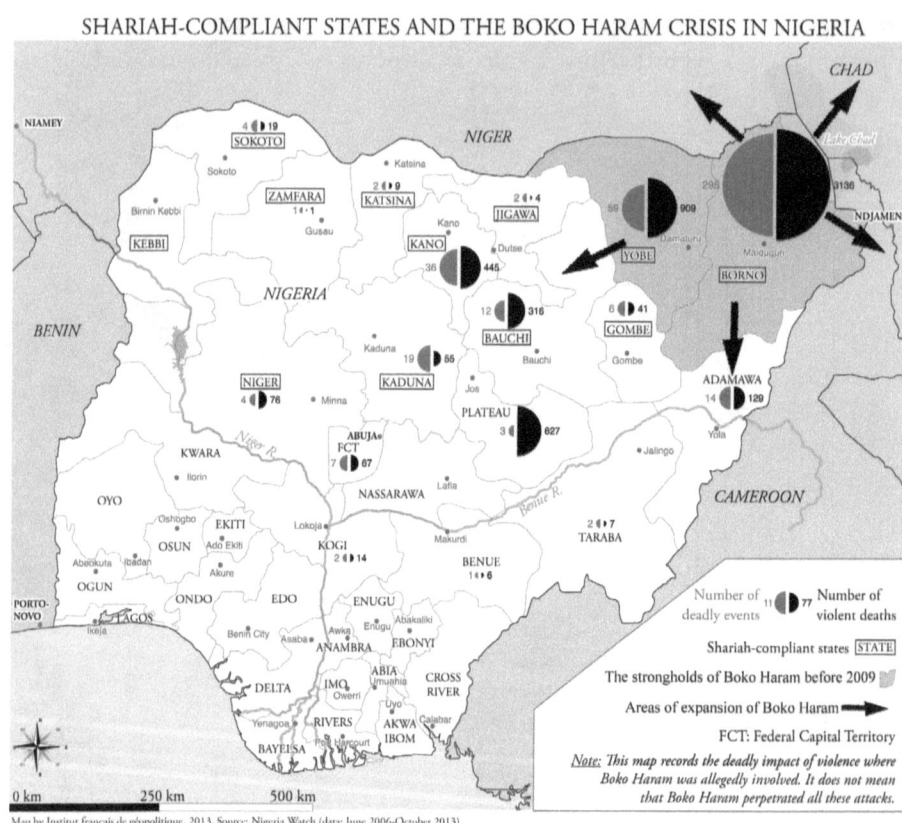

Figure 1.1 Map of Shariah-complaint States and the Boko Haram crisis in Nigeria

INTRODUCTION

As I write this introduction, Boko Haram is making the headlines. Paradoxically, it is seen in the media as clandestine and invisible, according to Nigerian President Goodluck Jonathan, who said he would not negotiate with "ghosts". The sect of Mohammed Yusuf was not always famous, however. When I began to investigate the so-called Taliban on the Niger–Nigeria border in 2005, no academics had written anything on Boko Haram. At that time, security analysts focused on violence in the oil-producing Niger Delta, and very few paid attention to a marginal group of extremists in remote Borno and Yobe states.

Since then, the sect has become a fashionable topic of research as well as an international issue. More so than the Maiduguri uprising of July 2009, the attack on the UNDP office in Abuja in August 2011 attracted much attention. Thus, a considerable number of articles on Boko Haram are now being written in the field of security studies. Many of them speculate on an Al-Qaeda franchise in Nigeria and possible links with AQIM (Al-Qaeda in Islamic Maghreb) in Mali.[1] Some even suggest that the US should fund the Qadiriyya and Tijaniyya brotherhoods to counter radical Islamism (Hill 2010). Such articles are oriented towards policy making. Accordingly, they make recommendations on the way to fight terrorism in the Nigerian context (see for instance Waldek & Jayasekara 2011; Aghedo & Osumah 2012; Forest 2012; Onuoha 2012; Idowu 2013; Sampson 2013). But they do not investigate Boko Haram from a political, sociological, religious, and anthropological, academic perspective.

Hence the necessity for a different type of analysis. Written by Nigerian, French, British, German, and American contributors, this book is the first of its kind. It not only offers different perspectives from northern and southern Nigeria, but also combines fieldwork and theory, qualitative and quantitative analysis. Moreover, it is not just another monograph study on Boko Haram; rather, the following chapters investigate how radical Islamism destabilises the

Nigerian state and challenges its secularity. In a pluralistic society, the jihad of Boko Haram raises many fears regarding Shariah, freedom of religion, the clash of civilisations, and the prospect of a civil war with Christians. Yet, all these issues are usually oversimplified in the rhetoric of the war on terrorism.

Shariah, for instance, is a whole way of life for Muslims. It should not be reduced to criminal law. Likewise, jihad is first and foremost an internal spiritual struggle, rather than a holy war against Christians (Cruise O'Brien & Coulon 1988; Westerlund & Rosander 1997; Levtzion & Pouwels 2000; Vikør 2005; Soares 2007; Hefner 2011). As for freedom of religion, it is often understood by legal practitioners as a right to follow a rite, to preach, to express religious beliefs in public, and, more generally, to be allowed to build a church, a mosque, or a temple. However, argues the French philosopher Rémi Brague, it is also the freedom to enter... or to leave a religion (AED 2013: 13). It is the right to convert, to be an atheist, or to dissent within a religion, drawing the limits to a core doctrine, up to "excommunication", anathema, and apostasy.

In this regard, Boko Haram is above all a challenge to mainstream Islam in Nigeria. The sect tells the story of a dissent and a fight between Muslims. So, it would be misleading to understand Boko Haram as a struggle to convert Christians to Islam. From its very beginning in the late 1990s, the sect mainly aimed to enforce a strict form of Shariah law. It began to target Christians at a much later stage, since 2009. In other words, the classical views and fears about a Nigerian war between religions reveal a very poor understanding of the doctrine and the fundamental drivers of Boko Haram. The secretive, mysterious, and stunning nature of the sect does not help either.

In fact, analysts do not even agree on the name of the group. Followers of Mohammed Yusuf see themselves as the "People Committed to the Propagation of the Prophet's Teachings and Jihad" (*Jama'atu Ahlis-Sunnah Lidda'awati Wal Jihad*). Boko Haram, explains Andrea Brigaglia, is only a nickname which "captures all the stereotypes that have daily currency in islamophobic discourses": obscurantism, primitivism, and the essentialist ferocity of Muslims (2012: 38). Moreover, specialists contest the meaning of *Boko Haram*, which is often translated as "Western education is a sin". According to Roman Loimeier, for instance, 'sin' is a Christian concept that does not exist in Islam, and the Arabic term *haram* should be translated as "forbidden", with a meaning of shame attached to it (2012). *Boko*, adds linguist Paul Newman, does not come from English and never meant 'book'; it refers rather to a sham, a fraud, and the Western type of education, *karatun boko* in Hausa (2013).

Another challenge is to find reliable and relevant evidence on Boko Haram. Since 2009, the volatile security environment makes it very difficult to access Borno and Yobe states in order to conduct interviews and cross-check oral testimonies. The problem is also to analyse the sketchy material on the sect: writings, audio and video recordings, communiqués, and so on. Mohammed Yusuf's only book is an important source, but authors do not agree on the date of its publication—sometime between 2005 and 2009. As for public statements, few researchers have attempted to use them as primary data (for an exception, see Eveslage 2013). Many communiqués of Boko Haram in Hausa or Arabic are not properly and fully translated by the media. As a result, their analyses are sometimes misleading. Professor Ricardo Laremont, for instance, claimed that in 2010 the head of the sect, Abubakar Shekau, pledged allegiance to AQIM leader Abdelmalek Droukdel, when actually he expressed his solidarity only with jihadist fighters in northern Mali (2011: 245).

The same problem applies to Ansaru, the dissident group of Boko Haram, whose self-proclaimed spokesman, Abu Ja'afar, had to send an email to correct distortions in the translation of their video in the Nigerian newspaper *Desert Herald* on 1 June 2012 (McCaul 2013: 16). The controversy concerned the fate of Christians, who were indeed a prime target of Ansaru—unlike those of Boko Haram. To set the record straight, it was thus necessary to add in the Annexes to this book translations directly from Hausa and Arabic of the original video and charter of *Jama'at Ansar Al Muslimin Fi Bilad al-Sudan*, a.k.a. Ansaru, respectively by Nathaniel Danjibo (University of Ibadan) and Mathieu Guidère (University of Toulouse).

Regarding both Ansaru and Boko Haram, secondary sources and oral testimonies are also rather confusing. As a matter of fact, they often contradict each other. For instance, there are different versions of the burial of the Boko Haram victims of a car accident that led to a first clash with the security forces in June 2009 and, ultimately, to the uprising in July. At the time of the event, the press reported that the police shot at members of the sect but killed no one. Since then, however, some analysts refer to a number of fatalities during the burial, without providing any evidence so far.

Military propaganda and the war on terrorism have also contributed to blurring the line between reality and fantasy. Security is a profitable business, and some attacks have been credited to Boko Haram without clear evidence and with no judicial follow-up. Popular rumours have also played a role. The fear of jihad and a Muslim invasion of the South sell well in Nigerian and international media. In Europe, for instance, attacks on Christian minorities in the North often make the headlines, but the massacres of Muslim communities go underreported. The same bias exists within Nigeria, where the press is based mainly in the South. In other words, there is always a marked difference between oral interviews in the North and written material in the South. Narratives from the North and the South are conflicting and confuse the whole story (Adibe 2012).

Developed in the first part of this book, a major challenge is thus to understand what exactly Boko Haram is from the available evidence we have. Writing from the North-East, Mohammed Kyari brings an important insight in this regard, showing that the radicalisation of the sect of Mohammed Yusuf paralleled the brutality of its repression by Nigerian security forces. Both contributed to the escalation of violence, up to the emergence of Ansaru and a modern global form of terrorism. Of course, local politics also played a role. Writing from Yobe State, Johannes Harnischfeger analyses how Muslim clerics and politicians were deeply entangled in a "web of corruption" that linked villagers with the Nigerian administration. That might explain why Boko Haram did indeed enjoy some popular support. Yet the doctrinal vision of Mohammed Yusuf was so extreme that it had very little appeal. In fact, Boko Haram divided and weakened the Muslim community.

Such views obviously contradict current stereotypes on jihad, forced conversion, imported terrorism, and a Muslim invasion of the South. Using the case of Kano, for instance, Hannah Hoechner argues that there is no evidence to substantiate the claim that Quranic students (*almajirai*) are the "foot soldiers" of Boko Haram. There is no predisposition to terrorism, only prejudice against the poorest elements of society. As for Henry Mang, he analyses Christian perspectives from Plateau State, a place where recurrent fighting with Muslim minority communities also exacerbates stereotypes, misunderstandings, hard feelings, and the rhetoric of the "clash of civilisations". The perception of "Islam's bloody corridors", he writes, changes according to various Christian schools of thought, with a vast spectrum from conservative to liberal views. In the same vein, Portia Roelofs shows that competing discourses over the meaning of the Boko Haram uprising in 2009 are characterised by different conceptions of the state. In the media, some argue for a government that should provide development and order, but others emphasise the state's secular role in containing expansionist Islam and helping mainstream Islam to control deviant sects.

Hence, the issue is not only to know what Boko Haram is, but also to understand what it stands for. In the second part of this book, we analyse the relationship of the sect to the ruling class and investigate how the fear of terrorism has transformed the political game. I argue that, despite its religious background, Boko Haram is political in nature because it contests Western values, challenges the secularity of the state, and reveals the corruption of a system that relies on a predatory ruling elite. Yet, its leaders have never actually proposed a political programme to establish a caliphate and govern Nigeria according to Shariah law. In this regard, Boko Haram is first and foremost a challenge to a divided *ummah* that never succeeded in setting up a party to play the democratic game and contest elections with a religious programme instead of resorting to violence as an alternative channel for reform.

Writing from the National Defence College in Abuja, Freedom Onuoha then focuses on the international context of the global Salafi Jihadist ideology rather than on local dynamics. He shows that the professionalisation and the radicalisation of the sect now pose significant threats to sub-regional security, beyond Nigeria. In his view, the audacity of Boko Haram reflects the weakness of the Nigerian state and its inability to build government legitimacy, to deliver public goods, to strengthen moderate Islam, and to implement a robust programme on countering ideological support for extremism and terrorism. By the same token, Rafael Serrano and Zacharias Pieri, from the University of South Florida, focus on the brutality of the JTF (Joint Task Force) and its inability to contain the sect and conduct a coherent strategy in an asymmetric war. In their chapter, the authors show that Nigeria ranks highest in terms of the ratio of militant to security force deaths compared with other counter-insurgency operations, in Northern Ireland, Colombia, and Chechnya. Their quantitative investigation also reveals that the ratio between arrests and killings has increasingly shifted towards killing, with a corresponding rise in abuses and collateral damage amongst civilians.

In the final chapter, Gérard Chouin, Manuel Reinert, and Elodie Apard examine the targeting of Christians by Boko Haram. They first caution us against a quick reading of the body count. It is often difficult, they explain, to identify victims and perpetrators. In addition, the faith of most victims remains unknown. As a result, it is extremely perilous to discuss the relative percentage of victims amongst Muslims and Christians. The authors did not find any reports about Boko Haram attacks against Christians before the crisis of July 2009. They had to combine demographic studies and a careful analysis of fatalities recorded in the Nigeria Watch database up until December 2012 to provide some of the most refined tools available so far to discuss such a sensitive issue. Their findings suggest that the majority of the victims—around two thirds—were Muslims. Although it cannot be denied that Christians have been subjected to targeted attacks from Boko Haram militants since July 2009, their conclusion challenges the common wisdom on the crisis as a war between religions.

Notes

1. See for instance the papers of Sean Gourley, Valarie Thomson, and Shannon Connell in the special issue of *Global Security Studies* Vol. 3, No. 3, 2012. Without any evidence, authors like Robert Crowley and Henry Wilkinson even connect Boko Haram to drug trafficking in Mali (2013). As for Michael McCaul *et al.*, they lobby so much for the sect to be listed as a Foreign Terrorist Organization that they quote Nigerian journalists of *Vanguard* (who never went to Mali) to pretend that Boko Haram participated in the attack on the Algerian consulate in Gao in 2012. In this same report, however, the US representatives admit that the explosives used by the group within Nigeria were not supplied by foreigners but probably stolen from mining operations in the Middle Belt or construction sites in Yobe (2013: 18). In any case, the French military of Operation Serval in 2013 did not find any Boko Haram training camp in northern Mali, just a few individuals hailing from Nigeria. Very few witnesses can actually testify to a physical link between the two organisations. UN Special Envoy to the Republic of Niger and Canadian diplomat Robert Fowler is one of them (2013: 398). He was kidnapped by AQIM in 2008 and saw in their ranks a single unidentified Nigerian, presumably from a Boko Haram cell in Kano. For an opposite view according to which Boko Haram is unlikely to be a trans-national organisation because the vast majority of its attacks and threats is directed against domestic targets, see also Eveslage (2013) and Pérouse de Montclos (2012).

References

Adibe, J. (2012), "Boko Haram: one sect, conflicting narratives", *African Renaissance: Terrorism in Africa* 9(1): 47-64.

AED, ed. (2013), *La liberté religieuse est-elle dans l'impasse? Retranscription des interventions de la conférence du 12 avril 2013 à l'Assemblée nationale*. Paris: Aide à l'Eglise en détresse.

Aghedo, I. & O. Osumah (2012), "The Boko Haram Uprising: how should Nigeria respond?", *Third World Quarterly* 33(5): 853-869.

Brigaglia, A. (2012), "Ja'far Mahmoud Adam, Mohammed Yusuf and Al-Muntada Islamic Trust: Reflections on the Genesis of the Boko Haram phenomenon in Nigeria", *Annual Review of Islam in Africa* 11.

Crowley, R. & H. Wilkinson (2013), "Boko Haram: une nouvelle menace en Afrique de l'Ouest". In: OCDE, ed., *Conflits liés aux ressources et terrorismes: deux facettes de l'insécurité*. Paris: Club du Sahel et de l'Afrique de l'Ouest, pp. 101-116.

Cruise O'Brien, D. & C. Coulon, eds (1988) *Charisma and Brotherhood in African Islam*. Oxford: Clarendon, p. 223.

Eveslage, B. (2013), "Clarifying Boko Haram's Transnational Intentions, Using Content Analysis of Public Statements in 2012", *Perspectives on Terrorism* 7(5): 47-76.

Forest, J. (2012), *Confronting the Terrorism of Boko Haram in Nigeria*. MacDill Air Force Base (Florida): The Joint Special Operations University Press, p. 178.

Fowler, R. (2013), *Ma saison en enfer: 130 jours de captivité aux mains d'Al-Qaïda*. Montréal: QuébecAmérique, p. 440.

Hefner, R., ed. (2011), *Shari'a politics: Islamic law and society in the modern world*. Bloomington: Indiana University Press, p. 329.

Hill, J. (2010), *Sufism in northern Nigeria: force for counter-radicalization?* Carlisle, PA: Strategic Studies Institute, US Army War College, p. 56.

Idowu, A.A. (2013), "Security Laws and Challenges in Nigeria: The Boko Haram Insurgency", *Journal of Applied Security Research* 8(1): 118-134.

Laremont, R.R. (2011), "Al Qaeda in the Islamic Maghreb: Terrorism and Counterterrorism in the Sahel", *African Security* 4: 242-268.

Levtzion, N. & R. Pouwels, eds (2000), *The History of Islam in Africa*. Oxford: James Currey, p. 591.

Loimeier, R. (2012), "Boko Haram: The Development of a Militant Religious Movement in Nigeria", *Afrika Spectrum* 47(2-3): 137-55.

McCaul, M. et al. (2013), *Boko Haram: Growing Threat to the US Homeland*, Washington DC, US House of Representatives, p. 39.

Newman, P. (2013), "The Etymology of Hausa *boko*", Nanterre: Mega-Chad Research Network, p. 13.

Onuoha, F. (2012), "From Ahlulsunna War'jama'ah Hijra to Jama'atu Ahlissunnah Lidda'awati Wal Jihad", *Africa Insight* 41(4): 159-175.

Pérouse de Montclos (de), M.-A. (2012), *Boko Haram et le terrorisme islamiste au Nigeria: insurrection religieuse, contestation politique ou protestation sociale?* Paris:

Centre d'études et de recherches internationales, Question de Recherche No. 40, p. 33.

Pérouse de Montclos, Marc-Antoine (2014), "Nigeria's Interminable Insurgency? Addressing the Boko Haram Crisis", London, Chatham House, Research Paper, 36p. http://www.chathamhouse.org//publication/nigerias-interminable-insurgency-addressing-boko-haram-crisis.

Sampson, I.T. (2013), "The dilemmas of counter-bokoharamism: Debating state responses to Boko Haram terrorism in northern Nigeria", *Security Journal* 26(3).

Soares, B., ed. (2007), *Islam And Muslim Politics In Africa*. Basingstoke: Palgrave, p. 288.

Vikør, K. (2005), *Between God and the sultan: a history of Islamic law*. London: Hurst, p. 387.

Waldek, L. & S. Jayasekara (2011), "Boko Haram: the evolution of Islamist extremism in Nigeria", *Journal of Policing, Intelligence and Counter Terrorism* 6(2): 168-178.

Westerlund, D. & E.E. Rosander, eds (1997), *African Islam and Islam in Africa*. London: Hurst & Co, p. 347.

Yusuf, M. (n.d.), *This is our faith and our Da'wa*. Maiduguri: Al Farba, p. 166.

PART I

WHAT IS BOKO HARAM?

Some Evidence & a lot of Confusion

1
THE MESSAGE & METHODS OF BOKO HARAM

Kyari Mohammed
Modibbo Adama University of Technology, Adamawa State, Nigeria

Boko Haram emerged from a tiny group of Islamist militants who openly challenged the Nigerian state between December 2003 and October 2004 without success. Thereafter, the remains of the group joined Mohammed Yusuf, who had returned from self-imposed exile in Saudi Arabia and proselytised in Borno until 2009, when the movement turned openly violent and was militarily suppressed. The group evolved, remodelled itself, and changed its tactics and strategies after a year's lull, essentially in response to the state's high-handed and brutal force. It moved from the *dawah* (proselytisation) phase marked by fiery speeches to the armed struggle phase in July 2009. Following a severe military crackdown and changing sub-regional dynamics in the Sahel, Boko Haram increasingly adopted the tactics of global Salafi Jihadist groups, including targeted assassinations, suicide bombings, and hostage taking. Although it emerged as a home-grown group with local grievances, developments in Mali and the international scene are increasingly drawing it into regional and global jihadi networks.

INTRODUCTION

Boko Haram is an Islamist movement which operated in north-eastern Nigeria and came to prominence in 2009. It was a fringe group under the leadership of Mallam Mohammed Yusuf, a fiery scholar resident in Maiduguri, who had not fully committed to violence before 2009. Through subtle and open harassment, Boko Haram was goaded into an open confrontation with the Nigerian state and violently suppressed in July 2009. Thereafter, it went underground, rebuilt, and resurfaced in October 2010 with a remarkable prison break at Bauchi and has since changed its tactics to targeted assassinations, drive-by shootings, suicide bombings, and massive deployment of improvised explosive devices (IEDs), vehicle-borne IEDs, and, lately, kidnapping and hostage taking.

The message of the movement has transformed over the years. Before 2009, it was characterised by the blistering speeches of its leader Mohammed Yusuf. This period was characterised by proselytisation (*dawah*), which included verbal assaults on secular authority, both traditional and modern–democratic. However, from 2010 onwards, Boko Haram committed itself to asymmetric warfare. Since its re-emergence the group had tried to mimic and adopt the tactics and strategies of global Salafist movements such as Al-Qaeda. Although heavily influenced by the message of Al-Qaeda and external developments, Boko Haram's grievances remained local at inception; however, there have been attempts to link local grievances to international developments in Mali and beyond.

Three distinct and yet overlapping phases can be discerned in the evolution of Boko Haram. The first phase is what can be termed the Kanama phase (2003–05), when a militant jihadist group waged war on the Nigerian state but was repelled with casualties on both sides. This group was led by Muhammad Ali, a Nigerian who was radicalised by jihadi literature in Saudi Arabia and was believed to have fought alongside the *mujahideen* in Afghanistan. The second phase began with the collapse of the Kanama uprising and ended with the suppression of Boko Haram proper in July 2009. This period, which can be dubbed the *dawah* phase, was devoted to intensive proselytisation, recruitment, indoctrination, and radicalisation of its members. This phase involved extensive criticism of the extant secular system; debates with opposing *ulama* (clerics) on the propriety or otherwise of Western education, Westernisation, democracy, and secularism; and unceasing criticism of the corruption and bad governance under Governor Ali Modu Sheriff (2003–2011) of Borno State, as well as the conspicuous consumption and opulence of the Western-educated elite in the midst of poverty. The third phase began with the 2009 suppression of the movement and the killing of its leadership in gory and barbaric form by Nigerian security agencies. Boko Haram went underground, re-organised, and resurfaced in 2010 with a vengeance. They not only targeted their perceived opponents, but indiscriminately attacked security officials, politicians associated with the ruling All Nigeria Peoples Party (ANPP) government in Borno State, and resorted to bombing high profile targets in Abuja such as the Nigerian Police Headquarters as well as UN offices, in June and August 2011 respectively. As the military crackdown intensified, they became desperate and more militant, thereby resorting to more desperate measures, which they had despised in the past, such as the burning of school buildings, attacking telecommunications base stations, the killing and kidnapping of foreigners, the slaughtering as opposed to shooting of opponents, and the killing of health officials at routine vaccination clinics, as well as the random shooting of pupils and teachers at schools.

This chapter attempts a reconstruction of the message and methods of Boko Haram before and after 2009, indicating the ebbs, flows, and nuances, as well as the contours of both the message and the methods. Boko Haram emerges as an amoebic group, continuously shaping and remodelling itself and its message to changing local and international developments.

HISTORICAL BACKGROUND

Nigeria's pre-colonial history and mode of incorporation into the global capitalist system under British colonial rule determined, to a large extent, the pattern and development of its geo-cultural and religious influences. The northern areas of the country are predominantly Muslim due to centuries of contact with Muslim North Africa through trans-Saharan trade, the agency of the Kanem-Borno empire prior to the nineteenth century, and the Sokoto Caliphate since the 1804 jihad. In contemporary times, modern means of mass communication and globalisation have opened up the country to foreign influences at an incredibly rapid rate. The southern part of the country is predominantly Christian, with a substantial Muslim population. This is partly due to prolonged contact with European influences dating back to the fifteenth century. However, there are substantial and vibrant minorities and animists in both regions. Colonial policies of divide-and-rule reinforced perceptions of North–South separateness, thereby not only blocking the emergence of a pan-Nigerian movement against colonial rule, but also fossilising the differences and separateness. The emergence and consolidation of a tripodal regional structure and ethno-regional political parties in the late 1940s solidified these positions. These regional identities and policies continue to shape Nigerian politics and governance to this day (Osaghae 2002).

Muslim identity and thought in Nigeria derive from the Sufi brotherhoods of Qadiriyya and Tijaniyya, primarily as a result of the historical role of the Kanem-Borno and Sokoto caliphates in the spread of Islam. The Sufi orders and the *Izalatul Bidi'a wa Ikhamatis Sunnah* (People Committed to the Removal of Innovations in Islam; hereafter Izala) are the two dominant contemporary Muslim foci of identity. The disdain towards and fear of *boko* (Western education) arose from its historically close association with the colonial state and Christian missionaries. This also suited colonial educational policy well, as the British had no intention of widespread education anyway. The aim of colonial education, particularly in northern Nigeria, was to maintain the existing status quo by "imparting some literacy to the aristocratic class, to the exclusion of the commoner classes" (Tukur 1979: 866). By the 1930s, colonial education had produced a limited cadre of Western-educated elite, who were conscious of their education and were yearning to play a role in society. Mainly children of the aristocratic class, the type of education they received was "different from the traditional education in their various societies, and this by itself was enough to mark them out as a group" (Kwanashie 2002: 50). This new education enabled them to climb the social and economic ladder over and above their peers who had a different kind of education, Quranic education. This was the origin of the animosity and distrust between the traditionally educated and Western-educated elite in northern Nigeria. Though subordinate to the Europeans, these educated elite were perceived as collaborators by their Arabic-educated fellows. Thus the antagonism towards Western education continues in many northern Nigerian communities, which have defied government campaigns for school enrolment to this day. Mohammed Yusuf simply resurrected and built on an existing historical narrative.

EVOLUTION OF BOKO HARAM

The first open challenge to government authority in this area was by a tiny group of people who withdrew from the urban landscape of Maiduguri to rural Kanama in the Yunusari local government area of Yobe State in north-eastern Nigeria in December 2003. They referred to themselves as the "Nigerian Taleban" [sic]. Their choice of rural Kanama as camp was made with an eye for military details. This site was carefully chosen for its remoteness and defensibility. The Kanama camp was forested and ensconced between two bodies of water near the Nigeria–Niger border. Trenches were dug and camouflaged across the only two access roads from Kanama and the exit road to Niger Republic, and sandbags were used to reinforce the defences.[1] The militants then launched attacks on police stations and government buildings and generally wreaked havoc on the Yunusari, Tarmuwa, Borsari, Geidam, and Damaturu local government areas of Yobe State between 21 December 2003 and 1 January 2004.

Between January and September 2004, this tiny group resurfaced and terrorised the inhabitants of Damaturu, the Yobe State capital and Damboa, Bama, and Gwoza in the neighbouring Borno State, attacking police stations and attempting prison breaks (Cook 2011: 10). They finally took a last stand atop the Mandara Mountains, from where they were dislodged by the Nigerian military using artillery shells (Cook 2011: 10). In October 2004, they took 12 policemen hostage in Kala Balge and not much was heard of the captives for a long time.

Members of this group were mostly young people in their twenties. This was a very diverse group, which also included females assigned domestic chores such as cooking and fetching firewood and water. Some of them were children of notable public figures, including a nephew of the then serving Governor of Yobe State, a son of the secretary to Borno State government, and five children of a local wealthy contractor.[2]

Mohammed Yusuf was neither an active physical participant nor a prominent figure at Kanama.[3] However, he shared the same ideology as the group. The remainder of those who survived the Kanama misadventure joined Mohammed Yusuf upon his return from exile in Saudi Arabia in 2005 to swell the group. The survivors of Kanama became the hawks within the *Yusufiyya* movement. Muhammad Ali, the leader of this incipient group, was in part responsible for initiating Mohammed Yusuf into militant jihadi ideology and world view.[4] Yusuf's conversion from the mainstream Islam prevalent in his area of operation to the fringe Islamic movement, which he nurtured and led, occurred *c.* 2005. Even though Muhammad Ali was the dominant influence in the indoctrination of Mohammed Yusuf, it was the years under Sheikh Ja'afar Mahmud Adam that radicalised as well as apparently legitimised the *dawah*. This largely accounts for the sense of betrayal and the stupendous energy expended in attempts to dissuade Yusuf from his new-found ideology and chosen course by very prominent Wahhabi scholars such as Ja'afar Mahmud Adam, Sheikh Muhammad Abba Aji, and Imam Ali Gabchiya. Mohammed Yusuf usually agreed with Sheikh Ja'afar on the shortcomings and baselessness of his position in private disputations but reverted to his original position as soon as he conferred with his followers.[5]

THE *DAWAH* PHASE

The period between the Kanama fiasco and the violent suppression of Boko Haram in July 2009 may be referred to as the second or *dawah* phase. Mohammed Yusuf returned from his self-imposed exile in Saudi Arabia after a rapprochement with the state, brokered by Borno State deputy governor, Adamu Shettima Dibal, and Sheikh Ja'afar Mahmud Adam, during the 2005 pilgrimage in Mecca, Saudi Arabia. According to Sheikh Ja'afar, Mohammed Yusuf had assured them that he was not a party to the Kanama uprising and swore never to espouse such violent jihadi ideology.[6] This was the basis upon which Mohammed Yusuf was permitted to return to Nigeria, where he continued to preach in and around Maiduguri. At this time and up to the July 2009 crushing by the Nigerian state, the *Yusufiyya* movement had no official name for itself.[7] It referred to itself as *dawah*, identified its mission as a return to the *Ahlus Sunnah wal Jama'a* (Adherents to the *Sunnah* and the Community of Muslims), and referred to its members as "brothers". The first reference to its current preferred name of *Ahlus Sunnah liddawa'ati wal Jihad* came in the aftermath of the Bauchi prison break in September 2010 (ICG 2010: 36 & n; Adamu 2012: 32-3).

The *dawah* is a major feature of radical Islam in the Muslim world. It is, in the words of Emmanuel Sivan:

> [an] Islamist term which denotes a combination of propaganda, education, medical and welfare action—and its practitioners. Yet the *da'awa* has an importance beyond that of being a possible cradle for violence. It is bringing about change in many Muslim societies, and sometimes plays a role—albeit indirect—in politics. (2003: 27)

Mohammed Yusuf had adopted the *dawah*, a major plank of Islamic jihadi strategy, very early in his peripatetic career. The narratives of the movement and the counter narratives were all developed at this stage in the evolution of the movement.

THE NARRATIVES OF BOKO HARAM

The message of Boko Haram, as outlined by Mohammed Yusuf, derived from and fed into the extant discourse and ideology of Islamism worldwide. Boko Haram narratives were framed within the radical Islamic discourse with which Mohammed Yusuf had become conversant. The main narratives of the sect, as outlined in Yusuf's sermons, were distributed widely throughout northern Nigeria via the Islamist media of choice (audio tapes) and through open-air sermons. The rejection of secularism, democracy, Western education, and Westernisation were the major planks of the narratives.

The rejection of secularism and the pursuit of its replacement by Shariah is a current in radical Islam that goes back to the fourteenth century Damascene scholar Ahmad Ibn Taymiyyah (1268–1328 CE). Ibn Taymiyyah wrote much on jihad and even elevated it above the Islamic pillars of fasting and pilgrimage (Bukay 2006: 4). Many modern scholars have used his *fatwas* (rulings) urging Muslims to rise against the Mongols to justify suicide bombings today (Bukay 2006: 4). However, the rejection of Western democracy partly derives from the same rejection of secularism but was further sharpened by the Saudi Arabian establishment's aversion to democracy's subversive element and the potential threat it could pose to the monarchy if unchecked. Therefore, Saudi scholars such as Sheikh Bakr Ibn Abdallah Abu Zaid (1944–2008) consistently attacked democracy and the freedoms it flaunted as anti-Islamic. Incidentally, none of Yusuf's opponents in the various debates took him up on the issue of democracy, therefore making its un-Islamic nature look settled. They all concentrated on the issue of Western education, Westernisation, and the propriety or impropriety of working for government institutions.

The *Yusufiyya dawah* was built around a close-knit group of followers, who believed in the justness of their cause and offered unalloyed loyalty to their leader. Mohammed Yusuf believed in what he preached and constantly exhorted his followers that the road will be rough and tough, and only a select few who persevere and are rightly guided by Allah will make it. In a sermon delivered on 30 June 2006, he said:[8]

> In this *dawah* we agreed that we are going to suffer like Bilal[9] was dragged on the ground, just like Ammar Ibn Yasir[10] was tortured, just like a spear was thrust unto Summayyah's vagina.[11] These are trials we are awaiting ... These are the hurdles we want to cross. Anyone who dies in the process goes to Paradise. This is our *dawah*.

He prepared the minds of his followers for possible consequences of their decision thus:[12]

> In the process they will abuse you, call you names and some of you may even die. They will shoot some of you, and we will just pray "may Allah give you *aljanna*" [Paradise] and proceed without any qualms. Can we endure? We ought to endure. May Allah give us the will to endure? This is how our *dawah* is. Patience: this is what we need, brothers. And perseverance upon the truth. Allah is watching us. Victory is certain. What we lack are the helpers. We are not yet primed for victory, but we are working towards getting ready for victory. This is what we are looking for, brothers. This is an incipient *dawah*, but it cannot be crushed. It cannot be killed. If we really stand by what the Prophet says we should stand by, even if we die in the process, this *dawah* will continue—even after a hundred years. Once the truth comes out, you[13] are in trouble.

The main planks of Yusuf's narratives were framed, though not exclusively, around the following issues or variants of them: (1) the concept of *taghut* (idolatry), including secularism, democracy, and partisan politics; (2) Western education and Westernisation; (3) working for an un-Islamic government; and (4) repudiation of the charge of Kharijism levelled against them by the local *ulama*, especially his former colleagues in the Wahhabi group in Borno. The fight with the local Borno Izala in the run-up to the 2009 crisis was extremely acrimonious, but is outside the scope of this chapter.

The concept of *taghut* and its rejection and replacement by Shariah is a current in radical Islamic discourse that goes back to Ibn Taymiyyah, the scholar after whom the *Yusufiyya* named their mosque, *Markaz Ibn Taymiyyah*.[14] Ibn Taymiyyah was a puritan Salafi scholar, who strove to ensure Islam's adherence to Shariah, eradicate alien innovations, and rejuvenate correct Islamic thought and practice. Ibn Taymiyyah's ruling on the Mongols has infused radical Islamic movements from Hassan al-Banna to Osama bin Laden (Euben & Zaman 2009). Mohammed Yusuf was heavily influenced by Ibn Taymiyyah, as seen by the copious references to him in his only book (Yusuf 2009a) and his sermons.

Quoting copiously from Ibn Taymiyyah, Mohammed Yusuf describes *taghut* (idolatry) as any form of executive, legislative, or judicial function derived from a secular constitution rather than from Islamic Shariah law. This is at the root of his opposition to secularism, democracy, and partisan politics as practised in Nigeria, and it led him on a collision course with Nigerian authorities on several occasions, culminating in the 2009 crisis. As far as he was concerned, fidelity to the constitution of the Federal Republic of Nigeria and subjecting oneself to the institutions created by it amount to unbelief.

> Those who formulate evil laws in their parliaments have made themselves partners to Allah, whether or not they feel it, whether or not they agree to this or disagree, whether or not they meant it ... Those who follow the legislative [sic] system and agree to take their cases to these courts are in agreement with *taghut* and are idolaters. (Yusuf 2009a: 66)

Even the symbolic bowing to the mace in the legislature did not escape Mohammed Yusuf's censure, who insisted:

> Parliamentarians and members of assemblies have combined between [sic] them making themselves gods and ascribing partners to Allah. This is because their mace is their object of worship in various ways such as bowing to it, subjecting themselves to it, loving it and using it as a symbol of *shirk* [apostasy], as they do not pass any bill or make decisions without it. [Without the mace] such decisions are unacceptable and has [sic] no legal backing. (2009a: 67)

Therefore, in Mohammed Yusuf's conception, anyone who superintends or abides by the laws and regulations within Nigeria's secular system is an unbeliever *simpliciter*. This was the cause of the protracted and often acrimonious debate with the Izala in the run-up to the 2009 violence.

The rejection of Western democracy derives from the same rejection of secularism but was further sharpened by the Saudi Arabian establishment's aversion to democracy's subversive streak and the threat it posed to the Saudi monarchy if unleashed. Saudi scholars such as Sheikh Bakr Ibn Abu Zaid consistently attacked democracy and the freedoms it flaunted as anti-Islamic. Mohammed Yusuf was heavily influenced by the writings of Saudi-based scholars such as Bakr Ibn Abu Zaid, Sheikh Abdul Aziz Ibn Abd-Allah Ibn Baaz (1910–99), and Sheikh Muhammad al-Amin ash Shanqiti (1907–73). As mentioned before, all of Yusuf's opponents side-stepped the issue of democracy being un-Islamic, thereby making the issue appear incontestable or settled.

For the same reason that a government not based on Shariah is illegal, serving such a government is also illegitimate. Yusuf said:

> Our call refuses employment under the government which does not rule by what Allah has revealed such as the French law, the American law, the British law or any other constitution or system that goes against the teachings of Islam and negates the Qur'an and Sunnah. (2009a: 111)

The legality or otherwise of Western education (Hausa: *boko*) and of serving in government became the main points of contention and debate with the Izala preachers. Yusuf was categorical that *boko* and serving the extant government were abhorrent and could lead to unbelief. When pressed to the wall in the debates with Isa Ibrahim Ali Pantami (Pantami-Yusuf 2006) and Idris Abdul Aziz Bauchi,[15] Mohammed Yusuf was definitive that they are *haram* ("forbidden"). Among types of knowledge which he decreed as *haram* are the physical and applied sciences, which deal with subjects such as Darwinism, evolution, and rainfall.

The rejection of Western education and Westernisation were the twin pillars which defined the movement. There exists a strand of anti-Western education views in Islamist discourse, but its trenchant manifestations are relatively new. Many prominent leaders of the Islamist movement in other parts of the Muslim world, such as Sayed Qutb (1906–66) and Hassan al-Banna (1906-49) in Egypt and Abu'l-Al'a Mawdudi (1903–79) in Pakistan, were trained in modern secular institutions and not traditional madrassahs (Euben & Zaman 2009: 10).

The aversion to Western education was derived in part from local conditions in northern Nigeria, and in part from the views of Saudi scholars, including Sheikh Bakr Ibn Abu Zaid. When asked what his views on Western education were in the debate with Sheikh Isa Pantami, Mohammed Yusuf responded thus:

> There are three perspectives on knowledge in Islam. The first is knowledge which is in line with what the Quran and the *Hadith* taught. The second perspective is where such knowledge differs with what the Quran and the *Hadith* contain. The third is a neutral perspective—which neither contradicts nor supports the Quran and *Hadith*; for as the Prophet said in a *Hadith* relating to People of the Book—"If they bring to you anything agreeable to the Quran, accept it; but if they bring anything that contradicts Islam, reject it; and if they bring anything that neither contradicts nor supports the Quran, it is your choice to accept or reject it." Well, this is the perspective I accept. If any form of knowledge is to be pursued for its sake, not following the structure of any government form of education, then I have my own reservations. (CD, Pantami-Yusuf Debate, 2006)

Mallam Yusuf is clear about the colonial origins of Western education. He argues:

> Western education is the body of knowledge that came to us through European colonialists, and includes medicine, technology, geography, physics and so on. And of course the English language. They can all be used if they do not clash with the teachings of the Prophet Mohammed (may the peace and blessings of Allah be upon him), and we can teach these subjects to our own children in our own schools, so long as they do not contradict Islamic teachings. If they do, then we should discard them. (CD, Pantami-Yusuf Debate, 2006)

There are some subjects, such as geography, geology, and sociology, which Mohammed Yusuf categorically says are forbidden (*haram*).

> I have a book that discusses the knowledge of geography, geology, and sociology. These branches of knowledge are not knowledge but full of unbelief. Even those studying it are aware if they are fair to Allah, except if they haven't studied Islam. If you have read geography, you'll know that in geography there is danger. If you have studied Islam, you'll know, whoever you are, that in sociology there is danger. (Yusuf tape, 30 June 2006)

An unrepentant and fiery Yusuf insisted that Western education amounts to unbelief:

> We are ready to debate any one on this creed. Western education is destructive. We didn't say knowledge is bad but that the unbelief inside it is more than its usefulness. I have English books in my possession which I read regularly. I didn't say English amounts to unbelief but the unbelief contained therein and the polytheism inside. In the process of becoming educated, you become a *mushrik* (idolater). This is our only fear ... Destruction is destruction, whoever it comes from. Because it is the white man that brought it, does it amount to civilisation? Yes, our own is traditional, as you call it, but yours is 'shirkasiation'.[16] (Yusuf tape, 30 June 2006)

The charge of Kharijism, levelled against them by the local Izala group, was the most painful and apparently distasteful to Boko Haram. The spirited attempt to repudiate this charge was perhaps the main reason that compelled Mohammed Yusuf to write his book *Hazihi Aqeedatun wa Minhaju Da'awatuna*.[17] Both the charge and the repudiation did not seriously enter the debates, since most of the debates took place in 2006, three years before the allegations became public knowledge. The allegations of Kharijism emerged in the debates and audio-taped responses in the run-up to the July 2009 eruption of violence in Maiduguri. It is remarkable to note that the charge of Kharijism was mainly a local affair.

However, the ease with which they label other Muslims as unbelievers, the lack of distinction between sin and unbelief, the quarrelsomeness and predisposition to easily kill for even minor infractions—all these mirror Khariji inclinations.

By early 2009 Mohammed Yusuf had openly attacked the local Izala *ulama* for hobnobbing with the corrupt and kleptocratic government of Governor Ali Modu Sheriff of Borno State. Yusuf had on numerous occasions addressed Governor Ali Sheriff as *taghut* and condemned the excesses of the government as un-Islamic and autocratic. The *ulama* that were patronised by and in the good books of the government were equally chastised for serving the *kuffur* (non-believing) government. Essentially, for this reason the local Izala, led by Mallam Bashir Mustafa (alias Kashar'ra), dubbed Boko Haram as Kharijite, especially because they easily label any sinner an unbeliever. The characterisation as Kharijites legitimised their killing. Thus, many scholars, but especially Bashir Kashar'ra, openly called on the state to exterminate them.[18]

The repudiation of this charge of Kharijism was the subject of many sermons and a book. Mohammed Yusuf says in the preface to *Aqeedatun*:

> When I saw some people talking about us and our call attempting to relate us to some beliefs—which Allah knows we are innocent of—such as al-Khawarij, Shi'ite, Quraniyun, or some secret groups ... I set out to explain our belief and method of call/propagation because this is what explains the way for us and for anyone who wants fairness for himself and for others.
>
> I have entitled the book "This is Our Belief and Method of Call", and in it attempted to explain what we believe in regarding Allah, His Angels, Books, Messengers, the Last Day, destiny (good or bad). I explained in it that we are together with Ahl al-Sunnah wa al-Jama'a [mainstream Islam] in the principles of belief and method of worship and conduct and Shariah. This is social justice: that a person expresses himself and his belief, conduct and method of his predecessors. (Yusuf 2009a: 10)

And he chastised his opponents for the wrong accusations thus:

> It is not fair for someone else, unrelated to him, who has neither heard from him nor read his book or treatise, to relate him to any belief that person wants. This is injustice and it is unfair and Islam prohibits it. (Yusuf 2009a: 10)

In spite of spirited attempts to dispel the accusation of Kharijism, it has stuck. Developments since the killing of Mohammed Yusuf and the targeted killing of Muslim *ulama* and many others seem to have confirmed Boko Haram's Kharijite tendencies.

Government service was another interesting area of discourse on which disagreement with the Izala came to the fore. Yusuf likened working for an un-Islamic government not based on Shariah as amounting to unbelief. This was the source of a polemical debate with the Izala, who, even though better armed with proofs and evidence, could neither convince Mohammed Yusuf nor dissuade his members because of the widespread disenchantment with government. The important issue was not who had better reasoning but the appeal of the message. In this, Mohammed Yusuf had the upper hand because he was not only a gifted demagogue and persuasive debater, but the government was perceived by most citizens to be corrupt and insensitive.

In part because of their puritan views, Boko Haram have perceived Christians and those Muslims who do not share their world view as enemies, and therefore legitimate targets of attack. Boko Haram has been attacking Christians and their places of worship and creating social tension and disharmony between Christians and Muslims in the northern states of Nigeria, and between northerners and southerners. Some southerners perceive Boko Haram as a mechanism for Islamising the country. The leadership of the Christian Association of Nigeria (CAN) has also seen the insurgency as a ploy to impose Shariah law and Islam on the country. According to Human Rights Watch (2012: 44), Boko Haram attacked at least 18 churches and killed 127 Christians between 2010 and 2012. These figures may be understated, as a Christian leader told Human Rights Watch that, in Borno State alone, not fewer than 142 Christians were killed between 7 June 2011 and 17 January 2012 in what appears to be a "systematic plan of violence and intimidation" (HRW 2012: 44). The main aim of Boko Haram in killing Christians is to "start a full scale war between the Muslims and the Christians" (HRW 2012: 45). It seems their ploy has worked, as CAN seems to blame Muslims and Muslim leaders for the actions of Boko Haram.

While Boko Haram undoubtedly attack Christians, there are rogue elements acting on their own that are also attacking Christians using Boko Haram-style tactics. The case of Lydia Joseph and the "Miya Barkate Eight" in Bauchi State indicate that some Christian elements also attack churches in the name of Boko Haram, especially in areas with a history of inter-religious violence, either to stir up discontent or to settle scores due to intra-religious disputes. On 29 August 2011, Lydia Joseph was apprehended while trying to burn St. John's Cathedral in Bauchi.[19] Similarly, on 9 January 2012, eight young men, all Christians, were apprehended attempting to bomb the Church of Christ in Nigeria (COCIN) at Miya Barkate in Bauchi State.[20] This could have successfully passed as a Boko Haram attack, and some Boko Haram "spokesman" might even have claimed responsibility if it had succeeded. In spite of the fact that the perpetrators were caught in the act, Rev. Lawi Pokti, the Bauchi State CAN chairman, absolved his men of responsibility. However, he confirmed that there was an argument within the church over the location of its headquarters between Tilden Fulani and Miya Barkate.[21]

The national leadership of CAN seems to fuel the crisis. Fortunately, Christian leaders in the North, especially Bishop Matthew Hassan Kukah and Bishop Josiah Idowu Fearon, have continuously called for restraint against reprisal attacks. Bishop Kukah condemned the "grand standing, demagoguery, rave and rant" by some religious leaders. He asked rhetorically:

> When Christians or Muslims claim self-defense, are they replacing the Commander-in-Chief of (all) the Armed Forces of Nigeria? Do these religious leaders who make such calls have a judiciary to try suspects, or a Barracks/Posts to hold suspects? Do these religious leaders believe they can resolve political and administrative problems of law enforcement and justice? Or are they calling on their people to take the laws into their hands? (Kukah 2012)

Like most issues in Nigeria, the Boko Haram insurgency has been politicised along ethnic, regional, and religious lines. The recent withdrawal of the Catholic Church from CAN may not be unconnected with the open partisanship and inflammatory statements of CAN President Ayo Oritsejeafor, who has fanned the embers of hatred rather than seeking solutions. The Catholic Church gave as its reasons for withdrawal the "polarizing statements of some Christian leaders" and the need to "promote Christian unity and peaceful coexistence with Christians and non-Christians alike", an obvious reference to the quarrelsome leadership of Oritsejeafor.[22]

THE DYNAMICS OF ISLAMIC RADICALISATION

The drivers of radicalisation of Islamic groups include both internal and external developments. Although the grievances of Boko Haram are largely local, its major influences have been foreign. The influential scholar that most shaped the thinking of Mohammed Yusuf, as mentioned earlier, was Ahmad

Ibn Taymiyyah. The basic message of radical Islam, whether in the Middle East, North Africa, or northern Nigeria, is the same: it is the duty of Muslims to revolt against and change apostate rulers and governments in order to help re-establish a proper Islamic state. The main differences among radical groups are in the methods and not the ideals.

Internal factors of Islamic radicalisation in Nigeria go back to the onset of colonial rule, when Islam became the focal point of opposition to the British take-over of the Sokoto Caliphate. British occupation of the caliphate began with the sacking of Bida in 1897 and was completed with the occupation of Sokoto in 1902. By 1903 all emirates had been conquered, even though there were still pockets of resistance. For the leadership of the caliphate there was the problem of how to respond to this new anomalous situation—by resistance, collaboration, or emigration—while for the British the problem was the difficulty of administering an Islamic society on the basis of a secular and non-Islamic ideology.

On the debate as to whether to collaborate or emigrate, the Gwandu jurist Ahmad Ibn Sa'id compared the situation in Sokoto to the Qaramanthian invasion of Mecca in 930 CE and the Mongolian invasion of Baghdad in 1258 CE and concluded that an interim compromise with the colonial state was possible as long as they did not interfere openly with practice of the faith. Collaboration with the British, he posited, did not amount to unbelief "as long as the resident does not himself become an unbeliever. It is disobedience if done voluntarily, but permissible if done under compulsion" (cited by Al-Hajj 1973: 162; See Adeleye: 1968). Thus, for most of the early colonial period a policy of non-cooperation, known as *taqiyya* ("dissimulation"), became the main pillar of resistance against colonial rule. After 1906, most emirs who had not been removed had grudgingly accepted their subordination.

In spite of the acquiescence of the emirs, the citizenry still remained sceptical of British intentions, and avoidance remained the preferred policy. This partly accounts for the disdain for Western education. The need to domesticate Islam and administer a Muslim society through indigenous institutions rather than by brute force was the most important consideration in the introduction of the colonial policy of indirect rule. The disdain for Western education is as old as the imposition of colonial rule, but the resort to violence to overturn it is entirely new.

The birth of the Wahhabi inspired Izala in 1978 under Sheikh Mahmud Abubakar Gumi (1922–92) was a major impetus in the radicalisation of Muslims in northern Nigeria. Although not anti-establishment, the Izala became critical of traditional rulers, of corruption in government, and of declining moral values of the society, without calling for a wholesale overthrow of the system.

The 1979 Iranian Revolution, which overthrew the Pahlavi dynasty and established an Islamic republic in its place in spite of US resistance, became another major source of Islamic radicalisation. It created the impression and instilled in many Muslim youths the possibility and practicability of using Islam as a vehicle for political and social transformation. The 1980s witnessed a proliferation of Iranian revolutionary literature in Nigeria, which inspired the Islamic Movement of Ibrahim El-Zakzaky. The revolutionary ideas of the Islamic Movement derived from Sayed Qutb's famous jihadi book *Al-Ma'alim fi'l-Tariq*, which has been rendered in English under the title of *Milestones* (1964) and which became a basic primer for its membership. Qutb's thesis of irreconcilable difference between Islam and *jahiliyya* (pre-Islamic unbelief) was central to shaping the group's thought. Many students who were radicalised in the Islamic Movement later on ended up in mainstream Sunni groups.

The introduction of Shariah law, with a full range of criminal law punishments, in Zamfara State and its whirlwind adoption by eleven other northern Nigerian states since 2000 accelerated the pace of radicalisation. The protagonists of Shariah created the impression that it would lead to a qualitative improvement in the lives of the inhabitants of Shariah states. However, the operation of Shariah as an adjunct to, and its subordination to, the secular constitution was anathema to radical Islamists, who now demanded a full complement of Shariah law as against the Zamfara model, which Boko Haram ridiculed and rejected. The inability of the Shariah states to implement the law in full led to the rejection of the Zamfara model of Shariah by Boko Haram, who insisted on a full Shariah or nothing. The imposition of full Shariah has remained a consistent demand by Boko Haram.

American foreign policy in the Middle East and especially its unalloyed support for Israel, along with the Israeli suppression of Palestinians, are important reasons for the radicalisation of Muslims in northern Nigeria. Nigerian Muslims are conversant with Islamic literature, which continuously condemns these actions. Closely related to this were the 11 September 2001 attacks on US soil and the reactions thereto, which also fed into an existing radicalisation channel. The militants of Kanama and Mohammed Yusuf were all aware of and incensed by the US invasion and occupation of Afghanistan and the declaration of a "global war on terror". These events and the war on terror were perceived as a war on Muslims and their religion—and this further fed into the radicalisation process (Mohammed 2004).

While these external factors fed into the radicalisation of Muslims, and especially those of fringe Muslim groups in northern Nigeria, the main drivers of radicalisation leading to violent conflicts are primarily internal. The retreating state and declining economic fortunes of the 1980s, consequent upon structural adjustment programmes, had further pauperised Nigerians. These conditions and the mismanagement of the limited resources and crass display of wealth by the ruling class, in the midst of widespread poverty, are all conducive to anger and frustration, which are expressed in religious terms. The poor existential condition of people in the northern states of Nigeria, in both relative and absolute terms, has been documented (Mohammed et al. 2000). These factors, coupled with a large, unemployed youth population, feed into a vicious circle of poverty.

In times of crisis and uncertainty, Muslim societies naturally react in religious terms. Indeed, Mohammed Yusuf's evangelism began in the form of a Muslim social movement: catering for orphans, widows, and the vulnerable. The excluded, especially the *almajirai* (itinerant students) who had flocked in large numbers to the urban areas owing to rural destitution, became a ready pool for recruitment and mobilisation. In difficult times, the vulnerable and excluded can be easily mobilised, especially by a movement such as Boko Haram, which preaches the brotherhood of all Muslims while attacking a system that has evidently excluded them as irreligious. This message has a natural appeal.

SECURITY AGENCIES AND THE ESCALATION OF VIOLENCE

The metamorphosis of Boko Haram from a *dawah* to an arms-bearing sect was in part the making of security agencies, which approached the situation as one of 'law and order' and responded as such, with disastrous consequences. There was no attempt to perceive the issues raised by the movement in its broader multi-faceted prism as political, social, and economic. The crisis in Borno State began over a contest for ownership of a place of worship with the Izala at Monguno in December 2008. Boko Haram members had been thrown out of Izala mosques as a result of a complete break with the Izala over the Izala's inability to dissuade Mohammed Yusuf from his firmly held convictions.

Owing to the close association between the two groups up to this period, and because they had worshipped together in the same mosques before then, the ownership of mosques became the subject of bitter disputes. In one such incident, while on their way to Monguno to reclaim a mosque from the Izala, 67 Boko Haram members, including Abubakar Shekau, were arrested and locked up at the Maiduguri prison by state authorities, apparently at the instigation of their rivals. Mohammed Yusuf vowed to recover the disputed mosque through due process.[23]

The security agencies serially mismanaged the crisis from the outset, and in the process pushed the movement to the extreme end of the spectrum. First was the setting up of the joint military operations, code named Operation Flush II, which tried to draw Boko Haram out for a fight by harassing members going to or returning from *dawah*, as they called their preaching activities. Restriction of movement of motorcycles at night and the attempt to enforce the use of crash helmets were all aimed at achieving this. The mandatory use of crash helmets by motorcycle riders, although a national policy, was not enforced in other places with the same zeal. In fact, the enforcement policy stopped once the movement was crushed in July 2009.[24]

Second was the onslaught on Boko Haram by Operation Flush II, and the shooting of its members at the Gwange cemetery in June 2009, which precipitated the violence at Maiduguri. Boko Haram members were going to bury their dead, who had died in a car crash, when security agents shot and wounded 17 of them. They were further provoked by being refused access to the wounded in hospital. This action was seen by Boko Haram as a declaration of war (Yusuf 2009b).

Third, the massive onslaught on the sect and the killing of its members and the extrajudicial killing of the sect leadership, including Mohammed Yusuf and other members, further radicalised members. Those who fled either went for further military training or went into hiding without renouncing their beliefs. These extrajudicial killings and the widespread dissemination of the video footage locally and its broadcast by the Al Jazeera cable satellite network further enraged members.

Once the sect was militarily crushed and their headquarters, the *Markaz Ibn Taymiyyah*, burnt and razed to the ground, the remainder of the leadership went underground while most members either fled or melted into the local population. The state compelled traditional rulers not to conceal Boko

Haram members in their domain and in the process many were identified and handed over to security agencies. However, lack of confidentiality within the security system and Boko Haram's intelligence network ensured that they got to know who gave information on them to state authorities. The first phase of resurgence was marked by targeted killings of ward and village heads that had collaborated with state security agents, prison officials whom they accused of torturing or poisoning their members in detention, prominent politicians of the ruling All Nigeria Peoples Party (ANPP) government of Borno State, and all security officials.

The successes recorded against security officers in urban warfare and the fear instilled in them and the general public seems to have further emboldened Boko Haram and cowed their opponents. The inability of the state to guarantee the security of citizens—in fact, their failure to defend even their own installations and officers—not only emboldened sect members, but had the effect of remobilising passive members into action. Thereafter, they used the cowed civilian population as a shield to perpetrate their activities. Anyone who challenged Boko Haram in the community was killed, and the state had no capacity to defend such people or identify and punish the culprits.

The tactics of Boko Haram and those of the military differed. While Boko Haram was, at least at inception, committed to not harming those who had not antagonised them and alerting people in areas where they intended to fight, the security agencies were known for their brutality in retaliation against the population for the actions of their opponents, especially where the agencies had incurred fatalities. The military Joint Task Force-Operation Restore Order (JTF) functioned like an army of occupation. Unable to distinguish Boko Haram members from unarmed civilians, they resorted to taking vengeance on the whole civilian population. This had the effect of alienating them from the community. In fact, the strategy of Boko Haram was to provoke the military by attacking and killing them, knowing full well that the military would kill defenceless citizens. This tactic has worked very well, such that local communities now openly affirm that Boko Haram, in spite of its excesses, is better than the military. The 19 April 2013 killing of at least 185 unarmed civilians and the burning of over 2,000 houses by the military, after their patrol vehicle was attacked and sustained fatalities at Baga in Kukawa local government area of Borno State, clearly demonstrate the pattern of military response.[25] Boko Haram will consciously provoke the military, knowing full well that the military will retaliate against the local population. According to an informant, Boko Haram says: "When we kill the big unbelievers, they will kill the lesser unbelievers."[26] The big unbelievers are military personnel, and the lesser unbelievers are the local population: Muslim or Christian.

There are numerous cases of documented atrocities by the JTF, including extrajudicial killings, arbitrary dragnet arrests, illegal and arbitrary detentions, arson, rape, and stealing (see Amnesty International 2012; HRW 2012).[27] The following incidents illustrate the pattern of military response in Maiduguri.

On 9 December 2010 soldiers stormed the Zannari zone of Maiduguri and arrested sixty men shortly after their patrol vehicle was attacked in the area.[28] Similarly, in the Jajiri ward of Maiduguri, Sheriff Bukhari recounts how "soldiers broke into homes waking people up, seizing money and cell phones" and lamented "it is unfortunate that the people deployed to protect us have turned against us".[29]

Following a skirmish between Boko Haram and security forces at the Kaleri ward of Maiduguri on 9 July 2011, security operatives killed more than forty people and underdeclared the number of those killed as only eight Boko Haram (*Tell*, 26 July 2011). Saudi and Habiba, widows of Mohammed Abdul, recounted how their husband was dragged out of his room and killed in cold blood (*ibid.*). Talatu, widow of Adamu Fulani, said soldiers not only killed her husband in the presence of his children but ransacked his room and stole N 250,000 (*ibid.*). Adamu Abdullahi, a staff member of the University of Maiduguri, was killed in the Kaleri incident in spite of his having identified himself to security officials.[30] In the Budum area of Maiduguri, 23 people were killed, the Budum market was burnt, and parked cars were sprayed with bullets when an IED planted by sect members exploded and injured three soldiers. There were numerous such incidents at Dala Alamderi, Bulum-Kuttu, and Baga Road Fish Market. The situation is similar in other settings, such as Damaturu, Potiskum, and Kano.

The Borno Elders and Leaders of Thought pressure group condemned these excesses and called for the withdrawal of troops from Maiduguri, but to no avail. They accused the JTF of "killing innocent young men and raping of married women and young girls by soldiers".[31] The JTF, not unexpectedly, denied all these allegations and insisted that all those "killed were members of the Boko Haram sect".[32] The JTF, through its spokesman Col. Victor Ebhalome, resorted to cheap blackmail by accusing all those alleging gross violations against them as "sponsors, sympathisers and members of the sect aimed at discrediting the task force so as to have a field day to operate".[33]

Aminu Sani, chairman of the Borno State branch of the Nigerian Bar Association, condemned the killings and called on the federal government to set up a judicial commission of inquiry to "probe the genocide and extrajudicial killings of innocent civilians". He also called for troop withdrawal.[34] Kashim Zannah, chief judge of Borno State, also deplored the extrajudicial killings and all attempts to infringe people's rights, no matter what the temptation. According to Justice Zannah (2011), "peace cannot be restored by means of injustices through departure from the rule of law and breach of due process", and he concluded that such actions can lead only to "hunting innocent persons, alienating the citizenry and aggravating the security situation". He ended rather prophetically, saying that "justice is the only route to enduring peace and security" because "injustice breeds insecurity" (Zannah 2011).

In January 2012, the federal government declared a state of emergency in 15 local government areas of four affected states, which gave security officials extra powers without legal encumbrances.[35] These emergency powers further emboldened the JTF, which had been accused of serious rights abuses. An unintended effect of the new military strategy of amassing troops in the urban areas is the export and escalation of the violence to rural areas where military presence is low. Most areas of northern Borno State are not under effective government control now, as Boko Haram move about and terrorise peasant farmers and herders unhindered. Local government functionaries have all abandoned their duty posts and taken refuge in the state capital owing to insecurity in the outlying provinces. Boko Haram have some toehold in the following ten local government areas of Borno State, far from government presence: Marte, Magumeri, Mobbar, Gubio, Guzamala, Abadam, Kukawa, Kaza, Nganzai, and Monguno.[36]

The security agencies have completely lost the hearts and minds war through high-handedness and brutality. The sentiment of the residents of Maiduguri and its environs is echoed by 60-year old Adamu Mohammed of Bulum-Kuttu: "We don't have a problem with Boko Haram; our problem is the police and the military that harass and kill our innocent people. They call every Muslim a Boko Haram".[37]

CHANGING TACTICS AND SHOPPING FOR CAUSES

Boko Haram changed its tactics, remodelled itself, and shopped for causes as the security forces continued to pummel them and seemingly diminished their capacity. Since mid-2010 their *modus operandi* has changed and they have become unpredictable. Old methods, such as the targeted killing of traditional ward and village heads, security officials, prominent politicians, and opposing *ulama*, continued unabated, but new fronts were also opened in the fight. They now targeted media houses and journalists, schools (including teachers and pupils), telecommunication base stations, and, recently, kidnapping of locals and foreigners.

The burning of schools was a new weapon employed by the group. A number of schools were burnt in the July 2009 violence in Maiduguri as symbols of government and Western education, which they abhor, along with police stations and other government buildings. However, the burning of schools in retaliation for the ill treatment of Quranic school teachers and pupils is a new development. The group insist they are attacking schools in retaliation for JTF atrocities. According to its spokesman, Abul Qaqa:[38]

> We attacked the schools because security operatives are going to Islamiyyah schools and picking teachers. We are attacking the public schools at night because we don't want to kill innocent pupils. Unless [Islamic school teachers] are allowed to be, we would be compelled to continue attacking schools.

However, the attack on schools, school teachers, and pupils has forced many schools to close down in Maiduguri since February 2013.

It seems Boko Haram is losing its initial focus as old members are lost and security forces close in on them. As the situation changed on the ground, Boko Haram changed its methods and style. Kidnapping, a style they had rejected and vehemently denied using, now became acceptable. They dissociated themselves from the kidnapping of Chris MacManus and Franco Lamolinara, two Europeans killed in a botched rescue attempt at Sokoto in March 2012. Up to this period, Boko Haram was not involved in kidnapping. According to its spokesman Abul Qaqa: "[W]e have never been engaged in hostage taking and it is not part of our style, and we never ask for ransom".[39] It seems an affiliate or a splinter group which operates in central and north-western Nigeria, or a criminal gang which is in the business for money, may have been responsible for the kidnappings.

There has been an upsurge in the killing and kidnapping of foreigners by Boko Haram since 2012, indicating a change of tactics arising from desperation. There are numerous such incidents in the north-east of Nigeria. These include the killing of road construction workers and Korean doctors in Borno and Yobe states, the kidnapping and subsequent killing of employees of a construction firm, Setraco, in Jama'are town of Bauchi State, and the kidnapping of the French family of Tanguy Moulin-Fournier, his wife, brother, and four children at Waza National Park in Northern Cameroon.[40] All these indicate both a change of tactics and further splintering of the movement into smaller groups, arising from internal and external developments.

The weakening of Boko Haram positions and the damage done to their capacity in Borno and Yobe states pushed them out to the outlying areas, out of reach of the military. Thus, the kidnapping and killing of foreigners may be another tactic to expose the weakness of the Nigerian state by showing its inability to protect both its citizens and foreigners alike. Besides, the kidnapping of Europeans is newsworthy and adds to their profile in Salafist jihadi circles. The Algerian incident, where foreign oil workers were rescued, albeit with a large number of casualties, seems to have sent signals that kidnapping may be an acceptable weapon among some jihadi groups.

THE ANSARU CHALLENGE

There has been tension both within the membership of Boko Haram and between it and outsiders over tactics and cruelty by some of its militants against the civilian population. The Kawar Maila killings, where 11 members were slaughtered for informing on their fellow members, and the tensions between members native to Borno, who can easily evade capture by melting into the local population, and non-natives indicate cracks within the movement. The issue of targeting non-combatants by Boko Haram has also worried some members. These tensions had been building up for a long time but came to the fore with the Kano attacks of 20 January 2012, when over 180 people lost their lives.

The formation of *Jama'atul Ansaru Muslimina fi Biladis Sudan* (Vanguard for the Protection of Muslims in Black Africa), which was announced on 26 January 2012, was both "a reaction to the loss of Muslim lives" as well as a desire for change of tactics by a splinter group within Boko Haram.[41] Ansaru is a splinter from the main body of Boko Haram and has its nucleus around northwest and central Nigeria, as distinct from the main body with its main strengths in the north-east epicentre of Boko Haram insurgency.

Ansaru shares the ideology and doctrines of Boko Haram, although there are differences in tactics. First, unlike Boko Haram, even from inception Ansaru committed itself to not harming innocent Muslims except in self-defence. Second, Ansaru condemns the killing of "innocent security operatives", a group which Boko Haram has attacked serially and with relish since July 2009. Third, Ansaru proclaimed itself the defender of Islamic interests all over West Africa and indeed Africa as a whole, as distinct from Boko Haram's localisation in the north of Nigeria.

Although Ansaru was newly formed, it had formerly existed and operated under different names. Apparently, it was the same group which had earlier called itself "Al-Qaeda in the Lands Beyond the Sahel", a group which had claimed responsibility for the kidnapping of Chris MacManus and Franco Lamolinara in May 2011. The targeting of foreigners and foreign interests was the main direction of Ansaru's development. As early as December 2012, the group warned France that it would target its citizens for "its ban on Islamic veil and its 'major role' in the planned intervention in Northern Mali".[42]

Ansaru also claimed responsibility for the kidnapping of seven construction workers in Jama'are in Bauchi State, which it said it had killed in retaliation for the anti-Islamic activities of European nations in Mali and Afghanistan. French military engagement and Nigeria's deployment of troops to Mali seem to have further excited a section of Boko Haram, which provided them an opportunity to present themselves as regional and global players.

CONCLUSION

The development of radical Islamist ideology in north-eastern Nigeria has drawn its inspiration from both internal and external sources. The external factors include the worldwide resurgence of radical Islam owing to the US global war on terror and the general decline in the living conditions in Muslim-majority countries, coupled with internal economic problems of urban destitution and rural decay in this part of Nigeria. A large pool of the *almajirai* and urban unemployed were conducive to the emergence of Boko Haram.

The state's inability to manage the crisis at inception and its stoking of the embers of discontent through serial mismanagement, coupled with an all-out military assault, all added to the conflagration. Massive military deployment and tactics akin to that of an army of occupation alienated the civilian population and worsened the state of insecurity. Although the spate of bombings has declined, the theatre of conflict has widened to encompass other outlying urban and rural areas, including Kano and Kaduna. The solution to the challenge posed by Boko Haram lies in an integrated holistic approach to addressing the issues raised. The state must also live up to its role of providing jobs and other basic amenities and guaranteeing the lives and property of the citizenry. The current approach of military force is unlikely to resolve the insurgency. The problem can only be solved through a negotiated settlement with moderate members of the group.

Notes

1. Interview: Anonymous, security officer who took part in the investigations at Kanama, 11 April 2010.
2. Nephew to Bukar Abba Ibrahim, Governor of Yobe State (1999–2007), now a serving senator; son of Abbagana Terab, secretary to the Borno State government; and five sons of Alhaji Kambar Adam. Interview: Anonymous, security officer who took part in the investigations at Kanama, 11 April 2010.
3. Mohammed Yusuf's role along with Abu Umar and Ibrahim Abdulganiyu was talent spotting, recruitment, and indoctrination of members; however, he escaped to Saudi Arabia and remained there throughout the uprising. Interview: Audu Maisaje, Maiduguri, 13 February 2010.
4. Interview: Ali Mowar, Maiduguri, 10 November 2009.
5. Interview with several Wahhabi scholars in Maiduguri between 2009 and 2011.
6. Sheikh Ja'afar Mahmud Adam, taped sermon on his relationship with Mohammed Yusuf, dated 6 June 2006. This tape was released by Mohammed Yusuf. However, the tape must have been released by Ja'afar earlier, probably in 2005. Copy in my possession.
7. This was the name by which they were known. They later adopted the name *Jama'atu Ahlus Sunnah Lidda'awati wal Jihad* (People Committed to the Removal of Innovation and Jihad), as against the popular but derisive *Boko Haram*, which they abhor.
8. Audio tape, dated 30 June 2006, in Hausa language. All translations are mine.
9. Bilal Ibn Rabah al-Habashi (580–640 CE), an African slave companion of the Prophet Mohammed, who endured serious torture upon his conversion to Islam but still remained steadfast.

10. Another convert and companion of the Prophet, who along with his mother, Summayyah, was tortured for his conversion.
11. Summayyah bint Khayyat, mother to the aforementioned Ammar Ibn Yasir. She did not survive the tortures and is considered the first Muslim martyr.
12. Muhamad Yusuf sermon, audio tape, dated 30 June 2006.
13. Reference to his adversaries, which at this time included Sheikh Ja'afar Mahmud Adam, the staunchest critic of Mohammed Yusuf in his lifetime.
14. Ibn Taymiyyah Centre.
15. This DVD was created in February 2008, and the debate may have taken place in January or February of the same year (Adamu 2012: 22).
16. Derived from *shirk*, the Arabic word for apostasy or unbelief.
17. Translated as "This is Our Belief and Method of Call" by A. S. Abdul-Mumini, who has graciously allowed me to use his translations, which are still in progress. Adamu (2012) translates the same work as "This is Our Manifesto and Our Path".
18. The Kharijites (Arabic: *Khawarij*, sing. *Khariji*), literally "those who went out", is a generic term for Muslim dissenters in the early history of Islam. They challenged the authority of Caliph Ali Ibn Abu Talib. They are usually known for their extreme position of declaring other Muslims unbelievers at the slightest transgression and thereby justifying their killing.
19. "Police arrest prostitute over alleged attempt to burn down church", *Vanguard News*, 30 August 2011. www.vanguardngr.com/2011/08/police-arrest-prostitute-over-allaged-attempt-to-burn-down-church [Accessed 23 April 2013].
20. "Suspects of church bombing moved to Abuja", *Daily Trust*, 1 March 2012. www.dailytrust.com.ng/index.php/news-news/9302-suspects-of-church-bombing-in-bauchi-moved-to-abuja [Accessed 23 April 2013].
21. *Ibid.*
22. "Nigerian Catholic Church 'Temporarily' Withdraws Membership of CAN", 23 January 2013. www.saharareporters.com/news-page/nigerian-catholic-church-'temporarily'-withdraws-membership-can [Accessed 23 April 2013].
23. Interview: Masta'a Monguno, 10 October 2010. Mohammed Yusuf vowed to revenge this unlawful act and urged his supporters to use the prison to proselytise.
24. The use of motorcycles has been banned in a number of urban areas, including Maiduguri, since June 2010. This is because of the ease with which Boko Haram used motorcycles as getaway vehicles after targeted assassinations or in planting IEDs.
25. "Bloodbath in Maiduguri: 185 killed as soldiers, Boko Haram clash", www.vanguardngr.com/2013/04/bloodbath-in-maiduguri-185-killed-as-soldiers-

boko-haram-clash/ [Accessed 23 April, 2013].

26. Interview: Anonymous, Maiduguri, 11 February 2013.
27. The atrocities of both Boko Haram and the JTF have been documented. See Amnesty International (2012), *Nigeria: Trapped in a Cycle of Violence*. London; Human Rights Watch (2012), *Spiraling Violence: Boko Haram Attacks and Security Force Abuses in Nigeria*. Chicago. See www.hrw.org.
28. *Newspublisher*, 27 December 2010.
29. *Ibid.*
30. At least four professors of the University of Maiduguri have been killed by Boko Haram in the last two years: Murtala Mohammed Aliyu (d. 4 November 2011) in Damaturu; Adamu Abdullahi (d. 9 July 2011); Mohammed Shettima Larduma (d. 28 November 2011); and Mohammed Murtala in Maiduguri (d. 31 March 2013). Meanwhile, Dr. Abba Kagu (abducted 26 February 2013) and Dr. Mohammed Mai (abducted 20 April 2013) have been kidnapped and are being held hostage, presumably by Boko Haram.
31. *Daily Trust*, 15 July 2011.
32. *Ibid.*
33. *Ibid.*
34. *Peoples Daily*, 15 July 2010.
35. The affected local government areas are the following: Maiduguri Metropolitan Council, Jere, Ngala, Bama, and Biu in Borno State; Damaturu, Geidam, Potiskum, Gujba, and Bade in Yobe State; Jos North, Jos South, Barkin Ladi, and Riyom in Plateau State; and Suleja in Niger State.
36. "Boko Haram taking over Northern Borno", *Weekly Trust*, 20 April 2013. www.weeklytrust.com.ng/index.php/top-stories/12338-boko-haram-taking-over-northern-borno [Accessed 22 April 2013].
37. *Tell*, 26 July 2011.
38. *Daily Trust*, 29 February 2012; Amnesty International (2012), *Nigeria: Trapped in the Cycle of Violence*, p. 17.
39. "Boko Haram Denies Kidnapping and Killing European Citizens Involved in Botched Rescue", *Sahara Reporters*, 9 March 2012.
40. The French family was released unharmed and returned to Paris on 19 April 2013.
41. *Vanguard*, 1 February 2012.
42. *ThisDay*, 24 December 2012.

References

Adeleye, R.A. (1968), "The Dilemma of the Wazir: The Place of the Risalat al-Wazir'ila Ahl al ilm Wa'l-Taddabur in the History of the Conquest of the Sokoto Caliphate", *Journal of the Historical Society of Nigeria* 4(2): 285-98.

Adamu, U.A. (2012), "Insurgency in Nigeria: The Northern Nigerian Experience", being the text of a paper presented at Eminent Persons and Expert Group Meeting on Complex Insurgencies in Nigeria, 28–30 August, at National Institute for Policy and Strategic Studies, Kuru, Nigeria.

Al-Hajj, M.A. (1973), "Mahdist Tradition in Northern Nigeria", PhD Thesis, Abdullahi Bayero College/Ahmadu Bello University, Kano.

Amnesty International (2012), *Nigeria: Trapped in a Cycle of Violence*. London: Amnesty International.

Bello, E. (2009), "Boko Haram Crisis: Crisis was not Religious—Gov. Sheriff", *Leadership Newspaper*, 8 August.

Bukay, D. (2006), "The Religious Foundations of Suicide Bombings Islamist Ideology", *Middle East Quarterly*, Fall, 27-36. Available at: www.meforum.org/1003/the-religious-foundations-of-suicide-bombings [Accessed 21 March 2012].

Cook, D. (2011), "Boko Haram: A Prognosis". James A. Baker III Institute for Public Policy, Rice University. 16 December.

Human Rights Watch (2012), *Spiraling Violence: Boko Haram Attacks and Security Force Abuses in Nigeria*. Chicago: Human Rights Watch.

International Crisis Group (2010), *Northern Nigeria: Background to Conflict*. Africa Report no. 168. 20 December.

Kwanashie, G.A. (2002), *The Making of the North in Nigeria, 1900–1965*. Kaduna: Arewa House.

Kukah, M.H. (2012), "Come Holy Spirit, Come Message of Pentecost", in www.ngrguardiannews.com/index.php?option=com content&view=article&id=87 318:come-holy-come-message-of-pentecost&&catid=175:kaleidoscope&itemid=702. 27 May. [Accessed 23 April 2013].

Mohammed, A.S., S.H. Adamu & A. Abba (2000), *The Living Conditions of the Talakawa and Sharia in Northern Nigeria*. Zaria: CEDDERT.

Mohammed, K. (2004), "Religion, Federalism and the Shariah Project in Northern Nigeria". In: E. Onwudiwe and R. Suberu, eds, *Nigerian Federalism in Crisis: Critical Perspectives and Poltical Options*. Ibadan: Programme on Ethnic and Federal Studies, University of Ibadan, Nigeria, 147-164.

Osaghae, E.E. (2002), *Crippled Giant: Nigeria since Independence*. Ibadan: John Archers.

Pantami and Yusuf Debate entitled *Muqabala kan Matsayin Karatun Boko da Aikin Gwamnati a Najeriya* (The Place of Western Education and Working for Government in Nigeria) took place on 25 June 2006 at Bauchi, apparently on the invitation of Isa Ali Pantami. It was conducted in Hausa language.

Qutb, S. (1964), *Milestones*. Cairo: [no publisher].

Sivan, E. (2003), "The Clash within Islam", *Survival*, 45(1): 25-44.

Tukur, M.M. (1979), "The Imposition of British Colonial Domination on the Sokoto Caliphate, Borno and the Neighbouring States, 1897–1914: A re-interpretation of Colonial Sources", PhD Thesis, Ahmadu Bello University, Zaria.

Yusuf, M. (2009a), *Hazihi Aqeedatun wa Minhaju Da'awatuna* [This is Our Belief and Method of Call]. Maiduguri.

――― (2009b), *Budediyar Wasika ga Gwamnatin Taraya*, [Open Letter to the Federal Republic of Nigeria, recorded on VCD]. 11 June.

Zannah, K. (2011), Speech delivered by Honourable Justice Kashim Zannah, Chief Judge of Borno State on the Occasion of the Ushering in of the New Legal Year and Commencement of Appeals Session for the Year 2011, 14 February, Maiduguri.

2

BOKO HARAM & ITS MUSLIM CRITICS

Observations from Yobe State

Johannes Harnischfeger
University of Frankfurt, Institute of African Studies

The campaign to transform state and society on the basis of Shariah was begun by Muslim politicians in 1999, when military rule ended and power shifted to the Christian South. Although the pious campaign was mainly a matter of political intrigues, it established a paradigm that still frames political debates. Few Muslims in the far north of Nigeria would openly question what the *imams* are preaching: that the will of God takes precedence over man-made laws and constitutions. Like most other Islamic organisations, Boko Haram refers to this principle. With its call for a consequent Islamisation, it seeks to achieve what Muslim politicians in the North have promised, but failed to deliver. This makes it difficult to denounce the aims of the rebels, and the Islamic establishment appears unable to formulate a coherent counter-paradigm. —My article will take a closer look at the disputes which Boko Haram has provoked among Muslims. In doing so, I will draw on recent observations in some rural communities in Yobe State. Mohammed Yusuf, the founder of Boko Haram, and Abubakar Shekau, its present leader, hail from Yobe; here and in neighbouring Borno, the insurgents enjoy some popular support.

Yet my impression is that Boko Haram's vision of a caliphate has very limited appeal. Most people do not want to live under a strict Shariah regime. However, Muslim critics of Boko Haram are themselves deeply divided. The two dominant religious organisations in north-east Nigeria, the Tijaniyya brotherhood and the Salafist Izala, cannot agree on an alternative model of an Islamic society which they might set against the orthodoxy of the militants. Concepts of divine justice are vague and contradictory, and there are no clear boundaries between moderate and radical Muslims. In order to appease Boko Haram, villagers suggested a more consequent application of Shariah by eradicating drinking and gambling and by placing females under stricter supervision. However, they have shown little interest in using the divine laws to reform the dysfunctional public administration. Most citizens, including Izala and Tijaniyya functionaries, are entangled in the web of corruption that links villagers with the local government administration. They complain about the hypocrisy of politicians, who do not obey the laws they profess, but resemble them as they break their religious obligations at will.

Keywords: Boko Haram, Shariah, Izala, Tijaniyya, Popular Discourses

RELIGIOUS POPULISM

What Boko Haram is fighting for—the Islamisation of state and society through a strict application of Shariah—was propagated by Hausa and Fulani politicians more than ten years ago. They suddenly declared that the moderate form of Shariah which had been in force in most northern states since Independence in 1960 was no longer acceptable: state governments should enact proper Shariah. Attempts to extend the competence of Islamic Law courts had long been central to the disputes between Muslims and Christians, and the political elites in the North knew that the introduction of harsher Islamic laws would spark violent conflicts. When 'Shariah clashes' in February and May 2000 killed an estimated 2,000 people, President Obasanjo appealed to the authorities in Zamfara, Kaduna, and other northern states to suspend the new legislation in order to prevent more bloodshed. Yet the political establishment in the Far North stood firm. After intensive consultations, the pro-Shariah line prevailed, and most political and religious leaders declared that a moderate form of Shariah was not compatible with their religious convictions: God's law must not be restricted to cases of inheritance, matrimonial affairs, and other civil matters, but had to be practised in full. In order to achieve this religious mission, some politicians went as far as demanding total commitment and self-sacrifice. Muhammadu Buhari, the most prominent politician in the Far North, assured his followers: "I can die for the cause of Islam",[1] and the Governor of Yobe State, Bukar Abba Ibrahim, added: "If necessary, we are prepared to fight another civil war. We cannot be blackmailed into killing Sharia".[2]

Buhari, Shagari, Balaraba Musa, and all the other big men who enlisted their support for the Shariah project knew that Governor Ahmed Sani of Zamfara, who had begun the process of passing strict Islamic laws, had done so for self-serving reasons. As one of Babangida's henchmen, with a lucrative position in Nigeria's central bank, Sani had become accustomed to living a life of luxury and lust. After the end of military rule, when he refashioned himself as an "apostle of Sharia",[3] he openly renounced his former life of sin and apologised for having stolen public money. But when asked whether he would repay the money that he had embezzled, he said no.[4] Campaigning on a Shariah ticket in 1999 had enabled him to oust a formidable contender: former National Security Adviser Lt. General Aliyu Gusau. Following Governor Sani's success, other politicians also depicted themselves as uncompromising fighters for the cause of Islam. Jumping on the Shariah bandwagon was, above all, a means to advance their political careers. Shariah, however, was also used to strengthen the position of the northern political establishment as a whole. After power had shifted to the South, northerners used Shariah as a "bargaining chip" to put pressure on the Christian president.[5]

The government of Zamfara promised that "all spheres of public life are being transformed into Islamic oriented institutions".[6] However, these transformations did not make the authorities any more responsive to the plight of the people. In some respects, the situation in Zamfara had even deteriorated: "Reports of forceful acquisition of land and other properties of the less-privileged by those in authority, particularly village and district heads, have reached [...] alarming proportion[s]".[7] As in other parts of Nigeria, poverty has increased while the ruling elites, behind a façade of Muslim piety, have continued to enjoy the way of life to which they are accustomed: "[W]e have formed a habit of sending our girlfriends to London and Paris to make their hair and do shopping in London and America. We steal the money from the oil".[8]

TURNING SHARIAH AGAINST THE ELITES

Young militants in Maiduguri or Kano have good reasons to hate the representatives of the state. Their rebellion is born out of poverty, illiteracy, and unemployment; it is a response to corruption and social neglect. Given the shocking disparities in wealth, analysts in the West have argued that government, in order to stop the violence, has to address the root causes of the crisis. It has to reach out to those it has alienated and offer them employment, better education, and other services to raise the standard of living. A top official in the US State Department, who was calling for political reforms, claimed that "[r]eligion is not driving extremist violence in Nigeria"; instead, he blamed "the underlying political and social economic problems in the north".[9] However, interpreting the rebellion as a protest against deteriorating living conditions is at odds with the statements of Boko Haram leaders, who insist on the religious motives of their insurrection: "[T]his is a war between Muslims and non-[M]uslims. [...] this is not a tribal war, nor is it [...] a war for financial gains, it is solely a religious war".[10] Commentators in Europe and North America, writing for a secular readership, have sought to make this war comprehensible by identifying poverty and social injustice as the real causes of the rebellion. However, it does not lead to a deeper understanding of Boko Haram (and Muslim resistance to it) when analysts leave aside that the rebels, when responding to the Nigerian crisis, seek a *religious* solution to it:

> The group's preaching—available on cassettes across the region—concerned almost exclusively detailed points of religious doctrine and what actions can and cannot be permitted within Islam. While this did include debates on the relations between democracy and Islam, it would be incorrect to think that Yusuf [the founder of Boko Haram] was a social reformer or was overly concerned with corruption. His concern was a pure interpretation of Islamic texts. (Crisis Group, *Northern Nigeria*, 38)[11]

For most Muslims in the North it makes sense to turn to religion in order to liberate themselves from decades of moral and economic decay. Secular institutions, which were brought to Africa by white colonisers, have failed, particularly in northern Nigeria, where citizens are disillusioned with Western ways of development. A vast majority no longer believes that democracy, human rights, and a market economy offer a way out. Nigeria's Fourth Republic was modelled along the lines of the US Constitution, but its citizens have not been able to make use of its democratic institutions to submit their rulers to public control: "Not a single one of those Northern governors has deemed it his duty to worry about [the] plight of the people".¹² The number of people living on less than 2 USD a day has increased, although the governors in the North (like their counterparts in the South) have received far more revenues from the federation account than in the late 1990s, under General Abacha, when a barrel of oil sold for 10 USD.

Since citizens have never found ways to control their rulers, they can only hope that politicians will submit at least to the authority of God. Theocratic rule is regarded as an alternative to democracy; it derives its attraction from the sense that Western concepts of modernisation have led to a dead end. While party democracy seems to encourage strife and ruthless competition, Shariah is conceived as a force that may check the excesses of the ruling class. The immutable law of God, which is the same all over the world, will be the yardstick by which all segments of the society, rich and poor, must be judged. Thus, the arrogant elite would be integrated into a moral community, in which rulers and ruled are united by a shared culture, as they had been in the mythical beginnings of Islam.

It was rumoured that the Sultan of Sokoto, like many other Muslim dignitaries, was unhappy with Shariah, but he could not openly declare that God's law should no longer be binding. At the height of the Shariah campaign, most political and religious leaders in the Far North supported the introduction of harsher Islamic laws, yet made sure that these laws were implemented only in a selective and half-hearted way.¹³ Boko Haram's militancy is, in part, a reaction to the cynical game of politicians who mobilised religious sentiments in the interests of their political ambitions. By posing as campaigners of an Islamic renewal, they have discredited themselves. To make matters worse, by declaring that their states must be run according to divine laws, they have empowered religious experts who can speak more competently about the will of God. This counter-elite has turned into a dangerous rival, because *imams*—especially those who stress their radical distance from the political class—have the capacity to mobilise the masses against the hypocrisy of the big men. One way of putting pressure on politicians is to insist that they abide by the standards of rectitude enshrined in the divine law. All sections of the *ummah* (the community of the faithful) had committed themselves to these standards when they insisted, against Christian pressure, on the necessity of living according to Shariah. Thus Shariah can be used against the same elites who propagated it. No prominent Muslim politician has dared to confront religious leaders by suggesting that the Shariah laws passed between 2000 and 2002 be scrapped. This makes it difficult for the Islamic establishment to denounce militants like Boko Haram, who are simply demanding what politicians promised but failed to deliver.

SHARIAH AS A DIVIDING FORCE

Ordinary Muslims are disillusioned with the selective form of Shariah implemented by politicians. However, the idea of Shariah, as depicted by *imams*, is still popular among them.[14] This does not mean that radicals like Boko Haram, who fight for an undiluted form of divine law, can count on widespread support. Most Muslims in the North do not want to live under a Taliban-like regime, although they find it difficult to formulate a counter-model when distancing themselves from the militants. Ideas about Shariah are diverse and often vague. Adherents of the Tijaniyya brotherhood, the dominant Muslim grouping in the North-East, tended to be lax in matters of Islamic Law and came under attack from more zealous Muslims who entered the scene in the 1970s: preachers with a certificate in Islamic studies (acquired in Saudi Arabia or at some university in Nigeria), who toured the countryside in order to impose, with the followers they gained, their purist version of a righteous life, often inspired by Salafist ideas or by Shia publications from Iran. Against these foreign doctrines, adherents of Tijaniyya tried to defend what little personal freedom they still had. However, their rejection of undue religious interference does not mean that they were fighting for tolerance and equal rights. Like other Muslims in the North, they want a society dominated by Islam, where infidels and women know their place.

The other major organisation, the Salafist Izala (Society for the Eradication of [un-Islamic] Innovations and the Establishment of the *Sunnah*), comes closer to Boko Haram in that it emphasises the necessity of scrupulously following God's commandments as revealed in the Quran and the *Sunnah*. Yet, a literal interpretation of the holy texts, as suggested by Izala, does not necessarily lead to a strategy of violence: instead of attacking the state apparatus, as Boko Haram suggests, it is better to take it over. By engaging with the state, Muslims have a chance to Islamise it, pushing for reforms that will gradually expand the official, state-enforced Shariah legislation. If they are to enhance their political influence, Muslims have to acquire Western-style education; without school certificates they cannot apply for senior positions in the state bureaucracy. This reformist apology of appropriating secular education and accepting jobs in an un-Islamic government appeals to those who have found employment, especially if they are young and better educated. But it is less attractive to the millions of jobless youths. Most of them just attended Quranic schools, where they learnt little else but to copy and memorise *suwar* (sing: *surah*) written and pronounced in a language they did not understand (Arabic). Products of an *almajiri* education used to stick to the teachings of the two main Sufi brotherhoods (*tariqa*), the Qadiriyya and Tijaniyya, yet they are also drawn to the message of Boko Haram: that Western schools, by spreading alien, materialist values, have corrupted society and must be banned.

When comparing the statements of religious organisations, it becomes clear that there is no major ideological difference between moderates and radicals. I will illustrate this, at the end of this contribution, by looking at three topics which have been at the centre of controversies generated by Boko Haram: the rejection of Western education; the declaration that some fellow Muslims are infidels who may be killed with impunity; and the attacks on Christians. In reconstructing some features of these debates, I will quote from newspaper articles and other materials available on the Internet, and I will draw on my own observations in 2011 and 2012 when I spent a few months in some remote locations in Yobe (and Borno) State.[15] In these rural towns and villages, questions of religious doctrine were widely discussed among both local government employees and illiterate farmers. However, theological disputes are just one aspect of the present crisis. They reflect social divisions between old and young, between illiterate and Western-educated Nigerians. In addition, they are shaped by political interests and intrigues. Thus, I will first discuss the political setting within which groups like Tijaniyya, Izala, and Boko Haram operate. Then I will look at the social composition of their members, their relationship with the political class, and the bitter antagonisms among these groups: not just between Boko Haram and the religious establishment, but also between Izala and Tijaniyya.

Given these deep divisions, it is unlikely that Muslims in northern Nigeria will direct the rigour of God's law against their oppressors. Clerics may decry a depraved and godless ruling class, but the faithful will not muster the common strength to confront those who are mainly responsible for the social and economic decline. Another reason why the project of a religious renewal of society will fail is the absence of credible leaders, as many *imams* have an ambivalent relationship towards the political establishment. Even Yusuf, the founder of Boko Haram, was close to the corrupt authorities in Borno State, sometimes working with them and sometimes confronting them. Although he was preaching jihad, his political patrons still bailed him out in January 2009 when he was detained in Abuja. On his return to Maiduguri, where he received a triumphant welcome, the streets at the reception venue were lined with exotic cars.[16] There is a further reason why religion will fail to domesticate the political elite: despite popular resentment of the rapacious elites, there is considerable complicity with them. Politicians and citizens work hand in hand to defraud the state, and they both take a very selective interest in Shariah. They observe their ritual obligations and maintain some Islamic decorum but have few qualms violating the holy injunctions against adultery and other vices.

THE FAILURE OF DEMOCRACY

Elections in Nigeria are very competitive, with a high turnover of incumbents. However, citizens have little influence on this process, as crucial decisions are taken by cliques of politicians behind the scenes. During the Shariah campaign, however, it looked as if ordinary people would be able to have some effect on government policies. In Borno, for instance, the incumbent governor lost out in 2003 to his rival within the ruling All Nigeria People's Party (ANPP), Modu Sheriff, who promised to be serious about the implementation of Shariah and who won the backing of Islamists like Mohammed Yusuf, the Boko Haram leader. After being elected, Sheriff created a ministry of religious affairs and put a close confidante of Yusuf in charge of it (in return for the support Boko Haram gangs had rendered him during the election campaign). But aside from that, he did not care much about divine justice. In early 2011, when his two terms drew to a close, the main concern of the ruling party was keeping the governor's family in power. Political controversies revolved around the question of whether Sheriff's cousin or his younger brother would succeed him. Pro-Shariah activists felt tricked: Sheriff had turned into a traitor; he had sided with the secular government in Abuja and called in the soldiers and policemen who murdered Yusuf in 2009.

The elections of 2011 were greeted by many international observers as an important step in consolidating democracy.[17] The chairman of the Independent Electoral Commission had clearly been independent, and there was less rigging than during the Obasanjo era. However, in those rural settlements of Yobe State where I witnessed the election campaign, people did not have much choice. Civil servants had been warned not to support the main opposition party, and some who did lost their jobs. On election day, the higher ranks of the administration, including chiefs and village heads, were expected to display their ballots so that everybody at the polling stations could see where they had cast their vote. After the incumbent governor had been confirmed in office, he consolidated his hold on power by cancelling local government elections and appointing ANPP men as caretaker chairmen and councillors. Many citizens were upset about the high-handedness of their governor, but they knew that his main challenger, a businessman who had bought the PDP governorship ticket, was not any better. I learnt that he normally lived abroad and only flew in for the election campaign. Even when inside the country he preferred spending his time in Abuja to visiting the state he wanted to rule.

People were fed up with party politics. They complained that everything had become politicised: the distribution of jobs, the sale of subsidised fertiliser, and the appointment of village and ward heads. Whatever resources state officials were dishing out were turned into a means to build up political patronage. A man who benefited from an ANPP politician was bound to him and could not support the main opposition party. Even a night watchman or a borehole operator risked losing his job if he did. Or a farmer might find himself without protection when wealthier neighbours tried to push him from his land. Although people grumbled about the rot in the local government and state administration, they did not unite to force politicians to stick to the laws. They preferred to participate in misappropriating public funds, if given a chance. And they were willing to back corrupt politicians, if they received something in return. The poor and vulnerable especially could not afford to antagonise the big men. They were too much concerned with individual survival to form a common front against those on whose generosity they depended. There is not much solidarity among impoverished farmers and jobless youth. As they compete over the means of survival, they are rivals for the favours of the rich and powerful.

Ordinary people and those in authority were accomplices in the embezzlement of public property. Their behaviour was guided by similar maxims; thus, it was difficult to take a principled stance against social vices. Both rich and poor presented themselves as pious Muslims but took a very limited, selfish interest in the law of God. Most kept their wives in purdah but had little compunction committing adultery with unmarried girls.

MUDDLING THROUGH

Boko Haram was perceived, above all, as a nuisance, because the insurgency made life more difficult. Economic activities were hindered, travelling became inconvenient owing to the many roadblocks, and the enhanced presence of policemen brought more chicanery and extortion. However, much of the blame for the insecurity was placed on the federal government, as it was widely assumed that President Jonathan could reach a settlement with Boko Haram, if only he wanted to. The rebels—I was told—were ready to make a deal with the government, just like the militants in the Niger Delta, who had attacked oil installations in order to extort money from the federal authorities. Such assertions about the aims of Boko Haram were of course mere speculation, for people had no direct contact with the insurgents. They followed the news on BBC and Voice of America, and some had seen interviews with Yusuf on Nigerian television. A few men were known to harbour sympathy for Boko Haram, but they kept a low profile since they had been interrogated by the state security service and warned not to make a mistake. Many others, in particular the younger ones, may have secretly admired Boko Haram's courageous attacks on the hated authorities. However, the general attitude towards the insurrection was rather negative. When discussing the attacks in the state capital Damaturu and other towns, it was often pointed out that innocent people had to suffer from the cycle of violence and counter-violence, although some commentators held that Boko Haram's ruthless attacks might, in the end, have a beneficial effect: the escalation of violence made it clear that the rotten political system in the North was no longer sustainable. The ruling elite had to completely change its ways and assume responsibility for the masses, improving the living conditions and bringing social justice. Otherwise, Nigeria would fall apart, and the political class would lose its sources of income.[18]

Whatever the outcome of the conflict, it seemed best not to be drawn into it. The majority of the people wanted to be left alone, and this was only possible if they did not offend either side. Local authorities had a similar interest. Thus they convened, at the instigation of the Yobe governor, town and village meetings in order to discuss what could be done to appease the rebels. I learnt that those who contributed to the discussions reiterated their commitment to Islam and their support for Shariah. It was suggested that the community get tough on gambling and drinking, which were still tolerated behind the scenes.[19] Moreover, it seemed advisable to tighten control over women and no longer allow them to talk to men when in public. One of the conveners of the meetings declared that any man who impregnated a girlfriend should marry her. Everybody knew of course that this was not the orthodox way of dealing with adultery, but they hoped that Boko Haram would spare them if they maintained some semblance of Islamic piety.

The rejection of Boko Haram's narrow Islamist vision was not born out of democratic convictions. People found it legitimate to impose an Islamic order on the state, and Shariah was accepted, in principle, as the appropriate means to strengthen the Islamic identity of their towns and villages. Christians were not seen as members of the community, even if they had been living there as farmers or artisans for two or three decades. They were not allowed to construct churches along the main roads but had to ask for a piece of land on the outskirts of town or in the bush.

THE QUEST FOR ORTHODOXY

All Muslim organisations that operated in Borno and Yobe State rejected the separation of religion and politics and welcomed the strict Shariah laws adopted in 2000.[20] Yet, they were polarised over the implementation of these laws and argued over the composition of Hisbah vigilantes that were meant to enforce them. Boko Haram has rekindled these controversies, as it brought the quest for an orthodox Shariah back onto the political agenda. Some twenty or thirty years ago, matters of doctrine had played a minor role, and most people outside the urban centres had not been aware that rival forms of Islam existed. The indigenes of those peripheral settlements, where I followed the debates on Boko Haram, were members of ethnic minorities, and Islam had spread among them only in colonial times. Until the 1980s, village chiefs had been in the centre of rural Islam, although they were illiterates with only rudimentary knowledge of religious doctrines. Being a Muslim made only modest demands on their way of life. The faithful had to participate in communal prayers, observe Ramadan, and wear some form of Islamic dress. Otherwise, they were not much curtailed by religious prescriptions. A few itinerant *mallams*, sent by the Shehu of Borno, toured these outlying regions, but they did not challenge the authority of the chiefs. Islamic teachers were expected to support the traditional rulers. Thus, it was acceptable for a newly elected chief to dismiss the *imam* of his predecessor and bring in a new one. Tijaniyya, as long as it was not challenged by other Muslim organisations, gave traditional rulers much latitude. They could continue to participate in ancient rites, as long as they supported the spread of Islam.

All this changed in the 1990s, when Izala entered the scene. Inspired by Wahhabi doctrines, it sought to purify a lax and adulterated Islam. Its activists polarised town and village communities because they drew a clear line between themselves and members of other Muslim organisations. Whoever did not follow their literal interpretation of Islam was ritually impure. It was therefore prohibited to eat with such a person or to submit to his authority. This message of a religious self-purification attracted, above all, young and educated men, who used the language of orthodox Islam to distance themselves from their elders, blaming them for not being consistent in their rejection of pagan traditions. While the old village culture, with its exuberant festivals and lavish sacrifices, appeared to be steeped in magic and superstition, Islamic Law, as Izala presented it, was rational, transparent, and straightforward. It taught the faithful to avoid needless expenses and reject pompous ceremonies and ostentatious displays of wealth.[21] Bride price payments and other social obligations should be modest, so that every man could afford to create a family. Such rules favoured the young, as did some of the legal reforms advocated by Izala. The Islamic law of inheritance, for instance, appeared preferable to many, because it divided the land of the deceased among the family members and gave each heir full control over his or her share, including the right to sell it. 'Traditional' law, by contrast, treated farmland as family property and kept it intact under the supervision of the eldest son or some other relative. Each family member was allotted land for farming, but he or she was allowed only to cultivate, not to sell it. The new system instead allowed for individual initiative and facilitated the sale of land.

For young people, the Izala programme was attractive because it levelled social differences. Nobody should bow before his parents and other authorities, and nobody should command respect only because of his wealth. What mattered, when measuring the status of a person, was piety and religious knowledge—characteristics which anybody could achieve, irrespective of his social origin. By de-emphasising social differences, the teachings of Izala also sought to obliterate ethnic antagonisms. All faithful, no matter what their tribal background, should live according to the same set of rules. This rejection of cultural diversity was attractive for Muslims from ethnic minorities, especially those who were willing to renounce their tribal heritage and assimilate to the dominant Hausa culture. When becoming Hausa, they entered a stratified society where differences of birth continued to be of importance. In most places, the Hausa, and to a greater extent the Fulani, forget neither their own origins nor those of others. Ethnic outsiders, by contrast, wanted a level playing field, and this fit with the radicalism of Izala and other reformers, who denounced ethnic prerogatives as un-Islamic:

> [A]ll Muslims, irrespective of race, language or nationality, must constitute a single brotherhood, one Umma. [...] the Umma, from one end of the world to the other, is but one single nation, its diverse peoples sharing but one faith, one law, one culture and one destiny".[22]

However, the universal law of Islam is not as clear and unequivocal as Salafist clerics suggest. In 1990 Izala split, and the two hostile factions were shouting at each other with loudspeakers. An old woman, whose house stood close to an Izala mosque, told me that she tried not to listen to the preaching, but the noise was so enervating that she had gone to the Izala leaders a couple of times to curse at them. She wanted them to pack up and go. She explained to me that there was no religion she hated more than Izala because it undermined family ties: "When your father cuts a ram, and you are not allowed to eat it, what religion is this?" A titleholder whose five children had all joined Izala also deplored that the youth turned away from their parents: "We [elders] slaughter our animals according to Islamic Law, yet our children call us infidels and do not touch our food." Moreover, the children no longer asked them about the history of their family or their village. The transmission of knowledge from one generation to the next had stopped, because "Izala tells them not to listen". Encouraged to acquire book knowledge and study the Quran, they judged with it the crude and hybrid Islam of their fathers.

For adherents of Tijaniyya it was difficult to distance themselves from Izala, because its doctrine seemed to follow scrupulously the original message of the Prophet. All those who deviated from such orthodoxy ran the risk of being branded insincere Muslims. A Tijaniyya *imam*, who was the vice chairmen of a Shariah implementation committee, acknowledged that it was difficult to justify his more lenient form of Islam. In order not to expose himself to Izala criticism, he had adopted many demands formulated by the purists: women should not work on farms, and their whole body should be covered when in public. Yet he defended the ancient naming and burial ceremonies which used to be costly social events. The Quran, he argued, did not talk about these exercises; thus they were not prohibited. Boycotting them, as Izala did, was not—in his eyes—based on religious considerations, but motivated by a wish to save money and to evade social obligations.

In its official pronouncements, Tijaniyya shared Izala's position that all aspects of public and private life have to conform to Islamic injunctions.

However, Nigeria's brotherhoods, like other religious movements, assemble people of diverse persuasions, many of whom would disagree with the official self-representation of their leaders. An elderly Tijaniyya *imam*, for instance, defended some of the traditional agricultural rituals, such as fertility rites, which had been more effective than mere prayers to Allah. He bemoaned that the village authorities, under Izala pressure, had stopped participating in the rain-making processions which had benefited the whole community. The *imam's* defence of his ancestral heritage went hand in hand with a meticulous observance of his ritual obligations under Islam. From his perspective, Izala members were bad Muslims because they prayed in a simplified, "incorrect" way. They entered mosques without covering their head, wearing blue jeans and t-shirts: "They are just like pagans." Since most young people were attracted by this informality, he assumed that his own dignified form of Islam would be pushed aside: "Izala will win." He also identified another reason for their superiority: "They are stronger, because they have money, and their people are in government. Governors, commissioners are all Izala."

A RELIGION FOR THE DISPOSSESSED

Others judged the prospect of the Tijaniyya less pessimistically: "As long as there are *almajirai*, the brotherhoods will have a large following." Students of Quranic schools spend years copying and memorising God's revelation in its original Arabic form, but most of them never learn to properly read and understand the meaning of these alien words. To them, an organisation like Izala that stresses the value of literacy and the exegesis of holy scriptures has little appeal. They are more at ease with the old brotherhoods, which are less concerned with rigid dogmas but allow for mystical experiences. Tijaniyya *mallams* sell charms to their customers and facilitate contact with the spirit world. However, for many illiterates—and especially for the uprooted urban youth who hope for a radical change—Boko Haram may also be an attractive option. By internalising the message that Western education is corrupt and that true knowledge can be acquired without it, young men without literacy (and other vocational skills) may recover some dignity. For those who join Boko Haram, an *almajiri* background is not a stigma; it does not hinder them making it to the top. The group's founder Yusuf, like its present leader Shekau, started as an *almajiri*, but made an impressive career by diligently acquiring Islamic knowledge. Like millions of other young men without school certificates,[23] Yusuf suffered from constant humiliations. Fellow Muslims derided him an as "amateur cleric"[24] and ridiculed his insufficient knowledge,[25] although it was clear from his lectures and interviews and his participation in public debates that he was an erudite man. As a favourite disciple of the famous Sheikh Ja'far Adam,[26] he was a member of Izala (until 2000), yet was barred from preaching at certain occasions because he did not possess a certificate from a university in Saudi Arabia or some other prestigious Islamic institution.[27] Yusuf refused to accept this discrimination; he insisted that he was guided in his words and deeds by a comprehensive knowledge of the holy scriptures. Unlike Maitatsine, the leader of an Islamist uprising in 1980, he did not make it easy for his critics to dismiss his teachings as heterodox. While Maitatsine styled himself a prophet and abrogated long-standing rituals such as praying five times a day, Yusuf took great pains to convince fellow Muslims that his call for a jihad resulted from a meticulous reading of the sacred texts. In his attempt to present himself as a custodian of Islamic orthodoxy, it was helpful to copy the rhetoric and outward appearance of transnational jihadists (a possibility Maitatsine did not have in 1980). His successor Shekau and other Boko Haram leaders, who lacked Yusuf's eloquence, knowledge, and charisma, took even greater care to accentuate these global models, claiming that they were "spiritual followers of al-Qaida".[28] Since Osama bin Laden was highly respected in Izala as well as *tariqa* circles,[29] it was difficult for the Muslim establishment to doubt the Islamic credentials of a Nigerian rebel group that acted like an affiliate of Al-Qaeda. Styling themselves in the image of international jihadists had still other advantages for self-made religious leaders like Yusuf and Shekau. It provided them with an organisational model that sanctioned obedience and a culture of self-sacrifice.

DINING WITH THE RICH

Boko Haram, as a "spiritual off shoot" of Izala,[30] has maintained a number of features which are characteristic of Izala's preaching, such as the hostility to Tijaniyya and its Sufi "mysticism". However, the emergence of Boko Haram also marked a break with Izala; it was a protest against clerics who appeared too friendly with corrupt politicians. Izala acted as an anti-establishment movement that articulated popular anger against the political class, yet on a local level politicians and religious leaders often found ways of getting along with and profiting from each other. In Yobe State, the governor and members of his cabinet attended Izala prayers (at least occasionally), and some local government chairmen paid allowances to Izala *imams* and donated public funds for the building of Izala mosques.[31] Certainly, most politicians and rich businessmen had little personal interest in the austere lifestyle propagated by the reformers, yet they had to appease religious critics by making religiously correct statements and by donating a part of their ill-gotten wealth to the construction of mosques and the subsidisation of Islamic clerics:

> These mosques are known colloquially as *Allah ga naka* (Allah here's your share)—and the owner may hire a young imam for the mosque as part of his 'good works'. Many young students go round preaching, or perform other ritual services for people (such as repeating for them 10,000 prayers). (Last 2008/9: 9)

Despite (or because) of its tendency to compromise, Izala had much support among intellectuals, university students, and civil servants who loathed Nigeria's dysfunctional state but were at the same time forced to live off it. This paradoxical attitude—abhorring the political system and being part of it—prevented them from being serious in their fight against corruption. And the same inner disunity haunted Izala. By spreading a message of moral rectitude and obedience to God, it was still the most important force of a spiritual renewal, yet it was tainted by its collaboration with the rich and powerful. I heard many stories about the greed and hypocrisy of individual Izala representatives. It was even said that Izala's split in 1990 was not motivated only by ideological differences but also by rivalry over the distribution of funds from abroad.[32]

A SAVIOUR

Religious associations offer citizens a chance to organise themselves outside the networks of political patronage; hence, these organisations could be used by Nigeria's discontents to submit the ruling class to public control. However, religious activists have not found ways to overcome their differences and cooperate. Even the campaign for a common goal—Shariah—failed to unite them. Ordinary Muslims often watched with disgust the petty strife among preachers competing for followers and/or political patronage. Some individual clerics with a reputation of scholarliness and integrity were held in high esteem, but none rose above religious factionalism. The only person who enjoyed almost universal support among the Muslims I met in Borno and Yobe states was Muhammadu Buhari, a former general who had ruled Nigeria from January 1984 to August 1985 and who had tried to become head of state again as an opposition candidate in the elections of 2003, 2007, and 2011. He combined a tough anti-corruption stance with a strong commitment to Islam. Moreover, he was known for carrying out his announcements without compromising them. Thus, he seemed capable of rising above his fellow politicians, forcing them to bow to the laws. However, the belief that a strong and upright leader like Buhari would be able to achieve what millions of citizens could not—checking the lawlessness of the ruling elites—is naïve. If he were elected president in 2015, militant Muslims might lay down their arms, trusting in his good intentions. But he would not have the means to radically transform the country. As an army general who ruled by decree, he had arrogated to himself the power to arrest and detain any citizen indefinitely. Government critics had been intimidated by extremely harsh laws. Whoever exposed army members and other state agents to public ridicule faced lengthy prison sentences.[33] In a democratic setting, Buhari would have to seek approval for all the measures he suggested as a president. As the present federal constitution, with its system of checks and balances, curtails the power of the executive, Buhari would have to accept compromises, accommodate political antagonists, and reconcile hostile factions. However, he is not known as someone who can listen to and win over his opponents. He was not even able to manage his own political parties and win the loyalty of ANPP and CPC politicians who had made him their presidential candidate.

During the Shariah campaign, Buhari alienated Christians when he demanded the spread of Shariah to all parts of the country,[34] and when he called on fellow Muslims not to vote for a Christian as president.[35] In the 2011 presidential election, he won a majority in the 12 Shariah states of the Far North but was defeated in all others. Although he had kept the implementation of Shariah and other religious issues out of his election campaign, many adherents perceived his defeat in religious terms: Christians (and their Muslim collaborators) had kept out of power the only candidate capable of bringing sanity to the decadent land.[36] In a deeply divided society, democracy does not work. Pious Muslims, as the losers of the election, were denied the right to be ruled by a fellow Muslim whom they could trust. Southerners, mainly Christians, had prevented them from purifying their social and political environment. Through their resistance to a sincere Islamic politician, Christians had aborted a project of self-purification that might have healed Nigeria's broken society.

HOW TO AVOID A RELIGIOUS CONFRONTATION

Passing Shariah laws that discriminate between Muslims and infidels, between men and women, and that impose penalties such as amputation and stoning, was a blatant breach of Nigeria's constitution.[37] When President

Obasanjo had to react to it, he consulted Benjamin Adekunle, a fellow officer during the civil war of 1967–70. Adekunle later disclosed that he suggested immediately sacking Governor Sani and imposing a state of emergency in Zamfara State.[38] As Nigeria's president, Obasanjo had sworn to defend the constitution, but I guess it was a reasonable decision by the head of state to let the Shariah campaign run its course, for it is unlikely that the intervention of a Christian politician would have stopped the agitation for Shariah and the emergence of groups like Boko Haram.

There is little that politicians in the South can do to end the violence in the North. They have prevented their angry young men from staging counter-attacks and killing members of the Hausa and Fulani communities living in Lagos or Enugu. Now it is up to the Muslim authorities in the North to prevail on their militants: "religious leaders must [...] call to order their followers who preach and promote violence".[39] It has often been alleged that Muslim leaders were afraid of speaking out against Boko Haram. However, many prominent Muslims have clearly condemned terrorist attacks. Some of the highest religious authorities stated that Islam preaches tolerance, and Governor Aliyu of Niger State reminded his co-religionists that "Islam is known to be a religion of peace and does not condone violence and crime in any form".[40] However, such declarations did not have much effect. Therefore, a Presidential Committee on the Security Challenges in the North-East recommended bolder pro-active measures, such as banning provocative, inciting preaching. In addition, it suggested that state governments engage "renowned Islamic scholars and jurists that could rationally challenge the doctrines of [Boko Haram] and convince them to renounce their beliefs".[41]

Western commentators have argued in a similar way: Muslim authorities should speak out more clearly and propagate a tolerant Islam. By engaging Boko Haram members and their sympathisers in an open debate, they should isolate the radical core, so that the moderates regain the initiative. However, such suggestions have ignored that "moderates" and "militants" have led intensive debates since the formation of the group. In a series of disputations with renowned scholars, Yusuf sought to justify his ideas on Western education and the necessity of a jihad. As the arguments and counter-arguments were recorded on video and audio cassettes, they became known to a wide audience of Muslim scholars as well as illiterate youth. Yet the results were not as encouraging as Western observers would have wished:

When the Boko Haram movement began to gather momentum [...]

the Ulama were fully aware of the trend. A number of initiatives from prominent Muslim scholars and Islamic organisations were put forward to intervene and resolve the misunderstanding amicably. Dialogues and debates with the Boko Haram leadership and their followers were staged to either use Islamic rationale to convince them to back down on their fatawah or to dissuade the influx of membership to them. [However] the debates drifted to being counter-productive in many incidences. Instead of achieving the desired response, therefore, the movement became more emboldened and they even won more public sympathy. (Mohammed 2010: 58-59)

The failure of religious leaders to restrain the militants is mainly due to their lack of moral authority. The Sultan of Sokoto has condemned violence against non-Muslims, yet the former army officer owes his office as the highest Islamic authority in Nigeria only to the fact that he, like all other sultans since 1815, is a direct descendant of Usman dan Fodio, a Fulani preacher, who in 1804 declared a jihad and established through a series of conquests the largest empire in West Africa. Official accounts of Islamic history still portray Usman dan Fodio as role model of a religious reformer, and the caliphate he founded is depicted as the culmination of Islamic civilisation.[42] The leaders of Boko Haram have taken up this tradition by calling on all Muslims to "fight for the restoration of the Caliphate of Usman Danfodio which the white man fought and fragmented".[43] By trying to "restore our lost glory",[44] the rebels present themselves as the true heirs of Nigeria's pre-colonial Islam, while the sultan and his emirs appear as traitors: "the Sultan is just a traditional ruler who revolted against the teachings of his ancestors and put the Nigerian Constitution ahead of the teachings of the Holy Qur'an".[45] Gambling with Shariah has discredited the religious establishment. After declaring that the law of God takes precedence over man-made law, they could not give plausible reasons for failing to push for a strict application of the divine prescriptions.

From the perspective of pious Muslims, it was just greed and opportunism that had destroyed the project of religious self-transformation. Political and religious leaders, who needed the oil wealth from the South to finance their extravagant lifestyle, continued to make deals with infidels and to collaborate with a godless state. Talking about 'peace' and 'tolerance' when denouncing Boko Haram did nothing for their credibility. Governors who operated armed gangs to intimidate their opponents were ill-qualified to lecture 'extremists' on the merits of non-violence. Given their lack of religious knowledge, it is unlikely that they will succeed in banning 'provocative, inciting preaching', as the Presidential Committee on the Security Challenges in the North-East recommended. Muslims will not accept that politicians and their cronies among the clergy supervise preachers by giving out licenses. How can representatives of a secular government decide which type of preaching is in line with Islamic doctrines? Furthermore, what is the true Islamic position on Western education? What do the holy scriptures have to say on the relationship with infidels? Is it a God-given dictum that all citizens have equal rights, as enshrined in Nigeria's Constitution? Or should Muslims reject Western notions of tolerance? Religious and political authorities, when challenging Boko Haram, have no clear message, as I will show in the remaining part of this chapter.

WESTERN EDUCATION

When the rebels began to attack schools and universities in February 2012,[46] many citizens were upset with what they saw as unwarranted interference in their life. Local elites and many others who wanted their children to get ahead sent them to government schools, as this was a prerequisite for a career in the state administration and other modern sectors. Apart from this personal interest in using the secular education system, they also believed that participation in the Western system of education was necessary for the welfare of the Muslim community as a whole: "If you do not want Christian doctors to attend to your wife when she gives birth, you have to make sure that Muslims are enabled to study medicine." Some Izala leaders blamed Boko Haram for spreading the misconception that Islam and modern sciences are incompatible.[47] However, Yusuf and his successor Shekau were not anti-modernists like Maitatsine. They declared that Muslims should use science and technology developed in the West, and reject only the un-Islamic ideas mixed into it:

> [T]he Prophet [Muhammad] said in his hadith concerning People of the Book, "if they bring to you anything that [is] agreeable in Qur'an, accept it; but if they bring anything that contradicts Islam, reject it; and if they bring anything that neither contradict nor support the Qur'an, it is your choice to accept or reject it." [...] Western education is the body of knowledge that came to us through European colonialists, and included learning medicine, technology, Geography, Physics and so on. [...] They can all be used if they do not clash with the teachings of the Prophet. (Mohammed Yusuf, in Adamu 2010: 15, 16)[48]

In this respect, Boko Haram did not differ from other Muslim organisations in the North. Izala clerics also maintained that Western education had been polluted by ungodly ideas and that the mixing of male and female students was immoral. Yet, as long as Muslims lacked the power to purge the school curricula, they grudgingly accepted secular education because it was indispensable to enhance their influence in the state apparatus. As a temporary measure, they could only supplement and partially correct the official syllabus by offering additional afternoon classes in Islamic studies. This pragmatic attitude of Izala appealed to Muslims who resented the immorality of the state but were forced to live on government jobs and contracts. It was less attractive, however, for the losers in modernisation, and these included not just the products of *almajiri* education but also many of those who had spent some years in Western-type schools without gaining any significant qualification.[49] To them, Western education might indeed look harmful as it only benefited those who had decoupled themselves from the fate of the ordinary people: "western-style education [...] equips you for the modern corrupt life of Nigerian politics and business".[50]

The resentment towards Western education dates to early colonial times and has often been fuelled by Muslims elites, such as Sultan Ibrahim Dasuki, a member of the Qadiriyya brotherhood, who led the *ummah* until 1996. As a scion of a royal family, he had studied at Oxford, and his son majored in political science at Harvard. Yet he warned his subjects against acquiring alien, non-Islamic knowledge: "Western education undermines our culture."[51] Another Muslim intellectual declared: "Western education is useless, it is polluted, it is immoral! [...] what do you need it for? You need it to work in the government service, and there are no longer government jobs."[52] For university graduates, it is difficult to find government employment, yet there is intense competition for it because positions in the civil service have become more lucrative since the transition to democracy. At the end of the military regime, policemen, teachers, and administrative officers had a basic salary equivalent to ten, twenty, or thirty dollars a month (and even these meagre salaries were often not paid). Two years after the death of General Abacha in 1998, state employees earned ten times more. This rekindled interest in school and university degrees so that dozens of new universities were hastily erected all over Nigeria. The standards of learning, however, have continued to decrease, as students are mainly interested in attaining certificates by whatever means. Some lecturers with a long teaching experience told me that many of those who had passed through primary school in the 1960s and 1970s were better educated than today's university graduates.[53] Aliyu Tilde, a Fulani politician, wrote a provocative essay in which he claimed that the lack of genuine interest in what is taught at school is a major drawback for northern Muslims:

> [W]e go to school only [to] obtain a certificate that will earn us a job without imbibing the principles and fundamentals that enabled the West to excel in such knowledge and technology [...] Our general contempt for knowledge is outstanding, making us to prefer ignorance as a companion. [...] we are culturally repulsive to any thing modern, from whatever direction it comes. Simply put, we are boko haram. Otherwise, what could explain our backwardness in every national endeavour, economic, social, political? Why do we have, for example, the lowest per capita income in the country, the lowest life expectancy, the lowest academic achievements [...] highest poverty and highest maternal and infant mortality rates? (Tilde 2009)

KILLING FELLOW MUSLIMS

Most victims of Boko Haram attacks have been other Muslims. In some cases it was obvious why the rebels had killed them; for instance, when they executed a comptroller of customs in his residence in Potiskum. People in Yobe State knew that the customs officer had issued an order to murder detained Boko Haram suspects, allegedly by poisoning their food or by driving nails into their head. In other cases, however, the victims had just committed minor offences such as playing cards, selling bush meat, or drinking in beer parlours. Boko Haram's leadership justified these executions, insisting that everyone must follow Shariah: "There are no exceptions. Even if you are a Muslim and you don't abide by Shariah, we will kill you. Even if you are my own father, we will kill you."[54]

Such extreme enforcement of Islamic Law alienated many Muslims. Critics pointed out that gambling and drinking, although forbidden in Islam, did not carry the death penalty, and it seems some Boko Haram leaders were aware that their arbitrary executions could not be justified in the light of Islamic orthodoxy. After an attack on a beer parlour, Shekau claimed that their aim had not been to punish drinkers but to kill security forces of the secular government:

> [W]e do not kill those who drink alcohol. It is mere propaganda that we attacked a beer parlour. We had heard that it was purely soldiers who gathered there to drink, and we confirmed it, that was why we went there and killed them. [...] we don't kill a Muslim; if you hear that we have killed a Muslim, we must have found out that he was collaborating

with the unbelievers [...] We are just fighting those who are fighting us, soldiers and police and the rest; and anybody, even if he is a learned Muslim teacher, if we confirm that he exposes us to the government, his children will become orphans and his wife will become a widow, in God's name. That is our way. But the ordinary people in town, we seek your forgiveness; I swear we will not harm you.[55]

Many Boko Haram operations show that great care was taken not to antagonise ordinary Muslims. When attacking police stations and other government institutions, the rebels urged passers-by to flee, lest they be hit by stray bullets. And when burning down schools, they also tried, at least initially, to avoid civilian casualties: "We are attacking the public schools at night because we don't want to kill innocent pupils."[56]

The Quran (in *Surah* 49, 10–11) forbids Muslims to kill fellow Muslims. But after the death of the Prophet, who had left no male heir, his disciples fought over the leadership of the caliphate; wars broke out, and the factions accused each other of not being genuine Muslims. In order to stop these intra-religious wars, which were threatening the very existence of the *ummah*, the great schools of Islamic jurisprudence sought to ban fighting over religious doctrines and the proper implementation of Shariah. They acknowledged that many faithful were lax Muslims who broke divine injunctions, but this did not make them infidels who merited death. Whoever claimed to be a Muslim should be treated as such. There were, however, exceptions, namely those who supported the enemies of Islam. For the early adherents of Islam it was obvious that they had the right to attack those who had betrayed the *ummah* and abandoned the cause of Islam.[57]

The most famous scholar and warrior in pre-colonial Nigeria, Usman dan Fodio, the founder of the Sokoto Caliphate, referred to this ban against traitors (or apostates) when he declared war against the kings of Hausaland, who claimed to be Muslims. He even justified the attack on the Sultanate of Bornu, the oldest Islamic polity in the central Sudan, on the grounds that the Mai of Borno had sided with the enemies of Islam.[58] In 1808, the jihadists destroyed the ancient capital of Borno and devastated the whole western half of the empire, taking away many of its inhabitants as slaves.[59] Given that Boko Haram has its home base in the Borno region, it is strange that its leaders have idealised the Fulani rulers of Sokoto and their jihad, calling on all Muslims to "fight for the restoration of the Caliphate of Usman Danfodio".[60] I suspect that Boko Haram leaders wanted to overcome the age-old divisions between the various Islamic regions and gain a foothold in north-west Nigeria. In former years, the legacy of Usman dan Fodio was claimed mainly by Fulani (and some Hausa) politicians, such as Ahmadu Bello, who was Premier of the Northern Region until his assassination in 1966. As a direct descendant of Usman dan Fodio, he often used the imagery of the jihad[61] and promised to continue the religious project of his famous ancestor: "[T]he work of salvation for all the people which he so nobly undertook has now been handed to me. I dedicate myself totally to its completion."[62] The tradition of Islamic militancy was also revived by religious leaders, such as Abubakar Gumi, who inspired the foundation of Izala. Calling for a purification of Islam, Gumi opposed the mysticism and the belief in miracles on the part of the Sufi brotherhoods, especially the Tijaniyya. Whoever adopted the prayer posture and the recitations of this group made himself an unbeliever, someone whom anyone was allowed to kill.[63]

THE STATUS OF CHRISTIANS

Boko Haram leaders chose their targets carefully. When operating in a Muslim environment, they were cautious not to harm ordinary people. School buildings, for instance, were burnt at night to ensure that pupils were not directly affected. When attacking Christians, however, they killed indiscriminately. Churches were bombed during Sunday services in order to produce as many casualties as possible: men, women, and children. Yet these attacks on infidels only began after the execution of Yusuf in July 2009, and the purpose of this new strategy has not become clear. In an interview with *Daily Trust*, Boko Haram's spokesman gave southern Nigerians, most of whom are Christians, an ultimatum to leave the North.[64] This call for a physical separation sounded like a prelude to secession. Yet in another statement, the group demanded that all Christians in Nigeria, including President Jonathan, convert to Islam.[65] And in a third statement, Abul Qaqa assured Christians that they would be protected under an Islamic state.[66]

Islamic orthodoxy prescribes that Christians (and Jews) enjoy security of life and property under a Muslim government. When Boko Haram's spokesman explained his organisation's policy towards Christians, he referred to this principle but insisted that it was not applicable in the present situation. Christians were not entitled to enjoy the peace assured by Islamic authorities because they had not asked to be placed under Islamic protection.[67] They were not ready to submit to Muslim rule but resisted the extension of Shariah and engaged in violent conflicts in order to stop it. It is understandable that many Muslims in the North were embittered by this resistance. The Christian minority in the North hindered them pursuing their dream of a religious renewal. Although Muslims formed a clear majority of the population, they were not allowed to shape their own social and political environment. In Zamfara State, where Christians were too insignificant in number to offer much resistance, Muslims could introduce far-reaching legal reforms; but in Kaduna State, where Christians accounted for at least a third of the population, only a restricted version of the Islamic penal code could be passed. Moreover, it was clear to the politicians who had initiated the Shariah project that the secular government in Abuja would not tolerate a consequent application of the new legislation. What they had promised—a far-reaching Islamisation of state and society—could not be achieved. Critics of this insincere, politically motivated Shariah—like Ibrahim Zakzaky, who had been inspired by the Iranian revolution—argued that the pious campaign was a farce. The instigators had known in advance that true Shariah was not possible as long as the power of infidels was not broken. Zakzaky assumed that the time was not ripe for an Islamic republic and that Nigeria's Muslims had to accept compromises when fighting to strengthen their position vis-à-vis infidels. His main rival, the Saudi-oriented Izala, also assumed that it would take a long time to transform Nigeria into an Islamic state. The Nigerian Supreme Council of Islamic Affairs, the most comprehensive umbrella organisation, concurred: "an Islamic State, [...] although desirable in the eyes of every Muslim, is not attainable in Nigeria, given the present realities of the country".[68] Boko Haram, by contrast, proclaimed that the secular government could be toppled and that Nigeria's Muslims should stop collaborating with it. The time had come to revive the jihadist tradition. However, there is nothing in the classical doctrine of jihad that would justify the deliberate killing of women and children. Islamic orthodoxy demands that violence be directed only against male combatants, while women and children, who form part of the war booty and may be enslaved, have to be spared.[69]

The Prophet, as he is remembered in the canonical texts, was not a campaigner for religious tolerance. When conquering Mecca, he desecrated the main 'pagan' sanctuary and smashed, with his own hands, 'idols' belonging to the shrine. According to the classical schools of Islamic Law, idol worship is a capital offence punishable by death. This view informed legislators in Nigeria when they began in early 2000 to enact "full Shariah". The Shariah Penal Code of Zamfara, which was largely adopted by most other Shariah states, decreed: "Whoever [...] takes part in the worship or invocation of any juju [...] shall be punished with death."[70] This paragraph of the new law has never been enforced.

Nevertheless, adherents of the indigenous African religions have learnt that they cannot count on protection from state authorities when their religious freedom is violated. Most of them have been put under pressure to abandon their ancient shrines, discontinue religious festivals, and give up dancing and drumming. Christians (and Jews), who worship the same Abrahamic God as the Muslims, are in a better position. The divine law, as it was reconstructed in Medina, Kufa, and Baghdad, grants them the right to retain their faith, though only with certain restrictions. They are not allowed to evangelise, to build new churches, and to display their religious symbols. They enjoy some autonomy when regulating internal affairs but otherwise have to accept the legal and political order established by Muslims.

Nigerian clerics, businessmen, and politicians, many of whom have gone on pilgrimages to Mecca, are aware that the strict regulation of public and private life, which Shariah prescribes, affects Muslims as well as non-Muslims, and that physical punishments such as flogging and amputation are meant for any offender, no matter what his faith. Why should a Christian thief be treated more leniently than a Muslim thief? However, Nigeria's Shariah campaigners found it advisable not to inform Christians about their legal status under Shariah, assuring them that they had nothing to fear: "all practicing Muslims know that God had said that there is no compulsion in religion. Therefore Shari'a will not be forced on anybody. It will only be forced on the Muslims."[71] However, the assertion that "Shari'a has never had anything to do with non-Muslims"[72] and that Christians have no reason to reject it is grossly misleading. Muslims "expected Christians to be ignorant of the status of non-Muslims according to the classical treatises on an Islamic state".[73]

The intricacies of Islamic Law were not known to most of the Muslims I met in rural Yobe. However, they generally agreed that infidels should not be granted equal rights and that public affairs should be determined by those who were guided by God. Christians were not perceived as part of one's community; they were an alien influence that had to be kept in check. The brunt of the resentment was directed against Igbo Christians from south-east Nigeria, who had settled all over the North as traders, artisans, and small-scale businessmen. They were widely seen as representatives of Western civilisation, who had brought with them all the vices of the West: greed, permissiveness, and lack of respect. As their way of life was supposed to have a corrupting influence on Islamic societies, it seemed best not to allow them to have any impact on public life. One way of excluding them was by stressing the Islamic identity of the indigenous population. If the Muslim majority decided to run its affairs on the basis of Islamic laws, then there was no place for infidels to participate in lawmaking and determine public life.

The Shariah paradigm does not contain principles that would give non-Muslims equal rights. It is true that Shariah in northern Nigeria has been enforced, at best, half-heartedly, and one can get away with breaking the law, but there are no legal safeguards that guarantee individual rights. Christians can only protect their rights granted by the Nigerian Constitution, as long as they are strong enough to contain the spread of Islamic Law. As the Catholic Bishop of Sokoto put it, there is "no alternative to democracy [and] secularity of the state".[74] Separating state and religion would limit the politicisation of religion, and it would make it easier for the adherents of different religions to get along with each other, provided that all sides felt bound to a secular arrangement. Religious communities would not be forced to compete for control of the state, if they agreed not to use the state apparatus to enforce their divine injunctions. However, it is unlikely that Muslims in the North will come to share this view. With the Shariah campaign, more than ten years ago, Muslim politicians, intellectuals, and religious leaders discarded the secular principles of the constitution; now they have no other rules on which a common polity with Christians and traditionalists can be built. When condemning Boko Haram, northern politicians said that Islam means peace, but they did not specify what a peace based on Islamic principles would look like.

THE WAY OUT

Western observers have called upon the Nigerian authorities to get serious about the eradication of poverty and social injustice. Instead of focusing on military repression, they should tackle the causes of the crisis and improve the living conditions in the backward states of the North. The governors of these states argued similarly, underlining the need for a sustainable development, mass economic empowerment, skills acquisition, and an effective administration. In order to achieve this, they demanded that the federal government give them additional funds. However, the problem with the North is not so much a lack of money but how it is spent. For nearly four decades northern politicians and army officers dominated the Nigerian state and appropriated for themselves the largest share of the oil revenues, yet their part of the country is the least developed. Giving them more money will not eliminate poverty. The governor of Borno, who called for a Marshall Plan in support of the impoverished North, promised to create half a million jobs.⁷⁵ However, this is neither realistic nor would it lead to a viable solution, because Nigeria's public administration already has too many employees on its payroll. Seventy-two per cent of the federal government's budget is spent on the salaries and pensions of its staff. Little money is left for investments in the country's infrastructure, yet the pressure on politicians to provide more jobs will not relent, because the Far North has virtually no industries to absorb the rising number of young men entering the job market: "[O]urs after all, is still an economy that imports everything including used underwear."⁷⁶ With the economy declining, state authorities will be confronted with a tidal wave of popular anger:

> Nigeria is sitting on a keg of gun powder if the population growth of the country continues to rise without putting in place deliberate policies that would provide job opportunities [...] From what I saw in the affected areas, hundreds of youths were still in the houses of their parents doing nothing.⁷⁷

Most factories in the urban centres have closed down, and even the agricultural sector is in crisis, as the country does not produce enough food to feed its own population. In Yobe State, arable land has become so scarce that peasants are driven off their property. Villages fight over boundaries; family members are cheated out of their plots; sons try to sell the land of their fathers, and fathers sell away family land that should have been inherited by their sons.

Nigerians cannot wait for their country and its citizens to become affluent. They have to find ways to contain the violence and get along with each other. However, an agreement that would end the insurgency in the North is not in sight. Boko Haram raised the question of a social transformation through religion; it brought Shariah back into the centre of political controversy, a Shariah that can be turned against the religious and political establishment. In order to end the crisis, Muslims in the North have to discuss what type of Shariah—if any—they want. This debate is largely an intra-Islamic affair, because Christians cannot contribute much to it. As infidels who have rejected the teaching of the Prophet, they cannot tell Muslims how to go about their religious obligations.

Muslim critics of Boko Haram suggested that the Supreme Council for Islamic Affairs and other mainline organisations "ought to be proactive in educating the masses about the true Islam".⁷⁸ The problem is that religious experts hold widely divergent views about Islam and the demands it may make on its adherents. Most ordinary Muslims agree that Shariah should play a role in the organisation of state and society, but they cannot agree to what extent the divine laws should govern their lives. Many politicians pay only lip service to Shariah and obstruct its implementation, but do not openly call for its abrogation. They cannot risk a confrontation with Muslim clerics, as they have discredited themselves with their Shariah gamble. Islam is a dangerous religion to play with. Since the political class started to campaign for the extension of Islamic Law, it has been snared in the Shariah trap. There is no easy way for it to extricate itself.

Notes

1. In Y. Olowolabi, "Anarchists Threaten Nation's Unity", *Tell* [print edition], 29 October 2001, 36.
2. Freedom House, *Talibanization*, 51.
3. Zamfara Government Advertorial, "Zamfara State One Year of Purposeful Leadership", *Hotline* [print edition], 4 June 2000, 24.
4. Maier, *This House*, 186.
5. Mazrui, *Shariacracy*, (chapter "Globalization and Islamic Revivalism"); Harnischfeger, *Democratization*, 112-54.
6. Zamfara Government Advertorial, "Zamfara State One Year of Purposeful Leadership", *Hotline* [print edition], 4 June 2000, 24.
7. Abdul-Azeez Suleiman, "Shari'a: Yarima vs. the Mallams", *Kaduna Weekly Trust*, 26 July 2003, in Paden, *Muslim Civic Cultures*, 166.
8. Maitama Sule, in N. Ebije, "FG Must Empower North", *Daily Sun*, 11 May 2012.
9. Johnnie Carson, Ass. Secretary of State for African Affairs, in [Anon.], "US Official: Violence in Nigeria Isn't about Religion", *Daily Trust* [print edition], 6 April 2012, 29.
10. Abubakar Shekau in a video message, in [Anon.], "Jos Bombing: Text of Video Statement by Jama'atu Ahlus-Sunnah Lidda'awati Wal Jihad", *Elombah*, 28 December 2010.
11. A detailed study on sermons, interviews, and debates between Boko Haram leaders and some of their Izala critics arrives at a similar conclusion: "misrule and poor governance resulting from the legendary corruption of Nigerian political leaders are not the explicit concerns of these discourses and counter-discourses on Boko Haram [...]. Yusuf was chiefly concerned with avenging his followers' injuries rather than raising Nigerian citizens' objections to the abuse of power by security forces, nor does he voice any criticism against the broader problem of poor governance and misrule by Nigerian political elites that many commentators

claim to be the explanation for the Boko Haram insurrection" ([Anon.], *Popular Discourses*, 119, 130-31).

12. Adamu Adamu, "Gazafication of the North", *Daily Trust* [print edition], 16 March 2012, 64.

13. Some governors made it clear that they dislike Shariah. In Kano, Rabiu Kwankwaso announced that no cleric could tell him what to do, "no matter how long his beard is" ([Anon.], "Paralysed by Fear", *The Economist* [print edition], 10 January 2004, 32). Yet he was forced to pass comprehensive Shariah laws and set up a Shariah vigilante. Moreover, he was voted out of office after just one term.

14. Crisis Group, *Northern Nigeria*, 21, 38; [Anon.], "Most Nigerians Reject Boko Haram", *Daily Trust* [print edition], 21 February 2012, 10.

15. The purpose of my visits to Nigeria, from January to April 2011 and 2012, was not to study Boko Haram, and I did not try to contact members of the group. I can refer only to conversations I had with ordinary Muslims, who often spoke about the rebellion and the state of emergency that had been imposed on parts of Yobe, Borno and a few other states.

16. Shehu Sani, *Boko Haram*, (chapter "His Threats").

17. Campbell: *The Morning After*.

18. I heard the same argument by northern intellectuals, for instance at the University of Maiduguri: Boko Haram, though a nasty organisation, may achieve through massive bombing what progressives in the North had always called for, namely good governance. Faced with the prospect that Nigeria might descend into chaos, the ruling class had no choice but to initiate a radical change lest they lose the basis of their existence: the oil rents.

19. Beer had become expensive; thus, villagers crossed into Gombe State and bought their bottles at a private club attached to the Ashaka Cement Company. Yet the club stopped selling alcohol when Boko Haram extended its bombing campaign into Gombe. This did not prevent rich people from getting their alcohol, while the poor had to accept that Shariah in Nigeria had a clear class bias. Instead of drinking alcohol, some men in the streets were sniffing glue. And on the university campuses, the ground was littered with empty bottles of cough syrup, which students drank to become intoxicated (see [Anon.], "Codeine Abuse Spreading Like Wild Fire", *Daily Trust*, 29 December 2012).

20. In a study of the Shariah campaign in Kano, T. H. Gwarzo (*Civic Associations*, 311-13) found that all Muslim organisations, from the conservative brotherhoods to the radical 'Shiites', called for the establishment of an Islamic state. M. Last (*Charia*, 143, 147) insisted that support for the extension of Shariah was not a matter of Islamic radicalism or 'fundamentalism': *"Parmi tous les musulmans, un consensus se fait autour de l'idée, que la charia est juste. [...] ceux qui soutiennent l'application de la charia ne sont pas des radicaux, mais plutôt des musulmans modérés"*.

21. Kane, *Muslim Modernity*, 136-38.

22. Sulaiman, *Islam and Secularism*, 11.

23. The Federal Ministry of Education estimated that "about 9.5 million school children are currently outside the conventional school system" ([Anon.], "FG and Almajiri Schools", *Daily Sun*, 13 April 2012).

24. Ahmad Sakida, "Reporting Terrorism in Africa", *Blueprint*, 19 April 2012.

25. [Anon.], *Popular Discourses*, 136-37.

26. Sani, *Boko Haram*, [Chapter: Who Are Boko Haram]; [Anon.], *Popular Discourses*, 122.

27. Pérouse de Montclos, *Boko Haram*, 6, 8, 16.

28. Abul Qaqa, spokesman of Boko Haram, in M. Mark, "Boko Haram Vows to Fight until Nigeria Establishes Sharia Law", *The Guardian* [London], 27 January 2012.

29. [Anon.], *Popular Discourses*, 133.—Following the attacks of September 11, 2011, 'Osama' became the most popular name for new born sons, just like 'Saddam' had become popular at the time of the Iraq war (Krings, *Osama Bin Laden*, 255-258; J. Nwokocha, "Gusau in the Grip of Extremists", *Vanguard* [print edition], 11 November 2001, 14). In 2010, a poll conducted by the Pew Research Global Attitudes Project (*Osama bin Laden*, 1) found that "confidence" in the Al-Qaeda leader was still high. Among Muslims in Nigeria as a whole, the approval rate was 48 per cent (and in the North probably higher). This was the highest rate in all countries analysed in the survey.

30. Ulama of the Caucus, in Alkali [a. o.], *Overview*, 13; M. Q. S. Isa, "Controversy over Proposed FG, Boko Haram Dialogue", *Daily Trust*, 15 June 2012.

31. See Alkali [a. o.], *Overview*, 30, for Borno and other states in north-east Nigeria.

32. The Bushawa faction, with its headquarters in Jos, followed the policy of Saudi Arabia by supporting President Bush's war against Iraq, while the Saddamawa faction, based in Kaduna, denounced the US intervention as an attack against fellow Muslims.

33. Diamond, *Nigeria*, 441-42.

34. Peters, *Islamic Criminal Law*, 55.

35. I. Bwala, "Riding the Sharia Tiger", *Tell* [print edition], 30 July 2001, 66.

36. In the riots following the 2011 presidential election, more than 400 churches were burnt or destroyed in northern Nigeria (United States Commission, *Annual Report*, 109). Angry protesters also set fire to the private houses of the Sultan of Sokoto, the Emir of Kano, and the Emir of Zaria, who were forced to go into hiding temporarily (Campbell: *The Morning After*).

37. The areas where Shariah contravenes the Nigerian Constitution are analysed in Peters, *Islamic Criminal Law*, 31-42.

38. I. Ibrahim, "How Obasanjo, IBB Created Boko Haram", *Insider Weekly* [print edition], 26 March 2012, 15.

39. Rev. Fr. Omonokhua of the Catholic Secretariat, in C. Omonokhua, "The Need for Inter-religious Dialogue", *The Guardian* [Lagos], 2 July 2012.
40. Dr. Mu'azu Aliyu, in *Wikipedia*, article on "Boko Haram" [Accessed 7 May 2012].
41. White Paper based on the report of the Ambassador Usman G. Galtimari committee, partly reproduced in T. Abbah, "White Paper on Insecurity: Report Links Boko Haram with London Scholar", *Sunday Trust*, 3 June 2012.
42. This official view has shaped the attitudes of Muslims in the Far North, no matter what their organisational affiliation: "most of the *Tarika*, Izala and Shiites interviewed view the 19th century Fulani Jihadist, Othman Danfodio's Hausaland as a model" (Alkali [a. o.], *Overview*, 29).
43. Abul Qaqa, spokesman of Boko Haram, in H. Idiris, "Boko Haram Says No More Talks with FG", *Daily Trust*, 21 March 2012.
44. *Ibid.*
45. Abul Qaqa, in H. Idris, "Boko Haram: Why We Won't Listen to Sultan", *Daily Trust*, 3 October 2011.
46. Human Rights Watch, *Boko Haram*.
47. Mohammed, *Boko Haram*, 41.
48. Shekau argued similarly: "We are not fighting Western education itself, what we are opposed to are the various un-Islamic things slotted into it" (in Zenn, *Radical Ideologue*, 14).
49. Prof. M. Modibbo, the executive general of the Universal Basic Education Commission, stated that "more than half of the teachers in some Northern states cannot read or write" (in [Anon.], "50% Illiterate Northern Teachers", *Blueprint*, 29 June 2012).
50. Last, *Pattern of Dissent*, 10.
51. Godwin Ugwu, "Educational Imbalance: The North and the Rest", *The Guardian* [Lagos, print edition], 24 May 1994.
52. Sani Hassan Kontagora, in M. Mumuni, "Western Education is Useless", *Tell* [print edition], 9 July 2001, 53.
53. Prof. Ben Nwabueze, a former minister of education, spoke of an "incredible decline in educational standards" and "near-illiterate university graduates" (in G. Oke, "The Mistakes Rotimi Williams and I Made about Nigeria's Constitution", *Vanguard*, 21 March 2013).
54. Abul Qaqa, spokesman of Boko Haram, in M. Mark, "Boko Haram Vows to Fight until Nigeria Establishes Sharia Law", *The Guardian* [London], 27 January 2012.
55. Abubakar Shekau, in I. Sheme, "'No Reconciliation' Boko Haram Leader Blows Hot in First Video", *Newsdiary*, 25 July 2011.
56. Abul Qaqa, in Human Rights Watch, *Boko Haram*.

57. Hodgson, *Venture*, 178, 197; Kenny, *Boko Haram*.
58. The ruling dynasty of the Borno Empire had been Islamic for more than 700 years. In the sixteenth century, Borno was seen as one of the four main sultanates in the Islamic world (Lavers, *Kanem*, 201). Its political and religious leader in the early nineteenth century, Shehu Al-Kanemi, wrote letters to Sokoto, protesting the invasion of his country, arguing that both empires, Borno and Sokoto, were Islamic and should not fight each other. The debate between the leaders of Sokoto and Borno over the legitimacy of the jihad is summarised in Brenner, *Jihad Debate*.
59. Brenner, *Shehus*, 25, 32.
60. Abul Qaqa, in H. Idiris, "Boko Haram Says no More Talks with FG", *Daily Trust*, 21 March 2012.—Abul Qaqa depicted the Sokoto Caliphate as a peaceful, thoroughly Islamic empire and thus as a counter-image to the present Nigerian nightmare of violence and corruption. This meant that the utopian world Boko Haram was fighting for had really existed and could exist again if Nigeria's Muslims mustered the determination of their forefathers: "peace will never reign until when Sharia as a complete way of life is restored 100 per cent; just like the way it was practiced during the period of Daular Usmaniyya" (Abul Qaqa, in H. Idris, "Boko Haram: Why We Won't Listen to Sultan", *Daily Trust*, 3 October 2011).
61. Reynolds, *Politics of History*, 56-60.
62. Ahmadu Bello, in Crampton, *Christianity*, 89.
63. Loimeier, *Islamic Reform*, 298.
64. Abul Qaqa, in H. Idris, "Boko Haram: State of Emergency Meant to Attack Muslims", *Daily Trust* [print edition], 2 January 2012, 7.
65. Walker, *Boko Haram*, 11; Abul Qaqa, in [Anon.], "No Going Back on Jihad, Dasuki Lied Says Boko Haram", *Sahara Reporters*, 10 July 2012.
66. Abul Qaqa, in M. Mark, "Boko Haram Vows to Fight until Nigeria Establishes Sharia Law", *The Guardian* [London], 27 January 2012.
67. Abul Qaqa, in [Anon.], "No Going Back on Jihad, Dasuki Lied Says Boko Haram", *Sahara Reporters*, 10 July 2012.
68. Dr. Lateef Adegbite, Secretary General of the Nigerian Supreme Council for Islamic Affairs, in Clarke & Linden, *Islam*, 172.
69. Hodgson, *Venture*, 191.
70. Zamfara State of Nigeria, *Shariah Penal Code*, Section 406.—The term "juju" is defined in Section 405: "'Juju' includes the worship or invocation of any object or being other than Allah".
71. Muhammadu Buhari, in [Anon.], "The Two Sides of Buhari", *Hotline* [print edition], 19 March 2000, 12.
72. Y. Mahmud, "Where Right Is Wrong", *Hotline* [print edition], 19 March 2000, 25.
73. Kenny, *Sharia*, 347.

74. Kukah, *Boko Haram*, 34.
75. Shettima, *Challenges of Insecurity*.
76. M. Al-Ghazali, "Boko Haram, CIA and Conspiracy Theories", *Daily Trust*, 28 February 2012.
77. Kashim Shettima, Governor of Borno, in [Anon.], "The Deserted Areas of Maiduguri", *Weekly Trust*, 7 July 2012.
78. Ujudu Shariff, in Mohammed, *Boko Haram*, 119.

References

Adamu, A.U. (2010), *African neo-Kharijites and Islamic militancy against authority: The Boko Haram/Yusufiyya Kharijites of northern Nigeria*. Paper presented to the Islam in Africa Working Group of the African Studies Center, University of Florida, Gainesville, 24 February [unpublished].

Alkali, M.N., A.K. Monguno & B.S. Mustafa (2012), *Overview of Islamic actors in northeastern Nigeria*, NRN Working Paper No. 2.

http://www.3.qeh.ox.ac.uk/pdf/nrn/WP2Alkali.pdf [Accessed 11 February 2013]

[Anonymous] (2012), "The popular discourses of Salafi radicalism and Salafi counter-radicalism in Nigeria: A case study of Boko Haram", *Journal of Religion in Africa* 42: 118-44.

Brenner, L. (1973), *The Shehus of Kukawa: A history of the Al-Kanemi dynasty of Bornu*. Oxford: Clarendon.

——— (1992), "The jihad debate between Sokoto and Borno: An historical analysis of Islamic political discourse in Nigeria". In: J.F.A. Ajayi & J.D.Y. Peel, eds, *People and empires in African history: Essays in memory of Michael Crowder*. London/New York: Longman, 21-43.

Campbell, J. (2011), "Nigeria: The morning after", *New York Times*, 2 May.

Clarke, P.B. & I. Linden (1984), *Islam in modern Nigeria: A study of a Muslim community in a post-independence state 1960–1983*. Mainz/München: Grünewald.

Crampton, E.P.T. (1979), *Christianity in northern Nigeria*. Second Edition. London: Chapman.

Crisis Group (2010), *Northern Nigeria: Background to conflict* (Africa Report N° 168 – 20 December 2010),

http://crisisgroup.org/~/media/Files/africa/west-africa/nigeria/168 Northern Nigeria - Background to Conflict.pdf [Accessed 11 February 2013].

Diamond, L. (1995), "Nigeria: The uncivic society and the descent into praetorianism".

In: L. Diamond, [a.o.], eds, *Politics in developing countries: Comparing experiences with democracy*. Second Edition. Boulder: Lynne Rienner. 417-91.

Freedom House (2002), *The Talibanization of Nigeria: Radical Islam, extremist Sharia law and religious freedom*.

http://www.freedomhouse.org/religion/pdfdocs/Nigeria%20Report.pdf [Accessed 12 November 2004].

Gwarzo, T.H. (2003), "Activities of Islamic civic associations in the northwest of Nigeria: With particular reference to Kano State", *Afrika Spectrum* 38(3): 289-317.

Harnischfeger, J. (2008), *Democratization and Islamic law: The Sharia conflict in Nigeria*. Frankfurt/New York: Campus.

Hodgson, M.G.S. (1977), *The venture of Islam: Conscience and history in a world civilization*. Vol. 1. The Classical Age of Islam. Chicago/London: Chicago University Press.

Human Rights Watch (2012), *Nigeria: Boko Haram targeting schools*, 7 March.

http://www.hrw.org/news/2012/03/07/nigeria-boko-haram-targeting-schools [Accessed 14 May 2012].

Kane, O. (2003), *Muslim modernity in postcolonial Nigeria: A study of the Society for the Removal of Innovation and Reinstatement of Tradition*. Leiden/Boston: Brill.

Kenny, J. (2012), "Can Boko Haram win?", *The Guardian* (Lagos), 27/28 February.

http://www.josephkenny.joyeurs.com/Guardian.htm [Accessed 14 May 2012].

——— (1996), "Sharia and Christianity in Nigeria: Islam and a 'secular' state", *Journal of Religion in Africa* 26(4): 338-364.

Krings, M. (2004), "Osama Bin Laden vs. George W. Bush in Nigeria. Zur lokalen Transkription globaler Ereignisse". In: C. Epping-Jäger, [a.o.], eds, *Freund, Feind & Verrat: Das Politische Feld der Medien*. Köln: Dumont, pp. 252-65.

Kukah, M.H. (2009), "Boko Haram: Some reflections on causes and effects", *Missio* 34: 21-35.

http://www.missio-hilft.de/media/thema/menschenrechte/studie/34-nigeria-de-en-fr.pdf [Accessed 3 May 2012].

Last, M. (2000), "La charia dans le Nord-Nigeria", *Politique africaine* 79: 141-152.

——— (2008/2009), "The pattern of dissent: Boko Haram in Nigeria 2009", *Annual Review of Islam in Africa* 10: 7-11.

Lavers, J.E. (1984), "Kanem and Borno to 1808". In: O. Ikime, ed., *Groundwork of Nigerian History*. Second Edition. Ibadan: Heinemann, pp. 187-209.

Loimeier, R. (1997), "Islamic reform and political change: The example of Abubakar Gumi and the Yan Izala movement in northern Nigeria". In: E.E. Rosander & D.

Westerlund, eds, *African Islam and Islam in Africa: Encounters between sufis and Islamists*. London: Hurst, pp. 286-307.

Maier, K. (2000), *This house has fallen: Midnight in Nigeria*. New York: Public Affairs.

Mazrui, A.A. (2001), *Shariacracy and federal models in the era of globalization: Nigeria in comparative perspective*, [Paper presented] at the conference on 'Restoration of Shariah in Nigeria. Challenges and Benefits', sponsored by the Nigeria Muslim Forum, and held in London, on 14 April 2001.

http://www.sharia2001.nmnonline.net/mazrui paper.htm [Accessed 30 April 2004].

Mohammed, A. (2010), *The paradox of Boko Haram*. Kano: Moving Image Limited.

Paden, J.N. (2005), *Muslim civic cultures and conflict resolution: The challenge of democratic federalism in Nigeria*. Washington, DC: Brookings Institution Press.

Pérouse de Montclos, M.-A. (2012), *Boko Haram et le terrorisme islamiste au Nigeria: Insurrection religieuse, contestation politique ou protestation social?* Centre d'études et de recherches internationales. Sciences Po.

http://www.sciencespo.fr/ceri/sites/sciencespo.fr.ceri/files/qdr40.pdf [Accessed 11 February 2013].

Peters, R. (2003), *Islamic criminal law in Nigeria*. Ibadan: Spectrum Books.

Pew Research Global Attitudes Project (2011), *Osama bin Laden largely discredited among Muslims publics in recent years*. 2 May 2011.

http://www.pewglobal.org/2011/05/02/osama-bin-laden-largely-discredited-among-muslim-publics-in-recent-years/ [Accessed 19 March 2013].

Reynolds, J.T. (1997), "The politics of history: The legacy of the Sokoto Caliphate in Nigeria". In: P.E. Lovejoy & P.A.T. Williams, eds, *Displacement and the politics of violence in Nigeria*. Leiden/New York/Köln: Brill, pp. 50-65.

Sani, S. (2011), "Boko Haram: History, ideas and revolt", *Newsdiary*, 3 August.

http:/www.newsdiaryonline.com/shehu_boko_haram.htm [Accessed 11 February 2013].

Shettima, K. (2012), "The challenges of insecurity in Borno State", *Leadership*, 15 May [reprinted in *Sunday Trust*].

http://www.leadership.ng/nga/columns/24704/2012/05/15/challenges_insecurity_borno_state_gov_kashim_shettima.html [Accessed 11 June 2012]

Sulaiman, I. (1986), "Islam and secularism in Nigeria: An encounter of two civilisations", *Impact International* [London], 24 Oct.–13 Nov. 1986, pp. 11-12.

Tilde, A. (2009), "We are Boko Haram", *Nigerian Village Square*, 20 August.

http://www.nigeriavillagesquare.com/articles/aliyu-u-tilde/we-are-boko-haram.html [Accessed 10 May 2012].

United States Commission on International Religious Freedom (2012), *Annual Report 2012*. March 2012.

http://www.uscirf.gov/images/Annual Report of USCIRF 2012(2).pdf [Accessed 14 March 2013].

Walker, A. (2012), *What is Boko Haram?* United States Institute of Peace, Special Report 308.

http://www.usip.org/publications/what-boko-haram [Accessed 27 July 2012].

Zamfara State of Nigeria. (2000), *Gazette. No. 1. 15th June, 2000. Vol. 3. Law No. 10: Shariah penal code law*. Gusau, Zamfara State: Ministry of Justice.

Zenn, J. (2012), "Boko Haram's radical ideologue: An in-depth look at northern Nigeria's Abu Shekau", *Militant Leadership Monitor*, Special Report, January 2012, pp. 13-17.

3

TRADITIONAL QURANIC STUDENTS (*ALMAJIRAI*) IN NIGERIA
Fair game for Unfair Accusations?

Hannah Hoechner
University of Oxford, Department of International Development

The enrolment of many boys and young men in traditional Quranic schools rather than in formal education has become an issue of growing concern in northern Nigeria. The *almajirai*, the students of such schools, have attracted attention in the context of increased attempts to universalise primary education and growing concerns about child welfare. They have also been discussed as potential 'foot soldiers' for violence in the context of Boko Haram. As systematic evidence does not exist to substantiate such claims, the link between *almajirai* and violence is often made with reference to the conditions of their upbringing. That the *almajirai* grow up defying the norms of 'modern' childhood is taken as proof of a violent predisposition. This chapter shows the problems of such reasoning. In terms of skills and future prospects, little differentiates the *almajirai* from other poor undereducated youth from rural households. Young people frequently move between different educational systems, which means few children are 'pure' *almajirai*. Lingering at the bottom of the status hierarchy, the *almajirai* often lack the power to refute unjustified accusations. These feed negative stereotypes, which may give rise to fresh accusations. Widespread prejudice and stigma are major concerns to the *almajirai*.

Keywords: almajirai, Boko Haram, education, madrassah, respect, youth

INTRODUCTION

The issues at stake

The enrolment of many boys and young men in traditional Quranic schools rather than in formal education has become an issue of growing concern in northern Nigeria. The students of such schools, many of whom while young beg for a living, have attracted attention in the context of increased attempts to universalise primary education and growing concerns about child welfare. The *almajirai*, as they are called, have also been rightly or wrongly associated with Islamic radicalisation, militancy, and the periodic riots that have blighted many northern Nigerian cities. The current spate of Boko Haram violence in northern Nigeria has carried such modes of thinking to the extreme. Many have jumped to the conclusion that the Islamist sect finds easy recruits in traditional Quranic schools. Nobel laureate Wole Soyinka (2012), for example, declared in an article in *Newsweek* magazine about Boko Haram that the "butchers of Nigeria":

> [have] been deliberately bred, nurtured, sheltered, rendered pliant, obedient to only one line of command, ready to be unleashed at the rest of society. They were bred in madrassas and are generally known as the almajiris. From knives and machetes, bows and poisoned arrows they have graduated to AK-47s, homemade bombs, and explosive-packed vehicles.

Other authors have declared the *almajirai*'s deprived living conditions responsible for violence. Former Minister of Education Aishatu Jibrin Dukku, for instance, found that "[m]ost of these children, because of the harsh realities they found themselves in, end up becoming juvenile delinquents and, subsequently, adult criminals" (Alkali 2009).

Some *almajirai* may well be, and probably are, amongst the followers of Boko Haram. But there is no systematic evidence to support such assertions. What empirical evidence exists, refutes the "simplistic application of economic deprivation theory" ([Anon.] 2012: 118). This chapter asks why, in the absence of sound data, the *almajirai* have become such a popular target for accusations and explores the mechanisms that make the *almajirai* convenient scapegoats.

I argue that the people participating in the *almajiri* system are often imagined to be opposed to 'modern' developments and even as the quintessential challenge to a 'modern' Nigeria because they defy the norms of 'modern' childhood as a protected phase of economic dependence, embedded within the nuclear family and the formal education system. Many take the fact that the *almajirai* do not conform to such blueprints of 'modern' childhood as a sure indication of their violent potential and inability to become functional members of society. There are undeniably problems and dangers related to the circumstances under which many *almajirai* grow up. Yet, many narratives construe negative outcomes as an automatic and inevitable result of *almajirci* (the practice of living as *almajiri*). As they over simplify matters, such narratives have little explanatory power

The argumentative logic underpinning most accusations against the *almajirai*, I argue, builds on problematic assumptions. Contrary to received wisdom, many *almajirai* and many parents of *almajirai* are anything but opposed to 'modern' education. Rather, they struggle to access 'modern' education that is affordable and of acceptable quality. While the link between *almajirai* and violence is often made with reference to their putative refusal to acquire 'modern' skills and knowledge, the *almajirai* are hardly alone in lacking skills to safeguard their economic futures, and educational disadvantage extends far beyond them. In brief, if educational disadvantage and opposition to 'modern' developments constitute the causal link between young people and violence, then we have little reason to conclude that our concern should focus merely on the *almajirai*. I argue in this chapter that they do not constitute the neatly separable social category they are often portrayed as. Clearly, we need to be mindful of the broader dynamics that produce problematic outcomes.

I argue in the second part of this chapter that, regardless of whether or not *almajirai* actually engage in problematic behaviour, for many it may be convenient to accuse them. They mostly lack the economic and cultural resources to participate in displays of status in their places of study. In addition, they often do not have social superiors to speak for them. Blaming *almajirai* carries little risk of stepping on the toes of powerful protectors, which makes them convenient scapegoats. What is more, low status can engender even lower status. As *almajirai* often lack the power to refute unjustified accusations, these feed negative stereotypes, which may give rise to fresh accusations.

Widespread prejudice and stigma against the *almajirai* is anything but inconsequential. Aware of the negative views people hold of them, the *almajirai* struggle to defend their sense of self and of purpose by embracing self-conceptions as devoted scholars migrating in search of sacred knowledge. In their experiences of being treated as underdogs and nuisances lies a source of frustration and alienation. Being shown respect as human beings would be as important for the *almajirai*'s well-being as improvements to their living conditions and access to 'modern' skills and knowledge. On a more general note, offloading the blame for violence and militancy onto the shoulders of the *almajirai* alone and thus framing the challenges the Nigerian nation-state is facing today in terms of the presumed backwardness and conservatism of a specific group is problematic. It risks obscuring widespread inequality, poverty, and alienation from the values 'modern' Nigeria has come to represent.

The remainder of this introduction discusses the methods and data collected and introduces the *almajirai* in more depth. The second section engages with the discourses surrounding the *almajirai*. The third section juxtaposes the discourses about the *almajirai* with their lived realities and experiences. The conclusion summarises the argument and emphasises the importance of an empirically informed analysis of the *almajiri* system.

Methods and data

The material for this chapter stems from media records (national and international English-language news, and internet sources including blogs and online forums), official narratives, institutional publications (from local and international organisations working with children), and local academic production. I collected the newspaper material through keyword searches ("almajiri") on individual newspapers' homepages,[1] including both Abuja- and Lagos-based newspapers, and via the online newspaper database *allafrica*. Most articles were published after 2009. I collected blog and online forum entries[2] via the Google search engine, using "almajiri" as a search term. As my searches yielded over 900 results, I conducted an NVivo word frequency query (search terms 'almajiri' / 'almajirai') to identify the most pertinent articles.

In addition, I build on 13 months of fieldwork that I carried out as part of my master's and doctoral research in Kano State between 2009 and 2011. My fieldwork included four months in Albasu, a small rural town in Albasu local government area in the east of Kano State. For the remaining time, I lived at Sabuwar Kofa within Kano's Old City. I collected data in the form of fieldwork observations, as well as semi-structured interviews, group conversations, and casual interactions with *almajirai*, their parents, caregivers, and teachers, as well as some former *almajirai*. Furthermore, I use translated and transcribed 'radio interviews' the young *almajirai* conducted amongst each other with my tape recorder and discussions of the photographs they took with disposable cameras.

In addition, I draw on data from the production process of a participatory documentary film/docu-drama about the perspectives of *almajirai* on their lives and the challenges they face.[3] This includes stories narrated or written down during the script-writing process, as well as discussions about the way they would like to see their lives and identities represented on screen. The nine participating youths were aged 15–20 years and came from three different Quranic schools in both urban and rural Kano, in which I had previously taught English.

Who are the almajirai? External ascriptions and internal self-conceptions

Many people conceive of young *almajirai* as "neglected", "exploited", or "abandoned", as "an eyesore or a pest" (Tilde 2009), and as a "generation lost" (Ekaette in Abubakar 2009). When they are adolescents, the *almajirai* appear in the public imagination as potential "[b]utchers of Nigeria" (Soyinka 2012) and "monsters" in the "breeding" ("Rehabilitating our almajiris" 2011). The *almajirai* that I conducted my research with conceived of themselves neither as "child urchins" (Olagunju 2012) nor as a "cancer" in society (Suleiman 2009, commentator). Rather, they saw themselves as *matafiyi mai neman ilimi* (Hausa: "those who have left their homes in search of knowledge"). I was told by *almajirai* that the syllable "al" in *almajiri* stood for Allah, whereas "ma" was short for the Prophet Mohammed, and "jiri" for the angel Jibril. While this interpretation does not reflect the word's actual etymology (*almajiri* derives from the Arabic word *al-muhajir*, which means "migrant"), it captures well how *almajirai* manipulate the word's meaning, making it a category still able to instill a certain degree of pride and self-worth. The gap between external ascriptions of what it means to be an *almajiri* and internal self-conceptions of those young people living as *almajirai* could hardly be wider.

Discourses about young people often address and open up for debate issues at the heart of the social imaginary (Durham 2004). Comaroff and Comaroff describe youth as:

complex signifiers, the stuff of mythic extremes ... simultaneously idealizations and monstrosities, pathologies and panaceas... [Y]outh stands for many things at once: for the terrors of the present, the errors of the past, the prospect of a future ... In all of these tropic guises, of course, they are figures of a popular imagination far removed from more nuanced social realities. (2006: 268)

The claim that children/youth are "lost" or, given the circumstances under which they grow up, have "lost out on" certain experiences deemed essential for their life stage may well reveal wider fears about the social reproduction of society (see Durham 2004: 591). But the *almajirai* are not only young but also male. Whitehead and Barrett suggest that:

whenever larger social and public concerns raise their head ... very quickly the issue of boys/men comes to the fore; usually how to change them, control them, provide them with purpose, or simply avoid the worst excesses of anti-social male behaviour. What emerges, in fact, is a moral panic around men and masculinity. (2001: 8)

Considering that prevailing ideals of childhood/youth and masculinity—and corresponding notions of deviance—bear the impress of wider societal concerns helps us understand and analyse popular discourses about the *almajirai*.

This chapter is about boys and young men self-identifying as *almajirai*—who may or may not conform to the mental picture that people have of them. What makes them *almajirai*, in their view, is that they are away from home and living with a Quranic teacher (*mallam*) to study the Quran. Using Arabic script, they learn to read, write, and recite it. They are young males from primary-school age to their early twenties, mostly (though not exclusively) from poor rural families. Their schools are largely beyond the state's purview and regulatory interventions, the teacher receiving no salary but living off the support given by the local community, the alms given in exchange for his spiritual services, the contributions of his students, and supplementary income-generating activities. Most teachers are not formally certified but are themselves products of the *almajiri* system. Many schools lack physical infrastructure beyond a canopied forecourt where the teaching takes place. The students do not necessarily sleep, eat, and bath on the actual school 'premises', but often cohabit in other spaces, for example mosques and neighbours'/employers' houses. To sustain themselves, the *almajirai* engage in a plethora of activities, ranging from begging for food and money, to farm work, petty jobs, and trade. Secular subjects do not form part of the *almajirai*'s curriculum, and Islamic subjects other than the Quran are the preserve of advanced learners.

Enrolment in Quranic schools all over Nigeria is estimated to exceed 9.5 million, with more than 8.5 million in the northern part of the country (UBEC 2010). How many of these students are *almajirai*, however, is subject to speculation, as the existing statistics do not differentiate between day-students (who stay with their parents, potentially attend 'modern' school in addition to Quranic school, and include females) and 'boarding' students. The most reliable estimate for Kano suggests that some 300,000 boys and young men—more than an eighth of all 6–21-year olds—live as *almajirai* in that state (Ministry of Education 2008).

MODERNITY, APPROPRIATE CHILDHOODS, AND THE FUTURE OF THE NATION

Almajirci as antipode of modernity/development

Concerned discourses about the *almajirai* can be traced back to the early years of the newly independent state, when modernist nation builders called into question the ability of the 'traditional' Quranic education system to forge a 'modern' citizenry for a united Nigeria. The British, during sixty years of indirect colonial rule in northern Nigeria, had neither reformed the Islamic education sector nor introduced secular education on any noteworthy scale. In this way they sought to avoid tensions with their Muslim subjects, as Christian missionaries provided most early secular schooling. But financial reasons and fear of self-assertive opponents to colonial rule (as had emerged in southern Nigeria from mission schools) also motivated their lack of engagement in the education sector (see Fafunwa 1974; Umar 2001). The needs of the colonial administration were met by employing secular-educated southerners and by offering 'modern' education only to a small section of society (Abdurrahman & Canham 1978).

Mustapha writes that regional differences in education had "a knock-on effect on the regional formation of human capital, and general economic development" (2004: 11) and that "a destabilizing inequality in educational attainment was built into the fabric of the Nigerian state" (*ibid*. 12). At the time of Independence, "Islamic education... appeared to many people to be a positive hindrance to the creation of a united and independent nation". In

1978, Abdurrahman and Canham wrote that "[t]his impression, which is often deliberately encouraged for political reasons, still persists in many areas of Nigeria" (1978: 63). More than thirty years on, discourses about the *almajirai* continue to reflect similar concerns.

Often, the *almajirai* are considered the quintessential challenge to a 'modern' Nigeria. "We are modern now; we don't send our children on *almajiranci*", I was told by an official of the local government education area in Kunchi when I asked whether any children in his family were *almajirai*. The *almajirai* are imagined as relics from the past, "stuck in a time warp" (Fabiyi 2008), their schools being likened to "typewriters" in an era of "computers" (Tilde n.d.). The *almajiri* system, it is claimed, needs "to be overhauled in order to conform with the new economy and modern realities" ("Almajiris: Towards Creating Brighter Future" 2012). It "has locked its students [out of modernity]", students who can neither "read newspapers nor partake in the running of government" (Tilde 2009). The *almajirai* are considered to lack "the practical skills required in the real world to contribute meaningfully to modern society, or even to earn a livelihood" (Suleiman 2009).

As a matter of fact, educational disadvantage in northern Nigeria extends far beyond the *almajirai*, as the low secular school enrolment rates for girls, or the poor achievements of even those children who do attend secular school, attest. According to the Nigerian Demographic and Health Survey, 35 percent of school-aged girls attend primary school in the North-West as compared with 47 percent of boys. In contrast, in the South-East 80 percent of both girls and boys attend. In Sokoto State, 91 percent of children aged 5–16 years cannot at all read a simple sentence in their preferred language; in Lagos State, on the other hand, 92 percent of children can either read the entire sentence or at least parts of it. Only 14 percent of children of that age group in Sokoto manage to add two single-digit numbers correctly (National Population Commission 2011: 44-59; 159-177).

In terms of skills and future prospects, not much sets the *almajirai* apart from other poor, undereducated youth from rural households. That the *almajirai* defy what have been argued to be globalised norms of 'modern' childhood today may contribute to the persistence/prevalence of the idea that they are in fundamental opposition to 'modern' Nigeria and that they, more than others, constitute a problem for development.

'Modern' children for a 'modern' nation

'Modern' Western ideals of childhood as a protected phase of economic dependence, embedded within the nuclear family and the formal education system, became a 'good' for "global export", Boyden says (1997: 190). These ideals have become enshrined in international children's rights legislation and have influenced social policy doctrines.[4] Also, I would argue that they have been embraced, in theory if not practice, by many 'modern', urbanised, better-off Nigerians. I would venture that the *almajirai*'s apparent defiance of 'modern' norms of childhood as a protected phase of economic dependence, embedded within the nuclear family and the formal education system, reinforces their association with 'backwardness' and 'conservatism'. Their failure to fit into blueprints of 'modern' childhood is construed as problematic. Supposedly, the *almajirai* grow up deprived of the "hopes and dreams of a normal childhood" and with "their humanity stolen" ("Picture Of President GEJ With Students" 2012)—as a "generation lost" (Ekaette in Abubakar 2009). They "experience lumpenhood with no substance of childhood", Amzat writes (2008: 57). *Almajirci* has been regarded as being on the same level as female circumcision and the killing of twins and child witches (Owuamanam *et al.* 2012).

As the *almajirai* do not live inside nuclear families, they are often considered to grow up outside appropriate adult care and control. Alternative upbringing arrangements are considered as being, *per se*, unable to provide sufficient support. The National Council for the Welfare of the Destitute, for instance, states that the "lack of parental participation in the moral up-bringing of the Almajiri pupils" predisposes them to become delinquents (NCWD 2001: 95). Jumare writes that many *almajirai* "have never known the love and care of parents, and living the hard life, they grow up generally without emotions or a humane side to them" (2012).

The fact that students often farm with their teacher and, if earning an income through other means, contribute financially to his livelihood has been equated with abuse. Ahmed Bello of the Nigerian National Agency for the Prohibition of Traffic in Persons is quoted as saying the *almajirai*'s provision of free labour on their teachers' farms amounts to "sheer exploitation" (Abubakar 2009). Begging, in particular, has been criticised for being "harmful to both [the *almajirai*'s] physical and mental health with attendant physical and psychological consequences" (Okoye & Yau 1999: 45).

The street as a corrupting space is a recurrent theme. According to Aluaigba, a researcher at Bayero University Kano, street begging exposes *almajirai* "to all sorts of vile and deviant behaviors and immoral acts because they interact freely with people of low virtue like prostitutes, drug addicts and gamblers" (2009: 22).

Defying the norms of 'modern' childhood, the *almajirai* are described as a threat to the project of the 'modern' Nigerian nation in its entirety. President Goodluck Jonathan calls them "dangerous to national development" (Kumolu 2012) and adds that "the time has come for the nation to build on the moral foundations of the traditional school system by providing the Almajiri with conventional knowledge and skills". An article in the *Nigerian Tribune* is titled "Almajirai, street kids and a nation's future", implying an immediate connection between the three (Olagunju 2012). M.E. Fabiyi, a blogger on NigeriaWorld, claims that "[i]t is imperative for Nigerian unity to ensure that the Northern Almajirai are provided with every opportunity to advance themselves" (2008).

It is widely acknowledged that many *almajirai* grow up in difficult conditions. However, we need to be careful when drawing conclusions about what this implies. Not every child living away from his parents is "abandoned"; not every form of work carried out by children amounts to "exploitation"; not every begging child falls prey to corrupting influences. What is more, for many poor children in Nigeria—and elsewhere—contributing to their families' subsistence through work (both within and outside the household) is a matter-of-course feature of everyday survival (see Boyden, Ling & Myers 1998). It is a widespread practice in West Africa to place children with guardians other than their biological parents, not only to forge links with other households, but also to ease the family's subsistence burden and to allow children to seize educational or income opportunities absent at home (see Goody 1981; Bledsoe 1990; Notermans 2008). To consider economic dependence and the setting of a nuclear family as necessary ingredients of a 'proper' childhood means to dismiss the lived realities of the vast majority of young people around the globe as pathological.

Backward and neglectful parents; rogue and gullible children

The notion that the parents of *almajirai* wilfully forfeit 'modern' careers for their children is a recurrent theme in discourses about *almajirci*. Often, the parents are described as hostile to change and ready to "defy every effort aimed at addressing" the system (Kumolu 2012). Moreover, *almajirai*'s parents are frequently depicted as negligent and oblivious of their parental duties. Bala Muhammad, then head of a Kano State directorate created to promote morals and good behaviour, for instance, chides "parents who have more children than they can afford and see Koranic schools as a means to rid themselves of the extra burden" (Abubakar 2009; see Sule-Kano 2008).

As their parents are dubbed backward and neglectful, the *almajirai* themselves are considered gullible and rogue. The circumstances of their upbringing are often presented as sufficient conditions to make them inherently dangerous. Saudatu Sani, a federal legislator from Kano State, claimed about the *almajirai* that "[t]he pathetic life they live... breeds heartless criminals" (Abubakar 2009). It has been asserted that, "[h]ungry and angry", the *almajirai* can easily be mobilised to engage in lootings and killings during ethno-religious clashes so as to pay society back (Abubakar 2009). Awofeso *et al.* writes of the "immense" "terrorist potential of having about one million hungry and gullible children roaming aimlessly in Nigeria's northern cities, from whom any fanatic, religious or otherwise, could readily recruit disciples for antisocial purposes" (2003: 320).

To my knowledge, the claim that the *almajirai* participate in violence, whether interreligious or sectarian, has been investigated systematically only on one occasion, namely in the aftermath of the Maitatsine crisis of the 1980s. A federal government-constituted Tribunal of Inquiry established that children aged 10–14 years, unaccompanied by their parents, were amongst Maitatsine's followers.[5] Yet, it would be hasty to conclude from this that *almajirai* are violent *per se*. Assuming that violence results automatically from some inherent feature of the *almajiri* education system aborts prematurely the search for more meaningful explanations of violent behaviour. Some 9.5 million boys and girls all over Nigeria attend Quranic schools, either in addition to attendance in a secular school, or as their only educational experience (UBEC 2010). Clearly, little is gained by suspecting all Quranic students indiscriminately of becoming violent militants. On the contrary, such general suspicion may even be dangerous as it can alienate the constituencies of the traditional Quranic education system.

Last argues that it is easy to declare disengagement from the national project to be "backward'"and "conservative", "but that is to take on, unthinkingly, the perception of the modernising faction in the country, with its different moral values and modes of living" (2009a: 4). Those parts of society commonly associated with the new Nigeria, amongst them non-Muslims, 'southerners', the nouveaux riches, and 'modern youth', often do not conform to Muslim/Hausa codes of behaviour, which emphasise "truthfulness, restraint (in words and actions), courtesy to others including strangers, [and] deference to seniors" (*ibid.* 6). To juxtapose "Muslim/Hausa values" with "modern Nigerian values" assumes that they can be told apart neatly and overlooks their historical entanglement. But there is an argument to be made about the disjuncture between the norms (if not behaviour) reigning among many 'commoners'/poor (*talakawa*) in Hausaland—among them the constituencies of the *almajiri* system—and the more cosmopolitanised Nigerian middle and upper classes (be they Hausa/Muslim or not) that have larger stakes and a greater presence in the 'modern' Nigerian project.

Framing the challenges the Nigerian nation-state is facing today in terms of the presumed backwardness and conservatism of a specific group carries the danger of dismissing alienation from the values 'modern' Nigeria has come to represent as a mere cultural defect. If having a "non-modern", "conservative", or "backward" childhood can explain problematic behaviour and even violence, one is spared having to look further for reasons accounting for the current crisis, and especially for reasons that might be corollaries of specifically 'modern' developments in Nigeria—such as the growing inequalities and individualism brought about by economic change. As long as the inadequacies of the *almajiri* system can serve to explain the Boko Haram-related violence, it is possible to blank out more complicated questions about poverty, inequality, and alienation.

THE ALMAJIRAI'S LIVED EXPERIENCES

Complex social realities defying one-dimensional narratives

The narrative of 'backward' parents refusing their children access to 'beneficial' knowledge is easily digestible. It does not call into question the set-up of Nigerian society or dominant conceptions of appropriate 'development' interventions (such as universal basic education). It also suggests that apposite policy responses to the *almajiri* system are an uncontroversial and straightforward choice. Could the 'problem' posed by the *almajirai* not be 'solved' with a ban on the system? The Northern Traditional Rulers' Council at least suggests such a ban (Folaranmi 2011), as does Senate President David Mark (Ogunmade 2013). Plateau State outlawed street begging by school-aged children in 2009, and on the federal level a similar law is in the legislative pipeline. Unfortunately, however, social realities are more complex than the dominant narrative suggests, making punitive and abolitionist approaches a problematic choice.

It is a commonplace that the parents enrolling their children as *almajirai* do not appreciate secular knowledge. Yet, throughout my research, I have not actually met anyone who considered secular education as principally *haram* (forbidden) and met very few who thought it not particularly desirable (see e.g. Brigaglia 2008). Appreciation of different forms of knowledge is reflected in children's educational trajectories. Many young people do not live as *almajirai* throughout their childhood and youth, but—voluntarily or forced by circumstances—switch between different educational options. Their schooling trajectories may, for example, include episodes in so-called *Islamiyya* schools. These are modernised Islamic schools that teach the Quran but also other Islamic, and in some instances 'modern'/secular subjects. Many *almajirai* also attend secular school for a couple of years before enrolling as Quranic students and plan to further their secular education in the future. Former *almajirai* are likely to make up a large part of the clientele of adult evening schools.[6]

Various people in Albasu informed me that in the past people did not value secular education, but now most had come to understand its benefits. Yet, increasing acceptance on principle has been thwarted by state withdrawal from the education sector since structural adjustment (Umar 2003; Baba 2011). While basic education is officially free, in reality it involves recurrent expenses: for textbooks and writing materials, uniforms, transportation where necessary, levies for the rehabilitation of school facilities (which are often in a deplorable state), levies to buy chalk, brooms, report cards, and such sundry running costs. Post-primary education in particular has its price—beginning with the bribe sometimes required to secure one of the limited places[7]— and often requires students to commute/board. Poor-quality teaching (see Johnson 2010), costs—including lost opportunity costs in terms of foregone children's work (see Tomasevski 2005)—insecurity about transitions to the next level of schooling, and more than insecure pay-offs in terms of future opportunities: all these make parents wonder whether secular school is quite worth the investment.

Admittedly, my research may underestimate remaining resentments on ideological grounds against secular education, as people opposed to anything 'Western' may have avoided meeting me/talking to me, and as interviewees may have concealed critical views thinking they would make me, a secular school product, uncomfortable. Several people I spoke to felt that secular knowledge comes second in importance to religious knowledge. Whereas parents may find it excusable to let their children's *boko* education slide, most felt strongly about ensuring their wards acquire at least a modicum of Quranic knowledge. But whatever the role of remaining resentments against *boko* education, given the financial difficulties poor parents face attempting to enrol and sustain their children in secular education, we cannot jump to the conclusion that it is necessarily a dislike for secular education that makes children drop out of secular school / enrol as *almajirai*. Also, to dismiss critical views on *boko* education out of hand as 'backward' is problematic. It ignores the fact that negative attitudes towards *boko* education originate, in part at least, in contemporary social and political conditions. Boko Haram, for example, links its rejection of *boko* to the corruption and depravity of today's elites, most of whom are 'modern' school products (see Last 2009b).

People make reasoned decisions based on the options available to them, and costly and poor-quality secular education may not make for a particularly attractive choice. The *almajiri* system, on the other hand, offers redress for a number of situations. Gathering the resources to launch an adult career—that is, to build a room for prospective bride(s) and children, and to marry—affords a real challenge to adolescent boys and young men in an eroding rural economy where opportunities to earn cash income are scarce. Seasonal or permanent migration to the cities, which offer petty income opportunities as street vendors and odd-job men, promises redress. Migration, especially during the agriculturally unproductive dry season, is indeed a common strategy of Sahelian peasant households to reduce their subsistence burden and allows boys to acquire livelihood skills appropriate to the ecology of the region (Mustapha & Meagher 1992; Mortimore 1998).

Divorce is frequent and easy to attain in Hausaland. In 1959, Smith wrote that "[t]he average Hausa woman probably makes three or four marriages before the menopause" (1959: 244). The repeated efforts of Kano State governor Rabiu Kwankwaso to marry off divorcees suggest that divorce continues to be pervasive ("Another 1,000 divorcees, widows up for wedding in Kano" 2013; see also Solivetti 1994). Many marriages end in divorce because husbands fail to take care of the basic subsistence needs of their families, or because of fights between/over co-wives. In the case of divorce, the need may arise to re-accommodate children. Divorced mothers, who are expected to re-marry soon, can rarely move into new marriages with children from previous ones. Children left with fathers are at risk of suffering neglect and of abuse from stepmothers.

High maternal mortality also renders children motherless (Federal Ministry of Health 2011). For boys, the *almajiri* system offers a way out under such constrained circumstances.

In summary, multiple economic, cultural, and religious factors interact together to make some parents prefer *almajirci* over other options. Poverty is a major factor constraining choice; 'modern' secular education often does not constitute a meaningful option; high divorce rates necessitate the re-accommodation of children. Norms about the gender-appropriate upbringing of children, religious beliefs in the need to prepare for the hereafter, and a concern with boys' acquisition of livelihood skills appropriate to the peasant economy and ecology of the region—all these factors also play a role in enrolment decisions. To shrug off all cultural/religious motives for *almajirci* as 'backward' means to dismiss the potential for change that lies in understanding them. What is more, an exclusive focus on the *almajiri* system as a putative radicalising agent in young people's lives overlooks the fact that the *almajirai* do not constitute the neatly separable social category which they are often portrayed as. Many young men are not 'pure' products of the *almajiri* system, but have also experienced other strands of education. Any serious assessment of processes of Islamist radicalisation and militancy needs to take into account the sum total of these experiences.

Meanwhile, it is convenient for many to point accusing fingers at the *almajirai*. The next section explores why this is the case and what the consequences are for the *almajirai*'s well-being and sense of dignity.

Scapegoats at the bottom of the status hierarchy

Most *almajirai* do not know that the media write about them as "cancer" (Suleiman 2009, commentator) and about their schools as "breeding grounds" for "monsters" ("Rehabilitating our almajiris" 2011). But they know that the people in the urban neighbourhoods to which they come to study talk about them as urchins and hoodlums. While they felt fairly well accepted within their rural communities, most *almajirai* I worked with—from very young ones to almost-adults—had experienced rejection and contempt in urban areas, ranging from insults, to 'donations' of spoilt food, to physical assaults. They were painfully aware of negative opinions about them and frequently voiced their distress about being denied even a minimum of respect as human beings. Bashir,[8] an *almajiri* at Sabuwar Kofa in urban Kano (12 years old), felt they were treated as even less than animals, for no reason other than being *almajirai*:

> Some of them don't think *almajirai* are human. To some, a dog is better than an *almajiri*[9] ... To some, an *almajiri*, as long as he is an *almajiri*, they just take him to be a bad person. They think he is an animal, that a donkey is even better than an *almajiri*.

As newcomers/strangers at their places of study, the *almajirai* feel they are vulnerable to abuses they would not be exposed to back home, and which young *'yan gari* (children of the town), youngsters living at home with their parents, are not exposed to. In a society in which individuals derive their social standing from the people they 'belong' to, be it family members or patrons, being unable to display such belonging means to be vulnerable/defenceless.[10] The term *gata* connotes a person whom you can legitimately expect to stand up, as well as provide materially, for you. The *almajirai* I conducted my research with often explained the abuses they suffered with reference to the apparent absence of such guardians/protectors. During the script-writing process for the film, for instance, the participating boys noted that *almajirai* are often mistreated because

> people see he [the *almajiri*] doesn't have a guardian/protector [*gata*]; and if they mistreat him, nothing will happen to them. And the *almajirai*'s teachers want to live in peace with the people from town. That's why even if *almajirai* have been mistreated, they'll tell them to have patience. (Script-writing, 22 July 2011)

I would not go so far as to suggest that it is considered legitimate to treat someone badly for lack of *gata*, but as an explanation for bad/heedless treatment it makes immediate sense to people. Command over / claims to other people's respect, I would venture, inhere not in the individual but in the social hierarchy she/he belongs to. To fend off assaults on their dignity, the *almajirai* participating in the film project declared they too had their supporters/protectors, rather than demanding that everyone should be treated with respect and dignity irrespective of whether or not he has *gata*. Buhari, for example, an *almajiri* in Albasu and part of the crew with whom I produced the film/docu-drama about the lives of *almajirai*, proclaims at the end credits where the *almajirai* spell out their messages to the public:

> I want those people who abuse *almajirai* to understand that they [the *almajirai*] also have people who care about them (*gata*).

There are other sources of vulnerability for *almajirai*, apart from their difficulties in displaying 'belonging'. Unlike in a village context where nearly everyone knows nearly everyone else's family background, in an urban environment, anonymity characterises many encounters. Displays of belonging have thus been complemented with novel ways of signalling one's status. Demonstrations of wealth are of course a popular default option for those wishing to make claims to high rank: posh cars are the preserve of the rich; flashy mobile phones and glamorous clothes belong to the symbolic repertoire also of the somewhat less-lavishly endowed. Finally, shows of one's mastery of prestigious and hard-to-attain forms of knowledge—for example, conversing in English (preferably in the presence of Hausa-only speakers!), reciting the Quran in the *qira'a* of Hafs (rather than the "folk" Warsh version), or at least greeting (*Assalamu alaikum wa rahmatullah he wa barakatuhu*) with an Arabic accent—work effectively to create instantaneous hierarchies. Unfortunately, most *almajirai* lack the economic and cultural capital required to participate in such new styles of differentiation. For the most part, they do not command the financial resources for displays of wealth, and 'modern' forms of knowledge are difficult to acquire, especially for those attending Quranic school only.

On top of this, their often precarious access to food compounds the *almajirai*'s low status. In Hausaland, the language of food is often used to express social relationships. Eating (*ci*) plays a central role in metaphors of power, the word "eating" being used to describe situations such as winning a victory, conquering a place, or having coitus with a woman (see Last 2000a: 374). Having stable/secure access to food signals status. *Almajirai*, conversely, often toil to find enough food for the day. "Not to eat is to experience what it is to lack power," Last writes (*ibid.*). Not to be in a position to choose whose food to accept and whose food to refuse means to lack leverage to signal discontent, protest against bad treatment, or pass moral judgement. Social harmony is sealed/expressed by the exchange of food. Refusing somebody's food, on the contrary, subtly signals dissent in a culture where open confrontation is shunned. Yet, this option is not always open to *almajirai*. The *almajirai* I befriended knew of fellow students who are so hungry that they would dry and re-boil food that had gone off. Food is usually eaten communally, and refusing to share with the members of one's community is hardly legitimate. Going hungry means to be excluded from the benefits of community membership.

Altogether, there is little to protect the *almajirai* from lingering at the bottom of the status hierarchy. This makes them easy prey to those searching for scapegoats. The *almajirai* involved in the film project were upset about having to serve as scapegoats for all kinds of incidents in their neighbourhoods.

Without someone answering for them close by, they felt they had become fair game for unfair accusations. Auwalu, for example, stated during the script-writing for the film:

> Some offences, it's not an *almajiri* who committed them; it's the people/kids from town [*'yan gari*]. But they'll just say an *almajiri* committed it. If there's a school close by, they'll just go and tell the *mallam* [Quranic teacher]: "Look what your *almajirai* did"; whereas it wasn't them who did it. The people from the neighbourhood don't see their own children's faults. (Script-writing, 22 July 2011)

It is handy for people to blame *almajirai* for petty incidents in their neighbourhoods, as it carries little risk of stepping on the toes of powerful protectors. The children in my neighbourhood at Sabuwar Kofa had understood this very well. On two occasions, I witnessed how young thieves in my house attempted to put the blame on the *almajirai* studying with my neighbour, a teacher of the Quran, after they had been discovered. Low status, then, can engender even lower status: since *almajirai* often lack the power to refute unjustified accusations, these feed negative stereotypes.

Struggling to come to terms with prejudice and stigma

What are the consequences of widespread prejudice and stigma for the young people living as *almajirai*? Aware of the negative views people hold of them, they struggle to defend their sense of self and of purpose. The *almajirai* I got to know well embraced time and again self-definitions as devoted scholars migrating in search of sacred knowledge, in order to challenge narratives that cast them and their fellow students as the product of parental neglect and poverty. During the script-writing for our film/docu-drama, for example, the boys involved in the film project invoked any number of social, cultural, and religious arguments to justify enrolment as an *almajiri*:

- At home, he [a child] becomes stubborn, quarrelsome with other children and disrespectful towards elders. If he's told to go to school, he doesn't go. He just goes for a stroll, annoying the people in the neighbourhood.

- Some are worried about the kind of kids their children associate with. That is why they decide to take them to school. Because if they left them at home, they might become spoiled; but if they take them to school, someone is looking after them because it's the *mallam*'s work to look after them.

- Parents want their children to get to know their religion, and know people, and know how to live together with people.

On other occasions, the *almajirai* categorically refuted explanations invoking poverty or difficult conditions at home as reasons for *almajiri* enrolment. Nasiru, for instance, an *almajiri* at Sabuwar Kofa (15 years), contended that

> especially now that there is *boko*, if you come for *almajirci*, some people think it's because you don't have food in your house: that's why you come out to beg. But it's not like that; it's because you're searching for knowledge.

Habibu (15 years) refuted the claim of parental neglect, suggesting that

> people bring their children to Quranic school not because they hate them, but because they want them to have the knowledge.

Being vilified as miscreants leaves its mark on the young people living as *almajirai*. How strongly a concern respect was felt by the *almajirai* participating in the film project becomes apparent in the messages to the public they included in the end credits of the film. Six of the nine participants voice respect as their biggest worry and call for a more sympathetic view on *almajirai*. For example:

- I want those who think *almajirai* are bad people, to know that they aren't. Either speak good about us, or keep quiet. (Kabiru Idris)
- I call upon you to stop accusing *almajirai* of things they didn't do. Please inquire first before you just accuse the *almajirai*. (Naziru Usman)
- I call upon those people who insult us, who think we are useless, to stop as of today, for the sake of Allah. (Auwalu Mahdmud)

Elsewhere, I have described how the *almajirai* struggle to maintain their sense of self and self-worth in this context of rejection and denigration (Hoechner 2011). The young people I got to know during my research embraced an explicitly moral conception of what it means to be an *almajiri* that allowed them to take pride in their identity as *almajirai* despite widespread societal disapproval. To know that they knew how to 'behave well' and possessed the 'moral knowledge' society often claimed they lacked helped them to maintain dignity in the face of negative attitudes. By asserting their moral superiority over their traducers—for example, behaving well and properly when treated in an obviously ungodly way—they could win at least a moral victory. Also, the *almajirai* frequently shifted (justifiably or not) the blame they felt was unfairly offloaded unto their shoulders to *'yan daba*, the members of urban ward gangs (see Casey 2007, 2008). Yet, such strategies cannot dispel completely the frustration caused by repeated confrontation with negative attitudes. The *almajirai* I spent considerable time with during the film production were quite frustrated with the rich and ruling classes, who in their view did not live up to their obligation to provide for the *almajirai* in the same way as they provide for the students of *boko* school (*'yan boko*).[11] As citizens (*'yan kasa*), the *almajirai* felt that they deserved to be accorded the same rights (*'yanci*).

CONCLUSION

Since the violence related to Boko Haram has escalated in northern Nigeria, the *almajirai*, already low in the social status hierarchy before the crisis began, have emerged as a popular target for accusations. Many think that traditional Quranic schools supply the "cannon fodder" for Boko Haram ("Rehabilitating our almajiris" 2011). So far, however, there is no conclusive empirical evidence to justify such conclusions. This chapter has probed why the *almajirai* are nevertheless so commonly associated with Islamist militancy and violence. I have argued that the *almajirai*'s apparent defiance of the norms of 'modern' childhood is often interpreted as a wilful rejection of 'modern' institutions and developments. Judging the conditions of their upbringing as unsuitable for children, many predict pathological results for the *almajirai*. Yet, such reasoning overlooks that the blueprints for 'modern' childhood prove unattainable for many poor children. It also hides from view that often it is poverty and the absence of meaningful secular education rather than a rejection of *boko* that makes parents enrol their sons as *almajirai*. What is more, if inadequate formal and vocational skills cause violence (as many discussing the *almajirai* as thugs- and militants-to-be assume), we are ill-advised to focus our attention merely on the *almajirai*: educational disadvantage in northern Nigeria extends far beyond them.

The second part of this chapter illustrated the practical mechanisms that make the *almajirai* convenient scapegoats. The *almajirai* are at the bottom of the status hierarchy and lack guardians to speak for them in their places of study. Blaming *almajirai* carries little risk of stepping on the toes of powerful protectors. But accusations that are experienced as unfair not only alienate and frustrate those whom they target, they also develop a reality of their own. As *almajirai* often lack the power to disprove unfounded accusations, these accusations remain in the air and feed negative stereotypes, which may lead to fresh accusations.

To improve the *almajirai*'s situation, rethinking stereotypes is necessary. Rather than reviling the system, viable alternatives need to be made available to poor rural households. The *almajirai* (and other poor undereducated youth) must be offered opportunities to further their education and to find work. These are more demanding tasks for governments than simply drafting legislation to ban the system. This chapter aimed to show that the presumably easy answers provided by punitive and abolitionist approaches to the *almajiri* system are chimaeras. Banning the system without providing alternatives will not help the current crisis in Nigeria's North. Blaming the *almajiri* system for negative outcomes without thinking about the larger societal forces underpinning the crisis—inequality, poverty, and alienation from the values 'modern' Nigeria has come to represent—may well compound rather than solve Nigeria's problems.

Notes

1. Among them, *234NEXT* (Lagos); BBC Africa; *Business Day* (Lagos); CNN; *Daily Times* (Lagos); *The Guardian* (Lagos); *Leadership* (Abuja); *The Nation* (Lagos); *Punch* (Lagos); *Sun News* (Lagos); *ThisDay* (Abuja); *Nigerian/Saturday Tribune* (Ibadan); *Daily/Sunday Triumph* (Kano); *Daily/Weekly/Sunday Trust* (Abuja); and *Vanguard* (Lagos).
2. Among them, Nairaland; Nigerian Village Square; and gamji.com.
3. Available online at: http://www.qeh.ox.ac.uk/research/video/video-hlg.
4. Nigeria is a signatory to the United Nations Convention on the Rights of the Child since 1991. Owing to resistance from different segments of society on religious and cultural grounds, it was not domesticated until 2003. To date, not all states have passed the Child's Rights Act into law. Norms prohibiting child trafficking are frequently considered applicable to the *almajirai* (e.g. Amali 2005; Olujuwon 2008).
5. Federal Republic of Nigeria (1981): *Report of Tribunal of Inquiry on Kano Disturbances (Maitatsine)* (cited in Awofeso, Ritchie & Degeling 2003).
6. This impression is based on visits to two different adult evening education centres in Kano City and on information from older/former *almajirai*.
7. I was told on several occasions that children did not proceed to secondary school, even though they would have liked to and had performed well in primary school, because they could not secure admission. I was told that admission certificates—a scarce and prized item, as the number of secondary school places is limited—are

often distributed based not on merit but on 'purchasing power'.

8. I have changed the names of informants where I felt it necessary to protect their identity. Where informants were comfortable with statements being publicised in their name and where I considered this safe for them, I have left names unchanged.

9. Unlike cats, which may be kept as pets, dogs entertain little sympathy in Hausa society. They are considered polluting, and Prophet Mohammed also disliked them (personal communication with Murray Last, 7 December 2010).

10. Conversely, being unable to protect one's 'own people' is a sign of weakness. Last argues with reference to the Biafran war that "[t]o kill a leader's defenceless, dependent women and children is to strike where he is most vulnerable, and to inflict on him maximum hurt ... their weakness is his weakness. To attack them is not seen necessarily as immoral" (Last 2000b). The threat of Boko Haram spokesperson Shekau to retaliate against policemen's women and children is a case in point (http://www.youtube.com/watch?v=kBemHl-tnsc [Accessed on 27 January 2012]).

11. Given the low standards and limited resources of most government *boko* schools in northern Nigeria, it is somewhat ironic that someone would envy them for the support they receive.

References

Abdurrahman, A.M. & P. Canham (1978), *The ink of the scholar: the Islamic tradition of education in Nigeria*. Lagos: Macmillan Nigeria.

Abubakar, A. (2009), "Nigeria struggles to curb rise in child beggars", *The Telegraph*, 18 November. http://www.telegraph.co.uk/expat/expatnews/6596232/Nigeria-struggles-to-curb-rise-in-child-beggars.html [Accessed on 25 September 2013].

Alkali, A. (2009), "10 Million Kids Beg in the North—Minister", *Leadership*, Abuja, Nigeria, 22 November. http://allafrica.com/stories/200911231395.html [Accessed on 25 September 2013].

"Almajiris: Towards Creating Brighter Future for the Street Kids" (2012), *ThisDay*, 22 April. http://www.thisdaylive.com/articles/almajiris-towards-creating-brighter-future-for-the-street-kids/114304/ [Accessed on 25 September 2013].

Aluaigba, M.T. (2009), "Circumventing or superimposing poverty on the African child? The Almajiri syndrome in Northern Nigeria", *Childhood in Africa* 1(1): 1-37. http://www.afrchild.ohio.edu/CAJ/articles/AluaigbaCAJ2009.pdf [Accessed on 25 September 2013].

Amali, A.U. (2005), "Almajirci as Child Trafficking", *Daily Trust*, 14 October. http://allafrica.com/stories/200510140663.html [Accessed on 25 September 2013]

Amzat, J. (2008), Lumpen Childhood in Nigeria: A Case of the Almajirai in Northern Nigeria, *Hemispheres* 23: 55-66.

[Anonymous] (2012), "The Popular Discourses of Salafi Radicalism and Salafi Counter-radicalism in Nigeria: A Case Study of Boko Haram", *Journal of Religion in Africa* 42: 118-144.

"Another 1,000 divorcees, widows up for wedding in Kano" (2013), *Premium Times*, 23 May. http://premiumtimesng.com/regional/135915-another-1-000-divorcees-widows-up-for-wedding-in-kano.html [Accessed 25 September 2013].

Awofeso, N., J. Ritchie & P. Degeling (2003), "The Almajiri Heritage and the Threat of Non-State Terrorism in Northern Nigeria—Lessons from Central Asia and Pakistan", *Studies in Conflict & Terrorism* 26(4): 311-325.

Baba, N.M. (2011), "Islamic Schools, the Ulama, and the State in the Educational Development of Northern Nigeria", *Bulletin de L'APAD* 33.

Bledsoe, C. (1990), "No success without struggle: social mobility and hardship for foster children in Sierra Leone", *Man* 25(1): 70-88.

Boyden, J. (1997), "Childhood and the Policy Makers: A Comparative Perspective on the Globalization of Childhood". In: A. James & A. Prout, eds, *Constructing and Reconstructing Childhood* (2nd ed.). London: Falmer Press, pp. 190-229.

Boyden, J., B. Ling & W.E. Myers (1998), *What works for working children*. Stockholm, Sweden: Rädda Barnen.

Brigaglia, A. (2008), "'We ain't coming to take people away': A Sufi Praise-song and the Representation of Police Forces in Northern Nigeria", *Annual Review of Islam in Africa* 10: 50-57.

Casey, C. (2007), "'Policing' through violence: fear, vigilantism, and the politics of Islam in northern Nigeria". In: D. Pratten & A. Sen, eds, *Global Vigilantes*. London: Hurst, pp. 93-124.

——— (2008), "'Marginal Muslims': Politics and the Perceptual Bounds of Islamic Authenticity in Northern Nigeria", *Africa Today* 54(3): 67-92.

Comaroff, J. & J. Comaroff (2006), "Reflections on youth, from the past to the postcolony". In: M.S. Fisher & G. Downey, eds, *Frontiers of Capital: Ethnographic Reflections on the New Economy*. Durham: Duke University Press, pp. 267-281.

Durham, D. (2004), "Disappearing youth", *American Ethnologist* 31(4): 589-605.

Fabiyi, M.E. (2008), "Misconceptions in analyzing northern Nigeria and the implications for Nigerian unity: contextualizing & addressing the almajirai challenge", *NigeriaWorld*. http://nigeriaworld.com/feature/publication/fabiyi/121908.htm [Accessed 23 July 2012]

Fafunwa, B.A. (1974), *History of education in Nigeria*. London: Allen and Unwin.

Federal Ministry of Health (2011), *Saving Newborn Lives in Nigeria: Newborn Health in the Context of the Integrated Maternal, Newborn and Child Health Strategy* (Revised 2nd edn.). Abuja, Nigeria: Federal Ministry of Health, Save the Children, Johns Hopkins University's Health Organisation.

Folaranmi, F.Y. (2011), "Fallout of Boko Haram bombings: Emirs spit fire", *Sun News Online*, 19 November. http://www.sunnewsonline.com/webpages/news/national/2011/nov/19/national-19-11-2011-09.html [Accessed 14 January 2012]

Goody, E. (1981), *Parenthood and social reproduction: fostering and occupational roles in West Africa*. Cambridge: Cambridge University Press.

Hoechner, H. (2011), "Striving for Knowledge and Dignity: How Qur'anic Students in Kano, Nigeria, Learn to Live with Rejection and Educational Disadvantage", *European Journal of Development Research* 23(5): 712-728.

Johnson, D. (2010), *An Assessment of the Professional Working Knowledge of Teachers in Nigeria: Implications for Teacher Development, Policy and Implementation*. Kano, Nigeria: Education Sector Support Programme in Nigeria.

Jumare, F.I. (2012), "Almajiri : The Invisible Child", *The Politico*, August. http://the-politico.com/development/almajiri-the-invisible-child/ [Accessed 25 September 2013].

Kumolu, C. (2012), "Almajiri education: Modern gang up against ancient tradition?", *Vanguard*, 26 April. http://www.vanguardngr.com/2012/04/almajiri-education-modern-gang-up-against-ancient-tradition/ [Accessed 25 September 2013].

Last, M. (2000a), "Children and the Experience of Violence: Contrasting Cultures of Punishment in Northern Nigeria", *Africa: Journal of the International African Institute* 70(3): 359-393.

—— (2000b), "Reconciliation and Memory in Postwar Nigeria". In: V. Das, ed., *Violence and Subjectivity*. London: University of California Press, pp. 315-332.

—— (2009a), "Nation-breaking & not-belonging in Nigeria—withdrawal, resistance, riot?", Leipzig. http://www.uni-leipzig.de/~ecas2009/index.php?option=com_docman&task=cat_view&gid=57&Itemid=24 [Accessed 25 September 2013].

—— (2009b), "The pattern of dissent : Boko haram in Nigeria 2009", *Annual Review of Islam in Africa* 10: 7-11.

Ministry of Education (2008), *Educational Sector Analysis*. Kano, Nigeria.

Mortimore, M. (1998), *Roots in the African Dust*. Cambridge: Cambridge University Press.

Mustapha, A. (2004), *Ethnic structure, inequality and governance of the public sector in*

Nigeria. UNRISD (United Nations Research Institute for Social Development). http://www.unrisd.org/unrisd/website/document.nsf/240da49ca467a53f802 56b4f005ef245/c6a23857ba3934ccc12572ce0024bb9e/$FILE/Mustapha.pdf [Accessed 25 September 2013].

Mustapha, A.R. & K. Meagher (1992), "Stress, Adaptation, and Resilience in Rural Kano", *Capitalism, Nature, Socialism* 5(2): 107-117.

National Population Commission (2011), *Nigeria Demographic and Health Survey (DHS) EdData Profile 1990, 2003, and 2008: Education Data for Decision-Making*. Washington, DC, USA: National Population Commission and RTI International.

NCWD (2001), *Almajiri and Qur'anic education*. Kaduna, Nigeria: National Council for the Welfare of the Destitute, Almajirci Directorate.

Notermans, C. (2008), "The Emotional World of Kinship: Children's experiences of fosterage in East Cameroon", *Childhood* 15(3): 355-377.

Ogunmade, O. (2013), "Mark Urges Northern Govs to Ban Almajiri System", *ThisDay*, 23 May. http://www.thisdaylive.com/articles/mark-urges-northern-govs-to-ban-almajiri-system/148259/ [Accessed 25 September 2013].

Okoye, F. & Y. Yau (1999), *The condition of almajirai in the North West Zone of Nigeria*. Kaduna, Nigeria: Human Rights Monitor & UNICEF.

Olagunju, L. (2012,), "Almajirai, street kids and a nation's future", *Nigerian Tribune*, 20 April. http://tribune.com.ng/index.php/the-friday-edition/39559-almajirai-street-kids-and-a-nations-future [Accessed 7 June 2012].

Olujuwon, T. (2008), "Combating Trafficking in Person: A Case Study of Nigeria", *European Journal of Scientific Research* 24(1): 23-32.

Owuamanam, J., S. Aborisade, O. Ubabukoh & D. Attah (2012), "Almajiri schools: Civil rights group disagrees with Afenifere, ACF", *The Punch*, 13 April. http://www.punchng.com/education/almajiri-schools-civil-rights-group-disagrees-with-afenifere-acf/ [Accessed 25 September 2013].

"Picture Of President GEJ With Students Of The New Almajiri School In Sokoto—Politics (4)—Nairaland" (2012), *Nairaland Forum*. http://www.nairaland.com/912445/picture-president-gej-students-new/4 [Accessed 12 July 2012].

"Rehabilitating our almajiris" (2011), *234NEXT*, 22 June. http://234next.com/csp/cms/sites/Next/Opinion/5716077-146/story.csp [Accessed 22 July 2012].

Smith, M.G. (1959), "The Hausa system of social status", *Africa* 29(3): 239-252.

Solivetti, L.M. (1994), "Family, Marriage and Divorce in a Hausa Community: A Sociological Model", *Africa* 64(2): 252-271.

Soyinka, W. (2012), "The Butchers Of Nigeria", *Newsweek*, 16 January, pp. 1-5. http://www.thedailybeast.com/newsweek/2012/01/15/wole-soyinka-on-nigeria-s-anti-christian-terror-sect-boko-haram.html [Accessed 25 September 2013].

Sule-Kano, A. (2008), *Poverty and the Traditional Qur'anic School System in Northern Nigeria: The Politics of the Almajiri-phenomenon*. Paper prepared for the Conference on Nigerian Youth and National Development, Centre for Democratic Research and Training, Mambayya House, Bayero University, Kano, Nigeria, 5–6 August.

Suleiman, S. (2009,), "Iliya, the Almajiri", *234NEXT*, 25 September, pp. 1-6. http://www.saharareporters.com/index.php?option=com_content&view=article&id=3793:iliya-the-almajiri&catid=81:external-contrib&Itemid=300 [Accessed 23 January 2012].

Tilde, A.U. (n.d.), "The Future of the Almajiri (3)", *Gamji*. http://www.gamji.com/tilde/tilde107.htm [Accessed 26 September 2012].

———— (2009), "The Future of the Almajiri (2)", *Gamji*. http://www.gamji.com/tilde/tilde106.htm [Accessed 26 September 2012].

Tomasevski, K. (2005), "Not Education for All, Only for Those Who Can Pay: The World Bank's Model for Financing Primary Education", *Law, Social Justice & Global Development Journal* 9(1): 1-19.

UBEC (2010), *National Framework for the Development and Integration of Almajiri Education into UBE Programme*. Abuja, Nigeria: Universal Basic Education Commission, 1-26.

Umar, M. (2001), "Education and Islamic trends in northern Nigeria: 1970s–1990s", *Africa Today* 48(2): 127-150.

———— (2003), "Profiles of New Islamic Schools in Northern Nigeria", *The Maghreb Review* 28(2-3): 146-169.

Whitehead, S.M. & F.J. Barrett (2001), *The masculinities reader*. Cambridge: Polity.

4

CHRISTIAN PERCEPTIONS OF ISLAM & SOCIETY IN RELATION TO BOKO HARAM

Recent Events in Jos and Northern Nigeria

Henry Gyang Mang

Centre for Conflict Management and Peace Studies
University of Jos, Nigeria

The rhetoric on and around religious conflict in Nigeria has revolved around the two main religions of Christianity and Islam. Although the growth of the two religions in the country has afforded them the latitude of being instruments for broad national negotiations, the growing diversity within them has led only to growing antipathy between their adherents. This has been further worsened by the emergence of Boko Haram, a phenomenon which has not only added new perspectives to the discourse on religion and national unity in Nigeria, but has also encouraged strong desires for reciprocal action among those affected by the movement's violence, and a growing militancy within various agencies of Christianity. This work gauges the various perceptions and perspectives of Christians towards Islam in contemporary Nigeria, considering factors such as identity, geography, and the growing dynamism in Christian belief and doctrine concerning 'the other'. It argues that there are four main divisions into which Christianity in Nigeria has evolved based on issues surrounding Islam. These divisions (Conservative Hierarchical, Conservative Egalitarian, Liberal Political, and Radical) have presented various reactions based on their histories and present predicaments. And although it cannot be conclusively argued that Christians have a single, general point of view on Islam's 'bloody corridors', the increasing violence, which has affected Christians, has created an atmosphere in which the rhetoric can easily slide towards calls for revenge, even when there is no true logic for it.

INTRODUCTION

Recent violent events in northern Nigeria, and worldwide generally, seem to reaffirm Huntington's hypothesis of a "Clash in Civilisations". Although the phrase itself has attained cliché status from both its opponents and proponents, there is little denying the fact that historically dynamic identity leanings have become the major factors for conflict in contemporary times; and even where they do not seem to be present, they in one way or the other emerge subliminally in the wider configurations and designs of belligerents of almost all contemporary conflicts.

The case of Islam and Christianity in Nigeria presents a compelling thrust to this argument. In general, since 2001, after the World Trade Center bombings in New York, many Christians in Nigeria have joined in the fray of the narrative about "the bloody corridors" of Islam. This was significantly more so for Christians in the north-central state of Plateau. Just three days before the New York events, their own violent event occurred. The Jos Crisis, as it came to be known, occurred on a Friday, and significantly after the *Jum'maat* prayers of 7 September. Although different narratives, both remote and immediate, have been presented, quite a number of Christians in Jos conclusively alleged that a Muslim agenda to overwhelm a predominantly Christian area was in the offing. Hence, just before its internationalisation on 11 September 2001, the perceptions of Islam's bloody corridors had begun to sow a seed within the rhetoric in Jos and the neighbourhood of Central Nigeria. This ignored Christianity's own bloody past, a past upon which the average Nigerian Christian has hardly been enlightened. Christianity in Nigeria came with more of a promise of individual opportunity in Western values and systems than with the collective promise of heavenly bliss and community which Islam gave. Therefore, while Nigerian Christianity carried an air of civility, it looked down upon the traditionalism of Islam and its adherents—most especially in northern Nigeria—who had initially rejected Western opportunities. In contrast, northern Islam looked down on a people they saw as gullible to the West and its values. This conflict of perceptions, which should have phased out with time, has only been transformed into a variety of instruments which are now the roots of new conflicts and even new negotiations.

Although the symbolisms of the two religions have become the main instruments for broad negotiations and the general building of perceptions, these symbolisms present false pictures of strong unified religious civilisations, powerful enough to control their adherents and thereby holding forth the flag of their people. In reality, the religions do not hold forth these flags; instead, shattered fragments within them have torn apart their unity, dividing them into small groups in attrition, which, although bearing definite features of the religious civilisation, wave the different pieces of the flag to the gallery. These different flags, in relation to the perception of a religion being a unified civilisation, have primarily prompted the reasons by which conflicts have not only emerged but are escalated. Nigeria presents an interesting case in that its size and the proportions of the various adherents of the two religions have further increased the complication of its religious perceptions and determinations. This has further placed the nation's politics onto the platform of the two religions.

Modern Christianity, unlike Islam in most secular states, has come to terms uncomfortably with the realisation of modernism's anti-religious stance on society and on the apparatus of the state. Islam's theology, on the other hand, legitimately places it within the organs of society and state (Falola 1998). This has thereby placed it in direct conflict with secularism in quite a large number of states and with both modernists and peoples of other religions. In defining politics in Islam, there are considerations on whether one deals with the relationship between Islam, its history, and politics in societies as a whole (Hassan 2002), or singles out various cases and relationships observed from different circumstances of "dissent to dissidence" of some purveyors of the religion based on their desire for reform within the religion (Last 2013). In both cases, one thing stands out: the question of tolerance by Islam for certain Muslims or of Muslims for non-Islamic tendencies both politically or individually. In the latter case, what predicates an acceptable level of 'the other's' points of view by Muslims, and vice-versa? Do these determinations encourage a sort of reciprocity of perceptions between Muslims and non-Muslims, or does it plunge the two into polarities? Furthermore, how does the discourse around Islam in the case of Nigeria affect the credo and the perspectives of 'the others'?

For the most part, Nigeria's case brings to mind Huntington's "clash"—but is it the clash of "civilisations" or, as Abdu (2010) argues, of "identities"? The localised Nigerian conflict discourse has encouraged the migration of identity groups into the arena of 'civilisations'. It is common for most of the distinct (and even hardly distinguishable) linguistic groups to carry the mantra of a 'nation'. And since Nigerian Independence in 1960, smaller groups have continually struggled to 'emancipate' themselves from the narratives and perceived influences of the dominant groups. This struggle has propagated hybrids of identity which have relied on various re-creations of history and legend (Mang 2012). Among these various categories of identity delineations, Christianity and Islam have carved out not just polarising niches, but have also inscribed within their adherents new constructs about themselves and of 'the others'. These two religions have, in many cases, either fused with the narratives and traditions of the emerging 'civilisations' or 'identities' or, in other cases, have eased out conflicting narratives or traditions. These fused identities have helped to establish a larger Nigerian polarity between Christianity and Islam, and thus there is a convenience of symbolising most conflicts as either religious or carrying ethnic strings.

This chapter analyses Christian perceptions of the influence and impact of Islam on society since the 1999 issues of Shariah, and relates the various issues with the present events concerning Boko Haram. What do Christians perceive as the politics of Islam, in the light of what they assume are the emerging and re-emerging attempts at asserting Islam and Islamic values in northern Nigeria's polity and society?

The paper first briefly looks into historical cases of post-colonial Islamic dissent in northern Nigeria, discussing approaches towards dissension from secular authority and the immediate causes of uprisings which occurred. It also looks at how Christians and other non-Muslims have been affected in these cases. In relation to this, it further discusses the perceptions of contemporary Christian society and tries to relate how much their insight into the history of Islamic dissent in the country has affected their present perceptions since the emergence of Boko Haram. The chapter revolves around the following questions:

- Is there a general Nigerian Christian view of Islam's influence in politics? If there is, what is it?
- How much of the history of Islam in Nigeria has influenced these views?

- Do Christians see deprivation or the lack of "entitlements",[1] as is being asserted by many, as an integral reason for some Muslim scholars calling for dissent, or do they see the cause of dissension as arising from a broader agenda(s)?
- What is (are) the broader agenda(s)?
- What are the changing Christian perceptions of traditional Islam when considering the effect of violence by Boko Haram?
- Is contemporary Christian leadership (most especially the fast-growing Pentecostal Church) influencing a radical change in tolerance and dissension within Christian society and politics against political Islam?

There is a growing quantity of literature on Christian–Muslim relations in northern Nigeria, mainly historical and focusing on the central areas. This is based on the fact that the spread of Christianity in the area was in essence limited to areas that had less contact with Islam or where there were non-Muslim populations. Boer (1979: 161-163) and Crampton (1976: 72-80) describe the process by which access to various northern groups by missionaries was restricted, and how restrictions on missionary work or any show of Christianity were imposed within the emirates, with exceptions in areas designated as *sabon garuruwa* (Hausa for "visitors' quarters"; sing: *sabon gari*) and within Zaria. Ozigi and Ocho (1981: 18-27) give detailed accounts of the process in Zaria and other predominantly Muslim areas. In general, Christian scholars, whether from the West or Nigeria, have argued there was a concerted effort by the colonial authorities to sustain the status quo and support the Muslim North. In contrast, scholars such as Ayandele (1966: 129-133) differed on the Christian narrative of a concerted process by the colonial government to restrict Christianity and missionary activity in the North. He instead points out that there was a realisation of the possibility that liberal Christian perspectives would conflict with Muslim society—which had an organised, controlled hierarchy and social structure that provided a relatively better system of pre-colonial rulership than other areas, a situation which added value to colonial bureaucracy (Last 2008: 43-44).

Nevertheless, some authors, mainly northern Christian scholarly elites and largely from within the minority ethnicities (Ozigi & Ocho 1981; Turaki 1993; Logams 2004), have emphasised an obvious identity demarcation based on both ethnic and religious divides. Logams, for example, argues that Christian identity within the minorities helped foster a bond which was built upon the following tripod: Christian evangelism, which tried to homogenise the minority groups; Western medicine, which showed promise and worked its own miracles; and education, which helped to produce a new social class of egalitarian minorities, who saw themselves on a par and even higher than certain classes within the North (Logams 2004: 246-273). These elites of the Christian North regularly attempted to raise issues about the dominance of Islam and Islamic traditions, questioning the convenience of the relationship between the Muslim hegemony and colonial authorities. Even where the colonial authorities tried to balance these seeming imbalances,[2] animosities and complaints continued and, with time, various missionary and church organisations in these minority areas began to emerge as homogeneous monoliths, garnering collective support within a growing group. Although Christian populations in northern Nigeria are relatively fewer than Muslims, there are indications of a slight increase in the number of Christians between 1950 and the present (see Ibrahim 1991: 116; Ostien 2012: 3). Some have postulated that this growth might have been greater if not for the process establishing the colonial North, which protected and propped up Islam above other religions. This eventually continued even after Independence, restricting most of the North to Islamic tradition (Turaki 1993: 143-175).

These views of the protection and propping up of Islam and Islamic traditions to the disadvantage of Christianity have been held mainly by Christian scholars (most of them theologians, clergymen, and prominent northern Christian apologists). And at no other time before now did the narrative become louder than during the events propagating Shariah from 1999 onwards. Ostien bluntly (and rightly) states that Nigeria's Christians deplored the revival of Shariah from 1999 and have postulated "many theories about its causes" (Ostien 2006: 221). He further argues that "Christians missed an opportunity to settle with the Muslims the place of Islamic law in Nigeria on reasonable, honorable, and stable terms" by continuously fighting, from the time of Independence, against legislation which would have created a balance between the inherited British legal system and Shariah (Ostien 2006: 224-229). Whether this argument holds water, considering current events, depends on a sense of objectivity uncommon in the discourse on religion in Nigeria generally; but even more so, it depends on the various perceptions Christians have of Muslim reactions to, and narratives for, the insurgencies instigated by fundamentalists carrying the flag of Islam.

CHRISTIAN NARRATIVES AND VIEWS OF ISLAM

In recent times, Christian churches and umbrella bodies in northern Nigeria have found it difficult to agree on a common perspective on political Islam. Although there is a general perspective that Islam in Nigeria has historically had a violent past, with trickles of it still existing (Tyoden 1993: Logams 2004), Christians in Nigeria present a variety of narratives around issues of the theocracy of Islam in contrast to the 'Christian' attempt at separating religion and state. A large number point to issues of political dominance and, in some cases, violence indicative of Islam in the North. This seeming threat is interpreted differently within the Christian population in Nigeria. Most conservative Christians take a cautionary look at pockets of Islamic dissent as unitary actions which must be addressed as such, through either dialogue or soft threats. The more radical Christian groups present the narrative of a jihadist game plan to overwhelm Nigeria with a religious and ethnic agenda. The latter find dialogue rather deceitful, and this demography mainly comprises a largely youthful population that has grown up in a Nigeria that has acquired with time new identity constructions, which have revolved around ethnicity and religion.

The customary divide between Catholics and Protestants has given way to more fundamental Pentecostals or Pentecostal-like groups. The growth of Pentecostalism (which has virtually invaded both Catholic and Protestant churches) has inspired a growing extremism. With the Christian rhetoric of 'salvation' propped up with a heavenly mandate to conquer the world with God-given success, Pentecostals view themselves as placed between the nexus of salvation and conquering the world. A completely different worldview is found among the pious conservatives, who desire heaven as their final goal and see the world's pleasures as ephemeral (Marshall 2009: 81). Although, since colonial times, Western influences and modernism have influenced a perceived class elevation for Christians relative to Muslims, the relative poverty and deprivation evidenced in the North compared with the South has encouraged an illogical but evidentiary sense of advantage in one religion relative to the other. The dominant narrative of prosperity and success through faith attracted a "new thinking" and eventually new class stratifications (*ibid.* 84-85).

The value of Western education and exposure and other attributes of modernism have encouraged the relativism of dynamic or progressive religion mainly among Christians, both within the religion and outside it. The church in the North was even more prone to this, because, to many converts of Christianity in northern Nigeria, the religion came with these modern opportunities, thereby making it a rich alternative to Islam. Considering that most of the groups which accepted Christianity in these northern areas had one story or another of alienation from the Islamic establishment throughout history (Tambo 1978: 213; Turaki 1993: 63-79; Logams 2004: 29-53), the new religion did two things principally: firstly, it helped remove the nomenclature of denigration that had been used for a long time for the minorities; and secondly, Western education further elevated their social status. Most of the early missions were established in areas already exposed to Islam either through peaceful relations or through a history of conflict. Also, in most cases, these new Christians had, before conversion, been labelled "pagans" and "heathen" (Tambo 1978: 203-205; Ibrahim 1991: 116), and therefore Christianity not only presented itself as an avenue for finding God but also as an instrument for elevating these pagans and heathen up to a higher social class of monotheism and modern European values (Ibrahim 1991: 119). This narrative further helped to strengthen a pro-Christian identity within the minorities in the North. Thus, within the more evangelical groups which became established in these areas, there grew a commonality. These evangelical groups had a distinct identity leaning, from the more elitist Anglican and, in some cases, Catholic churches which had carried with them a large following from the South. In most cases (with exceptions in the case of the Church Missionary Society [Anglican Church] and Roman Catholic Missions in Zaria, Kano, and the Benue/Plateau areas) these churches had very little contact with natives in these northern minority areas. The more proactive Sudan United Mission/Sudan Interior Mission groups, both promoted by evangelical groups in the UK and US, and splinters of the Baptist, Lutheran, and Methodist missions, had greater depth within the remote areas of the minorities, with most of them working on and assimilating aspects of these societies with a blend of Christianity which more or less encouraged piety and submission.

This modernism associated with Christianity now turned the tables in terms of perceptions. The pagans and heathen now became an elite class, transiting from obscurity to an internationalised religious identity, comparable to Islam and with a padding of modernity. A large proportion of Christians, not only in northern Nigeria, but also in the South, have perceived the slow growth in modernity in most northern areas as a product of the peoples' adherence to a rigid Islamic tradition with restricted options for modernity. Western education was a prized prospect and was aggressively acquired by the minorities (largely Christian) relative to the Hausa and Fulani (mainly Muslim). This growing number of educated elites in these areas, further spurred by developments in the south of the country, encouraged a persona of 'Christian modernism', relative to 'Muslim inflexibility'.

The other issue, referred to earlier, is that of a common fear by most Christians of the theocratic character of Islam. Although evident throughout the late colonial era and most especially in relation to the politics of Independence and the First Republic, two events stood out over time. The first was the controversy surrounding Nigeria's membership of the Organisation of Islamic Cooperation (OIC) in 1986, with a resurgence of the issue in 2001 (Falola 1998: 69, 89-94). This controversy not only raised concerns about the secular identity of Nigeria, but also invigorated the claims by Christian apologists of the seeming growth and dominance of Islamism in Nigerian politics. These apologists and quite a number of non-Muslim intellectuals had fought throughout post-Independence against what they saw as a threat from Islam, first in the strength of a northern party led by an influential religious hegemony, and secondly, the already established Shariah judicial system which was prevalent in the North. Quoting Anderson (1976), Ostien presents the fact that modernity tried to overshadow a long-standing religious tradition unique in the Muslim world at its time:

> The case of Northern Nigeria was, indeed, almost unique, for up till [1960] this was the only place outside the Arabian peninsula in which the Islamic law, both substantive and procedural, was applied in criminal litigation—sometimes even in regard to capital offences. [Ostien (2006), citing Anderson (1976: 27-28)].

The growing modern (Christian) perspective, mainly among the largely non-Muslim educated elite, stifled any attempt at enabling a compromise between English law (generally perceived by the Muslim North as "Christian") and the existing Shariah (which was the norm). This was further worsened by the constitutionalism of 1976–78, which seemed to relegate Shariah to the realm of small, unitary, customary litigations and, worse, limit its space (Ostien 2006: 240-241). This "Debacle of 1979", in Ostien's view (2006: 241), spurred a re-strategising of options in 1999 and a new wave of discontent and fear of a subtle attempt at political Islamisation of the Nigerian state. Most Christians in post-Independence Nigeria, irrespective of their inclinations, have perceived Islam (more specifically, northern Islam) as an overwhelming force on the polity generally (Ibrahim 1991). It has become convenient to see any symbolism of Islam as a threat to an established modern and secular system. This is seen in the context where secularism in the Nigerian case revolves around the two main religions. Christianity and Islam dominate the religious system, and other beliefs, although not necessarily harshly discriminated against, hardly stand on the same level of recognition. Muslims in Nigeria, as with Muslims the world over, jealously guard their traditions; and this jealousy, combined with the strong influence which belief generally wields, often creates fear within other groups. Kukah (1993: 9) describes this jealous guarding of Islam in northern Nigeria by using Hiskett's (1975: 109) Islamic verse:

> *As for the Christian, what he desires is gain*
> *To cast you, our Mallams aside,*
> *And to cause you to stop applying our Sharia*
> *Which Allah sent down through our Prophet.*

This sort of rhetoric and the continuous issues around Nigeria's secularism and Shariah have increased the fears of Christians in Nigeria; and because of the contemporary history of Islam in the Middle East and North Africa bearing theocratic potency, Christian apologists and secular jingoists within the Nigerian state have harped on the likelihood of an Islamisation agenda, most especially in cases where structures and elements of the state open up to Islamic symbolisms.

THE POLITICS OF CHRISTIANITY AND ISLAM IN NIGERIA

In commenting on issues surrounding the Shariah controversy in 1978 (an issue we discuss in detail later), Laitin (1982: 412) pointed out with a somewhat visionary phrase that "the politics of religion, where there is no room for flexibility, can rock a political system to its very foundations". The Shariah controversy, since Independence, not only exacerbated tensions between the north and south of Nigeria, but seemed to be the groundswell to which outbursts of violence over issues like the unholy use of the Muslim holy book by a non-Muslim or the hullabaloo over a beauty pageant could be released. Although incomprehensible to Christians, it made perfect sense to quite a number of Muslims, who assume that the alleged abuse and decadence of non-Muslims in relation to Islamic symbols or the moral statutes of their religion goes to show the lacuna, which their loss of Shariah from colonial times had caused within the context of Islamic theocracy. Additional perceptions, of greater socio-economic leverage of the South relative to the North, and the convenient stereotype of southern educated and professional elite relative to peasant northerners, further opened doors to grievances (whether appropriate or not) towards both government and the largely Christian South.

Central Nigeria, or what is commonly called the Middle Belt, introduced a further dimension to the circumstances. The groups in this area, which had in pre-colonial times, and even during colonial times, been of little political value, began to become more assertive towards the time when Independence came. Their assertiveness gradually developed into antagonism, owing to the growth of Christianity in these areas. During the events leading to Independence in 1960, Logams (1993: 11-20) describes a concerted effort by the Hausa- and Muslim-dominated Northern People's Congress (NPC) to stifle any attempt at a growing opposition in the North, which was largely composed of ethnic minorities who were mainly either animists or Christians. A phrase he coined was "internal colonialism". Areas like the Tiv Division, which comprised the present Benue and Kogi states, saw a series of politically motivated acts of violence in the 1960s, among mainly Tiv groups. Their primary anger was what they saw as an attempt by the Hausa/Muslim-dominated NPC—using a few rogue elements from within the Tiv Division—to hijack the political structure of the United Middle Belt Congress (UMBC), then led by a Tiv Christian, Joseph Tarka (Logams 1993; 644).

In the Plateau area, on the other hand, the politics was more subtle. First of all, from the late 1950s, Sir Ahmadu Bello, the Sardauna of Sokoto (a Muslim), began a proselytisation drive in the central region. His main aim then was to convert the traditional heads, who would subsequently encourage the conversion of their subjects. A particular case in point is made by Joseph Garba, a prominent military officer from Plateau, whose father, a traditional ruler and animist, was caught in a dilemma as to whether or not he should convert to Islam after being entreated to by emissaries of the Sardauna, preceding a visit by the latter to Garba's domain. Mallam Garba felt he needed his son's advice, his son being educated and working as a top military officer (Garba 1982: 55-58).

From elder statesmen to local politicians, and from radical Christian clerics to youth leaders and even academics, there have been calls within the Middle Belt groups to fight these attempts at internal colonialism; and even though the area has been highly heterogeneous, their largely Christian identity has been a source of homogeneity.

In Plateau State most especially, the attempt at deconstructing Islam and its politics, and the problem of ethnic and religious conflict in the state, have become arduous. To make matters worse, the rhetoric and incursions of Boko Haram in recent times have only further bolted the hinges in the doors of Christian historical memory of a large concerted Islamic agenda. Since 2011, the perspective has been that the Muslim North in Nigeria has been uncomfortable with the politics of Plateau State. It is a fact that apart from Benue and Plateau states in the political northern Nigeria arena, in every other state either both the governor and his deputy are Muslim, or, in most cases, there is a compromise of one or the other being shared between Christians and Muslims (Imo 2001: 109). The case of Plateau is even more complicated by the sequence of changes in political dimensions and determinations. In earlier work (Mang 2012) I tried to highlight these dynamics in relation to changes in geopolitical space in Plateau State. Between 1967 and 1994, Plateau State was broken down into smaller states, and in all cases, most especially in the latter two, ethnic and religious instrumentations laced the geopolitics of the state, leading to a wave of gerrymandering (Mang 2012; 275-279).

The loudest chord was struck in 2011 in the contentious politics of Plateau State; and since then, the causes and dimensions of the violence have continually changed, and with them, the rhetoric. By 2008, the diameter of the violent arena had increased from the cities into villages, and also, the frequency of occurrences increased. The rhetoric, which had been political, between the autochthonous ethnic groups—the Afizere, Anaguta and Berom, and the Hausa—transited into one of Christians versus Muslims. Allegations on both sides described harrowing experiences of violence and other human rights abuses, dividing Jos and Bukuru, the main metropolitan areas, into pockets of religious identity communities. Furthermore, the violence in the villages between the Berom and Fulani was alleged to have escalated owing to the appearance of foreign mercenaries. Events led to the death of serving senator Gyang Dantong and member of the state house of assembly Gyang Fulani after trying to bury the dead from an alleged Fulani invasion, which took place on Saturday, 7 July 2012, leading to the death of over sixty people. Both men were of Berom extraction and prominent within the Plateau Christian community. This occurrence inflamed passions and further intensified the rhetoric of a grand Muslim design to overwhelm Plateau State as a whole through a concerted 'terrorist incursion' (Olagunju 2011; Online Nigeria 2013). With this, and over four incidents of bomb blasts in the state, for which Boko Haram itself claimed responsibility, Christians in Plateau State fed better on the narratives of a concerted Muslim agenda (The Messenger Voice 2012). This and the growing Boko Haram threat encouraged a new wave in which random violent attacks on any Islamic symbol or persons with such symbols became acceptable within the Christian community. The rationale to deconstruct the religion from its fundamentalism was lost, since as one pastor put it: "You can not distinguish Islam from its politics, so how can you distinguish it from its violence?"[3]

PERSPECTIVES OF CHRISTIANS ON FUNDAMENTALIST DISSENSIONS LIKE BOKO HARAM

There seems to be a convenience for Christians in alluding to the inflexibility of Islamic doctrine in cases where Islam (which is wrongly seen by many Christians as a unified system) seems to be imploding. The common assumption is that Muslims, unlike Christians who hold on to denominational values, are relatively more homogenous. This assumption is not necessarily true. The different sects and dogmas of these sects have caused more conflict within Islam than outside it (Last 2012). But even these (most especially in contemporary times) have been seen by Christians as plans gone awry. One common phrase, 'confusion in the enemy's camp',[4] dominated the interviews used for this work when questions were asked in relation to the fact that cases of violence (most especially in the case of Boko Haram) indicate that Muslims are the relatively more affected. The idea behind the phrase was that even though it was true that more Muslims have died, it was only indicative of a common plan gone awry owing to either clashes between ideologues and politicians or even between contending ideologues. This argument is commonly associated with the narratives surrounding the death of Mohammed Yusuf. Yusuf's death, most especially, has shaped new myths, not only among Muslims but also to a large extent among Christians, who, like many Muslims, build their knowledge on word from the street. The media too, in certain ways, has helped in hyping up the rhetoric of the birth, growth, and present nature of Boko Haram (Ayoob 2008; Idris 2011; Salkida 2011).

Most Christian respondents primarily rely on two mediums for information about Islam: the clergy or the growing number of para-clergy[5] that now wield various spheres of influence; and the news media. These two mediums, most especially the former, have highly influenced the Christian laity into taking an 'us' versus 'them' stance in the events related to the two religions and Boko Haram. Relatively few Christians in southern Kaduna and Plateau states distinguish Islam and Muslims from Boko Haram. In Plateau State particularly, in the few cases in which bomb blasts occurred and Boko Haram claimed responsibility, violent reprisals erupted against anyone suspected to be Muslim. In a 2012 focus group discussion with Christian youth involved in violence at Anguwan Rukuba and Gada Biyu (Jos), there was a clear indication that to be Christian primarily meant not being Muslim. By implication, one's Christian link or identity was a sort of shibboleth. He or she could choose to take on occult, 'magic', or 'primitive religious' agencies, if their cause was against any form of Islam.[6] Muslim converts or those with Muslim backgrounds were still not within the Christian circle, even though they were tolerated. To members of this group, Christianity and Islam were principally about identity and not necessarily about belief. As seen with the commerce of meat in Jos and its environs, owing to the agency of conflict, meat has built on an identity (Mang 2012).[7] And when the violence stretches out to these non-Muslims, the narrative harps on that as the main agenda. This narrative in the recent past has been further encouraged by the seeming silence or ambiguity of the Muslim *ummah* and *ulama* on the subject of violence against others. The argument here by some Christians is that Muslim violence is their personal matter; and whatever the cause may be, they should not drag Christians into it. Ibrahim (1991: 122-124) gives clear examples of these intra-religious crises which Muslims have been contending with for a long time. Christians have been aware of these and have, in most cases, been left out of them. After all, even Christian sects have these issues. But the disturbing issue has been the rhetoric and actions of Boko Haram against Christians. Considering the already built-in constructs by Christians of what they choose to see as "Islamic tendencies", Boko Haram appears as a mouthpiece for Islam, most especially in Nigeria's North. Rarely do Christians see the situation as the product of any sort of grievance that should affect them. That is why the once growing narrative of deprivation of the north-east of the country as a primary factor is rejected by most Christians. As one clergyman informant put it: "Poverty is like a common cloth in Nigeria; in fact, most Africans wear it, so they cannot bring the issue of too much poverty in their areas."

Poverty, although a predisposing factor to violence, cannot account for issues surrounding what Christians view as an Islamisation agenda by the North. This is not helped by the historical narratives of the proselytisation agenda of the late Sardauna of Sokoto from the 1950s in the minority areas (Garba 1982). This, and the largely one-track politics of the Hausa-dominated

Northern Peoples' Congress (NPC) after Independence, have only helped to shore up the already-fed fears of minorities, as expressed in the Willink's Commission Report (League for Human Rights 2003).

Owing to this general insinuation of a grand design, narratives within the various Christian communities are rarely presented only within the local situation. The narratives are extended to include the existing narrative of Islamic terrorism worldwide. This narrative expands most especially when dissidence by Muslims leads to large-scale violence against Christians, such as attacks on churches and specific targets in predominantly Christian domains. This allusion, which thrives with the increased violence perpetuated by groups like Boko Haram, ignores the fact that Christianity has also had its bloody corridors, and similar narratives can be linked to Christian violence. Why has the narrative on Islam increasingly become bloodied and given a highly generalised rhetoric, instead of being assessed as incidental?

STRANDS AND CORDS IN CHRISTIAN PERSPECTIVES OF ISLAM AND ISLAMISM

There is in truth no general Christian perspective on the influence of Islam on Nigeria's society and politics; and judging from recent conflicting comments by various members of the clergy, the Christian church is obviously divided into several strands of perspective, with the potential to form cords as the Boko Haram issue seems unlikely to abate. A further latency is provided by the silence or ambiguity of the Muslim *ummah* and *ulama* towards the violence which has affected Nigerian Christians.

Four observable strands seem to have emerged within the context of the Boko Haram issue among Christians in Nigeria. Although all express grievances towards violent actions against Christians, each strand argues a distinct view and process for making headway in these trying situations. I have grouped them into the following:

- Conservative Hierarchical
- Conservative Egalitarian
- Liberal Political Christian
- Radical Christian Identity

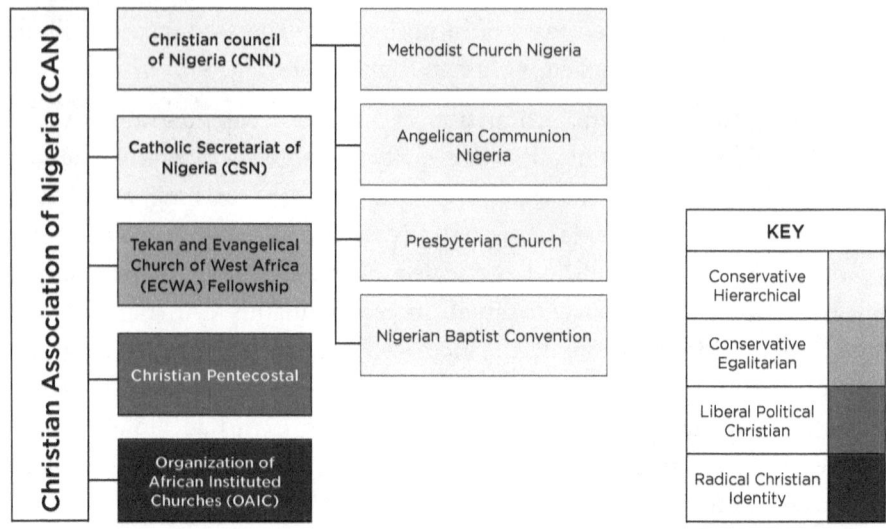

Figure 4.1 The divisions of Christian Association of Nigeria (CAN)
Source: Mang (2013)

Diagram showing the divisions of CAN, showing colours indicating the classifications discussed in this work

Conservative Hierarchical

Issues of hierarchy both within and between churches, and the level to which these hierarchies are influential on the laity, present us with this construct. But it does not just stop there. The level of exposure of those in this group is another determinant, because even within Christian groups that are seen to be egalitarian, hierarchies exist between institutors and guardians of doctrine, and the laity. Exposure is the strong point of this group. By exposure here, we refer to the levels to which these hierarchies have interacted with Islam and Muslims. For this group, their interaction with Islam is not just superficial; in most cases they have in-depth knowledge of Islam and its traditions. One can conveniently place the Nigerian Anglican Communion and the Nigerian Catholic Church within this group. Apart from their being some of the oldest church organisations in the country, their background knowledge both within and outside the Bible has encouraged a relatively higher sense of discretion when it comes to issues of inter-religious dialogue. These churches, owing to their history, growth, and following in Nigeria, have claimed a traditional sense of superiority over less-established churches. Their history has also encouraged the state to, in more cases than not, relate more with them where the need arises. They are seen as conservative in relation to the dynamic doctrinal and philosophical character of Pentecostals. In relation to Islam and its politics in Nigeria, this group presents a high sense of maturity in its desire for dialogue, even when it seems that the other side has the upper hand. Two significant pieces of evidence stand out for them: their calculated placements of significantly influential strategists in conflict-prone areas and in areas where Islamic power reigns.[8]

Conservative Egalitarian

These groups, in most cases, comprise localised church organisations based on certain identity leanings such as ethnicity, linguistics, or culture. They are in most cases Protestant evangelicals, brought up within the confines of certain mixed doctrines combining Christianity and traditions of their identity. To these groups, identity is quite important, even though they are open to outsiders in limited circumstances. With their common sense of identity arises a level of egalitarianism, and because they are relatively sparse geographically and are in many cases surrounded by larger Muslim communities, they are bound by the need to be cohesive and do not necessarily adhere to doctrinal or canonical restraints. This group is prominently influential in the minority non-Muslim areas of northern Nigeria. Their main perception of Islam in northern Nigeria, unlike that of the *Conservative Hierarchical* group, is one of an ethnicised religious domination which subjugates them. Their drive for equality has become influential in their changing theology; therefore, they have less desire for dialogue, even though they are open to it if it seems genuine.

Liberal Political Christian

This group comprises either clergy or non-clergy who build constructs which relate together the state, politics, and Christianity. When they become involved in politics, their primary constituents are usually Christians who purposely or inadvertently campaign using the rhetoric of domination or of an ungodly world which needs the reform that Christianity can supposedly give. This group refrains as much as possible from promoting any form of division which presents itself in the wider church. Instead, their rhetoric is filled with calls for Christian ecumenism as a starting point in fighting the "forces of evil". This group, being politically driven and ecumenical in its outlook, seeks dialogue with Islam only as a route to fostering political and religious power bases. Its whole agenda in the end is to produce what have come to be called "prominent Christian leaders or politicians", most of whom stand as symbols of Christianity within the secular system of the state, which itself has permitted the two religions (Christianity and Islam) to dominate.

Radical Christian Identity

This group thrives on the symbolism which Christianity provides and not necessarily on its significance or value. To them, Christian identity presents a vehicle for either ethnic or traditional authority or protest. By being Christian, they claim a commonality with others, while still pursuing other agendas. Even within this group there exist two distinct groups. One thrives on the syncretism of Christianity and local traditions, while the other thrives on its claim to a long history of Christian identity due to pre-colonial interactions with the religion through explorers and voyagers in the Niger Delta.[9]

STRANDS THAT SEPARATE

New issues surrounding Boko Haram have emerged since I began writing this chapter. The most prominent has been the call for an amnesty for the group, as an avenue of pacifying them and also as a means of correcting certain social issues attributed to influencing people to join the group.[10]

Calls to government for amnesty for Boko Haram were made by well-known Muslims, the most prominent being the Sultan of Sokoto. These calls sparked off a series of dismissals and counter-dismissals, and this drew a main dividing line between two sides. Christians, on the one hand, dismissed it as an excuse by the northern oligarchy to institutionalise the situation for economic advantage, following the line of the Niger Delta situation, which led to a similar amnesty. Some Christians have harped on the fact that a call for amnesty is callous, considering the fact that criminal elements have killed and maimed many innocent people, with the government doing hardly anything to provide proper restitution. Now it seems as if the same restitution will be given to the criminals in the form of an amnesty. Most Muslims, on the other hand, argue that the north-east of the country particularly has been underfunded within the federation, thereby fostering extreme poverty and leading to a high level of gullibility towards preachers and politicians, who in turn provided seemingly valid reasons for things being hard and society unfriendly. This lack of a social contract has been worsened by what most Muslim politicians and religious leaders see as the heavy hand of government through the use of its own instruments of violence.

The plan for amnesty helped to further broaden Christian perspectives about Boko Haram and Islam, introducing a cohort of philosophically inclined views, expressed mainly by the clergy and a number of politicians. These views have varied, and looked at from the perspective of the divisions created for this work, the discourse can be viewed thus:

The Christian Association of Nigeria (CAN), which has served as an umbrella for Nigerian Christians since the 1980s, became embroiled in a battle of wits since June 2010. Although CAN has always had its own dose of intrigues, 2010 introduced a new dimension. For the first time, the influence of the Pentecostal Church was being felt. Previously, the presidency of CAN revolved around the mould of the *Conservative Hierarchical* group. From Catholic archbishops to Anglican or Methodist primates, the authority of CAN revolved around these more accommodating elite of the clergy, and they found it convenient to moderately relate with government and Islam, with a sense of reciprocity.[11] The Pentecostal Church in Nigeria had during this time preoccupied itself with building a followership. Their growing numbers, which had emerged from the activity of adherents mainly of the more conservative churches, became their major pre-occupation until the political system provided an avenue through growing corruption and radicalism, a system which with time became highly influenced by the Pentecostals. With this new influence, a more politically Pentecostal movement emerged.

As an informant pointed out: "We [Pentecostals] have hardly been interested in politics or even ecumenism, but we realised that Christianity was not well represented in Nigerian politics."[12] The choice of Pastor Ayo Oritsejafor, a popular Pentecostal preacher from the South-South of Nigeria, had a strategic attraction. First of all, the fact that he was from the same region as the president encouraged a growing political support for Oritsejafor. Unlike the era of old, a large support grew from both the Pentecostal clergy and laity which could be found within the *Conservative Egalitarian* and the *Liberal Political Christian* groups. This triggered great discomfort within the *Conservative Hierarchical* group, which had previously held sway. This group had attained a political status quo which was acceptable to all groups, government and Muslims included. Their non-radical stance and their propensity for dialogue made them amenable and convenient for the politics of Nigerian religious dialogue. Unlike them, the Pentecostals had a narrower view, both of religious dialogue and tolerance, because they had a close-knit and family-like feature which encouraged a collective will. As Lamle (2013) puts it:

> Through the [Pentecostal] church, people that had come together from different socio-political and socio-economic status are brought together into one family. They come together in one brotherhood that helps them to withstand the socio-political and economic chaos in Nigeria. This bond becomes the crutch upon which the people are able to come together into one single-family unit and domesticate their problems together.

Thus, choices and debates, ranging from domestic issues to national politics, have been influenced by the nature of the bond which Pentecostalism—or as Lamle (2013) calls it, "neo-Pentecostalism"—has created, with its extension into the more established churches.

The June 2010 emergence of Oritsejafor[13] jolted the hierarchical groups. Before this time, all CAN presidents had emerged from the hierarchical group, and the doors revolved around them. In fact, when the growing rate of ethnic and religious conflict caused President Obasanjo to inaugurate The Nigeria Inter-Religious Council (NIREC) on 29 September 1999, the co-chairmanship on the Christian side was shared by two people, both of the *Conservative Hierarchical* group.[14] The subsequent emergence of the Catholic Archbishop of Abuja, Dr. John Onaiyekan, presented an opportunity for another from this group. Coincidentally, Onaiyekan was to co-chair with a new Muslim leader, Alhaji Muhammad Sa'ad Abubakar, the Sultan of Sokoto. The relationship between the sultan and the archbishop was a highly praised one; with these men at the helm of affairs, there was a high level of tolerance and wide acceptance of the need for dialogue. Thus, it was not surprising when, in a strategic move, one of the Nigerian church's most vocal and cerebral priests, Matthew Hassan Kukah, was appointed Bishop of Sokoto. Furthermore, the Vatican, under the papacy of Pope Benedict XVI, appointed Bishop Kukah as a member of the Pontifical Council for Inter-Religious Dialogue, a 13-member council primarily geared towards dialogue.[15] Kukah's academic and public profile has made him and the Catholic Church a veritable tool for dialogue in Nigeria. The church's nationwide presence has enabled it to gain wide acceptance from both government and the Nigerian Islamic community. But the Catholic Church's largest opposition seems to have emerged from two groups particularly: the *Conservative Egalitarian* and the *Liberal Political Christian* groups. Each group obviously had its own reasons for having reservations about the Catholic Church, but in the context of this chapter, both groups have had histories which places them at variance with religious dialogue. Mbachirin (2006a: 174-188), in discussing the history of CAN, introduces the arguments between various Christian groups on who should take the credit for the formation of CAN.

From the narrative he presents, there was a clear indication that the arguments were between the evangelicals (mainly present in northern Nigeria) and Catholics. The evangelicals from the North claimed that CAN emerged from the Northern Christian Association (NCA), an association which emerged from northern fears:

> Christian operation in the North was different from that in the South because the South was just mainly for church Unionism (meaning CCN's[16] attempt to form a Union Church) but the North saw the threat of the Sardauna's policies of Islam coming. So [the northern Christians] felt that for anything that had to do with Government, the Christians of all denominations must come together and speak with a similar voice. So, usually the Christian operation was relatively strong in the North and a little weak in the South because the problems were different. (*ibid.* 176)

Most Catholic and southern Nigerian scholars, on the other hand, saw CAN as emerging from the collaboration between the Christian Council of Nigeria (CCN) and the Catholic Secretariat of Nigeria (CSN), both of which financed and housed CAN at its inception and for a long time after its formation. With this parenting, it became traditional for these groups to share the leadership of CAN over the years. But the fight over claims of origin became a reason to wrench authority in 2010 when the competition for the presidency of CAN saw factions emerging. The *Conservative Hierarchical* groups were insistent on maintaining the status quo, while the *Conservative Egalitarian* and the *Liberal Political Christian* groups strove to change the pattern. The *Radical Christian Identity* had in most cases found it difficult to join the mainstream owing to questions about their integrity arising from the others; therefore, they had little influence in these determinations. The success of Pastor Ayo Oritsejafor over Archbishop John Onaiyekan indicates the growing strength of a more liberal leaning, even among the historically conservative. Two things have accounted for this. The first is what seems to be the growing threat of Islamism and, as earlier discussed, a threat narrated as a concerted process of Islamising Nigeria (mainly the North). The second is the growing Pentecostal Church, which has less tolerance for dialogue even with fellow Christian groups, let alone with Muslims. As Ojo (2007: 176) points out: "Ideologically, while Islamic groups seek to solve the problems of the ambiguities of the modern state, Pentecostal groups are concerned with solving problems confronting the individual." This can also be likened to the relationship between Pentecostalism and the other Christians in Nigeria. Pentecostalism in the north of Nigeria, as Ojo notes (*ibid.*

181), became highly politicised when its presence in northern universities during the 1970s and 1980s encouraged a radical defence of Christianity and Christian values against what they saw as the fundamentalist orientation of Muslim organisations in the institutions. Although the North's Christians had lived for a long time with this, their stance was primarily not one of collective physical violence against Muslims but either ideological or political rejection. Events which led to violence in institutions of higher learning were indicative only of radical Christians who saw themselves as having to fight to defend Christianity, very much unlike the generality of Christians in the North at that time. But this influence grew with the growth of Pentecostalism and the seeping of its values into the largely evangelical North.

Northern Christians, mainly within the evangelical groups, had for long been weary of what they perceived as the friendliness and tolerance of the *Conservative Hierarchical* groups towards Islam. Most clergy and laity from this hierarchical group in colonial times were either European, from English West Africa, or from Nigeria's South. These people were little influenced by the history of Islam, unlike the indigenous minorities who eventually converted to Christianity had been, and therefore, under the convenience of *Pax Britannica*, they held their own in northern Nigeria. The indigenous minorities, on the other hand, had to contend with both history and the colonial rhetoric of their being a lower class. The Catholic and Anglican churches did not experience as rapid a growth as the evangelicals owing to the former's search for convenient converts, while evangelicals took on the more uphill task of searching the interiors for converts. Therefore, the relationship of the *Conservative Hierarchical* groups with Islam was one of a sense of mutuality, while that of the *Conservative Egalitarian* and *Liberal Political Christian* groups with Islam was not. This could explain why it has been easier for the *Conservative Hierarchical* groups to emphasise the need for dialogue and tolerance, in contrast to the others.

Apart from the obvious attempt of the Catholic Secretariat of Nigeria to encourage dialogue and to present light at the end of the tunnel, Anglicans—primarily through the Archbishop of the province of Kaduna (northern Nigeria), Josiah Idowu-Fearon—have also argued for Christians to avail of the routes for dialogue. Being a co-founder of the Centre for the Study of Islam and Christianity at Kaduna, the archbishop has introduced a significant pathway for dialogue with Islam—but not without criticism. His background as an academic is a rare one in Nigeria. With a PhD in Islamic Studies and fluency in Arabic, Idowu-Fearon stands out amongst his peers in both religions. Like some bishops and archbishops of the Catholic Church, Idowu-Fearon has been highly criticised by the *Conservative Egalitarian, Liberal Political Christian,* and *Radical Christian Identity* groups as being rather romantic about the situation of Islamism in northern Nigeria, and their insistence on a less radical Christian approach (Mudashir 2012; Idowu-Fearon 2013; Midat 2013). He, like Onaiyekan and Kukah, has in recent times supported the call by the Sultan of Sokoto Alhaji Muhammad Sa'ad Abubakar for an amnesty to be granted to Boko Haram. While Onaiyekan and Kukah harp on the twin issues of politics and the economy as the primary cause of Boko Haram (Aminu 2013; PM News 2013), Idowu-Fearon argues that there is a growing intolerance among Christians, which he blames on individuals and groups with ethnic or economic agendas who use the platform of Christianity to influence even genuine Christians towards violence (Kawu 2012). Although these views are tenable, the meta-narrative amongst a large number of northern Christians has been that of a resurgence of Ahmadu Bello's proselytisation drives, but this time without the subtlety of the Sardauna. A series of events have helped intensify and strengthen perceptions supporting these sorts of narratives. With the return to a more extended version of the Shariah legal system in 1999, equating it with the inherited Western legal system, the coming of a new Shariah jolted most Christians, most especially Christians in the North. According to Alubo (2006)—who does not provide consistent data to support his claim—of thirty major violent incidents, based on magnitude, between 1999 and January 2012, only two were not in northern Nigeria and only one did not involve Muslims and Christians. Within the Middle Belt areas, continuous conflict between the mainly Muslim Hausa or Fulani majority and other ethnicities (in some cases mainly Christian) has further increased the fears of domination by a network of the more northern groups connected by Islam.

The *Conservative Egalitarian, Liberal Political Christian,* and *Radical Christian Identity* groups, most especially within the Nigerian North, have outrightly rejected the passive and discursive style of the *Conservative Hierarchical* groups. The divide created by the struggle for presidency in CAN showed this. Moreover, nationally and internationally, there were indications that individuals and not necessarily the organisations themselves were credited as defenders of peace, and it was alleged that Onaiyekan and the sultan had been nominated for the Nobel Peace Prize in 2012. Also, within that period, various awards were conferred on this duo. This served as a clear affront to CAN, considering that while the sultan in his capacity represented Islam in

Nigeria, Onaiyekan represented just one faction of Nigerian Christians, and this was at a time when Onaiyekan had stepped down as president of CAN. To a number of Christians, the relationship of this one group (the Catholic Secretariat) with Islam and its leadership provided a symbolic sign which showed that the Catholic Church was ready and available for dialogue, while the other Christian groups were not as friendly and therefore not ready for a path to peaceful coexistence.[17] These latter groups, from the general narratives in preparing this study, obviously have less tolerance for Islam and are clearly more weary of dialogue. But even with this, there seems to be a stronger desire for dialogue within the generally more accepting groups, rather than the whole. This partitioning in desire for dialogue has encouraged animosities amongst the Christian groups, with some even alleging a conspiracy by the Catholic Church to destroy CAN (Atonko 2013; Eyieyien 2013). Even though these assertions seem to hold some water, owing to the obvious conflict within CAN over the past few years, there is a need for a proper quantitative sampling of opinions from Christians to obtain confirmable data on these perspectives.

CONCLUSION

In summary, the clear fact is that Christians have become more apprehensive of Islam since the introduction of the Shariah regime of 1999. Democracy had not only provided freedom for society, but opened doors to a freer expression of grievances. This is now seen as weakened in the light of the stubborn implementation of Shariah and the violence between Muslims and Christians in Plateau and other north–central states, a violence that Christians view as being based on alleged hegemonic tendencies. Central Nigerian Christians, most especially, feel caught between the Biblical call to be at peace and the increasing threat coming from pockets of violence attributed to Islam. In their case, it is easy for narratives to trigger strong emotions.

This chapter has presented the four main divisions which Christianity has grown into based on issues surrounding Islam. These divisions (*Conservative Hierarchical, Conservative Egalitarian, Liberal Political,* and *Radical*) have presented various reactions based on their histories and present predicaments. It cannot be concluded that Christians have a single, general point of view, apart from their rejection of features of Islamism such as Boko Haram's violence. Reactions have varied, but with increasing violence affecting Christians, the rhetoric can easily slide towards calls for revenge, even when there is no proper logic for it.

Notes

1. Borrowing from Sen's (1982) work.
2. A case in point is what happened in 1955, when the British colonial administration instituted the formation of a minority Berom *Gbong Gwom* traditional institution in Jos. The area, although largely Berom, had traditionally been run by a Hausa chief, a process initiated by the British.
3. A. Dogo, pastor of a Pentecostal church. Interview by Henry Mang, Bukuru, 15 March 2012.
4. In two separate focus group discussions (one in Kaduna and the other in Jos) most Christian youth insisted that the Boko Haram issue was a calculated and largely organised plan by northern Muslims, with political and jihadist ends. To their minds, even though there has been more violence within Islam in northern Nigeria, this has occurred owing to what they see as the failure of evil plans.
5. Those whom Marshall refers to without "standardized or institutionalized process of accreditation of religious authority".
6. Focus group discussion with youths in *Anguwan Rukuba*/Tinna Junction area, with Henry Mang at Gondola, Jos North, 15 April 2012.
7. The study looked at the establishment of a new market in a community after aggrieved parties were relocated from another market owing to violent conflict in 2010. This new market creation was influential in inspiring similar occurrences in other markets and could lead to further replication in more areas. This is due to the fact that there are political and economic advantages to the aggrieved or disadvantaged actors, who through the connivance of their power brokers have created their own sphere of influence. In addition, the agency of religion and its position as an instrument within the meat market provides an interesting dimension to the use of religion for economic advantage. In applying systems which mirror the process of Muslim halal practice in the meat market, Christian butchers instinctively created a form of legitimacy for their meat, which was previously labelled as "unclean", thereby increasing the value of their business.
8. Bishop Josiah Idowu-Fearon and Bishop Matthew Hassan Kukah in Kaduna and Sokoto, respectively, are the cases in point. This is discussed in further detail in the coming section.
9. It is important for the reader to note that these strands are not necessarily clearly divided. They are present in the same way as all social stratifications: variables which interweave. This categorisation simply helps to provide an idea of the basic variables that help build perceptions by Christians in Nigeria of Islam and politics.
10. There are generally two broad points of view in the arguments on an amnesty for Boko Haram. The first looks at the antecedents of the group in relation to the socio-economy of the area and concludes that poverty, although not the most prominent factor influencing the group, has helped in the intensification of its actions and the growth in its following. The second line of argument looks at the

high-handedness of the government's use of instruments of coercion, at allegations of brutality towards members of the sect, and at the high level of collateral damage. These have led to much outcry from both within and outside Nigeria, indicating human rights violations and, in the case of the outcry within Nigeria, allegations of gross corruption and unaccountability having led to extreme poverty.

11. The case is seen in the 1980s demand by CAN for the sponsorship of Christian pilgrims to their holy lands in equivalence to Muslims who were benefiting from a similar service. See (CAN 1989: 12-20)
12. Interview with A. Dogo.
13. And his re-election, which occurred while writing this chapter.
14. They were Dr. Sunday Mbang, CON, the Primate of the Methodist Church of Nigeria, and Archbishop J. Akinola, CON, the Primate of the Nigerian Anglican Communion. Both were at one time presidents of the Christian Association of Nigeria (CAN). http://nirecng.org/history.html.
15. "A special department of the Roman Curia for relations with the people of other religions. Known at first as the Secretariat for Non-Christians, in 1988 it was renamed the Pontifical Council for Interreligious Dialogue (PCID)." http://www.vatican.va/roman_curia/pontifical_councils/interelg/documents/rc_pc_interelg_pro_20051996_en.html.
16. Christian Council of Nigeria, formed in 1929 as a mainly Protestant body and a mainly southern union, comprising Anglicans, Methodists, Presbyterians, etc.
17. Rev J. Bistu, S. Dasit, and P. Gyang: president and executive members of Youth CAN Plateau State. Focus group interview by Henry Gyang Mang at COCIN Headquarters, Jos, 18 January 2013.

References

Abdu, H. (2010), *Clash of Identities*. Kaduna, Nigeria: DevReach Publishers.

Alubo, O. (2006), *Ethnic Conflicts and Citizenship Crises in the Central Region*. Ibadan: PEFS.

Aminu, M. (2013), "Kukah: Boko Haram, Symptom of Failed State", *ThisDay*, Nigeria. http://www.thisdaylive.com/articles/kukah-boko-haram-symptom-of-failed-state/98217/ [Accessed: 4 May 2013].

Atonko, B. (2013), "Onaiyekan, Kukah can't speak for CAN", *Daily Trust*, Nigeria. http://www.dailytrust.com.ng/index.php/news-news/52367-onaiyekan-kukah-can-t-speak-for-can [Accessed: 4 May 2013].

Ayandele, E. (1966), *The missionary impact on modern Nigeria, 1842-1914*. London: Longmans.

Ayoob, M. (2008), *The Many Faces of Political Islam—Religion and Politics in the Muslim World*. Ann Arbor: The University of Michigan Press.

Boer, J. (1979), *Missionary messengers of liberation in a colonial context*. Amsterdam: Rodopi.

Crampton, E. (1976), *Christianity in northern Nigeria*. Zaria: Gaskiya Corporation.

Christian Association of Nigeria (1989), *Leadership in Nigeria to Date: An Analysis*. Enlightenment series 1 [report]. Kaduna: CAN.

Eyieyien, E. (2013), "The Catholic Church and the Christian Association of Nigeria", *Selah!*, [blog] 24 January. http://eghes.blogspot.com/2013/01/the-catholic-church-and-christian.html [Accessed: 4 May 2013].

Falola, T. (1998), *Violence in Nigeria : the crisis of religious politics and secular ideologies*. Rochester NY: University of Rochester Press.

——— (2002), *Nigeria in the twentieth century*. Durham, NC: Carolina Academic Press.

Falola, T., R. Doron et al. (2012), *Warfare, ethnicity and national identity in Nigeria*. Trenton, NJ: Africa World Press.

Gaiya, M. (2004), "Christianity in Northern Nigeria, 1975–2000", *Exchange: Bulletin of Third World Christian Literature* 33: 354-71.

Garba, J. (1982), *Revolution in Nigeria: Another View*. London: Africa Books Ltd.

Hassan, R. (2002) *Faithlines: Muslim conceptions of Islam and society*. Karachi: Oxford University Press.

Huntington, S. (1993), "The clash of civilizations?" Foreign affairs: 22-49.

Ibrahim, J. (1991), "Religion and Political Turbulence in Nigeria", *The Journal of Modern African Studies* 29(1): 115-136.

Idowu-Fearon, J. (2013), "Murder in the name of which God?", *Vanguard Newspapers Online*, 6 May 2012, Nigeria. http://www.vanguardngr.com/2012/05/bishop-idowu-fearon-asks-murder-in-the-name-of-which-god/ [Accessed 4 May 2013].

Idris, H. (2011), "FGs committee never addressed our demands—Boko Haram", *Daily Trust*, 29 September, p. 2.

Imo, C. (2001), "Christian-Muslim Relations in Jos Plateau", *Mandyeng: Journal of Central Nigerian Studies* 2(1), pp. 98-112.

Juergensmeyer, M. (2003) *Terror in the mind of God: the global rise of religious violence*. Berkley: University of California Press.

Kalu, U. (2011), "How Nur, Shekau run Boko Haram", *Vanguard Newspapers Online*, Nigeria, 3 September. http://www.vanguardngr.com/2011/09/how-nur-shekau-run-boko-haram/ [Accessed 8 October 2011].

Kalu, O., C. Korieh et al. (2005) *Religion, history, and politics in Nigeria*. Lanham, MD: University Press of America.

Kawu, I. (2012), "Bishop Josiah Idowu-Fearon: Advocate of co-existence", *Blueprint Newspapers*, 5 April. http://www.blueprintng.com/bishop-josiah-idowu-fearon-advocate-of-co-existence [Accessed 4 May 2013]

Kukah, M. (1993), *Religion, politics and power in Northern Nigeria*. Ibadan, Nigeria: Spectrum Books.

Laitin, D. (1982), "The Shari'ah Debate and the Origins of Nigeria's Second Republic", *The Journal of Modern African Studies* 20(3): 411- 430.

Lamle, E. (2013), "Pentecostalism and the Conflicts of Modernity Within Nigerian Cities: A Voice in the Wilderness?" In: A. Gambo & N. Lamle, eds, (n.p.) *Ethnicity, Religion and Peacebuilding in Nigeria*. 1st ed. Jos: CECOMPS, University of Jos, pp. 56-72.

Last, M. (2008), "The Search For Security In Muslim Northern Nigeria", *Africa* 78(1): 41-63.

—— (2013), *From dissent to dissidence The genesis & development of reformist Islamic groups in northern Nigeria*. Interfaith Relations in Northern Nigeria, Policy Paper No. 2. http://www3.qeh.ox.ac.uk/pdf/nrn/nrn-pp02.pdf [Accessed 27 May 2013].

League for Human Rights (2003), Proceedings at the Sir Henry Willink's Commission, Appointed to Enquire Into the Fears of Minorities and the Means of Allaying Them. [report] Jos: League for Human Rights.

Logams, P. (2004), *The Middle Belt Movement in Nigerian Political Development*. Abuja: Centre for Middle Belt Studies.

Mang, H. (2012), *Can We Meet at the Market Tomorrow? Commerce, Authority and Economic Power Relations After Violent Conflicts in Jos, Nigeria*. MSc thesis. University of Oxford.

—— (2013), "Minorities as a Political Majority: Power and Reciprocity Within and outside the Small Geographic Boundaries of a North-Central Nigerian State". In: M. Fois & A. Pes, eds, *Politics and Minorities in Africa*. 1st ed. Rome: ARACNE editrice S.r.l., 273-294.

Marshall, R. (2009), *Political spiritualities*. Chicago, IL: University of Chicago Press.

Mbachirin, A. (2006a) "The responses of the church in Nigeria to socio-economic, political, and religious problems in Nigeria: a case study of the Christian Association of Nigeria *(CAN)*". PhD thesis. Institute of Church-State Studies, Baylor University. https://beardocs.baylor.edu:8443/xmlui/handle/2104/4874 [Accessed 9 January 2013].

Mbachirin, A. & D. Davis (2006b), *The responses of the church in Nigeria to socio-economic, political, and religious problems in Nigeria.* Waco, Tex.: Baylor University.

Midat, J. (2013), "SOKAPU Tackles Bishop Fearon Over Killings In Southern Kaduna", *Leadership Newspapers,* Nigeria, 1 May. http://leadership.ng/person/josiah-idowu-fearon [Accessed 4 May 2013].

Mudashir, J. (2012), "Kaduna reprisal attacks call for concern, says Bishop Idowu-Fearon", *Daily Trust,* Nigeria, 27 June. http://www.dailytrust.com.ng/index.php/news-news/4365-kaduna-reprisal-attacks-call-for-concern-says-bishop-idowu-fearon [Accessed 4 May 2013].

NIREC (1999), *NIREC—Nigeria Inter-Religious Council.* http://nirecng.org/history.html [Accessed 12 March 2013].

Ojo, M. (2007) "Pentecostal Movements, Islam and the Contest for Public Space in Northern Nigeria", *Islam and Christian-Muslim Relations* 18(2): 175-188.

Nigeria70.com. 2013. "Plateau Burial Massacre: Security agents blocked our only escape route •Survivor-Rep alleges •Jos streets deserted as residents observe curfew •Senate, Reps adjourn in honour of Dantong", *Tribune Newspaper/Nigeria '70.* [online] July 10 2012: http://www.nigeria70.com/nigerian_news_paper/plateau_burial_massacre_security_agents_blocked_our/475191 [Accessed: 26 Sep 2013].

Ostien, P. (2006), "An Opportunity Missed by Nigeria's Christians: The 1976-78 Sharia Debate Revisited". In: B. Soares, ed., *Muslim-Christian Encounters in Africa.* 1st ed. Leiden and Boston: Brill, pp. 221-255.

———— (2012), Percentages By Religion of the 1952 and 1963 Populations of Nigeria's Present 36 States. Nigeria Research Network Background Papers: Oxford Department of International Development Queen Elizabeth House University of Oxford. http://www3.qeh.ox.ac.uk/pdf/nrn/BP1Ostien.pdf [Accessed 18 March 2013].

Ostien, P., ed. (2007) *Sharia Implementation in Northern Nigeria 1999–2006: A Sourcebook.* Ibadan: Spectrum Books.

Ozigi, A. & L. OCHO (1981), *Education in Northern Nigeria.* London: Allen & Unwin.

PM News (2013), "Onayekan, Kukah highlight Nigeria's twin monsters print", *PM News,* Nigeria, 4 May. http://pmnewsnigeria.com/2013/05/04/onayekan-kukah-highlight-nigerias-twin-monsters/ [Accessed 4 May 2013].

Salkida, A. (2011a), "Boko Haram: We have lined up over 100 militants for suicide bombings", *Blueprint Newspapers Online,* 26 June. http://blueprintng.com/index/2011/06/boko-haram-we-have-lined-up-over-100-militants-for-suicide-bombings/ [Accessed 5 October 2011].

Salkida, A. (2011b), "Face of UN House bomber", *Blueprint Newspapers Online*, September. http://blueprintng.com/index/2011/09/face-of-un-house-bomber/ [Accessed 5 October 2011].

ScanNews Nigeria (2012), "Poverty responsibility for Boko Haram activities says Borno Governor", *ScanNews Nigeria*. http://scannewsnigeria.com/news/poverty-responsibility-for-boko-haram-activities-says-borno-governor/ [Accessed 27 May 2013].

Sen, A. (1981), Poverty and famines. Oxford: Clarendon Press.

Tambo, D. (1978), "The 'Hill Refuges' of the Jos Plateau: A Historiographical Examination", *History in Africa (African Studies Association)* 5: 201-223.

The Messenger Voice (2012), "The Full Story of St. Finbarrs Bombing in Rayfield, Jos", http://themessengervoice.com/?p=1069 [Accessed 2 June 2013].

Trimingham, S. (1962), *History of Islam in West Africa*. London, New York: published for the University of Glasgow by Oxford University Press.

Turaki, Y. (1993), *The British colonial legacy in Northern Nigeria*. Jos: Fab Anieh Press.

Tyoden, S. (1993), *The Middle Belt in Nigerian politics*. Jos: AHA.

Vatican.va (n.d.), The Pontifical Council for Interreligious Dialogue. http://www.vatican.va/roman_curia/pontifical_councils/interelg_en.html [Accessed 12 March 2013].

Wallis, W. (2012), "Nigerian central banker calls for end to imbalances", *Financial Times*. http://www.ft.com/intl/cms/s/0/02ce9e7e-4837-11e1-b1b4-00144feabdc0.html#axzz2UTRtS8UA [Accessed 27 May 2013].

5

FRAMING & BLAMING

Discourse Analysis of the Boko Haram Uprising, July 2009*

Portia Roelofs

Competing discourses are involved in a meta-conflict over the meaning of the Boko Haram uprising in northern Nigeria in July 2009. These discourses are characterised by different conceptions of the state. This study analyses the struggle over the meaning of the uprising, using the theoretical framework of "meta-conflict" set out by Horowitz and Brass, and a discourse analysis methodology based on the work of Foucault, and Lakoff and Johnson. An analysis of media reports in the five weeks following the uprising reveals that embedded within reports on Boko Haram there are four competing conceptions of the state. The Socio-Economic discourse argues for the state as the provider of development, whereas the Political Agency discourse posits the state as the provider of order. The Religious Structural discourse emphasises the state's secular role in containing expansionist Islam, and the Religious Agency discourse calls on the state to help mainstream Islam maintain control over deviant sects.

INTRODUCTION

Research on violent conflict tends to focus on trying to answer the primary-level questions about the cause and nature of violence. Equally important, however, is how the idea of violence is constructed and instrumentalised to support wider political narratives. This chapter analyses how different actors have given different meanings to the violence related to the Boko Haram uprising in 2009, and how those meanings have been reproduced through discourse. The language used to describe the conflict represents divergent understandings of conflict. This study asks what metaphors are used to describe the Boko Haram uprising and what model of the causation is assumed by such metaphors.

As Boko Haram-related violence continues to be a central political issue in Nigeria and in Nigeria's relations with external states, the need for reliable empirical data on the violence, including details of the victims and transparency over government actions, is obvious. However, equally important is the need to understand what is at stake in discussions about Boko Haram. In talking about Boko Haram, commentators make implicit claims about how the state in Nigeria should operate. The main argument of this chapter is that the meta-conflict over the meaning of the July 2009 Boko Haram uprising in northern Nigeria is between competing discourses which are characterised by different conceptions of the state: the state as provider of development, the secular state, the state as provider of order, and the state as protector of the moral order. Each of the four major discourses employs metaphorical structures to imply different models of causation. Despite the differences in causation, all of them suggest that the state has responsibility to control the causes of violence. All argue that to solve the conflict, the state must perform its role better, but disagree over the state's proper role.

As such, this study uses the discourses about Boko Haram as a window to explore salient themes and tensions in Nigerian politics and the international political environment. An analysis of how people talk about Boko Haram, and the themes and tensions within different accounts of the conflict, is relevant to understanding and situating the Boko Haram conflict in wider concerns. Depending on whether one believes that the root causes of the conflict are underdevelopment and bad governance, a lack of police control, the expansionist desires of Muslims, or a lack of regulation of Islamic teachings, one will come to different conclusions as to how peace and stability can be returned to the north-eastern states. The analysis below demonstrates that such core beliefs are often not stated explicitly, but embedded in the language used to frame the Boko Haram conflict.

The chapter has five sections. The first sets out the theoretical framework, defining two key concepts: discourse and meta-conflict. The second section reviews the literature on the Boko Haram uprising in July 2009, highlighting the confusion and lack of clarity concerning the group's genesis due to uncritical use of sources. The third section sets out the methodology based on discourse analysis of newspaper reports between 26 July and 31 August 2009 and highlights the methodology's limitations. In the fourth section, I set out four major discourses about the meaning of the uprising: the Socio-Economic discourse, the Religious Structural discourse, the Political Agency discourse, and the Religious Agency discourse. The fifth section picks up on specific tensions between the discourses and highlights how discourse analysis allows for the identification of metaphors that mask questions of causation. The chapter concludes with a warning to commentators to critically examine the sources they use and the hidden assumptions of the discourses they employ in discussing the Boko Haram conflict.

For the sake of brevity and clarity I use the phrase "Boko Haram uprising" to describe the period of violence in northern states from 26 July to 30 July 2009. The label is misleading insofar as violence was perpetrated by a variety of actors, not just by those referred to as Boko Haram. Moreover, the word "uprising" has specific connotations of a unified political project with goals of overthrowing an oppressor. The appropriateness of this term is debatable, but beyond the scope of this article.

MEANING, REPRESENTATION, AND FRAMING

> There is the conflict itself, and there is the meta-conflict—the conflict over the nature of the conflict. Neither is coterminous with the other; neither can be reduced to the other.
>
> (Horowitz 1991: 2)

Discourse constructs the conceptual framework through which we interpret the world around us. Through the establishment of metaphors, exclusion of rival explanations and actors, and objectification of social groups into entities, discourses build up overarching narratives. In politics, discourse shapes how we conceive of our interests and identity (Horowitz 1991: 31). When conflict arises, discourse determines not only which side we take, but what we believe the conflict is about. This is evident in the current debates over Boko Haram: if the group is essentially a symptom of poverty and deprivation, then it is a conflict between those whose duty is to provide development (typically the state) and those who are the victims of their incompetence (in this case, unemployed northern youth). Alternatively, if the conflict is caused by deep religious antagonisms, then the only choice is whether to side with the Christians or Muslims. The scope of such discourses extends into the past to find causes for current violence and into the future by setting up expectations of future behaviour (Brass 1996: 2).

For some scholars, discourse is a pejorative term which denotes a gap between what is said and what is true. On this view, discourse is something which obscures truth and must be 'cut through' to get to the truth underneath. The resulting scholarly account will not be a discourse; it will just be a neutral analysis of the conflict (McGarry & O'Leary 1995: 1; Lemarchand 1996: 17). However, there is no way of escaping the need to interpret the world around us. The use of discourse is neither optional nor inherently deceptive. Mills emphasises that, following Foucault, discourse is a universal filter, or lens of interpretation (Mills 2003: 55-56).

The purpose of analysing discourse is not to find out which discourse has the best claim to truth, because the criteria by which we might measure truth are internal to specific discourses and cannot be used to evaluate various discourses from an external, "objective" standpoint (Mills 2003: 58). Rather, discourse analysis can help us to de-naturalise certain ways of interpreting the world and see things we would otherwise miss. Ordinarily, the ways in which discourse structures our understanding may seem so natural and automatic as to be invisible to us (Laclau & Mouffe 2001: 108).

The concept of meta-conflict originates in Horowitz's work on South Africa (1991), but has since been applied more widely to analyse the 1992 Los Angeles riots and the Troubles in Northern Ireland (McGarry & O'Leary 1995; Mac Ginty, Roger & du Toit 2007). The concept of a meta-conflict can be seen as applying the tools of Critical Discourse Analysis to discussions on violent conflict. All conflicts are accompanied by a struggle for their meaning, explanation, and cause. Brass defines a meta-conflict as "the struggle for control over the meaning" of acts of violence and for "the right to represent them properly". He argues that the struggle is not simply between parties to the conflict but includes the contributions to discourse from academics and journalists (Brass 1996: 1).

A meta-conflict is characterised by a "fundamental dissensus" about who is fighting whom and why (Horowitz 1991: 26). The different narratives interact in a conflictual manner. A key function of each narrative is to assign blame and responsibility. These are not just rival explanations which sit side by side; they actively attack the other explanations offered. Discourses seek to silence or marginalise other competing discourses, presenting rival explanations as attempts to whitewash the real causes of violence, or else discounting them as superficial and self-serving. This happens in two ways. Firstly, through rarefaction, discourse defines who has the authority to speak truth on a certain subject (Foucault 1982: 64; Mills 2003: 67-68; Foucault 2006). Secondly, via exclusion, discourse can exclude rival explanations. In addition to rarefaction and exclusion, discourse engages in objectification: the simplification of the messy and disparate elements of human experience into entities with defined properties as if they were physical objects.

An analysis of discourse is impotent without reference to the power struggles it relates to. For this it is necessary to have knowledge of the local context the discourse occurs in; otherwise, the significance of the 'words' and how they relate to pertinent local, national, and international interests will be lost.

Lakoff and Johnson argue that "our ordinary conceptual system, in terms of which we both think and act, is fundamentally metaphorical in nature". They give the example of an argument as a war. We do not simply talk about argument as if it is war; crucially, we also think about argument as if it is war. The linguistic framework of the metaphor structures our conceptual reality, that is, the way we think about the world (Lakoff & Johnson 1981: 3). The analysis of metaphorical language in descriptions of violence in news reports, often in subtle ways, is a key aspect of Critical Discourse Analysis. The discourses on Boko Haram present events via metaphors in order to simplify and explain them.

CONTESTED CHRONOLOGY AND UNCRITICAL USE OF SOURCES

There has been a steady increase in interest in Boko Haram from academics, government, and NGOs in the years since 2009, with an attendant increase in research output about the group. However, there is a lack of clarity over the chronology of events and the genesis of the group—what Eltringham calls the "factual chronicle" (2003). Not only are commentators interpreting events differently, but they do not even agree on what the events are.

There are a number of discrepancies in different descriptions of the history of Boko Haram. Onuoha says that "the exact date of the emergence of the Boko Haram sect is mired in controversy" (2010: 56), but a survey of the literature reveals confusion rather than disagreement. Writers unintentionally contradict each other. Accounts of how Boko Haram developed are so profoundly different as to indicate a general lack of clarity and knowledge about the group, rather than a range of interpretations of agreed facts. Many authors cite unverified media reports, without critically assessing the reliability of such sources. A pair of news articles in *Tell Magazine* in August 2009 are cited for large parts of the description of Boko Haram's activities and history by Adesoji (2011), Danjibo (2009), and Onuoha (2010), who are then cited, among others, in Bagaji (2012), Pham (2012), Aghedo and Osumah (2012), and Cline (2011), Ekanem *et al.* quote from Wikipedia (Ekanem, Dada & Ejue 2005: 190-191). Other articles do not use citations at all for key claims, such as when Essiet talks about the "raping [sic] of Christian women in Maiduguri" (Essiet 2010: 4). The Christian Solidarity Worldwide report on intercommunal violence in the years preceding the uprising attempts to evade the need for references by using phrases such as "it is widely held that" or "it appears that" (Christian Solidarity Worldwide 2004: 2).

Owing to the low visibility of the group before 2009, they attracted little academic interest before the uprising. Moreover, the difficulty of researching violent groups first-hand, combined with the escalating risks associated with doing research in the areas where Boko Haram operates in Borno, Yobe, and Bauchi states, means the prospects for empirical study of the group at present remain dim. Journalists, policy makers, and commentators should critically examine their sources when analysing Boko Haram and ensure that the confidence of any subsequent claims reflect the strength of the evidence available.

There is confusion over when Boko Haram first appeared. Onuoha presents one of the most detailed accounts. He quotes the Nigerian Director of Defence Information, who says the sect started in 1995 under Abubakah Lawan's leadership and then changed name several times from *Ahulsunna wal'jam'ah hijra*, to the *Nigerian Taliban*, to *Yusufiyya* sect, to *Boko Haram* (Onuoha 2010: 55). However, the group have never referred to themselves as Boko Haram, calling themselves first ahl al-sunna wa-l-jama'a wa-l-hijra, and then from late 2009 onwards, jama'at ahl al-sunna li-l-da'wa wa-l-jihad 'ala minhaj al-salaf (Loimeier 2012: 151-152). It appears that Yusuf and the group became associated with the phrase *boko haram* from 2005 onwards, thanks to

Yusuf's frequent decrying of "boko" in his sermons. However, up until 2009, press reports call group members "Nigerian Talibans" (Chouin, Reinert & Apard: this volume).

Aghedo and Osumah cite Onuoha for their historical overview section and yet say that Yusuf was the leader of the group since the mid-1990s (Aghedo & Osumah 2012: 858). Cook claims that Boko Haram first manifested in 2002, which is later than Onuoha's 2001 date for their establishment but before his estimate of their first attack, 2003 (Onuoha 2010: 56; Cook 2011: 9). Danjibo agrees that Boko Haram has at times been called the *Yusufiyya* sect but that it was Yusuf who established it in 2001, not Lawan in 1995, whilst Cline says that in 2002 Yusuf merely took over the group, despite using Danjibo as his reference (Danjibo 2009: 6; Cline 2011: 281)

Onuoha argues that the first public attacks by Boko Haram came in Kanama and Geidam, Yobe State, in 2003, before the group was "dislodged" by the army and dispersed, returning to set up base in Kanama in 2004. The same year, the group attacked police stations in Gwoza and Bama, Borno State, which was met with police counterattacks (2010: 56). Cook echoes the 2003 and 2004 Kanama stories, but asserts that there were two other attacks in 2004, resulting in deaths and arrests before this, which Onuoha does not mention, in Damboa and Damaturu (2011: 9-10). Cline says Boko Haram started armed operations in 2004, which could refer to Kanama, but he does not give details (2011: 281). Okpaga *et al.* and Boas suggest that Yusuf operated in Maiduguri, not Kanama, in that time period, with Boas presenting Boko Haram as a different group from the ones that launched attacks in 2004 (Okpaga, Chijioke & Eme 2012: 82). Boas suggests that whilst the other more violent groups were crushed, before 2009 Boko Haram appeared to be a "harmless" complex comprising of a school and mosque (Boas 2012: 3). Pham suggests that this period of "relative calm" only emerged sometime after they were repelled by security forces in 2004 (Pham 2012: 2-3).

According to Onuoha, skirmishes with the police continued at a low level until 2007, when Yusuf and a fellow member of Boko Haram were tried for terror-related crimes (Onuoha 2010: 56-57). However, Danjibo and Bagaji both cite an article from *Tell Magazine* in 2009 that claims Yusuf and others from Boko Haram were arrested as part of Operation Sawdust in 2005 and held in police custody until 2007 (Danjibo 2009: 15; Bagaji *et al.* 2012: 38). Onuoha says that Yusuf was arrested again in 2008 and held until January 2009, though Danjibo does not mention this (Onuoha 2010: 56). Cook and Le Sage do not mention any arrests and say that between 2004/2005 and 2009 there was a period of truce between Boko Haram and the government (Cook 2011: 10), or at least an "inactive phase" (Le Sage 2011: 7).

In terms of the July 2009 uprising, it appears that there was an initial incident at a funeral procession in Maiduguri in June 2009 where 17 Boko Haram members were shot and wounded by police after a confrontation over motorbike taxi drivers not wearing helmets (Last 2008: 7; Okpaga, Chijioke & Eme 2012: 82-3). A police raid in Bauchi town, advised by the Nigerian intelligence services, then came in early July, resulting in a shoot-out at a police station where some Boko Haram members who were arrested in the raid were being held. Soon afterwards, Boko Haram members began to congregate in Maiduguri in preparation for more confrontations (Last 2008: 7; Danjibo 2009: 15).

Recently, rigorous work has been done to establish a reliable chronology of events, both in terms of the group's development in the context of Islamic contestation in the northern states over a number of decades (Loimeier 2012), and in terms of lethal incidents in the Boko Haram conflict.[1] My aim in this study is not to resolve the discrepancies in the factual record but to analyse how the debate about the conflict illuminates wider political themes in Nigerian politics.

Despite the differences between different accounts of what happened, when, and why, there are three main events during the course of the uprising between 26 and 30 July that each discourse has to interpret. In rough chronological order they are the following: the uprising and associated violence perpetrated by Boko Haram between 26 and 30 July, whether in Maiduguri, Borno State, Bauchi, Bauchi State, Damaturu and Potiskum, Yobe State, or Wudil, Kano State; the response of the state, which involved immediate retaliation by police and then a military operation in Maiduguri starting on 27 July; and the death of the leader of Boko Haram, Mohammad Yusuf, in police custody on 30 July. In addition to these key nodes of analysis, articles refer to a range of other events in an effort to place the Boko Haram uprising in a broader context. This contributes to ideological discourses whose significance extends beyond the uprising.

METHODOLOGY AND LIMITATIONS

My analysis was conducted on 186 newspaper reports from a five-week window extending from 26 July to the end of August 2009. The vast majority of articles I looked at were news reports rather than analysis or editorials, meaning that the process of interpretation is manifested in how the author tells the story, rather than in explicit editorial opinions. Articles from outside that period, or from other news sources, are included where they help illuminate an overarching discourse, which articles from the time period fit into.

Discourse is not limited to the written word; however, for the purposes of this study, the primary sources selected come solely from the national and international newspaper press. Non-literate media, such as TV and radio, were excluded from the dataset, as were news sources such as BBC Hausa Service and Aminiya, which do not broadcast in English. There are difficulties in ascertaining the size of the readership of newspapers and thus in determining how representative of the views of the general population discourses reproduced by newspapers are. However, there are reasons to believe that newspapers reach a significant portion of the Nigerian population (Bakker 2011: 5-6). Copies are passed from person to person, around offices and workplaces, and archived in libraries.[2] Furthermore, this does not include online readership. This means the real readership is likely to be many multiples higher than the sales figures.

For domestic newspapers, I looked at *Daily Trust*, perhaps the largest-selling English-language newspaper in the North; *The Nation*, aimed at the business elite; *The Guardian*, secular and aimed at the educated elite; and *ThisDay*, with a similar audience and genre to *The Guardian* (Stanford University Libraries). Not all Nigerian newspapers have online archives going back to 2009, so I was unable to include *Punch* in my analysis, despite its apparently having the highest circulation. For others (including *The Nation* and *The Guardian*), archives were available only on news aggregation websites, meaning that they may have published articles which were not picked up by the website and thus not included in my analysis. Therefore I chose my sources based on the following criteria: whether they were available online, whether they had a significant readership, and whether across all the sources there was a good cross-section of the views available. Newspaper publishing is concentrated around Lagos, with the *Daily Trust* being the only major 'northern' newspaper included in the study. *The New Nigerian*, established by Sir Ahmadu Bello in 1963, was for a long time the mouth-piece of the northern establishment. In

2009 it was still active, yet archives are unavailable online and it is therefore not included in the analysis.

For foreign newspapers, I applied the added criteria of whether they discussed the Boko Haram crisis, as the coverage was patchy. From the foreign press, I looked at *Foreign Policy*, BBC News Online, Al Jazeera English, and the British newspaper *The Guardian* (from here on, *The Guardian* (UK)).

The Boko Haram conflict has expanded in geographic scope, number of causalities, and political and social consequences since 2009. Several different phases have developed, with substantial shifts in the leadership of the group, their methods, their communications, and their international links and outlook. Accordingly, the number of media and academic reports on the conflict has exploded. A full analysis of the meta-conflict over the meaning of the violence would take account of these growing bodies of discourse. Notably, some key discourses have emerged which are not touched on in this study but have been dominant in certain sectors: the discourse of foreign influence as the cause of Boko Haram violence; of Boko Haram being used as political thugs by ex-Borno State Governor Ali Modu Sherriff; and a growing discourse of civil war between Muslim North and Christian South, linking Boko Haram to violations of the Presidential zoning agreement. Rather, this study takes only a small snapshot of discourses that were in circulation in a limited number of newspapers very early on in the conflict. This snapshot is then used as an opening to analyse more general themes and concerns in Nigerian politics, through the lens of the Boko Haram conflict.

FRAMING AND BLAMING: DISCOURSES ON BOKO HARAM

In the media in the five weeks during and after the uprising, there are four major discourses on the meaning of the Boko Haram uprising: the Socio-Economic discourse, the Religious Structural discourse, the Political Agency discourse, and the Religious Agency discourse. All offer an explanation of the conflict whereby it fits with a broader worldview. The discourses locate the violence related to the Boko Haram uprising in different contexts, identifying its causes and assigning blame. Through this interpretive process each viewpoint contains a conception of the state which links context, cause, and blame to an implied understanding of how the state should respond to violence. These conceptions are in conflict: each discourse seeks to undermine rival discourses via exclusion and rarefaction.

Socio-Economic discourse: the roots of underdevelopment

The socio-economic view holds that the Boko Haram crisis is merely a symptom of the larger underlying problem of poverty and exclusion, which is at the heart of all violence in Nigeria whether in the Delta, Jos, or Maiduguri. *Foreign Policy* (FP) magazine summarises the socio-economic view:

> With Yusuf out of the picture, it would be silly to assume that the trouble is over. These sorts of episodes will keep popping up as they have throughout the North for the last decades until the root of the problem is fixed (Dickinson 2009a).

The discourse uses metaphorical language to suggest that all incidents of violence have the same cause. This objectifies the cause of violence into a single entity, like a root, and homogenises all violent incidents, as if they are plants linked by an underground root system. This is evident in phrases such as "these sorts of episodes", "uprisings like this", "this most recent eruption", and the description of Boko Haram as "the northern Nigerian version" of violence in the Niger Delta (Dickinson 2009a; Herskovits 2009).

The role of religion in the conflict is acknowledged but presented as epiphenomenal and relatively unimportant. The metaphors of depth are used to characterise the 'real' causes of violence, reinforcing the idea of the causes of violence as a root of a plant which spread below the surface. In contrast, rival accounts of the conflict are excluded by labelling them as superficial, using metaphors of shallowness. FP writes: "Religious violence is a much simpler answer—and on the surface, a correct one" (Dickinson 2009a). The 'surface' is irrelevant because the real cause—deprivation—"digs deeper" and it "stretches all the way back to Abuja" (*ibid.*). The root cause lies under the surface ready to be triggered: "the only question is what will trigger the next spate of armed mayhem, and where. It could be anywhere" (Herskovits 2009).

Even explicitly religious events cannot be explained with reference to religion, but by socio-economic factors. The cause of violence is socio-economic deprivation, and the blame lies with the corrupt political elite, which has failed in the state's primary task to provide development. Conflict should be seen in the context of Nigeria as a weak or failing state. For example, in 2000, "secular institutions were not delivering justice. Sharia, it was hoped, would do a better job" (*ibid.*). The FP blog argues that people were indifferent to Shariah "as a religious tool" but interested in it as a solution to a "backwards system" (Dickinson 2009a).

The solution is to replace the failing state with one that delivers development according to good governance models. The failure is not of the model of the state but of the individual office holders' inability to perform the functions required by the Western liberal free-market model of the state. The root cause of socio-economic deprivation would be solved if the state operated correctly. The opposition ANPP support this view, arguing that the problem would be solvable were different actors, namely the ANPP, in charge at a federal level (Bisalla 2009).

The socio-economic view criticises the government as part of a process of rarefaction. Officials are portrayed as incompetent and not a credible source of knowledge. FP calls the government "unprepared" and its views "silly" (Dickinson 2009a; Herskovits 2009). It mocks the president for going on a "jaunt" to Brazil during the uprising (Dickinson 2009b). This discourse is largely held by Western commentators, including *Foreign Policy* magazine and the United States government, who position themselves as experts or representatives of the state as providers of development.

It empowers those who can be presented as the victims of state-led underdevelopment, such as Boko Haram, because their grievances are seen as somewhat justified. The socio-economic view downplays the threat of Boko Haram and contrasts it with "the excessive force" of the state's response (Herskovits 2009; Kawu 2009). Descriptions of Boko Haram attacks are absent or brief and are referred to as "attacks on police stations" and then "clashes between" the group and the security services. In contrast, the focus is on the aggression of the police, saying that the military "compounded the misery of people in Maiduguri" thanks to the "indiscriminate killing of guilty and innocent alike" (Herskovits 2009).

Religious Structural discourse: Muslims versus the rest

The religious structural view presents the Boko Haram crisis as just one example of an intrinsic tendency within Islam, which causes periodic episodes of violence. The Boko Haram uprising is essentially a religious conflict, like past instances of communal violence in Jos and Kano. Conflict should be seen in the context of northern Nigeria as the site of repeated jihad, going back to 1804, and as part of a global struggle against Islamism and terrorism.

Violence is described in religious terms and with a focus on details which highlight the Islamic-ness of the actors involved—that they were "chanting 'God is Great!'" (Smith 2009a), or were "wearing long-beards"(Smith 2009b).

Muslims are objectified and portrayed as having essential characteristics. The specifics of Boko Haram are only relevant insofar as they uncover deeper, more essential characteristics that all Muslims share.

The objectification of Muslims can be seen in the wider literature on religious violence in Nigeria. Christian Solidarity Worldwide groups all Muslims into a single monolithic entity and then homogenises 'the rest', constructing a binary between Muslim and non-Muslims. "Non-Muslims" becomes a unitary actor which thinks and acts as one. For example, "the non-Muslims of Plateau State view the situation altogether differently" (Christian Solidarity Worldwide 2004: 1).

The entity of "Muslims" is extended in two directions to form a spectrum of "extremist" to "moderate" Muslims. At one pole are Al-Qaeda terrorists (Clark 2009) and at the other are everyday Nigerian Muslim social customs (Essiet 2010). Yet, because everything on the spectrum shares the same basic characteristic of being Muslim, the differences between them are presented as being of degree rather than categorical. On this view, extremists are therefore simply uninhibited moderates. Moderates and extremists share a desire to impose their beliefs, but moderates will not act upon them. This supports the idea that the threat of Islam is bubbling below the surface. An individual Muslim might appear to be moderate but beneath their inhibited, civilised front lie threatening Islamic tendencies: extremism can erupt from seeming moderacy. The religious structural view implies that violence will stop only when the underlying cause of structural religious antagonism is resolved.

Furthermore, the religious structural view merges state and society, to create an impression of Islam as all-consuming. Bagaji *et al.* use the phrases "secular state" and "secular society" interchangeably, both of which are presented as the target for Muslim aggression (Bagaji *et al.* 2012). Individual liberty and safety, therefore, are equated with a secular state. The conception of the state, this implies, can be seen in the following quote:

> The church, which blamed the Federal Government for the proliferation of the Boko Haram movement, urged government to take urgent steps to contain the current upsurge in religious militancy in the country as propagated by the sect. (*The Guardian* 2009c)

Therefore, the problem is one of religion, but it has a political solution for which the state is responsible. The biggest threat to society is the inherent expansionist tendency of Islam, and therefore the primary function of the state is to protect against it. The state can be judged by how well it protects its secular status to keep Islam at bay. But the major conflict is not between two religions—Islam and Christianity—but Islam and 'the rest'. Therefore the state's role is to protect its secular status, which mainly involves containing or repelling the expansionist tendencies of Islam. When the state fails in this role, the state is to blame for the violence, because it has neglected its responsibilities.

In terms of the wider power hierarchies reinforced by this discourse, Christian groups such as the Christian Association of Nigeria (CAN) gain authority to represent the conflict in such a way that it emphasises religious difference and position themselves as speaking for the innocent victims of the struggle against expansionist Islam. Newspapers like *The Guardian* often give column inches to Christian organisations condemning the violence (*The Guardian* 2009c). Muslims are seen as perpetrators of violence and Christians as peace-loving victims (*The Guardian* 2009f). *The Guardian* (UK) repeats four times in one article that Mohammad Yusuf said he and his followers will fight to the death, reinforcing the idea that he is mad or irrational (Smith 2009a). This excludes discourses which advocate negotiation with the group or appeasement through development in the North. This discourse undermines the ability of Muslims to speak with authority on the conflict, and of those who are seen as too politically correct to admit that the problem is Islam.

Political Agency discourse: the volatility of violence

The political agency view casts Boko Haram-related violence as part of the state's continuous efforts to maintain order against the forces of chaos and disorder. The state's purpose is to provide order, and this is threatened by the existence of violence, which is apt to spread by contagion. The language used suggests a metaphor of violence as a liquid seeping through gaps in the state's protection. The metaphor helps construct a binary between soft, chaotic, non-state violence and the hard control of the state. Like water, violence is fluid and evades control: it "spreads" (Idris *et al.* 2009), militants "proliferate", there are "upsurges" (*The Guardian* 2009b) and "outbreaks" of violence (*The Guardian* 2009f). In response to the unpredictable fluid movements of chaos, the police must "contain and repel" the threat (Abdulfattah 2009a). Any lack of control is characterised as loose, lax or volatile. Reports refer to poor policing as "exposing the country to danger", which reinforces the idea of danger as softness or an opening (*The Guardian* 2009e).

The political agency view presents violence by non-state actors as especially dangerous. Boko Haram's attacks are described in literal, evocative terms, focussing on the physical acts of violence: villages are "stormed" and "razed". "[A]nother civilian was burnt to ashes" as Boko Haram "used sharp knives and inflicted serious injuries on the necks and body parts of seven other police officers" (Idris *et al.* 2009).

In direct contrast to the visually evocative descriptions of Boko Haram, police are presented as rule-driven. The acts of state violence are described in orderly terms, and the police's physical actions are almost never mentioned. Instead, they are described as if in a constitutional document. They submit "comprehensive reports" (*The Nation* 2009a), continue "heavy bombardments", and "successfully crushed the uprising" (*The Guardian* 2009d). Furthermore, police officers are the frontline of the fight against violence, because they are the guardians of the forces of order (Idris & Haroun 2009).

In certain situations, however, the police or the government are to blame for failing to exert enough control. The state should not show signs of weakness—for example, indecision, unwillingness to be violent, or mercy—because these are as bad as the violence itself. The idea that violence is the result of weakness is echoed in the wider literature about terrorism. Forrest and Giroux use terms which denote softness or opening to describe the risks posed by terrorists: for instance, terrorists might find "sanctuary", "operational freedom", or a "safe-haven" (2011: 12). They describe a lack of government control as government "softness" (*ibid.* 12). Soft openings are bad because danger could penetrate the gaps, like water leaks through holes or weak points in fabric. This excludes discourses which focus on the causes or justifications for non-state violence.

For politicians, the solution is to impose more order. The plans proposed by a group of northern governors involve increasing government control in general. They "resolved to monitor the activities of all religious groups to forestall recurrence of unrest" [sic], and traditional rulers will be "empowered to enforce relevant laws that guide and regulate the establishment and activities of religious groups or sects" (*The Guardian* 2009f). All the verbs are all about control: *resolve, monitor, forestall, empower, enforce, guide, regulate.* The state should be synonymous with control and order; thus, the response to violence is to extend the control of the state. In the literature on terrorism, we can see similar conceptions of violence as the result of the state's failure to be strong and provide order. Forrest and Giroux write that terrorism could be addressed by helping African militaries and police services to "strengthen" themselves or encouraging "non-state actors... [to] undertake local policing duties" (2011: 12-13).

This discourse serves the interests of the police, because it marginalises members of Boko Haram as "dangerous lunatics" and "religious fanatics", who are "awfully superstitious", and justifies police killings of suspects. BBC News, *The Nation*, Al Jazeera, and *ThisDay* also reproduce this discourse.

Religious Agency discourse: deviance and order within Islam

The view put forward by some of the northern Islamic establishment is that the Boko Haram crisis is a religious issue, but one caused by an Islamic agent whose views and behaviour are an aberration, not the norm. The Arewa Consultative Forum and editorials in the *Daily Trust* newspaper present this view (Ebije 2009). It emphasises the benign nature of Islam in the North and focuses on the ways in which individuals such as Yusuf have manipulated normal Muslims to make them act in anomalous ways. Muslim leaders engage in a complex process of including and excluding Boko Haram from wider Islam. Mohammad Haruna writes in a *Daily Trust* editorial: "Billions of others, including his fellow Muslims, would equally disagree [with Mohammad Yusuf]". The idea of "fellow Muslims" who are in disagreement reflects this tension (Haruna 2009). On the one hand, they do not want Islam to be associated with violence, so they condemn Boko Haram as "un-Islamic" (*Daily Trust* 2009h), on the other hand, they want to resist the socio-economic view which labels religion as unimportant, a superficial symptom of underlying deprivation.

The Religious Agency discourse resolves this tension by saying Boko Haram is a religious problem which therefore needs a religious solution (Abubakar 2009; Ebije 2009; *The Guardian* 2009a). Contrary to the Socio-Economic discourse, religion is not epiphenomenal. The direct causes of violence are incorrect teachings and a lack of moral order. This empowers Islamic leaders as experts, who can solve the problem of bad religious teaching through producing CDs with authoritative preaching (*Daily Trust* 2009a) or religious radio programmes that "debunk the myths of Yusuf's teaching" (*Daily Trust* 2009b). The *Daily Trust* newspaper devotes large sections of news reports to quoting Islamic leaders' condemnations of the violence (*Daily Trust* 2009a). This sets up an opposition between a minority and the majority of Nigerian Muslims. Boko Haram is marginalised through the description of weird beliefs held by the group, which distinguish it from normal Islam. The *Daily Trust* notes that schools linked with Boko Haram taught children not to eat Maggi—a ubiquitous food brand—or wash with soap (Fidelis 2009).

Whereas the religious structural view presents the difference between extremists and moderates as a matter of degree, the religious agency view presents extremism as an aberration. Rather than Boko Haram being an "eruption" of underlying extremism, Yusuf's ideas are portrayed as externally imposed, like a sickness, a delirium, or a spell (Idris 2009). Boko Haram members are "misled" (Lalo, Agbese & Muhammed 2009) and "ill-informed, perhaps brainwashed" by Yusuf (*Daily Trust* 2009f), and "innocent children ... were unconsciously initiated into the sect" (*Daily Trust* 2009c). This discourse emphasises Muslim victimhood both in terms of the members of Boko Haram who "lost their lives" and the "bereaved" families they left behind without breadwinners (Gusau & Bashir 2009; Idris 2009).

The state, in its primary role as the upholder of moral order, should reaffirm and strengthen the proper forms of Islam, supporting mainstream Islam to overcome its misguided deviant fringes. This discourse is ambivalent towards the current government, at times blaming the police for anti-Muslim violence and, at others, seeking to harness the power of the state to license and control religious activities (Kwaru, Salkida & Idris 2009).

TENSIONS, METAPHORS, AND HIDDEN ASSUMPTIONS

Violence does not speak for itself; violence must go through a process of interpretation where it is turned into an event, with a cause and a context. The above analysis demonstrates that in the case of the Boko Haram uprising in 2009, there is dissensus over the meaning of violence. Where are the points of tension in the meta-conflict? How do the various discourses competing for dominance attempt to exclude and marginalise rival discourses? In this brief discussion section, I highlight how these tensions play out in practice, using the example of a specific discursive interaction between the Socio-Economic discourse as reproduced by Hilary Clinton and the Political Agency discourse as reproduced by the then President Umar Yar'Adua. Finally, I analyse two instances where metaphors are used to mask questions of causation and naturalise certain simplified ways of seeing the world. Such analysis is by no means exhaustive but illustrative of the ways in which discourse embeds certain assumptions.

Shared ground and areas of tension

In general, it is worth noting that the political agency view is most prevalent, finding widespread support among the Nigerian press and Yar'Adua. Internationally, the socio-economic view is most popular, whilst the religious structural view is held by a minority of foreign commentators and some Christian organisations in Nigeria. The religious agency view is the least prevalent, with support confined to Muslim commentators in the North. The four discourses at times overlap. In particular, all the divergent discourses are tinged with the political agency view, which focuses on the state maintaining control over the forces of chaos. Moreover, the first three are statist. They all present the state as the key to both the problem and the solution, whilst advancing competing views of the appropriate role of the state. The final view presents the state as an auxiliary actor in the solution, fulfilling only a supporting role to the northern Islamic establishment, whose role is to uphold the moral order.

Boyd says some resolution of the meta-conflict is necessary, and Horowitz argues that dissensus in the meta-conflict "increases the difficulty of finding ways for the parties to the conflict to seek accommodation and inclusion rather than hegemony and exclusion" (Horowitz 1991, 21; Boyd 1992). Indeed, the four conceptions of the state are not necessarily incompatible; there is a degree of shared ground where dialogue can happen. There could be a state that provides development and order, is secular, and ensures the upholding of multiple schemes of moral authority. But this is a tall order for a state which has low capacity, resources, and legitimacy. The different conceptions pull in different directions, and tradeoffs will require prioritisation of certain functions of the state over others. For instance, a discourse which emphasises the inevitability of conflict will counsel a different course of action from discourses which identify specific grievances as the cause of conflict. Where discourses pull in opposite directions, many of the available options will be not only undesirable but illegitimate for key sections of society. For example, the possibility of strengthening Muslim leadership in the North as a way of safeguarding against deviant forms of Islam would be a solution on the religious agency view, but for the religious structural view it would threaten the key secular role of the state.

A key example of these conflicting conceptions of the state is in the tension between the Socio-Economic discourse and the Political Agency discourse. Both present the state as a solution to violence, but their conceptions of the state differ. For the commentators in *Foreign Policy* and in the United States government, the state's primary offering is development; for many

Nigerian politicians, it is order and control. Hilary Clinton visited Nigeria as American Secretary of State for Foreign Affairs two weeks after the violence. Her comments emphasised conflict's socio-economic causes:

> The most immediate source of the disconnect between Nigeria's wealth and its poverty is a failure of governance at the federal, state and local levels ... Lack of transparency and accountability has eroded the legitimacy of the government and contributed to the rise of groups that embrace violence and reject the authority of the state. (*The Nation* 2009b)

At first glance, the then President Yar'Adua agreed with Clinton's analysis, saying that he "promised the United States that his administration would not falter in the war against corruption" (*The Nation* 2009c). However, Clinton's conception of the state as provider of development is met with a conception of the state as the provider of order. The president's conception is based around improving the state's strength and control—for instance, winning the "war against corruption" and not "falter[ing]" (Abdulfattah 2009b).

The Political Agency discourse, which portrays non-state violence as chaotic and unpredictable, contrasts with the Socio-Economic discourse, in which Boko Haram is portrayed as predictable and rational. Herskovits says that the violence "did not surprise the people of Maiduguri or anyone else in Nigeria". She suggests that Boko Haram's anti-state beliefs are widely held: "even established leaders of Islam in the north ... are aware of how government has failed Nigeria's young" (Herskovits 2009). More broadly, the tension between the socio-economic and political agency views can further be seen in the discussion of amnesty for Boko Haram. For the former it is a rational response to violence which expresses political grievances, but for the latter it represents weakness and permissiveness, going against the core purpose of the state. Under stress, the small area of overlap between the conceptions—for instance, the shared importance of the rule of law for the political agency and socio-economic views—will disappear as different actors cling to the core elements of their worldviews.

The discourses differ in how far they treat the police as an authoritative source of knowledge. Newspapers that reproduce the Political Agency discourse, like *The Nation*, *ThisDay,* and *The Guardian*, frequently quote police spokesmen uncritically. In contrast, the *Daily Trust* articles, representing the Religious Agency discourse, undermine the police as authoritative sources of knowledge by contradictory reports—for example, when paraded suspects protest their innocence (*Daily Trust* 2009d; *Daily Trust* 2009e; *Daily Trust* 2009g; Idris *et al.* 2009).

For both the Socio-Economic discourse and the Religious Structural discourse, the focus is on general, longstanding structural causes of violence. This allows commentators to explain the violence with little reference to local context and facts on the ground. Whilst the religious agency view puts local actors in a position of expertise—because they know the specifics of Boko Haram's teaching—structural views empower international commentators who are able to 'stand back' from the conflict and look to the wider, supposedly deeper, causes, whether socio-economic or religious.

Objectification of Violence and Social Groups

The discourses about Boko Haram exemplify how metaphors are used to think about different non-physical aspects of our experience in the same ways that we can think about physical objects and substances (Lakoff & Johnson 1980). Metaphors can obscure empirical questions about the cause of violence, by replacing causes with inherent causal properties of the metaphorical objects they create. For example, the Political Agency discourse presents the metaphor of violence as a fluid. In describing violence as if it is a disembodied phenomenon that can spread like water through a country, it becomes unlinked from its human agents. The fight against violence stops being a fight against other human beings, and the human cost of retaliation is sidelined. Such discourse naturalises state violence, making it comparatively invisible.

Just as violence can be discursively constructed into a physical object like water, social groups can be objectified into a single entity. The Religious Structural discourse objectifies social groups into homogenous categories of "northern Muslims" in Nigeria, and "Muslims" in general across the world. Therefore, the explanation offered for the violence relies on the assumed violent characteristics of "northern Muslims", masking the need to explain how frustration among that group leads to conflict. Within this metaphorical conceptualisation, Muslims react violently because they are the sort of thing that reacts violently. In seeking to simplify and explain the world, we must be cautious not to allow analytic categories to slip into being treated as "really existing" physical categories (Eltringham 2004).

Whilst the religious structural view objectifies all Muslims into a monolithic entity, the religious agency view highlights the individual agency of Muslims and the plurality of beliefs. For instance, the *Daily Trust* reports on ordinary people who tried to convince their relatives not to join Boko Haram. When Mohammad Yusuf was invited to Dumbulwa to preach, the local population is presented as going out of their way to prevent his visit, including climbing trees to remove the sound system (Idris 2009). Disaggregating the category of "Muslims" allows for a more nuanced ascription of motivations and interests to various individuals and communities who are affected by the conflict in different ways.

CONCLUSION

It is wrong to say that there are two conflicts in Nigeria, the conflict and the meta-conflict, because only the first is bounded by location. The second extends beyond the state's borders to encompass all those who contribute to the circulation of discourses which deal with the Boko Haram uprising. The media will inevitably use different frameworks or interpretive lenses for making sense of events in Nigeria and the rest of the world; neutral reporting is not an option. This article sets out the beginnings of a framework whereby commentators can tease out the underlying assumptions of different ways of telling the story of Boko Haram. There is no objective way of ranking the views, because they rely equally on material facts, normative beliefs, and subconscious assumptions about social realities. Journalists should be aware of the power hierarchies they are supporting when they subconsciously use certain metaphors to describe and explain the conflict, not just in editorials and analysis pieces but in 'factual' news reports. Rather than striving for our work to be neutral in its effects, we should seek to participate in the meta-conflict responsibly.

Notes

*   I am grateful to Marc-Antoine Pérouse de Montclos, Ruadhan Hayes, Manuel Reinert, and Gérard Chouin for their helpful comments. I would like to thank Bala Mohammad Liman, Athanasius Atta Barkindo, and Steve Itugbu for valuable discussions. This research would not have been possible without funding from the Economic and Social Research Council Overseas Institutional Visit programme, and the generous support of the School of Oriental and African Studies, University of London (SOAS) Queen's Anniversary Fund, which enabled me to pursue postgraduate study at SOAS, where this article was originally submitted as a Master's Dissertation on 14 September 2012.

1. www.nigeriawatch.org.

2. Newspapers are archived at, among other places, the Nigerian Institute of International Affairs, and the National Archives, in Ibadan, Kaduna, Enugu. For more information about the holdings of various Nigerian archives, see: http://archiveswiki.historians.org/index.php/National_Archives_of_Nigeria.

References

Abdulfattah, O. (2009a), "The Daily Trust (Nigeria)—AAGM: Yar'Adua Orders Security Agencies to Rout Boko Hara", *Daily Trust (Nigeria)*.

——— (2009b), "The Daily Trust (Nigeria)—AAGM: Yar'Adua Orders Probe of Sect Leader's Death", *Daily Trust (Nigeria)*.

Abubakar, M. (2009), "The Daily Trust (Nigeria)—AAGM: Akanbi Charges Muslims on Human Devt", *Daily Trust (Nigeria)*.

Adesoji, A.O. (2011), "Between Maitatsine and Boko Haram: Islamic Fundamentalism and the Response of the Nigerian State", *Africa Today* 57: 99-109.

Aghedo, I. & O. Osumah (2012), "The Boko Haram Uprising: How Should Nigeria Respond?", *Third World Quarterly* 33: 853-869.

Bagaji, A.S.Y., M.S. Etila, E.E. Ogbadu & J.G. Sule (2012), "Boko Haram and the Recurring Bomb Attacks in Nigeria: Attempt to Impose Religious Ideology through Terrorism?", *Cross-Cultural Communication (CS Canada)* 8: 33-41. doi:10.3968/j.ccc.1923670020120801.1370.

Bakker, P. (2011), "Not Dead yet—the Changing Significance of Newspapers Worldwide", In Cardiff. http://www0.caerdydd.ac.uk/jomec/resources/foj2011/foj2011-Bakker.pdf.

Bisalla, S.M. (2009), "The Daily Trust (Nigeria)—AAGM: Niger Delta, Boko Haram Resentments to Injustice, Says Gambo Magaji", *Daily Trust (Nigeria)*, 10 August.

Boas, M. (2012), "Violent Islamic Uprising in Northern Nigeria: From the 'Taleban' to Boko Haram II". NOREF: Norwegian Peacebuilding Research Centre. internal-pdf://boas.Boko.Haram-1676050945/boas.Boko.Haram.pdf.

Boyd, Jr. (1992), "Perspectives on South Africa's Future", *African Studies Review* 35: 105-113.

Brass, P.R. (1996. *Riots and Pogroms*. New York: New York University Press.

Christian Solidarity Worldwide (2004), "Recent Religious Violence in Central and Northern Nigeria". Christian Solidarity Worldwide. internal-pdf://Christian Solidarity Network-3337123073/Christian Solidarity Network.pdf.

Clark, N. (2009), "Nigeria's Sectarian Crisis—Inside Story", *Al Jazeera English*, 30 July. http://www.aljazeera.com/programmes/

insidestory/2009/07/200972913505618217.html.

Cline, L.E. (2011), "'Today We Shall Drink Blood': Internal Unrest in Nigeria", *Small Wars & Insurgencies* 22: 273-289.

Cook, D. (2011), "Boko Haram: A Prognosis". Rice University: James A. Baker III Institute for Public Policy, Rice University. internal-pdf://Cook 1-0921085441/Cook 1.pdf.

Daily Trust (2009a), "The Daily Trust (Nigeria)—AAGM: Boko Haram And Aftermath", *Daily Trust (Nigeria)*.

————— (2009b), "The Daily Trust (Nigeria)—AAGM: Boko Haram—Security Agencies Not to Blame, Says Cleric", *Daily Trust (Nigeria)*.

————— (2009c), "The Daily Trust (Nigeria)—AAGM: Muslim Leaders Condemn Mayhem", *Daily Trust (Nigeria)*.

————— (2009d), "The Daily Trust (Nigeria)—AAGM: The Sacking of Darul-Islam", *Daily Trust (Nigeria)*.

————— (2009e), "Police Detain Daily Trust Reporter", *Daily Trust (Nigeria)*, 30 July. http://nigerianbulletin.com/2009/07/30/police-detain-daily-trust-reporter-daily-trust/.

————— (2009f), "The Daily Trust (Nigeria)—AAGM: Tragedy of Negligence", *Daily Trust (Nigeria)*, August 3.

————— (2009g), "Photos Don't lie...Sect Leader Alive after Capture", *Daily Trust (Nigeria)*, 3 August. http://nigerianbulletin.com/2009/08/03/photos-don%E2%80%99t-lie-sect-leader-alive-after-capture-daily-trust/.

————— (2009h), "The Daily Trust (Nigeria)—AAGM: Boko Haram Hostages—Yuguda Releases 120 Women, Children", *Daily Trust (Nigeria)*, August 4.

Danjibo, N.D. (2009), "Islamic Fundamentalism and Sectarian Violence: The 'Maitatsine' and 'Boko Haram' Crises in Northern Nigeria". In: *IFRA Conference on Conflict and Violence in Nigeria*. Zaria, Nigeria: Institut Francais de Recerche en Afrique & Institute for Development Research, Zaria. internal-pdf://Danjibo-1072086017/Danjibo.pdf.

Dickinson, E. (2009a), "Mayhem in Nigeria", *Passport: A Blog by the Editors of Foreign Policy*. http://blog.foreignpolicy.com/posts/2009/07/31/mayhem_in_nigeria.

—————. (2009b), "Nigeria, a Week Later", *Passport: A Blog by the Editors of Foreign Policy*. http://blog.foreignpolicy.com/posts/2009/08/04/nigeria_a_week_later.

Ebije, A.I. (2009), "The Daily Trust (Nigeria)—AAGM: ACF Wants Compensation For Darul Islam Members", *Daily Trust (Nigeria)*.

Ekanem, S.A., J.A. Dada & B.J. Ejue (2005), "Boko Haram and Amnesty: A Philo-legal Appraisal", *International Journal of Humanities and Social Science* 2: 189-202.

Eltringham, N. (2003), "The Blind Men and the Elephant: The Challenge of Representing the Rwandan Genocide". In: P. Caplan, *The Ethics of Anthropology*, New York: Routledge, pp. 96-112.

——— (2004), *Accounting for Horror: Post-genocide Debates in Rwanda*. London; Sterling, Va.: Pluto Press.

Essiet, J.U. (2010), "The Maiduguri Boko Haram Religious Conflict in Borno State of Nigeria". Universitat Wien. internal-pdf://Essiet-2917586433/Essiet.pdf.

Fidelis, M-L. (2009), "The Daily Trust (Nigeria)—AAGM: Boko Haram School Closed in Jalingo", *Daily Trust (Nigeria)*.

Forrest, J.J.F. & J. Giroux (2011), "Terrorism and Political Violence in Africa: Contemporary Trends in a Shifting Terrain", *Perspectives on Terrorism* 5: 5-17.

Foucault, M. (1982), *The Archaeology of Knowledge; and the Discourse on Language*. New York: Pantheon Books.

——— (2006), *Madness and Civilization*. Routledge.

Gusau, I.U. & M. Bashir (2009), "The Daily Trust (Nigeria)—AAGM: Boko Haram Leader's in-Law Killed", *Daily Trust (Nigeria)*.

Haruna, M. (2009), "The Daily Trust (Nigeria)—AAGM: The Meaning of the Boko Haram Massacre", *Daily Trust (Nigeria)*.

Herskovits, J. (2009), "The Real Tragedy in Nigeria's Violence", *Foreign Policy*, 3 August. http://www.foreignpolicy.com/articles/2009/08/03/the_real_tragedy_in_nigerias_violence?hidecomments=yes.

Horowitz, D.L. (1991), *A Democratic South Africa?: Constitutional Engineering in a Divided Society*. Berkeley: University of California Press.

Idris, A. & H. Haroun (2009), "The Daily Trust (Nigeria)—AAGM: The Media And Deaths of Boko Haram Leaders", *Daily Trust (Nigeria)*.

Idris, H. (2009), "The Daily Trust (Nigeria)—AAGM: Travails of Boko Haram Families", *Daily Trust (Nigeria)*.

Idris, H., M.I. Kwaru, I.U. Gusau & A. Salkida (2009. "The Daily Trust (Nigeria)—AAGM: Violence Spreads to Other Northern States", *Daily Trust (Nigeria)*.

Kawu, I.M. (2009), "The Daily Trust (Nigeria)—AAGM: Boko Haram—Media Profiling And Extra-Judicial Killings", *Daily Trust (Nigeria)*.

Kwaru, M.I., A. Salkida & H. Idris (2009), "The Daily Trust (Nigeria)—AAGM: Muslims Shaved Beards to Stay Alive", *Daily Trust (Nigeria)*, August 5.

Laclau, E. & C. Mouffe (2001), *Hegemony and Socialist Strategy: Towards a Radical Democratic Politics*. London: Verso.

Lakoff, G. & M. Johnson (1981), *Metaphors We Live By*. Chicago and London:

University of Chicago Press.

Lalo, M., A. Agbese & A. Muhammed (2009), "The Daily Trust (Nigeria)—AAGM: It's Extra-Judicial, Barbaric—Sheikh Khalid", *Daily Trust (Nigeria)*, 3 August.

Last, M. (2008), "The Pattern of Dissent: Boko Haram in Nigeria 2009", *Annual Review of Islam in Africa* 10 (September): 7-11.

Le Sage, A. (2011), "The Evolving Threat of Al Qaeda in the Islamic Maghreb". July 2011. National Defense University: Institute for National Strategic Studies (INSS). internal-pdf://Le Sage-3118919169/Le Sage.pdf.

Lemarchand, R. (1996), *Burundi: Ethnic Conflict and Genocide*. [Washington, DC]; Cambridge; New York, NY: Woodrow Wilson Center Press; Cambridge University Press.

Loimeier, R. (2012), "Boko Haram: The Development of a Militant Religious Movement in Nigeria", *Afrika Spectrum* 47(2): 137.

Mac Ginty, R. & P. du Toit (2007), "A Disparity of Esteem: Relative Group Status in Northern Ireland after the Belfast Agreement", *Political Psychology* 28: 13-31.

McGarry, J. & B. O'Leary (1995), *Explaining Northern Ireland : Broken Images*. Oxford, UK; Cambridge, Mass.: Blackwell.

Mills, S. (2003), *Michel Foucault*. London; New York: Routledge.

Okpaga, A., U.S. Chijioke & O.I. Eme (2012), "Activities of Boko Haram and Insecurity Question in Nigeria", *Arabian Journal of Business and Management Review (OMAN Chapter)* 1: 77-99.

Onuoha, F.C. (2010), "The Islamist Challenge: Nigeria's Boko Haram Crisis Explained", *African Security Review* 19: 54-67.

Pham, J.P. (2012), "Boko Haram's Evolving Threat". Africa Security Brief 20: April 2012. The Africa Center for Strategic Studies. internal-pdf://Pham-3857129473/Pham.pdf.

Smith, D. (2009a), "Nigerian 'Taliban' Offensive Leaves 150 Dead", *The Guardian (UK)*. http://www.guardian.co.uk/world/2009/jul/27/boko-haram-nigeria-attacks?INTCMP=SRCH.

――――― (2009b), "Army Lays Siege to Nigerian 'Taliban' in Bid to Crush Rebels", *The Guardian (UK)*. http://www.guardian.co.uk/world/2009/jul/29/nigeria-boko-haram-islam?INTCMP=SRCH.

Stanford University Libraries. "Nigeria News": http://www-sul.stanford.edu/depts/ssrg/africa/nigeria/nigerianews.html.

The Guardian (2009a), "Ramadan May Begin on August 22, Say Clerics", *The Guardian*. http://nigerianbulletin.com/news-headlines/ramadan-may-begin-on-august-22-say-clerics-the-guradian/.

——— (2009b), "Fighting Rages, Death Toll Hits 300 in Borno", *The Guardian*, 30 July.

——— (2009c), "Catholics, Kumuyi Condemn Crisis, Urge Respect for Human Lives", *The Guardian*. July 31. http://nigerianbulletin.com/2009/07/31/catholics-kumuyi-condemn-crisis-urge-respect-for-human-lives-the-guardian/.

——— (2009d), "Calm Returns, More Troops in Northern States", *The Guardian*, 31 July. http://nigerianbulletin.com/2009/07/31/calm-returns-more-troops-in-northern-states-the-guardian/.

——— (2009e), "'Sectarian Crisis, Symptom of Failed State'", *The Guardian*, 3 August. http://nigerianbulletin.com/2009/08/03/sectarian-crisis-symptom-of-failed-state-the-guardian-2/.

——— (2009f), "Northern Govs Move to Stem Religious Crises", *The Guardian*, 4 August. http://nigerianbulletin.com/uncategorized/northern-govs-move-to-stem-religious-crises-the-guardian/.

The Nation (2009a), "Revealed: Boko Haram Leaders Trained in Afghanistan, Algeria", *The Nation*. http://nigerianbulletin.com/2009/08/06/panel-demands-reports-in-24hrs-on-sect-leader%E2%80%99s-death-the-nation/.

——— (2009b), "Governance Has Failed in Nigeria, Says Clinton", *The Nation*. http://nigerianbulletin.com/2009/08/13/governance-has-failed-in-nigeria-says-clinton-the-nation/.

——— (2009c), "Yar'Adua Promises to Fight Corruption", *The Nation*. http://nigerianbulletin.com/2009/08/13/yar%E2%80%99adua-promises-to-fight-corruption-the-nation/.

PART II

BOKO HARAM & THE NIGERIAN STATE

a Strategic Analysis

6

BOKO HARAM & POLITICS
from Insurgency to Terrorism

Marc-Antoine Pérouse de Montclos
French Institute of Geopolitics, University of Paris 8

Based on the case of Boko Haram, or *Jama'atu Ahlis-Sunnah Lidda'awati Wal Jihad* (People Committed to the Propagation of the Prophet's Teachings and Jihad) to give it its real name, this chapter introduces a general discussion on the relationship between Islam and politics in Nigeria. Unlike Hamas in Palestine, Hezbollah in Lebanon, or the Muslim Brothers in Egypt, Boko Haram is neither a political party nor a charity network. It is political because it contests Western values, challenges the secularity of the Nigerian state, and reveals the corruption of a "democrazy" that relies on a predatory ruling elite, the so-called "godfathers". But Boko Haram also remains a sect, now engaged in terrorist violence. From Mohammed Yusuf to Abubakar Shekau, its leaders have never actually proposed a political programme to reform and govern Nigeria according to Shariah. In this regard, Boko Haram raises an important question: why has Nigeria never had a religious political party, either Islamic or Christian? Federalism and the alleged 'neutrality' of military regimes do not explain everything. Compared with the situation in Northern Sudan, the structure and division of Islam also help us to understand why Nigerian Muslims have never succeeded in setting up a political platform to contest elections with a religious programme, and why violence became an alternative channel for reform.

INTRODUCTION

The Western media and many Nigerians see the terrorist attacks of Boko Haram as part of a wider global religious war between Muslims and Christians. The *New York Times*, for instance, claims that "the radical Islamist group ... has struck mostly at Christians and burned churches" (Worth 2012). As for the Christian Association of Nigeria (CAN), it insists on the possibility of a religious war, and it has found fault with President Goodluck Jonathan's statement that Boko Haram killed more Muslims than Christians (Akowe 2013). However, the first and main targets of the radical Islamist organisation were indeed the security forces and 'bad' Muslims, not Christian communities. The problem is that passions and a large variety of opinions confuse the analysis of the objectives and the evolution of an indigenous sect turned terror group. Depending on positions, Boko Haram is thus considered a political uprising, a religious organisation, a social movement, or a purely criminal affair.

As is to be expected, the official narratives of Nigerian security forces tend to reduce the radical Islamist group to a gang of armed robbers, devoid of any political or social leaning. The founder of Boko Haram, the late Mohammed Yusuf, is himself described as an opportunist and a religious entrepreneur who built a massive audience of followers and attracted donations to become influential and obtain material rewards. Many Nigerian politicians from the South also deny that the sect is a freedom-fighting movement cast in the mould of the MEND (Movement for the Emancipation of the Niger Delta) in Ijawland, the OPC (Oodua Peoples Congress) in Yorubaland, or the MASSOB (Movement for the Actualization of the Sovereign State of Biafra) in Igboland. Actually, Boko Haram is not ethnic based, even if its main stronghold remains in Borno. Moreover, it developed in a remote region, far from the resources of the oil-producing areas that fund most of the budget of the federal state. Hence, it does not have the same financial leverage to negotiate an amnesty or a political agreement with the central government. Last but not least, its militants are often said to be able to commit suicide attacks because they are poor people who have nothing to lose ... and to gain, unlike MEND fighters who struggled for their share of the 'national cake'.

However, religious authorities have different views on Boko Haram. On the one hand, some Islamic scholars simply deny that the followers of Mohammed Yusuf are Muslims. The nickname Boko Haram is quite useful in this regard, since it turns "the radical group into an exotic eccentricity and hides its embarrassing connection to the leadership of well-established Salafi organization", the Izala (Brigaglia 2012: 38). On the other hand, many evangelicals insist on the role of religion and Quranic schools in breeding violence. While pressing the US to declare the sect a foreign terrorist organisation, the President of CAN, Pastor Ayo Oritsejafor, argues for instance that the movement of Mohammed Yusuf is neither a political nor a social one. To him, Boko Haram is first and foremost an extremist group "fuelled by a religious fundamentalist ideology". He acknowledges that the sect indoctrinated the poor and was manipulated by politicians. But he claims that it was not driven by misery and compares Mohammed Yusuf to Osama bin Laden, who came from a very rich family.[1]

By contrast, I argue that Boko Haram is basically an indigenous uprising with a religious ideology, a political meaning, and some social support locally, unlike transnational professional terrorist groups that can strike anywhere in the world. Obviously, the sect is not the armed branch of a party. It does not have a political program as such, and its members did not attempt to contest elections. On the contrary, the followers of Mohammed Yusuf retreated from the state to dream of a Shariah-based caliphate. Yet I consider that they form an embryonic political group because of their targets, their rejection of Western values, their contestation of a secular post-colonial state, their manipulation by politicians, the legitimacy they built during the repression, and the fear they provoke in Borno and all over Nigeria. To facilitate the reading of this chapter, I use the name Boko Haram rather than *Jama'atu Ahlis-Sunnah Lidda'awati Wal Jihad* (People Committed to the Propagation of the Prophet's Teachings and Jihad), the real name of the organisation. I qualify the group as a sect because of its distinctive religious beliefs, its deviance from mainstream Islam, its intolerance, its claim to possess unique access to the truth, the selection of its members, their fanatic indoctrination, and the fascination exerted by their former guru, Mohammed Yusuf. I also describe Boko Haram as a movement because of its social basis. And I call "terrorist" the faction which began to plant bombs and resort to suicide attacks after the killing of Mohammed Yusuf in 2009. My position does not mean that I support the labelling of the whole movement as a foreign terrorist organisation, precisely because of its grassroots and its genesis.

A POLITICAL UPRISING: FROM INSURGENCY TO TERRORISM

Since the first recorded act of violence committed by the so-called "Taliban" in November 2003, Boko Haram has actually struck against political targets: police stations, which were sometimes the only effective presence of the state in remote villages; prisons, which were attacked to release militants; schools that symbolised Western education and the colonisation of the mind; mosques and Muslim scholars who contested the moral authority of the deviant sect; politicians and godfathers who were fraudulently elected and who were accused of failing to implement properly Islamic Law, etc. After the assault of the army and the extrajudicial killing of Mohammed Yusuf in Maiduguri in July 2009, the group then started to operate outside of Borno and Yobe, hitting churches in Jos in December 2010 and United Nations offices in Abuja in August 2011. At the time of completing this chapter in September 2013, it was also speculated that Boko Haram aimed to further destabilise Nigeria by going to the South to attack strategic targets such as bridges, power plants, the radar facilities of international airports, and radio and television transmitters. If it did not yet have the capacity to do so, this did not mean that it was not engaged in a full war against the government.

Meanwhile, the extension of the targets of Boko Haram to Christian communities has testified to the radicalisation and professionalisation of the sect. Indeed, this shift makes more sense for a terrorist group which seeks an international audience. In the Western media, first, it pays more to attack Christians rather than Muslims—hence a better chance to publicise the local struggle of an Islamist sect. Moreover, Boko Haram can now claim to be part of a global holy war (jihad) when it pretends to defend Muslims against Christian aggressors in Kaduna or Plateau States—and hence the possibility of external support from organisations based in Arab countries. Also, it is sometimes suggested that attacking Christians is a way to force Nigerian Muslims to take sides. In this regard, it is important to understand the implications of the rupture of July 2009, when the remnants of the group had to run away from Maiduguri and, once in exile, faced a higher probability of getting directly in touch with transnational jihadist movements that were clearly engaged against the Jews and the "Crusaders."

Before then, Boko Haram exclusively targeted the security forces and Muslims who did not strictly follow Shariah rules. Initially inspired by the Salafi doctrine of the Izala movement, Mohammed Yusuf was always very vocal against the African "perversion" of Islamic practices by the Sufi brotherhoods

(Loimeier 2012; Pérouse de Montclos 2012: 7). His attacks focused on the Tijaniyya, who were more popular than the Qadiriyya.[2] Mohammed Yusuf also condemned the corruption of traditional elders and emirs, even if he continued to pay respect to Usman dan Fodio and the jihad of 1804, which was linked to the Qadiriyya.[3] And he eventually fought against the Izala too, a movement which rebuked the teachings of the scholars (*Gardawa Mallams*) of the traditional Sufi brotherhoods, yet did not oppose violently Western education and the secularity of the Nigerian state.[4]

At that time, the only Christians targeted by Boko Haram were not communities but a few individuals who were killed because they informed the security forces, cursed Mohammed Yusuf, or infringed the Islamic ban on alcohol.[5] On 24 December 2003, the coordinated attacks of the Taliban faction against police stations in Yobe happened on Christmas Eve. But this symbolic date might have been chosen because the holiday period facilitated the operation. It had nothing to do with the Christian celebration as such. The fact that Christian communities in Borno are not very visible also played a role, for it was more difficult to besiege them. First, they are very scattered, unlike in Kano and Kaduna, where they usually live together in specific areas. Secondly, they are mainly made up of indigenous people who are more integrated in local communities than migrants from the South in north-western Nigeria. Thirdly, these native Christians are rather recent. As early as 1711, the Sacred Congregation for the Propagation of the Faith attempted to establish a Christian mission in Borno, but to no avail as the expedition eventually ended in Katsina. When the Sokoto Caliphate fell in 1903, the British then banned Christian missions and schools in the North. Thus, in Borno, most churches developed after Independence.

Of course, this relative 'invisibility' does not mean that Christian natives or migrants were spared from violence. The CAN claims that in February 2006, anger over the publication in Denmark of controversial cartoons of the Prophet Mohammed sparked riots by mobs of Muslims in Maiduguri, leaving about fifty Christians dead and many churches burnt. During the five days of violence in July 2009, it is also alleged that Boko Haram members killed 37 Christians, including three pastors, and torched or partially destroyed 29 churches in Borno State. However, these two events require clarification. In July 2009, Christians were not the exclusive targets of a more general fighting between Boko Haram and the security forces. And in February 2006, the press did not report any involvement of the sect; on the contrary, the assailants were assumed to be Hausa-Fulani who came from Kano, Katsina, and Sokoto because the indigenous Kanuri and Shuwa Muslims were too soft on the issue of Shariah (CSW, 2006: 9). According to local observers, the protest against the Danish cartoons was actually manipulated by politicians to express discontentment against President Olusegun Obasanjo, a Christian who was sidelining his Muslim Vice President, Abubakar Atiku, in an attempt to run for a third term in office.[6]

As far as we know, it is in December 2010 that, for the first time, Boko Haram really planned and organised the deadly bombing of churches in Jos and Maiduguri. The repression certainly contributed to this evolution. Mohammed Yusuf had not advocated the slaying of Christians, neither in his book nor in his sermons left on record (Yusuf 2005). It was after his extrajudicial killing that the remaining commanders of the sect, who wanted revenge, drew closer to the global jihadist narrative against "Crusaders". The role of Boko Haram is still disputed in some of the bombings of churches. Mohammed Yusuf's successor, Abubakar Shekau, did not claim or deny any of them in his video releases. Although the sect attempted to exploit communal tensions in the Middle Belt, there is no conclusive evidence that it was responsible for all the attacks it claimed responsibility for, especially against Christians in Jos (ICG 2012: 15). On the contrary, the 'original' Boko Haram's focus on Muslim targets caused the split off of Abubakar Adam Kambar and a dissident group, *Jama'atu Ansarul Muslimina Fi Biladis Sudan* (The Supporters for the Aid of Muslims in Black Africa), which emerged in 2012 to kidnap expatriates (see Annexes 1 and 2). From a doctrinal point of view, the leader of the new organisation, Abu Usamata "al-Ansari", disagreed with Abubakar Shekau because he considered that the 'real' enemies of Islam were essentially Westerners. As for the faction of Khalid al-Barnawi "Abu Hafsat", it regarded deadly attacks against innocent Muslims as a misinterpretation of Islam. It did not oppose talks with the government and eventually clashed with Abubakar Shekau, who accused it of treachery and organised the killing of its spiritual leader, Awwal Gombe, in 2012.[7] The Christian issue has thus been a source of dissent between the three leaders who took up the baton of Mohammed Yusuf and who have been designated by the US as global terrorists: Abubakar Adam Kambar, Abubakar Shekau, and Khalid al-Barnawi.[8]

In this regard, there are two ways—global and local—to understand the extension of the targets of Boko Haram. The first is to analyse this evolution as a strategic move to destabilise a government led by a Christian president, Goodluck Jonathan. Such a development is usually seen as going together with the internationalisation of the sect, its alleged involvement in northern Mali, and possible links with Al-Qaeda in the Islamic Maghreb (AQIM). A strategic alliance with Saudi Salafi groups actually remains doubtful because the doctrine of Mohammed Yusuf does not fit the Wahhabi model. One should remember that Boko Haram is itself a dissident group that broke away from the Izala, the main Salafi movement in Nigeria. In Abuja, courts could never prove that Mohammed Yusuf received funding from Saudi extremists after his two *hajj* trips to Mecca. Likewise, the Nigerian State Security Service (SSS) alleged in 2006 that Boko Haram had sent some children to an Al-Qaeda training camp in Mauritania and to some *mujahideen* fighters in the Republic of Niger. Yet the Kano businessman they arrested in connection with this, Mallam Muhammad Ashafa, was later released because no evidence could be laid against him regarding funding from Al-Qaeda Tabliqh Headquarters in Lahore, Pakistan. In 2007, again, an Abuja High Court had to drop charges against the proprietor of the *Daily Trust* newspapers' group, Mallam Muhammad Bello Ilyas Damagun, who had been accused of receiving funds from Al-Qaeda to train terrorists abroad and support the Taliban branch of Boko Haram.

In 2012, the fact that some Nigerians were said to have fought with AQIM in Timbuktu did not prove either that they were sent by Abubakar Shekau in order to extend and coordinate various attacks in the region.[9] In northern Mali, evidence of their nationality and their affiliation to Boko Haram remained weak. From a purely tactical point of view, it is very likely that the sect cooperated with foreign jihadist groups to train fighters and get supplies of weapons. In 2009, just after the death of Mohammed Yusuf, the acting leader of Boko Haram, Mallam Sani Umaru, was even reported to have signed a statement supporting Osama bin Laden to "carry out his command in Nigeria until the country is totally Islamised".[10] But this expression of solidarity did not mean that his successor, Abubakar Shekau, was to destabilise Nigeria under the supervision of Al-Qaeda. On the contrary, the extortion of local businessmen and the multiplication of armed robberies since 2011 tended to show that he had to continue relying on domestic funding. Moreover, Boko Haram was international from the beginning, since it operated from a region with porous borders.[11] At the end of the 1990s, Mohammed Yusuf first used the regional networks of Izala to extend his influence outside of Borno and his home state Yobe. This took him and his supporters towards neighbouring countries like Chad and the Republic of Niger, where the Nigerian Izala had begun to preach in the mid-1980s, launching their own organisation, Adini-Islam, in Niamey in

1993 (Zakari 2007). After Mohammed Yusuf broke his relationship with the Izala, his supporters still used neighbouring countries as rear bases, for instance in the region of Diffa in Niger and in the Mandara Mountains of Cameroon around 2003–06.

TERRORISM AND FEAR

Thus, the possibility of an operational connection with AQIM does not explain properly the spatial extension and the strategic move of Boko Haram against Christian communities to destabilise the Nigerian government. The internationalisation theory is more relevant when it refers to models of terrorism, rather than religious doctrines. As early as 2003, the first *mujahideen* fighters of Boko Haram called themselves "Taliban" even if they had no operational link with Afghanistan. Since then, some of them have made references to other jihadist battlefronts like Somalia. Yet the main change was, in 2011, to resort to suicide attacks after the model of Pakistan, Iraq, Lebanon, and Palestine. This is indeed a real novelty in Nigeria, a country where non-Muslim groups also used terrorist techniques and bombs against the military junta in the 1990s, but no suicide attacks. As such, the international dimension of Boko Haram is not a new phenomenon if we look at the history of Islamic protest in northern Nigeria. All the main Sufi brotherhoods had a foreign origin, while the Izala followed the model of Saudi Arabia, the *yan schi'a* of Ibrahim el-Zakzaky looked at Iran, and the leader of the Maitatsine, Muhammad Marwa, hailed from Cameroon. From a doctrinal point of view, it would also be spurious to claim that Mohammed Yusuf was more radical than other forms of Islamic protest in northern Nigeria, from Mahdism to Quranic integralism.[12] His rejection of Western modernity, for instance, was much more accommodating than the position of Muhammad Marwa, who forbade his followers even to ride a bicycle. Likewise, the deadly impact of Boko Haram has never reached the proportions of the Maitatsine insurgency in Kano, which resulted in the killing of more than 4,000 people in just 11 days in December 1980 (Hiskett 1987; Isichei 1987).

Definitely, the real novelty of the sect in Nigeria is to resort to suicide attacks and terrorist techniques that follow (but presumably do not obey) a global jihadist model. In this logic, targeting Christian communities makes sense because it creates panic and challenges the secularity of the state, especially regarding freedom of religion.[13] To get a national audience despite being based in the periphery of Nigeria, Boko Haram plays with the fears of southerners regarding forced conversion, the Shariah, and the jihad of

Usman dan Fodio in the nineteenth century. This is rather easy in a society which often perceives itself as being divided between a Muslim North and a Christian South. According to surveys conducted in Sub-Saharan Africa by the Pew Research Center, for instance, Nigeria is the country where a majority of people (58 per cent) see conflict between religious groups as a very important problem. Individually, however, respondents do not feel personally threatened by the other religion of the Book: only one out of five said that Muslims were hostile towards Christians, or vice-versa (Lugo *et al.* 2010: 43-4). But these perceptions vary widely across the country. Surveys conducted in 2001 and 2007 showed that the fear of Islam was stronger in regions where Muslims were a minority. A majority of respondents in non-Shariah states believed that the implementation of Islamic Law would increase ethnic, religious, and political conflicts. Yet there was a minority that thought so in Shariah states (Kirwin 2009).

In this context, Boko Haram fits quite well the terrorist model of insurgents who aim to create panic in order to destabilise the state. Since this chapter is written from a Western perspective, however, it is important not to overemphasise the rationality and the global logic of a sect which often targets outsiders to retaliate against attacks on its members. For instance, it is difficult to understand why the 'original' Boko Haram did not try harder to trigger a mass exodus of Christians from the North and revenge killings in the South. To provoke ethnic-cleansing and a religious all-out war, it would definitely make sense to focus attacks on Christian migrants in the North, instead of natives. In the past, such targets have caused retaliation that led to the Biafra secession in 1967 and riots in Aba and Onitsha in 2000. But today, the self-defence system of Igbo migrants in the ghettos of cities like Kano has developed so much that it helps to prevent Islamist attacks. It is also suggested that Boko Haram does not want to provoke retaliation that would drive large numbers of Muslim northerners out of the South, where they have settled to earn a living. The sect prefers to organise gradual and sporadic attacks on churches to intimidate and pressure the government to negotiate.[14]

Parallel to the internationalisation theory, local dynamics also explain the radicalisation of the group and the extension of its targets to Christian communities—the so-called Nassarawa in Hausa—that symbolise the intrusion of foreign powers. Indeed, the rejection of Western values—at least those which are seen as incompatible with Islam—is coherent with the demand for full Shariah and the utopian creation of a caliphate in Nigeria. Even if the followers of Mohammed Yusuf prefer to be called *Jama'atu Ahlis-Sunnah Lidda'awati Wal Jihad*, their nickname *Boko Haram* is quite telling when it is understood as a warning against the colonisation of the mind through 'bad, forbidden books'. The word *boko* refers both to deception and sorcery (*boka*) in Hausa, and possibly to *book* in English.[15] Today, Nigerian Islamic scholars are often trained in modern schools (see Annex 3). But in the past, many shunned all forms of Western education and its certificates based on false evidence (*shahadatul zur*). The words *amaryar boko*, for instance, refer to a fake bride in Hausa marriage customs, and apparently it was used by the Muslim ruling elite when the British introduced their system of education, as only Quranic teachings were regarded as true (Ayuba 2010: 263).[16]

More generally, Western education is accused of having failed to develop the North. This critique is not specific to Boko Haram and expresses a long-standing opposition between tradition and modernity.[17] To put this in perspective, it is worth quoting the views of Usman Muhammad Bugaje (1997: 85), a political activist from a secular party, the Action Congress. He indeed raises the question:

> Has this western system of education made [Nigeria] an any happier place to live in? The greatest promise of the imperial system of education, fully secured in its secular niche, has been material development. We must now ask, has it delivered; what with the crushing weight of corruption, inefficiency, poverty, disease and hunger on our frail shoulders? How much hope can we nurse today? Can the scholars of this western system of education deliver us from the prevailing tyranny and injustice that has today become our lot in the same way Muslim scholars and the Jihad leaders of the early 19th century delivered their society from the tyranny of the Hausa rulers?

To try to get an answer from the point of view of Boko Haram, a quick analysis of the doctrine of Mohammed Yusuf is necessary here. The rejection of Western modernity by his followers is often seen as an expression of their backwardness and lack of education. Mohammed Yusuf himself is described as a lunatic guru, amongst other things because he contested the Copernican Revolution and the assumption that the Earth revolved around the Sun in a system of planets named after pagan Roman gods: Saturn, Mercury, Venus, Jupiter, Pluto, Neptune, Uranus, and Mars. Yet the founder of Boko Haram did not reject all modern technologies. Unlike Muhammad Marwa, for instance, Mohammed Yusuf drove cars, used mobile telephones, had computers, and did not ban them for his followers. Moreover, his condemnation of Western values was rooted in local Muslim complaints against the colonisation of the mind through education. The targeting of modern medicine, for instance, echoed the rejection of polio vaccination by some *ulama* who feared a US conspiracy to sterilise Muslims after the death of several children in Kano due to unfortunate pharmaceutical tests by the American company Pfizer. This context gives more sense to the 'irrational' Boko Haram burglary and murder of a pharmacist in February 2011, the bombing of a medical store in June 2011 (both in Maiduguri), the assassination of three North Korean doctors in February 2013 (in Potiskum), and the killing of ten polio immunisation workers (in Kano), also in February 2013. David Cook (2011: 20) even sees the suicide attack against UN offices in Abuja in August 2011 as a form of protest against the World Health Organization.

A thorough analysis of the doctrine of Mohammed Yusuf offers a radical religious reading of the travails of Nigerian politics in this regard. Obviously, the fight against the corruption of traditional chiefs and governors does not mean that Boko Haram was to become a kind of "armed branch" of Transparency International. In his speeches, Mohammed Yusuf did not explicitly condemn the bad governance and the electoral fraud of the ruling class. In fact, we do not even really know if Nigerian Muslims reject modern corruption and if they consider Islam to be the best way to reform the moral economy. To the rural *talakawa* masses in Hausaland, for instance, colonisation and British taxes were seen as just a continuation of the oppressive exploitation of the Sokoto *Sarakuna* aristocracy, with another name and a new legal framework (Pierce 2006). But clearly, the Boko Haram dream of a 'pure' Islamic society and the blank refusal to be governed by a non-Muslim government reflected strong disillusion with post-colonial Nigeria, party politics, and the failure of the so-called "democrazy" since the return to a civilian regime in 1999. Unlike other Salafi groups that also wanted to establish a caliphate, Mohammed Yusuf did not accept the modern rule of a secular state as a temporary necessity. Consequently, he forbade his followers to accept employment in the government, especially in the areas of judiciary and law enforcement (more than in social services), and he did not recognise the authority of the present Sultan of Sokoto, a former military man (Anonymous 2012: 126).

AN AMBIGUOUS RELATIONSHIP TO THE STATE

In this logic, the demand for full Shariah, social justice, and Islamic purity could not be seen as compatible with a parliamentary regime in a plural society. Interestingly enough, other radical groups like the *yan schi'a* of Ibrahim el-Zakzaky came to the same conclusion, but without advocating armed struggle.[18] The main argument was that a secular government could not properly apply Islamic Law. The doctrinal and divine foundation of Shariah could not be placed under the supremacy of a constitution written by men. The basis for a 'secular' rule of law was weak indeed. Even in the South some scholars challenged the legality of the Nigerian Constitution because it was promulgated by a military decree in 1999. But the extension of Islamic Law by some northern governors clearly compromised the secular neutrality of the state, especially with regard to the condemnation of apostasy, which contradicted freedom of religion. In addition, the severity of Shariah punishments could not be reconciled with the proscription of cruel and inhuman treatment by various international human rights conventions to which Nigeria was signatory.

Contradictions were quite obvious. Shariah, first, was discriminatory because citizens were no longer equal before the law. At Independence, specific punishments for Muslims had generated little controversy since offences like adultery or the consumption of alcohol already existed in the Northern Nigerian Penal Code. But discrimination became more visible after 1999, when Shariah-compliant states extended the domain of Islamic Law and imposed a stricter penal regime on Muslims. For instance, a Muslim culprit who stole a bicycle would face amputation while his non-Muslim co-offender would be sentenced only to prison. Likewise, a Christian adulterer would not answer to any criminal charge, while a Muslim could be sentenced to death by stoning (Iwobi 2004: 149). From a political point of view, such discrimination dismissed the argument of conservative religious scholars, for whom the more rigorous penal regime sanctioned by Shariah would be regarded by devout Muslims as a benefit.

After the end of the military regime in 1999, the extension of Islamic Law definitely exacerbated the most visible contradictions of the Nigerian parliamentary system. In the North, for instance, Shariah was officially to be implemented by the corrupt and ineffective police force of a unitary federal government that forbade the creation of specific religious and regional militias like the Hisbah in Kano. The various interpretations and the uneven application of Islamic Law raised another problem, with different legal frameworks from one northern state to another (Ostien 2007; Naniya 2002). In addition, some of the governors who claimed to have banned alcohol did not refuse the *haram* (forbidden) money of their monthly federal allocation, which was partly funded by taxes on alcohol levied in the South. Up to now, this contradiction has not been resolved.[19]

An important issue after 1999 was actually to know whether it was the role of the state to extend, promote, and implement Shariah. Some Islamic scholars thought so and accepted playing the 'democratic' game by lobbying political parties and cooperating with the government. Indeed, many Nigerian Muslims considered that "an Islamic law system helps legitimize the state" (Laremont 2011: xx). But others did not agree. This does not mean that they followed the radical reasoning of Mohammed Yusuf. On the contrary, moderate and quietist Muslims thought that religion should not interfere with secular politics because it belonged to the private sphere. Historically, they argued, Shariah was not developed by states but by the population growth of the *ummah*, the necessity to formalise Islamic Law, and the expansion of the business of traders who needed universal standards to sign contracts and circumvent the variations of local rules.[20] Other scholars added that it was not possible to call for the political authorities to apply a uniform and codified version of Shariah, which had always coexisted with native customs and whose versions had been disputed by several legal schools since the eighth century. Using the Quran as the principal, or even the only, source of Shariah, as some Boko Haram members advocated, was not sustainable either. The text contains few explicit rules. Out of 6,235 verses, between 350 and 500 are said to be relevant from a legal point of view. Yet even these verses deal mainly with rituals, devotional issues, marriage, and trade. In the whole Quran, only thirty verses are really concerned with crime, prescribing specific punishments for the famous five *hudud* infractions: theft, drunkenness, fornication, defamation, and highway robbery (Hallaq 1997: 12; Vikør 2005: 32-7).

In other words, Boko Haram was not alone in rejecting the possibility of a secular state to apply Shariah. The difference is that Mohammed Yusuf did so with fiery arguments that precipitated violence yet did not solve ideological contradictions. Indeed, Shariah has historically been a moral and an ethical power, rather than a blueprint for government organisations. Thus, the sole demand for full Shariah, which was the main objective of Mohammed Yusuf, did not help in understanding the political meaning of his actions. Undoubtedly, Boko Haram has had an ambiguous and puzzling relationship to the Nigerian state. Scholars do not agree in this regard. Muhammad Sani Imam and Muhammad Kyari (2011: 29), for instance, argue that by calling for isolation from the government and the city, Boko Haram wanted to abrogate the state, which was regarded as satanic and off-limits (*taghut*). Meanwhile, Andrew Walker (2012: 9) claims that Mohammed Yusuf wanted to set up a parallel political organisation in order to, ultimately, "replace the actual state". Hence, he had a cabinet, a Supreme Council (*Shura*), specialised departments (*Lagina*), and various emirs posted according to the Nigerian administrative territorial units of local government areas. According to Micha'el Tanchum (2012: 79), this "alternative society" eventually formed a "miniature state within the state".[21]

From a political and ideological point of view, Boko Haram reveals many inconsistencies in this regard. As we have seen, Mohammed Yusuf and his followers did not hesitate to use modern technology imported from the West to carry on their struggle. In the same vein, they condemned entertainment, including cinema, but they broadcast videotaped sermons; before 2009, Mohammed Yusuf was even allowed to preach on the Borno television station. His Izala arch-rival Jafar Adam also noticed that the founder of the sect used a passport from the Federal Republic of Nigeria—the secular government Yusuf supposedly abhorred—to obtain the visa necessary to perform the holy pilgrimage to Saudi (Anonymous 2012: 138). Following the logic of Muhammad Marwa, Mohammed Yusuf should have refused to travel on roads constructed by the state with revenues from usury and taxes collected from alcohol manufacturers. Today, Boko Haram members are also incoherent. On the one hand, they condemn secular justice. On the other, they ask the government to punish the people responsible for the extrajudicial execution of Mohammed Yusuf and his unarmed followers. Likewise, they justify bank robberies because banks charge usury and are owned by big men who siphon public funds. Yet they steal and use *haram* money.

A POLITICISATION BY RECIPROCAL MANIPULATION

Do such inconsistencies mean that Boko Haram is not a political uprising, but just the irrational revolt of uneducated and lunatic, young fanatics from the poorest sections of the society, especially Quranic students? I do not think so, because of the way the sect has encountered the Nigerian state, which politicised the group through manipulation and repression. Of course, I would agree that political targets and religious grievances do not make up a political programme, no more than they make up a guerrilla movement. Bank robberies and retaliations on both sides have confused the political meaning of the attacks of Boko Haram. Many politicians, Muslim leaders, and traditional chiefs were assassinated by the sect to avenge the killing of its members rather than to implement a comprehensive strategy to destabilise the Nigerian state. Likewise, the security forces often went on the rampage to retaliate against the slaying of soldiers or policemen, without any counter-insurgency planning to win the hearts and minds of the people. This is precisely what killed Mohammed Yusuf.

But the sect has also played with local politics. In its love–hate relationship with the Nigerian state it both manipulated, and was manipulated by, its political sponsors. In Borno, it is on record that Governor Ali Modu Sheriff used Boko Haram to win the elections of 2003; in exchange, followers of Mohammed Yusuf were rewarded: Alhaji Buji Foi was promoted to Minister of Religious Affairs, and Abubakar Adam Kambar was released from jail, where he had been held for armed robbery. In fact, such kinds of 'deals' were not specific to the sect. Elsewhere in the North, after the end of the military regime in 1999, politicians also played with Islamic issues to get elected. Thus, in 2001, the leader of the opposition and the All Nigeria People's Party (ANPP), Muhammad Buhari, was reported to have called for the introduction of 'total' Shariah across the country.[22] Nicknamed Abacha People's Party after the former military dictator, who was a Kanuri from Borno, Buhari's group was strongest in the North, especially in Zamfara where Governor Ahmad Sani Yerima was the first to extend Islamic Law after 1999. Yet the ANPP was not the only party to advocate Shariah. Northern governors of the ruling People's Democratic Party (PDP) in power in Abuja, were quick to follow suit.

In this regard, Boko Haram exposed the misbehaviour of politicians who did not hesitate to manipulate Islam and hire private militia to kill their opponents. The sect certainly benefited from the lack of legitimacy of fraudulently elected leaders. Conversely, it contributed to delegitimise a mafia-like parliamentary regime that did not follow Islamic principles of government. More than poverty, bad governance in Borno helped Mohammed Yusuf to become popular and politicise his struggle.[23] The difference with the neighbouring Republic of Niger is quite striking. To William Miles (2003), who studied Hausaland on both sides of the border, radical Islamists actually developed more in Nigeria because of bad governance. By all standards, the Republic of Niger is much poorer, yet it is better managed and hence has a lower sense of alienation and social injustice. Such variations result not only from the French and British colonial legacies of direct or indirect rule. In the Republic of Niger, after Independence, local politicians did not try to set up private armies with traditional watchmen, the so-called *yan sintiri*, a Hausa word derived from the English "sentry". Likewise, the *yan daba*, who hailed from the Vanguard youth movement of the Nigerian Northern Elements Progressive Union (NEPU) in Kano, at Independence in 1960, did not transform into a political militia when they formed neighbourhood watches for self-defence in Niamey in the 1990s (Göpfert 2012).

By contrast, Boko Haram got involved in dirty politics as soon as Mohammed Yusuf became popular and was potentially able to bring votes to the governor of Borno. Today, it is quite unlikely that local officials still attempt to manipulate the remnants of the sect to win elections or destabilise opponents—a very risky operation. But Boko Haram has generated all sorts of conspiracy theories that have further contributed to delegitimise the parliamentary basis of a secular government. The press, the blogosphere, and street conversations speculate on who benefits from the insurgency. In the North, some believe that Boko Haram was first and foremost a plot by the PDP to destabilise the opposition. They argue that violence mainly affected ANPP states like Borno and Yobe, whereas in neighbouring Bauchi, Governor Isa Yuguda, who changed allegiance to the PDP in 2009, is suspected of having harboured members of the sect to avoid being attacked by them. Many Muslims from the North also claim that curfews and the war on terrorism prevented the opposition and Muhammad Buhari from campaigning in 2011 and that it would help the PDP to rig the elections in 2015.[24] Interestingly enough, such speculations mirror the opposite views of southern Christians, who think that Boko Haram is a Muslim conspiracy to destabilise President Goodluck Jonathan, or "a Frankenstein monster created by some elite of the North" (Okpaga *et al.* 2012: 85).

A POLITICISATION BY REPRESSION

In any case, all these theories exacerbate the North–South divide and expose the fragility of a weak state, which is precisely the objective of terrorists. In the same vein, the resilience of the sect challenges the capacity of the government to maintain law and order. Again, the repression of July 2009 was a major rupture. First, it showed the shortcomings of a military response, which triggered a terrorist reaction and failed to win the hearts and minds of the locals. Emeka Okereke (2012: 186), a Research Fellow at the National Defence College, thus acknowledged that

> contrary to the expectation that the destruction of Boko Haram headquarters in Borno State and the killing of its leaders could eradicate the threat of religious extremism in Nigeria, the sect transformed itself from a loose network of artisans, school dropouts and unemployed youths to an organised network of intellectuals and strategists, with strong national and international connections.

In addition, the brutality of the security forces and the massacre of innocent civilians led some people to believe that the Islamist organisation was a resistance group against occupying troops.

The police, which were the first target of Boko Haram from November 2003, are quite telling in this regard. All over Nigeria, they have a terrible reputation of being abusive, brutal, corrupt, and completely inefficient. In the North-East, they were involved in various human rights violations. In March 2005, for instance, they arrested six boys in different locations of Borno, charged them with armed robbery, and summarily executed them in the Ibrahim Taiwo Police Station in Maiduguri (Odinkalu 2010: 58). In other words, the population did not trust the Nigerian police even before the extrajudicial killing of Mohammed Yusuf. Boko Haram probably benefited from this suspicion, as it raised sympathy for Islamic justice against governmental repression. Indeed, the massacre of hundreds of unarmed, innocent believers in July 2009 came as a reminder of how brutal post-colonial forces could be. Such traumatic events were sometimes interpreted as a proof of the necessity for Muslims to defend themselves against an aggression led by officers who included Christian southerners in their ranks.[25] As a matter of fact, many policemen do not speak local languages because a national policy requires them to be posted outside of their native region. Moreover, Maiduguri does not accommodate the police headquarters of the zonal command of Borno and Yobe, which is in Bauchi. In July 2009, most of reinforcements sent to quell the Boko Haram rebellion were outsiders.

Of course, a sense of alienation and compassion for the victims of the repression do not mean that, all of a sudden, the youth felt an urge to join the sect or that the masses adhered to the extremist doctrine of Mohammed Yusuf. To be protected, for instance, local businessmen are sometimes forced to pay a tribute to the group, yet they have no sympathy with its ideology. However, coercion is not the only reason for refusing to fight against the 'terrorists'.

Because of ethnic affinities, Boko Haram members certainly found it easier to hide amongst the population in Maiduguri rather than in Kano, where they were seen as foreigners. In Borno, the locals avoided informing the security forces against their brothers and sisters, even if they were as much afraid of the terrorists. This *omertà* also reflected poor social control by traditional elders. Appointed by Governor Ali Modu Sheriff in March 2009, the new Shehu of Borno, Umar Garbai Abba Kyari, lacked legitimacy and never publicly condemned the atrocities committed by the army. As a result, he did not enjoy the popularity of the emirs of Kano or Zaria, two old Hausa cities where the population still cooperated with the security forces.

Although not a mass movement, Boko Haram has thus a social basis which has not been eliminated by the repression. Such support does not seem to have been impacted by a growing disillusionment regarding the capacity of Islamic Law to bring social justice and reform the government. The popularity of the demand for Shariah is certainly difficult to assess. It depends much on people's expectations. In Kano, for instance, members of the Hisbah militia see Islamic Law as the democracy of majority rules in a Muslim environment, while members of *yan daba* urban gangs emphasise the need for social justice and individual human rights through Shariah (Casey 2008: 81). Perceptions also vary according to education, ranks, status, regional origin, and, of course, religious creed. As we do not have data on the feelings of Muslims in Borno, it would be hazardous to speculate on a link between the demand for Shariah and the popularity of Boko Haram.

According to opinion polls conducted in 2001 and 2007, we know that the support for Islamic Law has not waned at the national level (Kirwin 2009). Movements that advocate Shariah are still vibrant. Surveys show that 56 percent of Nigerian Muslims do not belong to Sufi orders, which are known for their willingness to accommodate local traditions and their softer views on the application of Islamic Law. Amongst this majority, 11 percent identify with the Shia, 14 percent with the Tabligh, 11 percent with the Salafi, and 14 percent with the Wahhabi movements (Lugo *et al.* 2010: 147, 158, 315-7). Likewise, 35 percent of the *ulama* in northern Nigeria are said to be Izala, as against 24 percent for the Tijaniyya, less than 8 percent for the Qadiriyya, and almost 28 percent with no affiliation (Jega 2005: 97). But the alleged predominance of Salafi scholars does not mean that believers would accept a religious radicalisation. According to the same surveys, many Nigerian Muslims who want Shariah to become the official law of their land also support democracy and freedom of religion. In fact, only a minority of them advocate the death penalty for renegades who leave Islam, stoning for women who commit adultery, or cutting off hands for thieves—a much lower percentage than in many other African countries.[26]

POLITICAL PARTIES AND ISLAM IN NIGERIA

In other words, the radical form of Shariah that Boko Haram wants to impose does not correspond at all to the demand of a very large majority of Nigerian Muslims. By the same token, the sect appears to be extremely marginal. Despite some backing in Borno and a high terrorist profile in the media, it does not have the support of the masses that other reformist Islamic movements can claim in Egypt or Tunisia. Boko Haram used religious references to legitimise political grievances as a moral right. But it would not and could not transform into a party. Unlike the Izala, for instance, it never maintained that elections were more important than daily prayers or the pilgrimage to Mecca.[27] On the contrary, it contributed much to dividing further the Muslim community and the political North, a region which has not had a clear leader since the times of Ahmadu Bello at Independence.

The story of Boko Haram thus leaves room for a more general discussion on the politicisation of Islam and the Islamisation of politics. Despite the assumptions of the theory of a clash of civilisations between Muslims and Christians, Nigeria did not develop religious parties as such, either Islamic or Christian Democrat. In this regard, the most populated country of the continent is quite different from Morocco, Algeria, Tunisia, Egypt, Sudan, Somalia, Kenya, and South Africa, which have all experienced the formation of Islamic parties, with or without people's support and legal recognition. In Nigeria, the only exception was probably the Lagos-based United Muslim Party from 1953 to 1966. This very local organisation had no national audience and aimed only at protecting the interests of an urban minority group. At Independence, however, the two main political parties in the North were clearly linked with religious movements: the conservative NPC (Northern People's Congress) with the Qadiriyya and the aristocracy (*Sarakuna*) of the Sokoto Caliphate; the progressive NEPU (Northern Elements Progressive Union) with the Tijaniyya and the commoners (*talakawa*) of Kano. But their experience was short-lived. While NEPU remained in the opposition, the leaders of the NPC were killed during the first coup of 1966, and both parties disappeared during the military regimes that followed (Paden 1973; Dudley 1968).

The Second Republic (1979–83) was more confusing in this regard. If NEPU was reformed under the aegis of the PRP (People's Redemption Party), which maintained links with the Tijaniyya, the NPN (National Party of Nigeria) in power had no clear allegiance and received support from the aristocracy of Sokoto as well as the spiritual leader of Izala, Sheikh Abubakar Gumi, who was very close to President Shehu Shagari. In their formative period before their legal registration and the return to civilian rule in 1979, the Izala were on the verge of developing a political platform. Hence, their different names referred either to an Association (*Kungiyar*) or a Congress (*Jamiyyar*), as in Kaduna with the "Party for the Propagation of Islam" (*Jamiyyar Ada Addinin Musulunci*) (Yandaki 1997: 48). But in the end, the Izala did not transform into a political platform to contest elections.

Since then, the voting patterns of Nigerian northern Muslims have not confirmed the existence of Islamic parties in disguise, even with the ANPP. The zoning system, which is supposed to protect the federal character of the country, also did not reflect a rigid religious divide between a "Muslim North" and a "Christian South". During the presidential elections of 1993, for instance, the two candidates, Moshood Abiola and Bashir Tofa, were Muslims and the former was a Yoruba who won in the South. In 2011, again, Nuhu Ribadu and his running mate Fola Adeola, who contested the presidential elections for the ACN (Action Congress of Nigeria: the opposition), were both Muslims; yet their party did win a substantial number of votes among Christians in south-western states, and very few in the so-called "Muslim North".

A comparison with Sudan is interesting in this regard (see Annex 4). Unlike Nigeria, local Islamic scholars have not only run governments or participated in elections, but also created and controlled political parties in a hereditary system.[28] At Independence, for instance, the Mahdi family led both the Umma Party and the Ansar brotherhood. Likewise, the Mirghani led both the People's Democratic Party and the Khatmiyya. Banned by the military coup of 25 May 1969, they later on had to go into exile when the 'socialist' junta of Colonel Jaafar Muhammad Nimeiri promoted smaller Sufi brotherhoods and killed thousands of Ansar supporters of the Umma Party. However, they came back to power after the dismissal of the dictator on 6 April 1985, and they are still politically active today. As for the Islamist coup of 30 June 1989, it was very much an offshoot of the Muslim Brothers of Sheikh Hassan al-Turabi.

In the same vein, the use of Islam as the official law of the state has been much more institutionalised in Sudan. By a decree of 9 September 1983, Jaafar

Muhammad Nimeiri first imposed Shariah throughout the country, even in the South where Muslims were a minority and where this decision contributed to precipitating a second civil war under the aegis of the Sudan People's Liberation Army. After the fall of the dictatorship, the National Islamic Front then refused to endorse a peace agreement signed on 16 November 1988, precisely because the government had accepted repealing Islamic Law to satisfy the demands of southerners. Despite an informal approval by the Parliament to suspend Shariah on 3 April 1989, the military coup of General Omar Hassan Ahmad al Bashir did put an end to the negotiation and abrogated the constitution, dissolving political parties, banning trade unions, and closing newspapers. A state of emergency was declared and, on 5 February 1991, a decree re-established Islam as the only official law in Sudan. Adopted by 96 percent of the voters at a referendum organised on 30 June 1998, the new constitution was extremely strict in this regard, since its Articles 7 and 10 proclaimed jihad, defence of the country, and payment of *zakat* as a compulsory duty for all, including non-Muslims.

CONCLUSION

No such thing ever happened in Nigeria, where the secular British Common Law still prevails, even in the North. Since 1999, Shariah courts are not permitted to try Christians without their consent and they usually settle conflicts only between Muslims. In other words, Nigeria experienced a politicisation of Islam but not the extensive Islamisation of politics that affected countries like Sudan. A better balance of power certainly explains this. Nigeria's South is much more developed than the North, whereas in Sudan, the North is much more developed than the South. Unlike Jaafar Muhammad Nimeiri, moreover, the military regimes in power in Lagos and Abuja did not attempt to use Islam as their primary source of legitimacy. On the contrary, they always justified their coups and the suspension of the constitution by the necessity to ban ethnic or religious parties to restore law and order.

The federal and secular structure of the Nigerian state, however, does not fully explain why Muslims have never succeeded in setting up a political platform to contest elections with a religious programme. Notwithstanding the Yoruba Muslims in the South, this characteristic has also much to do with the internal divisions of Islam in the North. In this regard, Boko Haram should be understood as another disruptive factor within the *ummah*, much more than the trigger of a civil war and a civilisational clash between the so-called "Muslim

North" and "Christian South". Many analysts like to speculate on the collapse of the Nigerian state. But Boko Haram also reveals the failure of the Muslim community to unify, develop, and organise a common response to modernity. In reality, the sect of Mohammed Yusuf is a challenge to both the Nigerian state and Islam.

Notes

1. Interview by Eriye, Festus [30 Sept. 2012], "The Trouble with Nigeria", *The Nation*, 24, 25, 50.
2. According to surveys, 19 percent of Nigerian Muslims belong to the former, compared with 9 percent for the latter, while the majority (56 percent) do not identify with any Sufi order (Lugo et al. 2010: 147, 158, 315-7).
3. Almost all Islamist movements in Nigeria praise the historical figure of Usman dan Fodio. In this regard, it will be interesting to see if the breakaway faction of Boko Haram, Ansaru, will also refer to Shaikh Said bin Hayat, the great-grandson of Usman dan Fodio and the Mahdist leader of the Ansar community of Dumbulwa in Fika emirate in Borno. Said bin Hayat is said to have been the longest serving political prisoner of the British Empire, from his arrest in 1924 until his late release in 1959.
4. Actually, the Izala rather aimed to adapt and reform Islamic education to face the technical challenges of the modern world.
5. Various interviews in Maiduguri and Kano, October 2011; database www.nigeriawatch.org.
6. Agang, Sunday, "Why the Cartoon Protest turned Lethal in Northern Nigeria". http://www.gamji.com/article5000/NEWS5671.htm [Accessed 22 November 2012].
7. *Africa Confidential*, various issues, 2012 and 2013.
8. Abubakar Adam Kambar is said to have been killed by the Nigerian security forces during a raid on his hideout in Kano in mid-August 2012. As for Khalid al-Barnawi, he allegedly got closer to AQIM and was to supply funds to both Ansaru and Boko Haram. According to sources that could not be cross-checked, Abubakar Shekau appointed as his deputy a disciple of Ansaru and Khalid al-Barnawi, Babagana 'Assalafi', when the French launched their military operation in northern Mali in January 2013. The Nigerian army eventually claimed that Abubakar Shekau was wounded in a gunfight and died later on in Cameroon in August 2013. As for Ansaru, it followed the model of Al-Qaeda by kidnapping and killing expatriates, and it was proscribed as a terrorist organisation by the British Home Office in November 2012.
9. Relying on a single secret American source, journalist Serge Daniel claims that Boko Haram received 2 million euros (probably ransom money) and sent twenty

men to be trained by Al-Qaeda after signing a "pact" in June 2010 (2012: 204-6). US Representatives Michael McCaul *et al.* do not provide any further evidence in this regard, as they quote press reports of journalists who were not even in Mali. They claim that Boko Haram is funded by AQIM to recommend that it should be designated a foreign terrorist organisation. But they also admit that, to be able to make bombs, the sect had to steal commercial explosives and detonators used in quarries and mines within Nigeria (2013: 18).

10. http://www.vanguardngr.com/2009/08/boko-haram-ressurects-declares-total-jihad/#.

11. The sect also attracted curiosity. Before 2008, for instance, Chadian ministers of Finance and Transports, Abbas Mahamat Tolli and Abdelkerim Souleyman Terio, were said to attend Friday prayers at the Boko Haram mosque in Maiduguri and allegedly gave alms to Mohammed Yusuf. According to rumours that could not be confirmed, this connection eventually became a diplomatic case because Abbas Mahamat Tolli was a nephew of President Idriss Deby and Abuja pressed the Chadian government to dismiss him.

12. Amongst many academic works on the issue, see for instance Christelow (1985).

13. In Nigeria, secularity does not mean that the state is separate from religion, but that it is neutral in a multi-religious society.

14. I wish to thank Johannes Harnischfeger for this suggestion.

15. For an etymological analysis that contests links to the English word *book*, see Newman (2013).

16. For a reference to old anti-Western education songs in Hausa in Jos, see also Abdulkareem, Mohammed Babangida [2010], *The paradox of Boko Haram*, Kaduna, Moving Image Ltd., 50-1.

17. As Murray Last wrote (2005: 79), it is not sure in this regard that the Western education system would have been more acceptable for the conservative Sokoto Caliphate, had the British not colonised northern Nigeria.

18. In Katsina, for instance, the so-called *yan schi'a* taught students to disregard the national anthem and the flag because they eroded the faith of Muslims in Islam. They also encouraged them to ignore the school's time-table when it coincided with the five daily prayers. And they did not recognise the laws of Nigeria that did not conform with the Quran (Sulaiman 1997).

19. In *The Nation*, dated 10 April 2007, for instance, Akintola Benson, a Senior Special Assistant to the (Muslim) Governor of Lagos State, Babatunde Fashola, was calling for federal compensation because alcohol consumption represented a major share of the local revenue of Value Added Tax (VAT), yet funded northern regions.

20. See for instance the position of An-Na'im (2005: 333). The famous historian Marshall Hodgson also reminds us that if Shariah was born in the Arab garrison-town, it was mainly applied by merchants and travellers, rather than peasants

(1974 vol. 1: 319-347, vol. 2: 122).

21. See also Onapajo, Hakeem & Ufo Okeke Uzodike (2012), "Boko Haram terrorism in Nigeria", *African Security Review* 21(3): 28.
22. http://www.news24.com/xArchive/Archive/Calls-for-total-Sharia-in-Nigeria-20010827.
23. For an alternative perspective, claiming that youth unemployment is the main driver behind Boko Haram, see Meagher (2013). For an opposite view, showing that poverty is not limited to Borno and is even more or as severe in Sokoto and other Shariah-compliant states where Boko Haram is not very active, see Pérouse de Montclos (2012).
24. See for instance the stories carried in the Kaduna-based newspaper *Desert Herald*.
25. In Kano, for instance, the Nigeria Police is seen as an occupation force, yet with less suspicion, and 40 percent of its officers are allegedly Christians, even if Northerners dominate senior ranks (Hills 2012: 52).
26. Interestingly enough, the same proportion of Christians (70 percent) also favour making the Bible the official law of their country (Lugo et al. 2010: 11, 50, 288, 291-3).
27. At the time, the Izala leader Abubakar Gumi campaigned for the re-election of President Shehu Shagari and was reported to have made this statement in the *New Nigerian* of 3 April 1983.
28. See for instance Fluehr-Lobban (1987); Hunwick (1992); Pérouse de Montclos (2003); Warburg (2003).

References

Akowe, T. (2013), "Jonathan distorting facts on Boko Haram victims—Northern CAN", *The Nation*, 23 June, p. 1.

An-Na'im, A.A. (2005), "The Future of Shariah and the Debate in Northern Nigeria". In: P. Ostien, J. Nasir, & F. Kogelmann, eds, *Comparative perspectives on Shari☐ah in Nigeria*. Ibadan: Spectrum Books.

[Anonymous] (2012), "The Popular Discourses of Salafi Radicalism and Salafi Counter-radicalism in Nigeria: A Case Study of Boko Haram", *Journal of Religion in Africa* 42(2).

Ayuba, J. (2010), "From Yan Kalare to Boko Haram: Political Corruption and Violence in Northern Nigeria". In: A.O. Agwuele, U. Nnwankwo & O. Akinwumi, eds, *Multidisciplinary Perspectives on Overcoming the African Predicaments*. Berlin: Media Team IT.

Brigaglia, A. (2012), "Ja☐far Mahmoud Adam, Mohammed Yusuf and Al-Muntada

Islamic Trust: Reflections on the Genesis of the Boko Haram phenomenon in Nigeria", *Annual Review of Islam in Africa* 11.

Bugaje, U.M. (1997), "Some Reflections on the Development of Islamic Learning in Katsina (1300-1800 AD)". In: A.I. Tsiga & A.U. Adamu, eds, *Islam and the History of Learning in Katsina*. Ibadan: Spectrum.

Casey, C. (2008), "'Marginal Muslims': Politics and the Perceptual Bounds of Islamic Authenticity in Northern Nigeria", *Africa Today* 54(3).

Christelow, A. (1985), "Religious protest and dissent in Northern Nigeria: from Mahdism to Qur'anic integralism", *Journal of the Institute of Muslim Minority Affairs* 6(2): 375-393.

Cook, D. (2011), *Boko Haram: A Prognosis*. Houston: Rice University.

CSW (2006), *Findings of Visit to Nigeria, April 2006*. New Malden (Surrey): Christian Solidarity Worldwide.

Daniel, S. (2012), *Aqmi: l'industrie de l'enlèvement*. Paris: Fayard.

Dudley, B.J. (1968), *Parties and Politics in Northern Nigeria*. London: Frank Cass, 352 pp.

Fluehr-Lobban, C. (1987), *Islamic Law and Society in the Sudan*. London. Frank Cass, 320 pp.

Göpfert, M. (2012), "Security in Niamey: an anthropological perspective on policing and an act of terrorism in Niger", *Journal of Modern African Studies* 50(1): 53-74.

Hallaq, W. (1997), *A history of Islamic legal theories: an introduction to Sunnī uṣūl al-fiqh*. Cambridge: Cambridge University Press.

Hills, A. (2012), "Policing a Plurality of Worlds: The Nigeria Police in Metropolitan Kano", *African Affairs*, 111.

Hiskett, M. (1987), "The Maitatsine Riots in Kano, 1980: An Assessment", *Journal of Religion in Africa* 17(3): 209-23.

Hodgson, M. (1974), *The venture of Islam, conscience and history in a world civilization*. Chicago: The University of Chicago Press.

ICG (2012), *Curbing Violence in Nigeria: the Jos crisis*. Brussels: International Crisis Group.

Imam, M.S. & M. Kyari (2011), "Yusufuyya and the Nigerian State: Historicizing the Dynamics of Boko Haram Phenomenon", *Kaduna Journal of Liberal Arts* 5(1).

Isichei, E. (1987), "The Maitatsine Risings in Nigeria, 1980-85: A Revolt of the Disinherited", *Journal of African Religions* 17(3): 194-208.

Iwobi, A.U. (2004), "Tiptoeing through a Constitutional Minefield: The Great Sharia Controversy in Nigeria", *Journal of African Law* 48(2).

Jega, A., ed. (2005), Report of a Commissioned Study on the Ulama in Contemporary Northern States of Nigeria. Kano: Centre for Democratic Research and Training.

Hunwick, J., ed. (1992), *Religion and National Integration in Africa: Islam, Christianity, and Politics in the Sudan and Nigeria.* Evanston: Northwetsern University Press, 176 pp.

Kirwin, M. (2009), *Popular Perceptions of Shari'a Law in Nigeria*, East Lansing, Michigan State University, Afrobarometer Briefing Paper No. 58, 12 pp.

Laremont, R.R. (2011), *Islamic Law And Politics In Northern Nigeria.* Trenton (NJ): Africa World Press.

Last, M. (2005), "1903 Revisited". In: A.M. Yakubu, ed., *Northern Nigeria: a century of transformation, 1903-2003.* Kaduna: Arewa House.

Loimeier, R. (2012), "Boko Haram: The Development of a Militant Religious Movement in Nigeria", *Afrika Spectrum* 47(2-3): 137-55.

Lugo, L. et al. (2010), *Tolerance and Tension: Islam and Christianity in Sub-Saharan Africa.* Washington DC: Pew Research Center.

McCaul, M. et al. (2013), *Boko Haram: Growing Threat to the US Homeland.* Washington DC: US House of Representatives, 39.

Meagher, K. (2013), "The Jobs Crisis Behind Nigeria's Unrest", *Current History* 112 (754): 169-174.

Miles, W. (2003), "Shari'a as De-Africanization: Evidence from Hausaland", *Africa Today* 50(1): 51-75.

Naniya, T.M. (2002), "History of the Shari'a in Some States of Northern Nigeria to Circa 2000", *Journal of Islamic Studies* 13: 14-31.

Newman, P. (2013), "The Etymology of Hausa *boko*", Nanterre, Mega-Chad Research Network, 13.

Odinkalu, C.A. (2010), *Criminal Force? Torture, Abuse, and Extrajudicial Killings by the Nigeria Police Force.* New York: Open Society Justice Initiative.

Okpaga, A. et al. (April 2012), "Activities of Boko Haram and Insecurity Question in Nigeria", *Arabian Journal of Business and Management Review (Oman)* 1(9).

Okereke, N.-E. (2012), "Boko Haram Crisis of July 2009: Official Response and Public Reactions". In: E. Uchendu, ed., *New Face of Islam in Eastern Nigeria and the Lake Chad Basin.* Ibadan: Aboki.

Ostien, P., ed. (2007), *Sharia implementation in northern Nigeria 1999-2006: a sourcebook.* Ibadan: Spectrum Books, 5 vol.

Paden, J. (1973), *Religion and Political Culture in Kano.* Berkeley: University of California Press, 461.

Pérouse de Montclos, M.-A. (2003), "Le Soudan: une guerre de religions en trompe-l'œil". In: CEAN, ed., *L'Afrique politique 2002*. Paris: Karthala, pp. 33-49.

——— (2012), *Boko Haram et le terrorisme islamiste au Nigeria: insurrection religieuse, contestation politique ou protestation sociale?* Paris: Centre d'études et de recherches internationales, Question de Recherche No. 40.

Pierce, S. (2006), "Looking Like a State: Colonialism and the Discourse of Corruption in Northern Nigeria", *Comparative Studies in Society and History* 48: 887-914.

Sulaiman, M.D. (1997), "Islamic Fundamentalism: The Shi'a in Katsina". In: M. Tanchum (2012), "Al-Qa'ida's West African Advance: Nigeria's Boko Haram, Mali's Touareg, and the Spread of Salafi Jihadism", *Israel Journal of Foreign Affairs* 6(2).

Tsiga, A.I. & A.U. Adamu, ed., *Islam and the History of Learning in Katsina*. Ibadan: Spectrum, pp. 53-66.

Vikør, K. (2005), *Between God and the sultan: a history of Islamic law*. London: Hurst.

Walker, A. (2012), *What is Boko Haram?* Washington DC: United States Institute of Peace Press.

Warburg, G.R. (2003), *Islam, sectarianism and politics in Sudan since the Mahdiyya*. London: Hurst, 252.

Worth, R. (2012), "Al Qaeda-Inspired Groups, Minus Goal of Striking U.S.", *New York Times*, 28 October, p. A6.

Yandaki, A.I. (1997), "The Izalah Movement and Islamic Intellectual Discourse in Northern Nigeria: A Case Study of Katsina". In: A.I. Tsiga & A.U. Adamu, ed., *Islam and the History of Learning in Katsina*. Ibadan: Spectrum.

Yusuf, M. (2005?), *This is our faith and our Da'wa*. Maiduguri: Al Farba, 166 pp.

Zakari, M. (2007), "La naissance et le développement du mouvement Izala au Niger". In: H. Souley *et al.*, *Islam, sociétés et politique en Afrique subsaharienne: les exemples du Sénégal, du Niger et du Nigeria*. Paris: Rivages des Xantons, pp. 51-74.

7

BOKO HARAM & THE EVOLVING SALAFI JIHADIST THREAT IN NIGERIA

Freedom Onuoha

Centre for Strategic Research and Studies of the National Defence College, Abuja, Nigeria

Over the last three years, Boko Haram has evolved from a sect that waged poorly planned hit-and-run attacks on state security establishments to one that increasingly mounts audacious attacks on diverse military and civilian targets. To reduce its operational capability, the Nigerian government has adopted several counter-insurgency measures. Notwithstanding the government efforts, the sect has continued to mount deadly (sometimes suicide) attacks in northern Nigeria with the potential to penetrate into the southern region. Why is the movement proving increasingly difficult for the Nigerian government to root out? This is the central concern of this chapter. The chapter therefore examines the threat posed by Boko Haram, arguing that its growing audacity and resiliency can better be understood within the context of the transnational flow of the global Salafi Jihadist ideology. Salafi jihadism focuses on the use of violence to purge Islam of outside influences and strives for a return to the Islam practised by the "pious ancestors", that is Mohammed and the early Islamic community. The transnational flow of this fringe and violent ideology is emboldening Boko Haram, and it poses significant threats to sub-regional and national security. To effectively counter the threat posed by Boko Haram, there is a need for a robust combination of the use of force and political dexterity. This will require, among other measures, a political strategy that builds government legitimacy and effectiveness in delivering public goods to citizens, strengthening support for moderate Islam, and implementing a robust programme on countering ideological support for extremism and terrorism.

Key Words: Almajiri, AQIM, Boko Haram, Salafi Jihadism, Suicide Bombing

INTRODUCTION

The violent activities of the extremist Islamic sect, Boko Haram, have made Nigeria a country of serious security concern for the international community and a subject of research interest for scholars focusing on terrorism and violent extremism. Although the sect incubated in northern Nigeria from the mid-1990s, very little academic and security attention was paid to it until July 2009, when it engaged state security forces in a major uprising in five states in northern Nigeria. The revolt ended when its charismatic leader, Mohammed Yusuf, was finally captured and later brutally murdered by the police.

The events that occurred in 2009 are important for understanding the current phase of Boko Haram, particularly the cause of its grievance against the Nigerian government. The group felt that the killing of Yusuf in police custody was unjust and extrajudicial, and vied to avenge the death of their leader and other members who perished in the police shooting during the 2009 uprising. To this end, over the past few years, the group's tactics have evolved from poorly planned open confrontations with state security forces to increasing use of improvised explosive devices (IEDs), targeted assassinations, ambushes, drive-by shootings, and suicide bombings (Onuoha 2012a).

In order to reduce its operational capability, the Nigerian government has adopted militarised counter-insurgency operations, which include legislative, prosecutorial, security, and bilateral and multilateral initiatives. Notwithstanding the government efforts, the sect has continued to mount attacks in northern Nigeria. Why is the group proving increasingly difficult for the Nigerian government to root out? This is the central concern of this chapter. In this light, the chapter is organised in seven parts. Following this introduction, the next section addresses the philosophy, organisation, and sources of funding for the sect. The third section discusses the evolution of the sect, while the fourth examines its operational tactics. The fifth part highlights government responses to the Boko Haram threat, and the sixth interrogates the transnational flow of Salafi Jihadist ideology and alliances that sustain the sect in spite of government-repressive measures. The chapter ends with a conclusion.

UNDERSTANDING BOKO HARAM

The most common account of the origin of Boko Haram offered by local and foreign media traces it to 2002, when a charismatic preacher, Mohammed Yusuf, became the leader of the group. To the intelligence community in Nigeria, however, its true historical root harks back to 1995, when Abubakar Lawan established the *Ahlulsunna wal'jama'ah hijra* or *Shabaab* group (Muslim Youth Organisation) in Maiduguri, Borno State (Taiwo & Olugbode 2009; Adisa 2012). The group flourished as a non-violent movement until 2002, when Mohammed Yusuf assumed leadership of the sect. Over time, the group has metamorphosed under various names, such as the *Yusufiyya* sect, *Nigerian Taliban*, and lately as *Jama'atu Ahlissunnah Lidda'awati wal Jihad*.

Philosophy and ideology

The sect considers "western influence on Islamic society as the basis of the religion's weakness" (Sani 2011: 26). It opposes secular government, conventional banking, taxation, jurisprudence, and in particular Western education, which it believes is not founded on moral teachings. This explains why the sect is popularly known as Boko Haram (literally, "Western education is forbidden"). The term *Boko Haram* is derived from a combination of the Hausa word *boko*, meaning "book", and the Arabic word *haram*, meaning "forbidden". However, a statement released in August 2009 by a self-identified interim leader of the sect, Mallam Sanni Umaru, rejected the media description of it as Boko Haram:

> Boko Haram does not in any way mean "Western Education is a forbidden" as the infidel media continue to portray us. Boko Haram actually means "Western Civilisation" is forbidden. The difference is that while the first gives the impression that we are opposed to formal education coming from the West ... which is not true, the second affirms our belief in the supremacy of Islamic culture (not Education),

for culture is broader, it includes education but not determined by Western Education. (*Vanguard* 2009)

The sect instead prefers to be addressed as the *Jama'atu Ahlissunnah Lidda'awati wal Jihad*, meaning a "People Committed to the Propagation of the Prophet's Teachings and Jihad". Its ideology is rooted in Salafi Jihadism and its actions are driven by Takfirism. Salafism seeks to purge Islam of outside influences and strives for a return to the Islam practised by the "pious ancestors", that is Mohammed and the early Islamic community (European Commission's Expert Group on Violent Radicalisation 2008). It stresses adherence to a rigorist interpretation of the Quran and the *Hadith* and aims at reforming the personal behaviour of every Muslim. It also involves the duty to advise other believers to change their way of life in the same sense. Only "one specific interpretation of *Salafism* focuses on the use of violence to bring about such radical change and is commonly known as *Salafist Jihadism*" (European Commission's Expert Group on Violent Radicalisation 2008: 6). Adding to the Salafi Jihadist strain is Takfirism. At the core of Takfirism is the Arabic word *takfir*—pronouncing an action or an individual un-Islamic (Mneimneh 2009). As noted by Shahzad (2007), Takfirism classifies all non-practising Muslims as *kafirs* (infidels) and calls upon its adherents to abandon existing Muslim societies, settle in isolated communities, and fight all Muslim infidels.

Likewise, Boko Haram adherents are motivated by the conviction that the Nigerian state is a cesspit of social vices, and thus:

> the best thing for a devout Muslim to do was to 'migrate' from the morally bankrupt society to a secluded place and establish an ideal Islamic society devoid of political corruption and moral deprivation. (Akanji 2009: 60)

For the sect, all those who do not subscribe to its strict interpretation of Islam are regarded as *kuffar* (disbelievers; those who deny the truth) or *fasiqun* (wrong-doers), making such individuals and groups legitimate targets of attack by its members. Its mission is to overthrow the secular Nigerian state and impose its own interpretation of Islamic Shariah law in the country. It is reported that members wore long beards and red or black headscarves and shunned certain modern (purportedly Western) goods, such as wristwatches and safety helmets (Ajani 2011; Jimos 2011). The irony, however, is that they do not abhor or refuse to use Western products such as motorcycles, cars, cellular phones, AK-47 guns, and other innovations that have aided their violent operations.

Leadership, organisation, and membership

Before his death in July 2009, Mohammed Yusuf was the spiritual leader as well as commander-in-chief (*amir ul-aam*) of the group. Under his leadership, an executive cabinet and a *Shura* (decision-making) Council was instituted to oversee the affairs of the group. Yusuf was then assisted by two deputies (*na'ib amir ul-aam I* and *II*). Each state where they existed had its own *amir* (commander/leader), and each local government area where they operated also had an *amir*. The group appointed *amirs* in various locations across the area, including in the Kanuri regions of Niger and Chad, to oversee local activities. They also organised themselves according to various roles, such as soldiers and police (Da'wah Coordination Council of Nigeria 2009: 14). In its early stage, the sect was entrenched in Borno, Yobe, Katsina, and Bauchi states. Over time it has recruited more followers and established operating cells in almost all northern states, possibly nursing the intention to spread further south.

In the aftermath of Yusuf's death, one of his deputies, Abubakar Shekau, became the new spiritual leader of the sect. Abubakar Shekau inherited, if not modified, the organisational structure. Under Shekau, the sect maintains a loose command-and-control structure, which allows it to operate autonomously (Figure 7.1). Boko Haram now operates in cells and units that are interlinked, but generally, the cells take directives from one commander (Alli 2011). The *Shura* Council is Boko Haram's apex council and highest decision-making organ, and all cells of the organisation are represented in the council (Marama 2013: 5). Currently, Shekau heads the *Shura* Consultative Council, which has authorised the more coordinated and sophisticated attacks by various cells of the sect since the July 2009 revolt.

Boko Haram members come from diverse backgrounds: disaffected youths, unemployed graduates, former *almajirai*, and wealthy persons, mostly but not limited to northern Nigeria. It also draws members from beyond Nigeria: from Cameroon, Chad, Niger, and Sudan. Former *almajirai* (sing. *almajiri*) form a significant part of its foot soldiers. The term *almajirai* here refers to youths and sometimes children who, in pursuit of higher knowledge and Islamic purity, leave their homes and take up residency with a senior or elderly Islamic scholar. It is a popular and ancient Islamic practice whereby children are sent to live and study under renowned Islamic teachers in cities in northern Nigeria, such as Kaduna, Kano, Maiduguri, and Zaria (West Africa Insight 2010: 7). Sometimes this is voluntary, but in most cases children are forced into becoming *almajirai* by abject poverty or orphanhood. A study conducted by the Ministerial Committee on Almajiri Education in 2010 revealed that "there are 9.5 million Almajiris in Nigeria" (Ibrahim 2010: 11). Over 70 percent of these *almajirai* are concentrated in northern Nigeria and they live and study in appalling social and economic conditions.

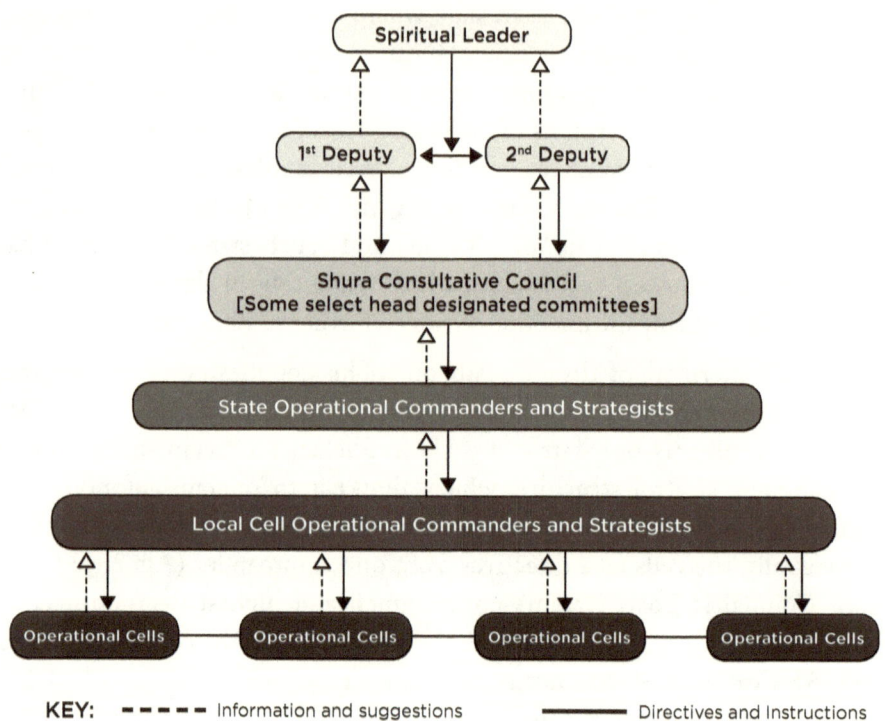

Figure 7.1 Hypothetical organisational structure of Boko Haram under Abubakar Shekau. Source: Onuoha (2012b: 3)

The practice of *almajirci* (living as *almajirai*) has been a contentious phenomenon which has generated different interpretations of its possible connections to insecurity in northern Nigeria. The *almajirai* have been rightly or wrongly associated with Islamic radicalisation, militancy, and the periodic religious riots that have blighted many northern Nigerian cities. The current menace of Boko Haram violence in northern Nigeria has accentuated the concern. While some writers have questioned the unfounded stigmatisation of this religious practice of acquiring education (Hoechner 2013), others have raised serious concern over its vulnerability to exploitation by extremist groups.

In this regard, four important features of the *almajirci* system that make it ideal for exploitation by terrorists or extremist ideologues have been identified:

> First, it involves children being relocated or separated from their family and friends to the guardianship of Mallams in towns. Second, it is restricted almost exclusively to boys. Third, the curriculum of the schools is concerned primarily with teaching the sixty chapters of the Koran by rote memorization. Fourth, each school serves 25 to 500, from the ages 6 to 25. These schools are largely autonomous from government oversight. (Awofeso, Ritchie & Degeling 2003: 314)

The *almajirai* are often cramped into shacks or makeshift homes and have little or no food or drinking water, forcing them to roam the streets begging for alms. Given their social and religious status, they are extremely vulnerable to religious extremism and financial influences.

Besides *almajirai*, the sect also has some well-educated, wealthy, and influential people as members. For instance, Alhaji Buji Foi (an ex-commissioner in Borno State), Kadiru Atiku (a former university lecturer), and Bunu Wakil (a very rich Borno-based contractor) are known to be members of the sect (Mukairu & Muhammad 2009; Idris 2011a; Sani 2011). The exact strength of its membership is not known, although an analyst gave an outrageous figure of "about 1.5 million followers" (Adele 2011: 64). There is no evidence that suggests that Boko Haram has such a huge number of fighters. At best, its militants will be in the region of a couple of thousand. Its method of recruitment is largely through indoctrination. It has also recruited among the escapees of prison jail breaks it has mounted in the past, in addition to using the Internet for the propagation of its extremist ideologies.

Sources of funds

Like other terrorist groups, Boko Haram sustains its operations through diverse sources of funding. However, four major financing streams stand out: membership dues, donations, external funding, and bank robberies. The payment of membership dues was initially the basic source of funding for the sect. Before Mohammed Yusuf was killed, members had to pay a daily levy of 100 naira to their leader. The known members then were predominantly peasant farmers, traders, road-side car washers, and commercial motorcycle riders or *okadas*. Some of the *okadas* were believed to be owned by Yusuf himself, who collected daily returns from them. But since the death of Yusuf, the activities of the sect have become more secretive, making it difficult for researchers to investigate the kinds of economic activities they are engaged in to generate funds and whether members still pay dues, as well as the significance of such dues to the group's sustainability.

Donations from businessmen, politicians, government officials, and other individuals and organisations within Nigeria have been another source of funding for the sect. On 5 January 2011, for instance, the Nigerian police celebrated what it described as a "landmark" achievement, when security operatives arrested Alhaji Bunu Wakil and 91 other persons. Alhaji Bunu Wakil, who is a contractor and an indigene of Borno State, was alleged to be a major financier of the Islamic sect (Idris 2011a). Also, on 21 November 2011, state security operatives arrested a serving senator representing Borno South Senatorial District, Mohammed Ali Ndume, who was subsequently arraigned before an Abuja High Court for ties with and sponsorship of Boko Haram (Abonyi 2011).

The sect is also alleged to receive financial assistance from foreign terrorist networks. In 2007, for instance, Mohammed Yusuf and Mohammed Bello Ilyas Damagun were tried for terrorism-related offences. Mohammed Damagun, the proprietor of the *Daily Trust* newspapers' group, was arraigned before the Abuja High Court on three charges: namely, belonging to the Nigerian Taliban; receiving a total of 300,000 USD from Al-Qaeda to recruit and train Nigerians in Mauritania for terrorism; and aiding terrorists in Nigeria. Mohammed Yusuf was arraigned on five charges, which included receiving monies from Al-Qaeda operatives in Pakistan to recruit terrorists to attack the residences of foreigners, especially Americans, living in Nigeria (Onuoha 2012c). However, the charges against Mohammed Bello Ilyas Damagun were later dropped by the court.

In an interview in January 2012, a self-identified spokesman for Boko Haram, Abul Qaqa, informed the *Guardian* newspaper that they are spiritual followers of Al-Qaeda and the late Osama bin Laden, and that their leader Mohammed Abubakar Shekau had met Al-Qaeda leaders in Saudi Arabia in August 2011 and was able to obtain from Al-Qaeda whatever financial and technical support they needed (Mark 2012). It is very difficult to ascertain the veracity of the claims by Abul Qaqa. This could be one of the propaganda tools Boko Haram wants to use to attract more attention or even scare the West. Although the issue of external financial assistance to Boko Haram remains uncertain, US Homeland Security Department officials contend that "groups like Boko Haram are being influenced and financed by extremist foreign religious leaders and groups" (Offor, Ogbonnikan & Okoro 2011).[1] Evidence in this regard emerged recently during the trial at the Federal High Court in Abuja of Kabiru Abubakar Dikko Umar, alias "Kabiru Sokoto", who masterminded the 2011 Christmas Day bombing of a church in Madalla, Niger State. A prosecution witness informed the court "that Sokoto included in his statement details of funding received by the insurgents from an Islamic group, *Musilimi Yaa'maa*, based in Algeria and how the funds led to the fragmentation of Boko Haram, following disagreements over the sharing of the money" (Soniyi, Bello & Akinsuyi 2013: 7).

Of late, Boko Haram has relied largely on criminality, such as directly raiding banks or supporting robbery gangs to raid banks, to finance its operations. A member of a robbery gang arrested by the police in 2011, Sheriff Shettima, confessed that his gang was responsible for some robbery operations in Borno State to raise funds for Boko Haram. He claimed that his gang raided the Damboa branch of First Bank Nigeria Plc on 12 October 2011, during which a policeman was killed and 21 million naira stolen (Bwala 2011). It is noteworthy that of about 100 bank branches in Nigeria attacked by armed robbers and Boko Haram in 2011, "over 30 of the raids were attributed to Boko Haram" (*ThisDay* 2011: 6). In this regard, Boko Haram militants subscribe to the principle of *Fa'i*, the religious arguments used by extremists to justify the robbing of banks and jewellery shops to finance their jihadist operations. Indeed, some arrested Boko Haram members have been arraigned for bank robbery in Nigeria.

Kabiru Abubakar Dikko Umar has also confirmed that the sect raises money for its operations through bank robbery. The loot is usually shared among five groups: the less privileged, widows of those that have died in the jihad, *zakat*, those that brought in the money, and the leadership (for use in prosecuting the jihad) (Alli 2012). As security agencies tighten the noose on its known funding streams, the sect may turn to other criminal activities, such as car theft, kidnapping, pipeline vandalism, illicit trafficking in arms and narcotics, and offering protection rackets for criminal networks to raise funds (Okereke & Omughelli 2012).

THE EVOLUTION AND INCARNATION OF BOKO HARAM

Although the movement had been incubating in north-eastern Nigeria since 1995, its transformation into an armed violent group can be traced to events leading up to the 2003 general elections in Nigeria. Shortly after the original founder of the sect, Abubakar Lawan, left for further studies in Saudi Arabia, a committee of clerics appointed Mohammad Yusuf as their leader in 2002. Afterwards, Mohammad Yusuf ousted the clerics who appointed him, on allegations of their corruption and failure to properly interpret the teaching of the Quran. In its early years, the group under Yusuf's spiritual leadership and command

> strove for self-exclusion of its members from the mainstream corrupt society by living in areas outside or far away from society in order to intellectualise and radicalise the revolutionary process that would ultimately lead to violent overthrow of the Nigerian state. (Isa 2010: 333)

Yusuf's preaching attracted unemployed youths from Yobe and Borno states, and even from neighbouring countries such as Niger and Chad. It was around this time that the group became known as the *Yusufiyya* movement.

As the followership expanded, the group became very attractive to politicians in the build-up to the 2003 general elections (Monguno 2013). On the eve of the 2003 general elections, politicians who sought to outsmart their opponents in the north-eastern states used several youth groups and militias established or funded by them as political thugs. Ahead of the polls, youths belonging to the *Yusufiyya* movement, as well as others operating under titles such as *Yan Kalare* in Gombe and *Sara Suka* in Bauchi, were armed with sophisticated weapons by political leaders contesting gubernatorial elections in Bauchi, Borno, Gombe, and Yobe states (Ohia 2009; Idris & Adebayo 2012; Patrick 2013). In Yobe State, for instance, the *Yusufiyya* movement was invited to the state

> during the build-up to the 2003 elections in the wake of Sharia implementation in some northern states. But due to the fact that the election never took the shape that those that invited them thought it would, the then state government subsequently gave [the group] the ultimatum to immediately quit. (Ohia 2009: 3)

In Borno State, however, it was reported that Ali Modu Sheriff employed the services of young men belonging to the ECOMOG and *Yusufiyya* movement during the 2003 election to snatch Borno State from then Governor Mala Kachalla. According to Monguno (2013), "Ali Modu Sheriff promised the group strict implementation of Shari'ah, 50 million naira reward, 50 motorcycles, and the office of the Commissioner for Religious Affairs in exchange for their support". The group then provided Sheriff with the name of Alhaji Buji Foi as their candidate for the position of the Commissioner for Islamic Affairs. After becoming governor, Sheriff created a Ministry of Religious Affairs and appointed Alhaji Buji Foi, *Yusufiyya*'s national secretary, as its first commissioner (Idris & Adebayo 2012).

Shortly after the election, there was a breakdown in the relationship between Governor Sheriff and the Mohammed Yusuf-led group over issues of strict implementation of the Shariah, although there could have been other personal reasons behind their parting company. Consequently, Mohammed Yusuf pressured Alhaji Buji Foi to resign from Sheriff's cabinet along with most of the other staff brought by Foi to the Ministry of Religious Affairs. At this point, Sheriff used rival group ECOMOG to confront the *Yusufiyya* movement. As the relationship deteriorated, Mohammed Yusuf became more vocal and belligerent in his preaching against the government (Monguno 2013).

The practice of arming youths, mainly unemployed, for electoral violence, and subsequently dumping them after elections is a well-established electioneering habit of most Nigerian politicians. In this connection, Ojo (2013) has rightly noted that south-eastern politicians used *Bakassi Boys* and members of the Movement for the Actualisation of the Sovereign State of Biafra (MASSOB), and South-South politicians used the *Egbesu Boys* as well as members of the Movement for the Emancipation of the Niger Delta (MEND) to deal with their political opponents. The political elite in the South-West used different factions of the Oodua Peoples Congress (remnants of the old Agbekoya Movement) and members of the Road Transport Workers Union, as well as street urchins known as "Area Boys", to deal with their perceived political opponents.

It is not surprising, therefore, that to influence or win elections

> Northern politicians used various groups such as *Yan Sara-Suka* in Bauchi, *Yan Kalare* in Gombe, *Yan Daba* and *Yan daukan amarya* in Kano, and *ECOMOG* in Borno and Yobe states. In Adamawa State, the political thugs are known as *Damagun Boys* and *Shinko Boys*. In Taraba State, they are called *Bani Israila*. (Ojo 2013:25)

As is typical of Nigerian politicians, the northern youths and militia that were armed by politicians during the 2003 elections were eventually discarded by their sponsors after the election since they could not continue funding them. With no visible means of legitimate livelihood and frustrated over their fate in the aftermath of the elections, some of these disillusioned youth and militias in northern Nigeria became very susceptible to the radical brand of Islam preached, at the time, by Mohammed Yusuf (Patrick 2013).

Mohammed Yusuf's mosque complex, the *Ibn Taimiyya Masjid*, named after the medieval Islamic scholar who virulently condemned Shia, Sufis, and the ruling Sunni elite, was both a staging post for his venomous attack on government, and a headquarters for his movement. By "naming his mosque after one of the Islamic scholars most often cited by *Salafi jihadists*, Yusuf signalled his hostility to the ruling Muslim elite as well as to traditional Nigerian Islam" (Tanchum 2012: 79). He ratcheted up his strident call for jihad to restore what he considered the pristine Islam of the early Islamic community, as well as began the construction of an alternative society. The group also managed farmland and engaged in micro-financing, and Yusuf functioned as chief adjudicator of this miniature state-within-a-state (Tanchum 2012).

Yusuf subsequently redefined the doctrine of the sect around an ideology that abhors Western education and the tenets of Western science. He centred his aspersion and criticisms on the failures and corrupt attitudes of *yan boko* (modern elites trained at secular schools) who have acquired Western education and are currently in positions of power. In the sect's view, "the system represented by the *yan boko* is unjust, secular and has no divine origin. It is therefore unIslamic, which in turn accounts for its ineptitude and corruptness" (Isa 2010: 332).

Subsequently, the movement first took up arms against the state establishment when, on 24 December 2003, it attacked police stations and public buildings in the towns of Geiam and Kanama, Yobe State. Members occupied the two buildings for several days, hoisting the flag of Afghanistan's Taliban movement over the camps. A joint "operation of soldiers and police dislodged the group after killing 18 and arresting dozens of its members" (Suleiman 2007: 25). On 31 December 2003 the group left the village and dispersed into other northern states after inscribing the word "Taliban" on a captured vehicle (Morgan 2009). In 2004 it established a "base called 'Afghanistan' in Kanama village in northern Yobe State, on the border with the Republic of Niger" (Awofadeji 2009: 8). With these developments, the sect became known as the *Nigerian Taliban*, which was used in a derogatory sense by local people who despised the ideology and teachings of the sect.

Yusuf's radical ideology, however, generated friction between himself and other moderate northern-based Islamic scholars like the late Ja'far Mahmud

Adam, Sheik Abba Aji, and Yahaya Jingir. In particular, bitter theological disputes characterised the confrontation between Ja'far Mahmud Adam and Mohammed Yusuf between 2004 and 2007 (the year of Ja'far Mahmud Adam's death). Ja'far Adam criticised Mohammed Yusuf's theological positions as "ignorant" and "stupid" and as dangerous for the political ambitions of Muslims in Nigeria. Contrary to Yusuf's position, Ja'far Adam advocated the importance of Western and secular education for Muslims, noting that "only the conscious adoption of Western and secular boko education would eventually enable Muslims to effectively fight the Western enemy" (Loimeier 2012: 149).

The dispute notwithstanding, Yusuf's charismatic skills endeared him to many young Muslims in northern Nigeria. Although Yusuf preached a simple, ascetic form of life for his followers, he enjoyed Western luxuries, including a Mercedes and imported delicacies (Onuoha 2012d: 27). The activities of his group became more worrisome in 2004 when students, especially in tertiary institutions in Borno and Yobe states, who constituted the sect's members, withdrew from school, tore up their certificates, and joined the group. By disassociating from society at large, members became more indoctrinated by the ideologues, who inculcated in them anti-secular ideologies. On 21 September 2004, members attacked Bama and Gworza police stations in Borno State, killing several policemen and stealing arms and ammunition. It maintained intermittent hit-and-run attacks on security posts in some parts of Borno and Yobe states until the famous July 2009 anti-government uprising.

The root cause of the July 2009 revolt can be traced to the fatal shooting of members of the sect on 11 June 2009 by men of Operation Flush.[2] Some members of the sect, riding on motorbikes on their way to a cemetery to bury four of their members that had died in a motor accident, were intercepted by a patrol team of Operation Flush. The affected members were temporarily detained for not wearing crash helmets as stipulated in the state traffic law. Other sect members were infuriated with the interception, which they interpreted as a provocation, given that they were in a funeral procession. The resultant altercation between the sect members and security forces led to the shooting of some of their members by men of Operation Flush. Reacting to this event, Mohammed Yusuf, though absent at the time,

> made a pronouncement through his well circulated Friday sermon in Maiduguri to retaliate the shooting of his men, boasting that his group would be prepared to confront all security agencies in the State as well as government which he described as the enemies of Islam. (Sani 2011: 29)

The security operatives later received a tip-off that the sect was planning to strike from their base in Dutsen Tanshi in Bauchi State. When "security operatives stormed the place, nine members of the group were arrested while items used in local production of bombs were recovered" (Ohia 2009: 6). In retaliation, the members attacked and destroyed the Dutsen Tanshi police station on 26 July. This attack was the curtain raiser for a wave of unrest that manifested in Bauchi, Borno, Kano, Katsina, and Yobe states. The revolt ended on 30 July 2009, when their leader, Mohammed Yusuf, was finally captured in a goat pen in his residence in Maiduguri. After a few hours in police custody, Yusuf was murdered extrajudicially by the police, although police officials claimed that he was killed while trying to escape. Over 800 persons, mainly sect members, were killed during the revolt, and hundreds of its members were arrested and detained for formal trial (Adesoji 2010; Sampson 2013). The way the 2009 revolt was repressed by the Nigerian state proved to be a critical factor in the deadly escalation of Boko Haram's violent attacks.

OPERATIONAL TACTICS OF BOKO HARAM

Following the death of Yusuf and the mass killings and arrest of many of its members, the sect retreated and re-strategised in two ways. First was the adoption of Yusuf's hard-line top deputy, Abubakar Shekau, alias "Darul Tawheed", as the sect's new spiritual leader. Second was the redefinition of its tactics, which involved perfecting its traditional hit-and-run attacks and adding new flexible violent tactics. As the sect retreated and regrouped, the new leadership began mobilising, recruiting, and radicalising members using martyrdom videos of the July 2009 revolt. They issued several radical messages in leaflets and audio and video tapes to the media, stating an intention to wage war on secular authorities and "enemies", as well as claiming responsibilities for deadly attacks. The sect has continued to perpetrate acts of violence against diverse targets, such as state security personnel, community and religious leaders, politicians, worship centres (churches and mosques), the United Nations building in Abuja, telecommunication facilities, and media houses.

Exact casualty figures of attacks since the July 2009 anti-government uprising are hard to come by. Nigeria's Chief of Army Staff Lt. Gen. Azubuike Ihejirika claimed in November 2012 that the Islamic sect had killed no fewer than 3,000 people since it began its terror campaign (Iroegbu, Adedapo & Shittu 2012). This figure is not inclusive of those allegedly killed by security forces while fighting the sect. Innocent people, including women and children, have been killed as a result of these attacks. There are other inestimable costs to the nation due to these attacks, such as discouraging local and foreign investments, disruption of social and academic activities, destruction of property, and internal displacement of persons. Their activities have equally undermined religious harmony. For instance, suicide bombing attacks on churches by the sect have precipitated reprisal attacks on Muslims by Christian youths in Kaduna and Plateau states (Akogun *et al.* 2012; Alechenu, Chiedozie & Onwuamanam 2012; Wooden 2012). Other consequences include the fracturing of family structures (creating widows, widowers, and orphans) and damage to the country's image.

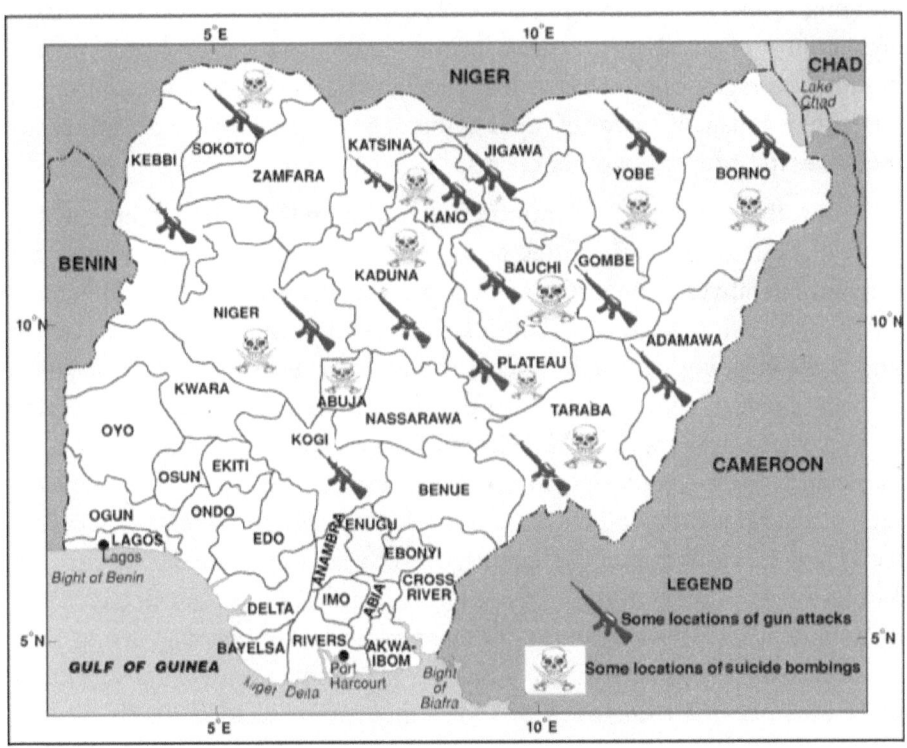

Figure 7.2 Locations of Boko Haram's attacks and suicide bombings in Nigeria
Source: Author

These attacks have occurred mainly in Maiduguri, the capital city of Borno State. However, several such attacks for which the group has claimed responsibility have occurred in Adamawa, Bauchi, Gombe, Jigawa, Kaduna, Kano, Kogi, Niger, Plateau, and Yobe states, and the Federal Capital Territory,

Abuja (Figure 7.2). Although the sect has concentrated its attacks mainly in northern Nigeria, it is speculated that it may extend its attacks to the Christian-dominated South as security agencies firm up counter-insurgency operations in the northern states (Onuoha 2012b: 9). Tactics such as targeted assassination, drive-by-shooting, use of IEDs, and suicide bombing have been used in the campaign of terror.

The choice of any of the above-mentioned tactics usually depends on the context, chosen target, and objective to be accomplished. The tactic of open armed confrontation is a key operational tactic Boko Haram has perfected since the July 2009 revolt. This is a modification of its traditional tactics of hit-and-run, which require appreciable numbers (10–60) of selected operatives engaging security forces in gun battles. The new method involves deploying a large number of members to mount surprise attacks on security establishments (stations, barracks, or prisons) or 'soft' civilian targets (markets and churches), where there is usually a large number of forces or people who can overpower its operatives if it adopts any other means.

Targeted assassination is another Boko Haram tactic. It is adopted when the sect is after a person(s) listed as an "enemy". The usual mode entails the assigned operatives trailing the target to a place where the individual is most vulnerable to being successfully killed. Boko Haram members usually use cars or motorbikes in going after such targets and shoot at a very close range (usually at the head, chest, or abdomen) to ensure that the chances of the victim surviving are very slim. In this way, Boko Haram has been able to kill several civilians, politicians, religious leaders, security agents, and community leaders that were outspoken against its ideology and activities. A notable example was the killing of engineer Modu Fannami Gubio, the governorship candidate of All Nigerians Peoples Party (ANPP) in Borno State for the April 2011 general elections. On 28 January 2011, Gubio, a cousin of then incumbent Governor of Borno State Ali Modu Sheriff, was killed along with Sheriff's younger brother and six others in his residence in Maiduguri by Boko Haram operatives (Idris 2011b).

Drive-by-shooting is a method that is very similar to targeted assassination in that some of the targets killed in the past have been executed through a process that involves operatives riding on a motorbike. It became a common tactic after the July 2009 revolt, and by mid-October 2010 no fewer than 21 people, including a top politician, had been killed by suspected members of the sect riding on a motorbike (*The Nation* 2010). One possible reason for adopting drive-by-shooting is to kill targets that have proven very difficult to track down to a spot where execution will be easy. It is a flexible method often adopted when operating in a built-up area or to kill target(s) that operate largely in the city centre. The convenience of this method is that the target can be shot at a very close range and the killers can easily manoeuvre their way out of the city without being apprehended by security agents.

The use of improvised explosive devices (IEDs) is another tactic that gained prominence after the July 2009 revolt. Such IEDs are configured in ways such that they can be detonated when thrown or can be set off through a timer or a remote control. Usually, the sect selects a particular place to plant the IED where it will have maximum effect upon explosion. They have been planted along roads, bridges, and rail lines, or deposited in bags or containers that are left behind in public places, including churches, drinking establishments, lecture halls, car parks, and bus stops. The size of the IEDs has ranged from small contraptions stuffed into used drink cans, to large containers such as drums fitted into the boot of a car if the intent is to mount a suicide attack.

The US Joint IED Defeat Organization revealed that Nigeria witnessed a nearly fourfold jump in the number of IED attacks in 2011. Nigeria saw 196 bomb incidents in 2011, compared with 52 incidents in 2010 (Straziuso 2012). The operational sophistication Boko Haram has attained in constructing IEDs is one of the main reasons why security experts believe it is receiving enhanced foreign support in the area of training and acquisition of explosives, possibly from AQIM. The IEDs are usually constructed using powerful explosive substances, such as trinitrotoluene (TNT), pentaerythritol (PETN), and ammonia (fertilisers). The use of IEDs is one of the greatest challenges the security forces are confronting in regard to the sect.

Particularly worrisome among the new tactics of Boko Haram is the adoption of suicide terrorism. Suicide terrorism refers to a form of extremely committed violence, carried out by someone who is intent on or deceived into taking his or her own life alongside killing or destroying the chosen target, in furtherance of a political, religious, or ideological goal. Seen in this light, the terrorist is fully aware that if he or she does not die, the planned attack will not be implemented. Thus the perpetrator's ensured death is a precondition for the success of the mission (Ganor 2001; Gunaranta 2002; O'Connor 2011). The method of suicide terrorism adopted by the sect is suicide bombing, which refers to any politically or ideologically motivated violent attack perpetrated by a self-aware individual(s) who actively and purposely causes his or her own death through blowing himself or herself up along with the chosen target.

Boko Haram is adept in mounting suicide bombing. At the time of writing, it has relied mainly on vehicle-borne improvised explosive devices (VBIED), twice on body-borne improvised explosive devices (BBIED), and once each on a motorcycle-borne improvised explosive device (MBIED) and a tricycle (popularly known as *Keke* NAPEP)[3]-borne improvised explosive device (TBIED). Table 7.1 provides one example each of the suicide bombing modes.

Date	Attacker	Mode	Target(s)	Effects
26 August 2011	Mohammed Abul Barra (27 years old)	VBIED (Honda Accord car)	UN House, Federal Capital Territory, Abuja.	On site for 10 months. The explosion killed 24 persons and injured over 100 others. The building houses over 400 staff of 26 UN humanitarian and development agencies. It was the sect's first attack on an international organisation
30 April 2012	Names not disclosed or reported	Motorcycle-borne (MBIED)	The convoy of Taraba State Police Commissioner, Jalingo, Taraba State	Three suicide bombers riding motorbikes rammed into the convoy of the Police Commissioner, killing at least 11 people
3 August 2012	Name not disclosed or reported	A suicide bomber packed his body with explosives (BBIED)	The Emir of Fika Alhaji Mohammed Abali Ibn Muhammadu Idrissa, at Potiskum mosque, Yobe State	Six people including three civilians, the emir's police orderly, and two other policemen sustained various degrees of injuries; the suicide bomber died in the incident
16 August 2012	Name not disclosed or reported	Tricycle, popularly known as Keke NAPEP (TBIED)	A patrol vehicle of the JTF in Custom area of Maiduguri	The suicide bomber on a bomb-laden tricycle missed his target and rode into a moving Mercedes Benz car. The blast killed the suicide bomber and a civilian, while two other people, including a soldier, sustained injuries

Table 7.1 Samples of Suicide Bombing Modes Mounted by Boko Haram (June 2011–November 2012). Source: Author's compilation

It has been noted that "between June 2011 and November 2012, the sect has staged at least 29 suicide attacks in northern Nigeria, with Borno State witnessing the highest number of attacks" (Onuoha 2012b: 7). Other acts of suicide bombing have been staged since then in northern Nigeria. While quite a number of these suicide attacks failed woefully, some were partially successful, and the majority have been largely successful when assessed on the basis of the number of lives lost, property damaged, and the international visibility they earned the sect. Its diverse targets of suicide attacks included security establishments (stations and barracks), international organisations, churches, mosques, telecom offices, and media houses. It is believed that some of the cars used in the suicide bombings were stolen.

Four factors could account for the adoption of suicide terrorism by the sect: the emergence of a more radical and hard-line leadership of the sect in the aftermath of the July 2009 revolt; the increased counter-insurgency measures put in place by the government to curtail its traditional tactics of open armed confrontation or placement of IEDs; improved funding from various sources within and outside Nigeria; and, more importantly, the sect's bond with foreign terror groups, leading to increased fanatic indoctrination of its members by experienced ideologues skilled in evoking visions of martyrdom to radicalise recruits.

GOVERNMENT RESPONSES TO THE BOKO HARAM THREAT[4]

To reduce the operational capability of the sect, the Nigerian government has adopted several measures, including prosecution of arrested members, deployment of special security forces, temporary closure of parts of borders in northern Nigeria, deportation of illegal immigrants, capacity building of security forces on counter-terrorism (CoT) and counter-insurgency (COIN) operations, installation of surveillance equipment, and collaboration with foreign partners.

The ramping up of violent attacks by the sect in the aftermath of the July 2009 revolt played a critical role in the enactment of Nigeria's first anti-terrorism legislation, the *Terrorism Prevention Act (TPA) 2011*. An important external factor that also contributed in this regard was the pressure from the US on the Nigerian government to expedite actions towards adopting comprehensive anti-terrorism legislation in the aftermath of the failed Christmas Day bombing of a US airliner by a Nigerian, Umar Farouk Abdulmutallab (Sampson & Onuoha 2011). The young Abdulmutallab, who had been trained in Yemen by Al-Qaeda, attempted to detonate an explosive device hidden in his underwear while on board Northwest Airlines Flight 253 en route to Detroit's Metropolitan Airport on 25 December 2009.

The establishment on 12 June 2011 of a Joint Military Task Force known as "Operation Restore Order" (JTORO), with headquarters in Maiduguri, Borno State, to counter the sect's growing terrorist potentials is a prominent dimension of the government response to the Boko Haram threat. The deployment of the JTORO has been partly successful, especially the use of military patrol vehicles equipped to detect hidden bombs and other weapons within a radius of 50 meters. The special security forces have also registered successes in terms of arrest and killing of Boko Haram operational commanders and strategists.

Notwithstanding the successes of the special security forces in northern Nigeria, their deployment has received criticism for harsh tactics that have injured civilians and damaged property. The approach taken by the security forces has led to unprecedented use of road blocks, cordon-and-search, and total blockade of some roads (especially those close to security establishments), often generating long traffic jams. Particularly worrisome is the accusation of unlawful killings, dragnet arrests, detention, intimidation, and extortion by the security forces. These real or alleged excesses undermine public support, especially in the area of providing tip-offs on Boko Haram members or hideouts. Sampson (2013: 17) has noted:

> [As] a result of these human rights abuses, the JTF has been severely criticised by a section of the Nigerian public over its violent counter-terrorism operations. Its use of disproportionate force has forced people, otherwise critical of the sect's activities, to renege on their earlier endorsement of military deployment.

Therefore, if the security forces are to be successful in the future, they must strike the proper balance of winning the hearts and minds of local people by offering security and using the 'stick' to weaken Boko Haram's operational capacity through arrests and prosecution.

Given the discovery that Boko Haram moves weapons and fighters in and out of Nigeria through Nigeria's porous international borders in the north, the federal government began an aggressive crackdown on illegal immigrants, repatriating around 11,000 foreigners as of 28 February 2012 (*Vanguard* 2012). Related to this was the decision to close part of Nigeria's northern borders and the establishment of two new defence intelligence missions in Niger and Mali in February 2012 to ensure better monitoring of the security situation in the Sahara–Sahel region. The Nigerian government has also scaled up training in counter-terrorism (CoT) and counter-insurgency (COIN) operations for state security forces in response to the growing audacity of the sect (Omonobi 2012). Training in special reconnaissance, close-quarters combat, urban warfare, amphibious operation, information operation and management, tactical communication, civil–military relations, and forensic analysis have equally been expanded in the training curricula of the armed forces and other security agencies (Musa 2012). This intervention is also supported by the acquisition and installation of technical and surveillance equipment, such as closed-circuit televisions, identification equipment for post-bomb blast investigation, and military patrol vehicles equipped to detect hidden explosives and other weapons.

The government has also embraced collaborative engagements with foreign states and international organisations to increase Nigeria's capacity to combat the Boko Haram threat. These include collaborations with organisations such as the UN, the EU, and the International Civil Aviation Organisation, as well as states like the US, France, South Korea, and Israel, geared towards ensuring that terrorist organisations do not establish strong footholds in Nigeria. For example, Nigeria established a collaborative framework with the UN known as the Integrated Assistance on Counter-Terrorism (I-ACT), under the aegis of the UN Counter-Terrorism Implementation Task Force. Although details of these collaborative efforts are not made public, they cover areas such as intelligence sharing, capacity building of security forces, and equipment support programmes.

In spite of the various measures adopted by the Nigerian government to reduce the sect's capability, Boko Haram continues to demonstrate resilience and modify its *modus operandi*. Since 2010, the sect has evolved into a more flexible, dynamic, and decentralised organisation, capable of changing and combining tactics, as well as expanding or re-ordering target selection. This situation has prompted debates concerning Boko Haram's ability to remain a potent force despite the losses it incurs from state security forces.

BOKO HARAM AND THE TRANSNATIONAL SALAFI JIHADIST THREAT

A fruitful way to understand Boko Haram's ability to continue to mount audacious attacks is to view it within the context of the transnational flow of ideological influence from global Salafi Jihadist Islamism. The term 'Islamism' means different things to different people. A more precise and analytically useful definition of Islamism describes it thus:

> a form of instrumentalisation of Islam by individuals, groups and organizations that pursue political objectives. It provides political responses to today's societal challenges by imagining a future, the

foundations for which rest on reappropriated, reinvented concepts borrowed from the Islamic tradition. (Denoeux 2002: 61)

Certainly, Islamism is politically heterogeneous, in the sense that different Islamist movements specialise in qualitatively different political activities depending on the context that underpins their emergence (Hegghammer 2009). Some oppose local regimes by non-violent means (radical Islamist); others try to topple regimes with terrorist tactics (jihadi Islamist); and still others wage armed resistance against occupation by non-Muslim powers (expellist Islamist).

Boko Haram belongs to the Salafi Jihadist Islamist stock, and it seeks to topple the secular Nigerian state. The sect's ideology and operational tactics derive from the global Salafist Islamic ideology, which seeks the imposition of its own interpretation of Islamic Law and a safe haven for jihadists. The *Salafiyya* movement identifies the problems of the contemporary world with deviation from the correct path delineated in the holy scriptures. Therefore, Salafis describe their activities as a struggle against innovations and *shirk*, or heresy (Rasheed 2012). Salafi adherents insist on the right of believers to interpret the fundamental texts for themselves through independent reasoning. There is often an analytical distinction between the *Salafiyya 'ilmiyya*, or "scholarly Salafis", and the *Salafiyya jihadiyya*, or "fighting Salafis". "Many *Salafis* are quite radical in their calls for a return to an authentic original form of Muslim practice without being at all oriented toward political activity, whether peaceful or violent" (European Commission's Expert Group on Violent Radicalisation 2008: 6). However, Salafi Jihadism, as noted earlier, focuses on the use of violence to bring about such radical change. It refers to the merging of a Salafi outlook and a jihadi call to violence. In other words:

> *Salafi jihadi* groups are motivated by a mix of religious and political objectives: they embrace a strict, literal interpretation of Islam, and combine it with an emphasis on *jihad*, understood here as holy war. They view *jihad* as the primary instrument through which their *Salafi* desire to 'return' to the original message of Islam will become reality. Unlike radical *Islamists*, they approach *jihad* as a global struggle that knows no borders, and that focuses on combating the West, in general, and the United States, in particular. They form an amorphous, transnational movement, and disseminate an ideology that is fundamentally hostile to modernity, to the secular, democratic nation-state, to the logic of globalization, and to peaceful coexistence of different cultures and religions. (Denoeux & Carter 2009: 86)

In this light, Boko Haram's Salafi Jihadist inclination became evident in the aftermath of the July 2009 revolt. In March 2010, for instance, Boko Haram declared that it was "joining Al-Qaeda to avenge the murder of some of its members and leaders in a series of explosions across Nigeria" (*The Jihadi Websites Monitoring Group* 2010: 14). In an interview with Al Jazeera television on 14 June 2010, the AQIM leader, Abdelmalek Droukdel, also known as Abu Musab Abdel Wadoud, confirmed that his group has been talking to Boko Haram and intends to supply it with weapons to "defend Muslims in Nigeria and stop the advance of a minority of Crusaders". He further noted that Al-Qaeda has an interest in Sub-Saharan Africa for "its strategic depth that would give it a bigger scope for manoeuvres" (*Stratfor* 2010).

Some analysts then dismissed AQIM's intent to bond with Boko Haram as mere wishful thinking or rhetoric. It was argued instead that "issuing statements claiming an alliance is easier than actually creating a meaningful accord and several factors complicate AQIM's intent to move into Nigeria" (*ibid.*). Indeed, there is clearly a distinction to be made not only between affiliation and solidarity, but also between tactics (common training and supply of weapons) and strategy (coordination of attacks under a central command). Notwithstanding, such a dismissive assessment downplayed the fact that both the AQIM and Boko Haram belong to the Salafi Jihadist ideological stock. Moreover, it overlooked the fact that global Al-Qaeda had attempted to draw localised conflicts (for instance, in Southeast Asia) into an evolving but loose network of transnational jihadism and may be bent on doing so in Nigeria. As Vidino, Pantucci, and Kohlmann (2010: 224) have rightly observed:

> Al-Qaeda and, more generally, the global jihadist movement, have repeatedly attempted to hijack conflicts that were largely nationalistic [local] in nature and turn them, both rhetorically and operationally, into battlefields of what they perceive to be a millenarian and global conflict between Islam and the world of infidelity. Local actors might maintain some of their parochial agendas, but by putting themselves under the banner of the global jihadist movement they benefit from outside support in terms of funding, recruits, propaganda, and military expertise. The global jihadist movement also benefits, as it can expand its influence and add credibility to its narrative that Islam is under attack from non-Muslims.

Evidently, Boko Haram began in 2010 to recast its grievances within the narrative framework of global jihad and employ rhetoric common to Salafi Jihadist groups around the world: that Islam is under attack by infidels in Nigeria. Given Nigeria's recent history of religious tension between Muslims and Christians, especially in northern Nigeria and the Middle Belt region, this was part of a strategy of whipping up religious sentiments to draw sympathy from impressionable Muslim youths to its cause. In February 2011, Boko Haram, in a message sent to the media, declared: "We are carrying out these attacks in order to propagate the name of Allah and to liberate ourselves and our religion from the hands of infidels and the Nigerian government" (Mshelizza 2011).

Earlier, in a published manifesto in July 2010, Abubakar Shekau linked the jihad being fought by Boko Haram with jihadist efforts globally, especially that of "the soldiers of Allah in the Islamic State of Iraq" (Pham 2012: 4). Shekau expressed solidarity with Al-Qaeda and threatened the US: "Do not think jihad is over. Rather jihad has just begun", he enthused (Pham 2012: 4). He also threatened attacks not only against the Nigerian state, but against "outposts of Western culture". This propaganda is archetypical of Al-Qaeda's global Islamist rhetoric of Islam being under attack by infidels. The ideological rhetoric signposts that Boko Haram aspires to share features of, and ties with, Al-Qaeda's Salafi Jihadist orientation, while at the same time retaining its own distinctive local organisation, character, and practice in Nigeria.

Given the brutal character of the Nigerian state, Boko Haram ideologues were convinced that the sect is largely impotent and must do the extraordinary to be able to liberate their religion from the hands of infidels in reference to the Nigerian state. As Ayoob has rightly noted:

> When and where the sense of impotence becomes very acute, it provides extremist elements with the opportunity to exploit the prevailing climate of despair to undertake terrorist activities. Extremist groups that arrogate to themselves the right to speak in the name of 'Islam' justify terrorism as the ... only strategy that can wrest the initiative from the hands of western powers and those perceived to be their surrogates in the Muslim world. (Ayoob 2005: 960)

The sense of impotence drove Boko Haram ideologues to establish links with like-minded Salafi Jihadist groups in Africa—in particular AQIM and Al-Shabaab—in furtherance of its ideological goal of Islamisation of northern Nigeria. To this end, many of their members fled to North Africa to train with Al-Qaeda in the Islamic Maghreb in the aftermath of the July 2009 revolt. The "*Boko Haram* men in the AQIM camp chose Abubakar Adam Kambar, as their leader" (*Africa Confidential* 2013: 5). During training with AQIM, Boko Haram members mastered the skills of bomb making:

> Boko Haram militants also attended Al Shabaab-owned training camps in Somalia. Members were taught how to construct and detonate improvised explosive devices, as well as employ the use of suicide bombers, which until participating in the training camps, Boko Haram did not engage such practices. (Connell 2012: 89)

In a statement released on 15 June 2011, Boko Haram boasted of its ties to the Somali-based terror group, Al-Shabaab:

> We want to make it known that our Jihadists (warriors) have arrived [in] Nigeria from Somalia where they got serious training on warfare from our brethren [Al-Shabaab] who made the country of Somalia ungovernable. We want to assure all security agencies that we would frustrate their efforts. By the grace of God, despite the armored carriers that they are boasting of, they cannot match the training we acquired in Somalia. (Safeafricagroup.com 2011)

The alignment and solidarity with AQIM and Al-Shabaab speaks for itself as a true shift of radical ideological expansion (Connell 2012). Having acquired the tactical and ideological tools, the sect began attacking targets it considers as infidels and surrogates: Christians, moderate Muslims, and secular (local and international) institutions in Nigeria. The suicide attack on a police headquarters on 16 June 2011 was a blatant signal of the training Boko Haram boasted it has acquired from established transnational jihadist movements in Africa. More than anything else, the 26 August 2011 suicide bombing of the UN building in Abuja was devastating evidence that the group aims to internationalise its acts of terror, in furtherance of the global jihadist agenda. In the aftermath of the UN bombing, a self-identified spokesman for Boko Haram claimed that they attacked the UN building because:

> all over the world, the UN is a global partner in the oppression of believers. We are at war against infidels. In Nigeria, the federal government tries to perpetuate the agenda of the United Nations. (Bashir 2011)

In another interview, Abu Qada disclosed Boko Haram's emerging ties to Al-Qaeda:

> Our relationship with Al Qaida is very strong. In fact, our leader [Shekau] and his team were in Mecca for the lesser Hajj to consolidate on that relationship. And we carried out the attack on the UN building when

he was about to go into a meeting with Al Qaida leadership in order to strengthen our negotiation position. (Salkida 2011: 42)

The UN bombing brought to the world's attention the growing danger Boko Haram poses to regional and international security. Prior to the UN bombing, there was very little awareness of, or attention paid to, the ideology driving the sect. In particular, there existed a collective security nescience concerning the growing ideological links between Boko Haram and other transnational Salafi Jihadist networks in Africa. Unlike earlier years when the debate was whether Boko Haram had links to other Salafi Jihadist movements, the current concern is on the extent of established ties and the consequences for national and regional security in Africa. The intelligence community has confirmed that Africa's top three Salafi Jihadist movements—Al-Shabaab, AQIM, and Boko Haram—are sharing funds, training, and explosive materials, which could possibly lead to the emergence of an "extremist triangle" in Africa (Shaughnessy 2012). The US AFRICOM Commander, Gen. Carter Ham, captured the threat thus:

> What really concerns me are the indications that the three organizations are seeking to coordinate and synchronize their efforts, in other words to establish a cooperative effort amongst the three most violent organizations. And I think that's a problem for America and for African security in general. (US Africa Command, 2012)[5]

Given that Al-Shabaab, AQIM, and Boko Haram subscribe to Salafi Jihadist ideology, it was possible for them to collaborate on certain areas of mutual interest such as training and weapons, while maintaining their distinctive local specificity and character shaped by the domestic environments in which they are operating. Recent developments in Mali confirm such connections. Mali slipped into instability after a coup led by Captain Amadou Sanogo overthrew President Amadou Toumani Touré on 22 March 2012. The coup created a power vacuum that enabled Tuareg rebels in the North, backed by a patchwork of Islamist forces—Ansar Dine, AQIM, and the Movement for Unity and Jihad in West Africa (MUJWA)—to take control of nearly two-thirds of the country. These groups, particularly AQIM and Ansar Dine, belong to the Salafi Jihadist stock.

Beginning from 11 January 2013, France deployed her forces in "Operation Serval" to stop the advance of Islamist groups who were intent on invading Bamako. French Mirage and Rafale fighter jets mounted air strikes across a wide belt of Islamist strongholds, from Gao and Kidal in the

North-East, near the border with Algeria, to the western town of Lere, close to Mauritania. French air and ground assaults on rebel strongholds have enabled French and Malian forces to retake Konna, Douentza, Gao, Timbuktu, and Kidal, with hopes of capturing more territories from the Islamists. Nigerian troops, in addition to other African forces, have joined French forces to roll back the Islamist occupation of northern Mali (Onuoha & Thurston 2013).

Nigerian President Goodluck Jonathan, as well as Chief of Army Staff Lt-Gen. Azubuike Ihejirika, have alleged that Boko Haram received training in Mali, making it imperative for Nigerian troops to join the international campaign to free northern Mali from Islamist militants. Some media reports carried further allegations:

> Hundreds of Boko Haram members stayed at training camps with Malian militants for months in Timbuktu, learning to fix Kalashnikovs and launch shoulder-fired weapons ... The Boko Haram members trained for about 10 months at what is now a bombed-out customs-police building on Timbuktu's desert fringe, intermingling with a local al Qaeda offshoot called Ansar Dine ... About 50 Boko Haram militants lived and trained at the customs building, and 50 more lived in an annex across a giant sandy lot, while others took up in other abandoned government buildings. (Pindiga 2013: 1)

Although concerns may be raised on the credibility of these latest allegations, they should be read against the backdrop of revelations that many Boko Haram members fled to North Africa after the July 2009 revolt to receive training in AQIM's camp (*Africa Confidential* 2013: 5). This evolving situation poses serious dangers to security in the Sahara–Sahel region, given possible fusion of movements that have strongholds or footprints in the region and share in the Salafi Jihadist ideology. In Niger, for instance, its southern part is dominated by the Hausa-speaking Izala-Salafi group, while its northern region, bordering Algeria and Libya, is dominated by the Tabligh Tuaregs. In Chad also, the *Ansar al Sunna* is an influential Salafi group which gets huge funding from donors in Sudan and Saudi Arabia (Rasheed 2012). As a result, the Sahara–Sahel region offers not only a potential safe haven and training ground for Salafi Jihadists, but also large ungoverned spaces for them to generate funds for their terrorist activities through complex shades of criminal activities such as kidnapping, drug trafficking, and arms smuggling. Worse still, the existence of porous borders and ineffective national security forces facilitates the ease of movement of jihadists across borders and the exchange of ideas, resources, and training centres. As Nigeria is surrounded by intrusive Salafi movements or influences, Boko Haram is gaining support from some Al-Qaeda-linked Salafist groups in the form of training, weapons, and ideological radicalisation of impressionable youths in northern Nigeria.

The tipping point in the radicalisation of Boko Haram has been traced to the extrajudicial killing of its charismatic leader, Mohammed Yusuf, as well as the gruesome murder of some arrested members in the aftermath of the July 2009 revolt. However, this factor rode on a groundswell of dissatisfaction, especially among Muslim youths in northern Nigeria, over governance failure on the part of the secular Nigerian state. Although political leaders from northern Nigeria dominated positions of leadership, such as presidents and heads of state, before the return to democracy in 1999 they did little or nothing to address the pervasive poverty and unemployment afflicting the northern region.

The frustrations created by poverty and unemployment played a critical role in making some youth fall victim to the appeals of violent, extremist ideologies. As rightly argued by Isa (2010: 333), the "movement used the term *Boko Haram* to mobilise and radicalise unemployed, unskilled and poverty-stricken youths to join its cause [and] dislodge the secular, *boko*-controlled state in Nigeria". The solution in the sect's view, therefore, is to overthrow the secular Nigerian state and introduce strict application of Shariah Law as a moral societal cleanser to effectuate the creation of an Islamic state devoid of corruption.

Boko Haram's Takfirist approach of cleansing the secular Nigerian state of infidels, however, has contributed in part to the emergence of a splinter group known as the *Jama'atu Ansarul Musilimina Fi Biladis Sudan* (abbreviated as Ansaru), which translates roughly as "The Supporters of Muslims in the Land of the Blacks". Arguably, ideological and personal differences between top leaders of Boko Haram contributed to the breaking away of Ansaru. At the root of the ideological differences is the issue of Takfirism. The Ansaru offshoot is believed to have sprouted from Boko Haram in January 2012, following the 20 January 2012 Boko Haram attack in the city of Kano that resulted in the death of at least 180 people, mostly Muslims. The group's existence, however, became more widely known from 2 June 2012, when its self-identified leader, Abu Usmatul al-Ansari, released a video proclaiming the creation of the sect and outlining its ideological stand (Onuoha 2013).

Security agents suspect that the name "Abu Usamatul Ansari" is a pseudonym for Khalid al-Barnawi, who is believed to be heading the group. As an erstwhile leader of Boko Haram, he is believed to have trained with AQIM in Algeria in the mid-2000s and led several AQIM-inspired kidnapping operations in Niger. It will be recalled that Khalid al-Barnawi was among the three leaders of Boko Haram designated as "global terrorists" by the US State Department on 21 June 2012. The other two were Abubakar Shekau, the current spiritual leader of Boko Haram, and Abubakar Adam Kambar, who was later killed by Nigerian security forces during a raid on his hideout in Kano on 15 August 2012 (*Africa Confidential* 2013).

Ansaru has become famous following a string of kidnappings of expatriates it has pulled off. Unlike the Shekau-led Boko Haram, which considers non-members as *kuffar* or *fasiqun*, making such individuals or groups legitimate targets of attack, Ansaru considers anybody that has accepted the *khalimatush shahada* (belief in one God and the Prophet Mohammed as the Messenger of Allah) as a Muslim who should not be killed, unless the person has committed an act that is punishable by death as stated in the Quran. In view of this, *"Ansaru detests Boko Haram's style of operations which it regards as inhuman to the Muslim Ummah. It claims that Islam forbids killing of innocent Muslims"* (Mamu 2012). This philosophical position, however, flies in the face of reality given the way some innocent foreigners abducted by the sect have been killed. For instance, on 9 March 2013, Ansaru released a communiqué and video claiming that it had killed the seven foreign hostages abducted from a Lebanese construction company, Setraco, in Jamaare, Bauchi State, on 17 February 2013. Ansaru justified the killing of the hostages after British warplanes were reported to have been seen in the northern Nigeria city of Bauchi by local journalists, possibly on a rescue mission. In keeping with its philosophical standpoint, it is possible for the group to claim that it acted in 'self-defence'.

The kidnapping and murder of the seven expatriates by the group remains the largest of its kind since the outbreak of terrorist violence in northern Nigeria. Before the February 2013 kidnapping, Ansaru was linked to the May 2011 kidnapping of Christopher McManus (a Briton) and Franco Lamolinara (an Italian) from their home in Kebbi State. They were held for months, before their captors killed them in March 2012 during a failed rescue mission by Nigerian security forces and British special forces in Sokoto. Given its ideological and operational outlook, as well as the known history of its suspected leader, Khalid al-Barnawi, analysts believe that Ansaru is strongly connected to AQIM (Bay & Tack 2013; Zenn 2013).

In terms of personal differences underling Ansaru's emergence, it is alleged that:

> one of the disputes between Al Barnawi and Shekau came over 40 million naira (US$250,000), which Al Barnawi donated to *Boko Haram* when he returned to Nigeria in early 2011. It was his share of an AQIM ransom. (*Africa Confidential* 2013: 5)

The ransom caused fierce disagreements within Boko Haram, with Shekau reluctant to give al-Barnawi any say in how the money should be spent. This offered al-Barnawi a reason to create a parallel group to burnish his own ideological interpretation of the jihadist struggle. In spite of their ideological and personal differences, it seems that the two have lately been growing closer, given the crackdown by Nigerian security forces against their members and the Franco–African onslaught against Islamists forces such as AQIM in northern Mali that have aided them in the past with financial and training assistance. Faced with similar challenges, it is possible that Boko Haram and Ansaru will tend to cooperate rather than compete with each other. As speculated by Zenn (2013: 8), "they may also collaborate on refining their tactics as well as expanding their areas of operations to locate new targets and eliminate Western and Christian influence from Nigeria and the region".

In this context, Boko Haram still poses a serious threat to security and stability in Nigeria, given the possible consequences of any successful large-scale attack in southern Nigeria. Although some analysts view this situation as a high-impact but low probability risk (de Pontet & Sparks 2013), several factors can serve as enablers rather than limiters for Boko Haram's penetration of the south-western zone. First, the substantial number of Muslim adherents in the zone offers Boko Haram broad room for incremental penetration. Second, and as a corollary to the above, the cosmopolitan nature of strategic economic cities such as Lagos, where substantial Hausa-speaking northerners tend to settle in particular communities, is another leverage for manoeuvre without being easily detected or suspected. Third, inchoate ideological rivalry between Islamic sects in the zone could be exploited to recruit impressionable youth into the Boko Haram fold. And fourth, the presence of strategic targets—embassies, oil tank farms, maritime assets, and international markets—could be so attractive that Boko Haram could partner with criminal or radical groups (such as Ansaru) to mount attacks. If successfully planned and executed, [such an] attack in southern Nigeria would also render a psychological victory for Boko Haram because it would show that the group could strike anywhere in the country and that Lagos, Nigeria's economic hub and Africa's most populous city, is in Boko Haram's targeting range. (Zenn 2012: 10)

It is safe to expect that such attacks are more probable in the form of planted IED or suicide bombing attacks than coordinated gunfights with security forces.

As hinted earlier, Boko Haram could also attempt to exploit incipient Islamo-ideological contestation between Sufi traditionalists and emerging Wahhabi Salafi adherents in the south-western zone to deepen its recruitment and radicalisation drives or establish a footprint in the zone. In recent times, Sufi traditionalists are being challenged by the emerging Wahhabi Salafis for the control of mosques across Yorubaland in the south-west zone (Rasheed 2012). The contest between the groups in the region is already evident in the struggles in mosques over how an *imam* or prayer leader should be chosen. Control over the mosques is critical in this respect, because the successful group stands in good stead to propagate its ideology in the region.

Even though Salafi Jihadism has not manifested in overt violence in any area of southern Nigeria, intelligence reports show that the penetration of the ideology is gradually manifesting across the South-West and Middle Belt zones (Rasheed 2012). Already, there have been cases of clashes between Islamic sects in the South-West, as was the case between the Izala sect and Tijaniyya group in the Sabo area of Ibadan, Oyo State. On 22 August 2010, disagreement on some Islamic doctrines saw the two groups using the public address systems to launch verbal attacks on each other. In the ensuing violent clashes, no fewer than 13 people were seriously injured and property, including buildings, three mosques, and four vehicles, was vandalised before policemen brought the situation under control (Adesuyi 2010: 6). As these confrontations unfurl over an environment of economic marginality, political exclusion, and social destitution, a potentially fertile ground for radicalisation and recruitment in the south-west zone is being created for Salafi Jihadist groups such as Boko Haram. The arrest of a top Boko Haram leader in Kano, who is believed to be a native of Ogbomoso, Oyo State (Salihu 2012), suggests that the sect can use such members as conduits to establish footprints in the South-West, where some young men are becoming very impatient with the secular Nigerian state over governance failure. Also, on 21 March 2013, security forces raided a hideout in

Ijora, Lagos State, where some suspected Boko Haram members were arrested, and bombs, AK-47 rifles, cartridges, and daggers were recovered (Utebor & Akinkuotu 2013). Any evidence that proves that the suspects are indeed Boko Haram members would confirm its potential expansion into the south-west zone. Given that in 2009 Boko Haram had threatened to attack cities such as Lagos in southern Nigeria (*Vanguard* 2009; Olupohunda 2013), its potential foray into southern Nigeria remains a major concern for the security agencies.

CONCLUSION

Although the Nigerian government has repeatedly promised to hold talks with Boko Haram if its leaders come forth, its kinetic response in the form of use of military force has recorded modest successes, such as the arrest and killing of some of the sect's members, strategists, and commanders. In spite of the government onslaught, Boko Haram has remained resilient, tapping strength from Salafi Jihadist ideology to further recruit and radicalise young impressionable minds and stage dramatic acts of terror in northern Nigeria. Evidently, Boko Haram is a manifestation of a fringe and violent ideology that underpinned many religious uprisings in the North in the past several decades, such as the Maitatsine revolt in the 1980s (Okanya 1995; Danjibo 2010). The problem is that even when the manifestation is destroyed, the ideology remains, leading to fears that in the future the ideology may sprout another manifestation with even more violent orientation (Rasheed 2012).

Therefore, a more sustainable approach to addressing the challenge in Nigeria is to deal with the underlying ideology of the sect as well as the formative environment that enables such ideology to flourish. As one scholar has rightly noted, the underlying ideology of Boko Haram

> is framed around issues that appeal to the people's grievances; hence, the environmental context is very critical to understanding what generates and sustains the grievances that are expressed through terrorists' tactics. (Sampson 2013: 22)

Defeating or countering such ideology could be achieved through the initiation of robust political, economic, and religious reforms. Political reforms would target strengthening governance processes and institutions to ensure transparency, accountability, and responsiveness in ways that increase the legitimacy of government at all levels in Nigeria. Economic reforms entail rolling out robust interventions that will drastically reduce the level of poverty, unemployment, and social destitution in northern Nigeria, which extremist ideologues have exploited in their recruitment and radicalisation drives. The religious aspect requires delivering a national project on countering ideological support for extremism and terrorism by the government, focusing on monitoring religious sermons, supporting moderate Islamic scholars to deliver enlightenment programmes, scrutinising foreign funding of religious undertakings, and encouraging the teaching of comparative religion in Nigerian schools—primary, secondary, and tertiary. If concerted efforts are not made to defeat the ideology behind the Boko Haram menace, the tendency for a different violent sect to emerge in the future is most probable, even if the Nigerian state succeeds in winning the fight against Boko Haram.

Notes

1. http://allafrica.com/stories/201101070435.html.
2. Operation Flush was a Borno State-owned security outfit established to combat armed banditry in the state.
3. Keke NAPEP refers to the motorised tricycle (*tuk tuk*) used for commercial transportation in cities across Nigeria. It was introduced in 2000, when President Olusegun Obasanjo's administration, through the *National Poverty Eradication Programme (NAPEP)*, partnered with the Autobahn Techniques Limited (trademark owners of the name KEKE NAPEP) to roll out the tricycle project as an intervention tool for job creation and poverty alleviation.
4. This section benefited from Onuoha, F. C. (forthcoming), "Assessing the Implications of Counter Boko Haram Operations by the Nigerian Government", commissioned by the Institute of Security Studies, South Africa.
5. http://www.africom.mil/getArticle.asp?art=8039&lang=0.

References

Abonyi, I. (2011), "Boko Haram: Senator Ali Ndume charged to court", *ThisDay,* 22 November.

Adele, B.J. (2011), "Boko Haram and democracy in Nigeria's fourth republic", *The Constitution,* 11(4): 58-70.

Adesoji, A. (2010), "The Boko Haram uprising and Islamic revivalism in Nigeria", *Africa Spectrum* 45(2): 95-108.

Adesuyi, G. (2010), "Islamist sects' clash: 9 suspects in police net", *Sun,* 24 August.

Adisa, T. (2012), "Boko Haram exposed, how sect was formed, training details, why it is changing tactics", *Tribune*, 12 February.

Africa Confidential (2013), "Nigeria: Taking the hostage road", 15 March, 54(6).

Ajani, J. (2011), "UN House bombing: The hunt for Maman Nur", *Vanguard*, 4 September.

Akanji, O. (2009), "The politics of combating domestic terrorism in Nigeria". In: W. Okumu & A. Botha, eds, *Domestic terrorism in Africa: defining, addressing and understanding its impact on human security*. Pretoria: Institute for Security Studies.

Akogun, K., A. Ogbu, Y. Akinsuyi, O. Nzeshi & J. Shiklam (2012), "Scores killed in Kaduna, Zaria bombings, Reprisal", *ThisDay*, 12 June. http://www.thisdaylive.com/articles/scores-killed-in-kaduna-zaria-bombings-reprisals/118205/ [Accessed 2 May 2013].

Alechenu, J., I. Chiedozie & J. Onwuamanam (2012), "Suicide bombers attack Gov Jang's church...", *Punch*, 27 February. http://www.punchng.com/news/suicide-bombers-attack-gov-jangs-church-%E2%80%A2-police-recover-explosives-from-christians-in-bauchi/ [Accessed 2 May 2013].

Alli, Y. (2011), "Boko Haram kingpin, five others arrested", *The Nation*, 29 September, http://www.thenationonlineng.net/2011/index.php/news/21273-boko-haram-kingpin-five-others-arrested.html [Accessed 30 September 2011].

――― (2012), "Kabiru Sokoto names Boko Haram's leaders", *The Nation*, 14 February, http://www.thenationonlineng.net/2011/index.php/news/36766-kabiru-sokoto-names-boko-haram%E2%80%99s-leaders.html [Accessed 16 February 2012].

Awofadeji, S. (2009), "150 killed in Bauchi religious crisis", *ThisDay*, 27 July.

Awofeso, N., J. Ritchie & P. Degeling (2003), "The Almajiri heritage and the threat of non-state terrorism in Northern Nigeria: Lessons from Central Asia and Pakistan", *Studies in Conflict and Terrorism*, 26(4): 311-325.

Ayoob, M. (2005), "The future of political Islam: the importance of external variables", *International Affairs* 81(5): 951-961.

Bakare, B. (2012), "Row over call for Hijab in public schools", *Nigerian Compass*, 6 April.

Bashir, M. (2011), "UN Building: Boko Haram names bomber, Abul Barra", *Daily Trust*, 2 September.

Bey, M. & S. Tack (2013), "The Rise of a New Nigerian Militant Group", *Stratfor*, 21 February.

Bwala, J. (2011), "Boko Haram wraps bombs as Sallah gifts", *Nigerian Tribune*, 3 November. http://www.tribune.com.ng/index.php/front-page-news/30668-

boko-haram-wraps-bombs-as-sallah-gifts-police-arrest-bomb-makers-recover-bombs-guns [Accessed 5 November 2011].

Connell, S. (2012), "To be or not to be: Is Boko Haram a foreign terrorist organisation", *Global Security Studies* 3(3): 87-93.

Da'wah Coordination Council of Nigeria (DCCN) (2009), *Boko Haram Tragedy: Frequently Asked Questions*. Minna: DCCN.

Danjibo, N.D. (2010), "Islamic fundamentalism and sectarian violence: The Maitatsine and Boko Haram crisis in northern Nigeria". http://www.ifra-nigeria.org/IMG/pdf/N-_D-_DANJIBO_-_Islamic_Fundamentalism_and_Sectarian_Violence_The_Maitatsine_and_Boko_Haram_Crises_in_Northern_Nigeria.pdf [Accessed 5 May 2013].

Denoeux, G. (2002), "The forgotten swamp: navigating political Islam", *Middle East Policy* 9(2): 56-81.

Denoeux, G. & L. Carter (2009), *Guide to the drivers of extremism*. US: United States Agency for International Development, p. 86.

de Pontet, P. & W. Sparks (2013), "The evolving threat of Boko Haram", *Foreign Policy*, 1 May. http://eurasia.foreignpolicy.com/posts/2013/05/01/the_evolving_threat_of_boko_haram [Accessed 2 May 2013].

European Commission's Expert Group on Violent Radicalisation (2008), "Radicalisation Processes Leading to Acts of Terrorism". A Concise Report submitted to the European Commission, 15 May.

Ganor, B. (2001), "Suicide attacks in Israel". In: International Policy Institute for Counter-Terrorism, *Countering Suicide Terrorism: An International Conference*. Herzliyya, Israel: ICT.

Gunaranta, R. (2002), "Suicide terrorism: A global threat", *Jane's Intelligence Review* 12(4): 52-55.

Gargon, F. & S. Bean (2010), "Northern Nigeria's Boko Haram movement: Dead or resurrected?", *Terrorism Monitor* 8(12): 2-6.

Hoechner, H. (2013), *Searching for Knowledge and Recognition: Traditional Qur'anic Students (Almajirai) in Kano, Nigeria*. Ibadan: French Institute For Research in Africa.

Hazzad, A. (2009), "Nigeria clashes kill over 50 in Northeastern city", *Reuters*, 26 July. http://www.reuters.com/article/newsMaps/idUSTRE56P24N20090726 [Accessed 1 August 2009].

Hegghammer, T. (2009), "Jihadi Salafis or revolutionaries? On religion and politics in the study of militant Islamism". In: R. Meijer, ed., *Global Salafism: Islam's new religious movement*. New York: Columbia University Press, pp. 244-266.

Ibrahim, Y. (2010), "FG to build 100 Tsangaya schools", *Daily Trust*, 13 December.

Idris, H. (2011a), "Boko Haram financier, 91 others in Police net", *Daily Trust*, 1 January.

——— (2011b), "Boko Haram: We killed Gubio", *Daily Trust*, 3 February.

Idris, H. & I. Adebayo (2012), "Boko Haram: Now, senator Sheriff, Zana clash on the truth", *Sunday Trust*, 28 October. http://sundaytrust.com.ng/index.php/top-stories/11845-boko-haram-now-senators-sheriff-zanna-clash-on-the-truth [Accessed 4 October 2012].

Iroegbu, S., A. Adedapo & H. Shittu (2012), "Boko Haram has killed 3,000 People, Says Army Chief", *ThisDay*, 6 November.

Isa, M.K. (2010), "Militant Islamist groups in Northern Nigeria". In: W. Okumu & A. Ikelegbe, eds, *Militias, Rebels and Islamist Militants: Human Security and State Crises in Africa*. Pretoria: Institute of Security Studies, pp. 313-340.

Jihadi Websites Monitoring Group (2010), "Africa Periodical Review", 2 March. http://www.ict.org.il/Portals/0/Internet%20Monitoring%20Group/JWMG_Periodical_Review_March_2010_No.2.pdf.

Jimos, A. (2011), "Nigeria: Boko Haram on a revenge mission", *Vanguard*, 2 April.

Komalafe, S. (2012), "Boko Haram: A crisis in search of strategy", *ThisDay*, 25 January

Lobe, J. (2012), "Nigeria: Three Boko Haram leaders put on US terrorism list", *Inter Press Service*, 21 June. http://www.ipsnews.net/2012/06/nigeria-three-boko-haram-leaders-put-on-u-s-terrorism-list/ [Accessed 22 June 2012].

Loimeier, R. (2012), "Boko Haram: The Development of a Militant Religious Movement in Nigeria", *Africa Spectrum* 47(2-3): 137-155.

Mamu, T. (2012), "Another Islamic Sect emerges…to counter Boko Haram", *Desert Herald*, 2 June. http://desertherald.com/?p=1526#more [Accessed 6 June 2012].

Marama, N. (2013), "We're yet to decide on amnesty—Boko Haram", *Vanguard*, 8 April.

Mark, M. (2012), "Boko Haram vows to fight until Nigeria establishes Sharia law", *The Guardian*, 27 January. http://www.guardian.co.uk/world/2012/jan/27/boko-haram-nigeria-sharia-law [Accessed 29 January 2012].

Mneimneh, H. (2009), "Takfirism", *Critical Threats*, 1 October. http://www.criticalthreats.org/al-qaeda/basics/takfirism [Accessed 4 February 2013].

Monguno, H. (2013), An indigene, resident, and security analyst in Borno interviewed by the author on board Ethiopia Airways, Abuja-Addis Ababa, 27 April.

Morgan, A. (2009), "Exclusive: Islamists on the rampage in Nigeria", *Family Security Matters*. http://www.familysecuritymatters.org/publications/id.3855/pub_

detail.asp [Accessed 12 August 2009].

Mshelizza, M. (2011), "Nigerian Islamist sect posters threaten uprising", *Reuters*, 2 February. http://af.reuters.com/article/topNews/idAFJOE7110GN20110202 [Accessed 4 February 2011].

Mukairu, L. & A. Muhammad (2009), "Another 43 Islamic fanatics killed in Yobe", *Vanguard*, 30 July, http://www.vanguardngr.com/2009/07/another-43-islamic-fanatics-killed-in-yobe/ [Accessed 3 May 2013].

Musa, M. (2012), "Nigeria: Understanding JTFs operation restore order in Borno State", *Daily Trust*, 2 April. http://allafrica.com/stories/201204020163.html [Accessed 4 May 2012].

O'Connor, T. (2011), "Varieties of suicidal terrorism", *Megalinks in Criminal Justice*, 3 August. http://www.drtomoconnor.com/3400/3400lect05.htm [Accessed 1 March 2012].

Ogbu, A. (2012), "FG Uncovers 1,497 illegal migration routes into Nigeria", *ThisDay*, 15 March.

Ohia, I. (2009), "Boko Haram killing: What was gov Sheriff's role?", *Desert herald*, 18 August.

Okanya, D.O. (1995), "Religion and violence in Nigeria: the Maitatsine rebellion explained". In: D.O. Okanya, ed., *Great issues in Nigerian government and politics*. Enugu: Department of Political Science, Enugu State University of Science and Technology.

Offor, C., F. Ogbonnikan & E. Okoro (2011), "Nigeria: FBI Links Al-Qaeda to Abuja Blast", *Daily Independent*, 6 January. http://allafrica.com/stories/201101070435.html [Accessed 12 January 2011].

Ojo, J. (2013), "Arming jobless youths to win elections", *Punch*, 15 May.

Okereke, C.N. & V.E. Omughelli (2012), "Financing the Boko Haram: Some informed projections", *African Journal for the Preventing and Combating of Terrorism* 2(1): 169-179.

Olupohunda, B. (2013), "How safe is Lagos from Boko Haram?", *Punch*, 4 April. http://www.punchng.com/opinion/how-safe-is-lagos-from-boko-haram/ [Accessed 12 April 2013].

Omonobi, K. (2012), "2,000 soldiers on counter terrorism training—Ihejirika", *Vanguard*, 14 March. http://www.vanguardngr.com/2012/03/2000-soldiers-on-counter-terrorism-training-ihejirika/ [Accessed 18 March 2012].

Onuoha, F.C. (2012a), "The Audacity of the Boko Haram: Background, Analysis and Emerging Trend", *Security Journal* 25(2): 134-151.

——— (2012b), "(Un)Willing to die: Boko Haram and suicide terrorism in Nigeria",

Report, Al Jazeera Centre for Studies, 24 December.

––––– (2012c), "Combating the financing of Boko Haram extremism in Nigeria", *African Journal for the Preventing and Combating of Terrorism* 2(1): 89-121.

––––– (2012d), "Boko Haram's tactical evolution", *African Defence Forum* 4(4):27-33.

––––– (2010), "The Islamist challenge: Nigeria's *Boko Haram* crisis explained", *African Security Review* 19(2): 54-67.

––––– (2013), "*Jama'atu Ansarul Musilimina Fi Biladis Sudan* or *Ansaru*: Nigeria's Evolving Terrorist Group", Report, Al Jazeera Centre for Studies, 14 March.

Onuoha, F.C. & A. Thurston (2013), "Franco-African military intervention in the Mali Crisis and evolving security concerns", Report, Al Jazeera Centre for Studies, 19 February.

Pham, J.P. (2013), "Boko Haram evolving threat", *Africa Security Brief* No. 20, April.

Pindiga, H.I. (2013), "Boko Haram training camps found in Mali—Over 200 Nigerians trained for 10 months in Timbuktu", *Daily Trust*, 6 February.

Punch (2013), "Nigerian al-Qaeda suspects arrested in Mali", *Punch*, 6 February.

Rasheed, O. (2012), "Hidden roots of Boko Haram...Why security Agencies are worried about South West", *Nigerian Tribune,* 17 February.

Safeafricagroup.com (2011), "Boko Haram calls off proposed talks, promises wider attacks using Somali-trained hit men", 16 June. http://safeafricagroup.com/2011/06/16/boko-haram-calls-off-proposed-talks-promises-wider-attacks-using-somali-trained-hit-men/ [Accessed 18 June 2011].

Salihu, M. (2012), "JTF arrests suspected Yoruba Boko Haram leader", *Punch,* 12 May.

Salkida, A. (2011), "Face of UN House Bomber", *Blueprint,* 5-11 September.

Sampson, I.T. (2013), "The dilemmas of *counter-bokoharamism*: Debating state responses to *Boko Haram* terrorism in northern Nigeria", *Security Journal* advance online publication, 18 February 2013.

Sampson, I.T. & F.C. Onuoha (2011), "Forcing the Horse to Drink or Making it Realize its Thirst? Understanding the Enactment of Anti-Terrorism Legislation (ATL) in Nigeria", *Perspectives on Terrorism,* 5(3-4):33-49.

Sani, S. (2011), "Boko Haram: History, ideas and revolt", *The Constitution* 11(4): 17-41.

Schweitzer, Y. (2001), "Suicide terrorism: Development and main characteristics". In: International Policy Institute for Counter-Terrorism, *Countering Suicide Terrorism: An International Conference.* Herzliyya, Israel: ICT.

Shahzad, S.S. (2007), "Takfirism: A messianic ideology", *Le Monde diplomatique,* 3

July, http://mondediplo.com/2007/07/03takfirism [Accessed 4 July 2012].

Shaughnessy, L. (2012), "Extremist triangle a growing threat to Africa and America", 25 June. http://security.blogs.cnn.com/2012/06/25/extremist-triangle-a-growing-threat-to-africa-and-america/ [Accessed 4 July 2012].

Soniyi, T, M. Bello & Y. Akinsuyi (2013), "Kabir Sokoto trial: Sharing of funds split Boko Haram", *ThisDay*, 10 May.

Stratfor (2010), "Nigeria: AQIM attempts to expand", 15 June. http://www.stratfor.com/analysis/20100615_nigeria_aqim_attempts_expand [Accessed 20 June 2010].

Straziuso, J. (2012), "African AQ-Linked groups using advanced IEDs", *The Associated Press*, 15 March. http://www.marinecorpstimes.com/news/2012/03/ap-military-jieddo-african-al-qaida-linked-groups-using-advanced-ieds-031512w/ [Accessed 17 March 2012].

Suleiman, T. (2007), "Terrorism unsettles the north", *Tell*, 26 February.

Taiwo, J. & M. Olugbode (2009), "Boko Haram leader killed", *ThisDay*, 31 July.

Tanchum, M. (2012), "Al-Qa'ida's West African advance: Nigeria's Boko Haram, Mali's Touareg, and the spread of Salafi Jihadism", *Israel Journal of Foreign Affairs* 6(2): 75-90.

The Jihadi Websites Monitoring Group (2010) *Periodical Review*, March (2).

The Nation (2010), "The Boko Haram kills Islamic cleric in Borno", 10 October.

This Day (2011), "Boko Haram, armed robbers attack 100 bank branches", 10 December.

Tisdall, S. (2009), "Nigeria clashes bode ill for West Africa", 30 July. http://www.guardian.co.uk/commentisfree/2009/jul/30/nigeria-islamists-africa [Accessed on 2 January 2010].

US Africa Command (2012), "Transcript: Ham discusses African security issues at ACSS senior leaders seminar", 27 June. http://www.africom.mil/getArticle.asp?art=8039&lang=0 [Accessed 4 July 2012].

Utebor, S. & E. Akinkuotu (2013), "100 Soldiers storm terror suspects' hideouts in Lagos", *Punch*, 22 March.

Vanguard (2009), "Nigeria: Boko Haram resurrects, declares total Jihad", 14 August. http://allafrica.com/stories/200908140646.html [Accessed 2 May 2013].

——— (2012), "Nigeria repatriates 11,000 foreigners over terror fears", *Vanguard*, 27 February. http://www.vanguardngr.com/2012/02/nigeria-repatriates-5000-foreigners-over-terror-fears/ [Accessed 1 March 2012].

Vidino, L., R. Pantucci & E. Kohlmann (2010), "Bringing global jihad to the Horn of

Africa: al Shabaab, Western fighters, and the sacralisation of the Somali conflict", *African Security* 3(4): 216-238.

Walker, A. (2011), "Maiduguri: Nigeria's city of fear", BBC News, 15 March. http://www.bbc.co.uk/news/worldafrica-12713739 [Accessed 2 April 2011].

West Africa Insight (2010), "Almajiris 'Street children' and sectarian conflicts in Northern Nigeria", 1(3): 6-8.

Wooden, C. (2012), "Church bombings, reprisal attacks, claim 45 lives in Nigeria", Catholic News Service, 19 June. http://www.catholicregister.org/news/international/item/14719-church-bombings-reprisal-attacks-claim-45-lives-in-nigeria [Accessed 2 May 2013].

Zenn, J. (2012), "Strategic Limitation of the Boko Haram in Southern Nigeria", *CTC Sentinel* 5(86): 9-13.

——— (2013), "Cooperation or Competition: Boko Haram and Ansaru after the Mali Intervention", *CTC Sentinel* 6(3): 1-8.

8

BY THE NUMBERS

The Nigerian State's Efforts to Counter Boko Haram

Rafael Serrano and Zacharias Pieri
Citizenship Initiative, University of South Florida

This chapter examines the interplay between insurgency and counter-insurgency elements within north-eastern Nigeria. We scrutinise the effectiveness of security force operations in increasing population security and managing or mitigating violence caused by the violent and extremist Islamist organisation Boko Haram. Key to the chapter is determining whether Nigerian security force operations have either helped or exacerbated problems associated with Islamist violence in the north of the country. To do so we have compiled data on both security force and militant fatalities since the outbreak of the violence and included historical case studies for comparison. Ultimately, this chapter will call into question whether Nigerian strategies for dealing with the problem are practicable and appropriate.

INTRODUCTION

Boko Haram, a self-styled Islamist movement, whose name has commonly been translated as "Western education is forbidden", and which has been ranked as a terrorist organisation by a host of governments across the world, has been engaged in a costly—both in terms of lives and property—insurgency/counter-insurgency battle with Nigeria's military and law enforcement elements, collectively operating under the Joint Task Force (hereafter JTF) framework. Boko Haram, which has its origins in and maintains its current stronghold in Nigeria's north-eastern provinces (Borno and Yobe), has increasingly utilised indiscriminate violence in pursuit of a radical social reform agenda, while the JTF have responded with heavy-handed tactics to quash the movement. The battle thus far, from the side of Boko Haram, has largely consisted of small-scale insurgent hit-and-run attacks on a range of government and civilian targets, followed by large-scale retaliatory military deployments from the state security forces, widespread urban lockdowns, door-to-door searches, and haphazard large-scale arrests. This dynamic has left much of the population of the north of Nigeria caught between Boko Haram brutality and JTF excesses of authority. The inability of the Nigerian military and the police elements of the JTF to effectively conduct more even-handed counter-insurgency operations in urban environments has created a situation where the constant ebb and flow of insurgent gains and systemic human rights abuses on the part of both insurgents and security forces make any substantial security improvements fleeting.

Security, as Okunola argues (2013: 4), is an imperative for Nigeria, as is the case for any society, and is one of the major needs of a population, particularly following physiological needs. Security allows for individuals to grow, engage in lawful and productive activities, and produce meaningful development in Nigerian society. As such, a primary duty of the Nigerian state is the provision of security to its citizens (*ibid.*).[1] Given this assertion, this chapter examines the Nigerian context by drawing upon elements of Hobbesian theory—that is, from the hypothesis that in the absence of strong central governance, where there is a mutually accepted covenant of trust between the government and the governed, situations emerge where there is a "war of all against all" (Hobbes 1988: 15). Moreover, key to the analysis of a state's struggle for security and stability is the point at which the actions of the state become part of the problem rather than the solution. In other words, when does the actor whose role it is to provide security, and often in the name of security implementation, become yet another element of insecurity in a seemingly never-ending cycle of violence (*ibid.*)? Whilst the context in Nigeria is not quite as stark as this, the emergence and continued activities of Boko Haram and its splinter groups, as well as generally high levels of violence across the country, suggest a fundamental breakdown in this covenant. At the same time, an overly violent central government or security force also has its part to play in perpetuating cycles of increasing violence and insecurity.

This chapter is a case study focused on the incidence of violence between the security services and the militant groups directly engaged in violence within Nigeria, namely Boko Haram and Ansaru. The chapter further touches upon examples of insurgency/counter-insurgency operations from other international conflicts as a means of contextualising our arguments. As such, the analysis will not substantively engage in larger issues of fatalities or patterns of violence suffered by either intended or unintended civilian or other government casualties (especially since clear designations are particularly difficult to definitively ascribe in Nigeria). Here we analyse the role of Nigeria's security forces as the primary proponents of state-sanctioned violence, to examine its attempts to (re)assert control over the state. How the Nigerian security forces respond to challenges to their central authority, both from internal non-state actors and other globalising influences, as well as how they exercise their desired monopoly over the practice of violence, represent the primary factors of analysis. As such, the central hypothesis is that the Nigerian security forces' ability or inability to exercise the required discretion in their use of violence determines the probability of successfully creating an atmosphere from which security and stability can emerge. If one accepts that a state of insecurity creates the opportunity for direct challenges to state legitimacy to arise and that overly repressive security tactics exacerbate the problem, then there is a need to determine whether the actions of the Nigerian state are resolving internal security issues or creating a growing sense of insecurity.

What this chapter argues is that the JTF response to Boko Haram and Ansaru has provided a platform from which these groups became successful in framing and re-framing longstanding local grievances in an organisationally advantageous way. This becomes evident in the fact that Boko Haram has been able to expand its support outside its original home base in the North-East. Further, we propose that this societal dynamic (namely the propensity to perceived grievances in the North-East) has been intensified by JTF operations in recent years, even though there has been no single linear trend to the changes over time. The chapter examines the back-and-forth battle between Boko Haram and the JTF, as well as its consequences.

In order to analyse the factors associated with security or insecurity, one needs to first establish reasonably reliable datasets from which to draw figures for comparison. In addition, one needs comparable historical case studies which provide a baseline for what can be considered effective or ineffective uses of state-sanctioned violence in response to direct challenges to authority. Moreover, reliable datasets provide the totals from which to identify broader trends and develop determinations for red-line points at which the rates of state-sanctioned violence begin to have adverse effects. In the case of Nigeria, data constitutes both the greatest requirement and the greatest impediment to empirical research, owing to poor data collection and management practices at all levels of government. As such, non-traditional methods of data selection and collection play significant roles in study and analysis. This type of research encountered two primary and significant obstacles. First, acquiring enough online media sources to reconstruct nearly a decade's worth of events with a reasonable amount of reliability proved extremely difficult and labour-intensive. Second, the politically charged atmosphere surrounding Boko Haram-related events made discerning between fact and propaganda immensely difficult and nearly impossible.

Using data collected from Nigerian online media sources, as well as from globally recognised news agencies such as the BBC, Reuters, AP, and AFP, we examine the details of events, fatalities, and evolutions within the militant insurgency in Nigeria to identify trends. For the Nigerian media sources we relied on all major reputable outlets but focused more on northern and central Nigerian-based media sources like *Leadership*, *Blueprint*, *Daily Trust*, and smaller outlets like the *Desert Herald* for linguistic and cultural reasons. Major southern-based sources like *Punch* and *Vanguard* were also used, but due to the heavily politicised nature of Boko Haram reporting, especially in terms of North–South divisions, this was an issue for which we attempted to account. Alternatively, *ThisDay* newspaper, which typically has the best access to the military elite, is a good example of a media outlet intimately tied, almost too much so, into the political and military elite, and therefore their reporting on certain events must be understood through that prism. Additionally, certain details, whether entirely accurate or not, once printed in one media outlet quickly become reproduced in others, creating a echo chamber effect that is easily mistaken for confirmation. For this reason, we chose to omit sources like *Osun Defender* and other such outlets which reproduce news instead of creating original content.

While this system is not the ideal source of empirical data, it is the most readily available in a country with noted deficiencies in transparency of reporting and record keeping. As such, best-faith efforts to cross-verify all reported data to ensure a reasonable level of consistency and accuracy have been made. Based on fatality totals reported by the JTF, we analyse the efficacy of JTF operations based on the numbers of suspected insurgents killed and how those killings affected Boko Haram's operations and organisational trajectory. The chapter further draws upon accounts and reported fatalities in other conflicts, as a means to determine the role security forces played in both the evolution of insurgencies and the creation of environments within which insurgencies continue to thrive. The total fatalities additionally allow us to further examine the overall transparency of JTF operations and scrutinize the attribution of insurgent status to victims of JTF operations.

This analysis will focus exclusively on the interplay between the security forces and the insurgents. The reason for this is the inherent difficulty in accurately assessing ultimate responsibility for fatalities in situations where victims are killed in an exchange of crossfire. Furthermore, we will rely only on estimates of "militant" fatalities collected by the authors, as part of an ongoing wider research study into conflict in West Africa. First, while there have been various reports on the alleged numbers of corpses stacked outside police facilities during the violent crackdowns in north-eastern Nigeria, there is no definitive evidence that the bodies were all militants. Despite this, some agencies have listed militant fatalities as the sum of corpses reportedly counted outside these police stations. Such numbers, while not impossible, are nonetheless largely improbable in sheer scale, based on comparative data we have from other such incidents both in Nigeria and around the world on numbers of "active militant" fatalities in combat over a similar period of time. Second, ascertaining which corpses were "actively" engaged in armed militancy is virtually impossible in a scenario where corpses are almost certainly not divided accurately into combatants and non-combatants. As such, while our estimates on militant and security force fatalities are lower than those released by the Nigerian government (Human Rights Watch 2010), we feel that they are reliable estimates for actual militant fatalities.

Beginning with the 2003 clashes in Yobe State and moving forward into the current operations under the rubric of "Operation Restore Order", we analyse both the JTF claims of militant killings and the reported loss of JTF members. In establishing solid estimates and comparing the data, we can scrutinise the figures for alleged Boko Haram members and reported JTF casualties and determine patterns of lethality associated with both insurgent operations and Nigerian state responses. The sum of alleged militant killings provides the basis for comparison with other such insurgencies in other parts of the world. Analysis of both Boko Haram and JTF fatalities, independent of the civilian casualties, will provide the opportunity to examine the internal dynamics of the struggle between Boko Haram and the JTF. This analysis will provide a level perspective and scale to the insurgency and present the data from multiple perspectives.

The chapter develops an understanding of where the JTF are in their attempts to dismantle Boko Haram and address the overall security situation that has arisen from the violence. Key analyses will focus on issues of proportionally appropriate violence, addressing underlying security factors, and decreasing federal legitimacy amongst affected populations. By determining the status of these factors one will be better able to ascertain how effective the JTF operations have been thus far and potentially determine where the operations have succeeded and failed to achieve their overall goals. Through this analysis we hope to highlight how and why the Boko Haram movement has both gained and lost support and legitimacy in the North-East, from its inception to its current manifestation. Finally, we develop a critical assessment of how the JTF has thus far engaged the threat to the Nigerian state.

INSURGENTS OR TERRORISTS?

Given the dramatic contextual shifts following the September 2001 attacks on the US, as well as subsequent terrorist attacks in Spain (2004) and the UK (2007), much non-state violent activity has come to be viewed through the securitised lens of the "war on terror". Groups and individuals that would once have been seen as guerrillas, insurgents, or revolutionaries have come to be defined as "terrorist" (Smith 2008). Whilst there are a number of overlaps between the definitions, it is important to highlight some of the differences as well as move away from crude labelling of groups as merely terrorist, a labelling that has often served a strategic function to increase counter-terrorism aid to certain governments from Washington (Smith 2008; Colombant 2012).

During the last few decades, religious and ethnic activists have been by far the most frequent non-governmental strategists of terror. Often they have called for autonomy; at times they have sought control of existing governments; but increasingly, they have struck directly at their religious and ethnic rivals (Tilly 2004: 10). But, just because a group utilises terrorist strategies as part of its repertoire of actions, does that make it a terrorist organisation? Charles Tilly, in his article *Terror, Terrorism, Terrorists*, asserts that "terror is a [political] strategy, not a creed" and thus represents "asymmetrical deployment of threats and violence against enemies using means that fall outside the forms of political struggle routinely operating within some current regime" (*ibid.* 11). For Tilly, terrorist strategies have a crude logic of their own, sending "signals that the target is vulnerable, that the perpetrators exist, and that the perpetrators have the capacity to strike again". These signals are often directed at three different audiences: "the targets themselves, potential allies of the perpetrators, and third parties that might cooperate with one or the other" (*ibid.* 9). For Tilly, terrorist violence is not an end in itself but rather is perpetrated in support of different demands: recognition, redress, autonomy, or transfers of power. Hence, for Tilly, terror is a strategy aimed at altering or inhibiting the target's disapproved of behaviour, fortifying the perpetrators' standing with potential allies, and moving third parties toward greater cooperation with the perpetrators' organisation and announced program (*ibid.*). This is certainly part of Boko Haram's wider repertoire of actions.

It is clear that Boko Haram utilises terrorist strategies as part of its repertoire of actions—however, to define it as simply a terrorist organisation is to fall short of an adequate analysis of the group's wider activities. This chapter argues instead that Boko Haram should be analysed within the wider lens of insurgencies and counter-insurgencies. For R. Scott Moore, insurgencies seek fundamental change

> [to] the existing political or social order through the use of sustained violence and political disruption. It is a long-term form of warfare in which military actions are carried out by guerrilla cells and terrorists, often targeting civilians and infrastructure. (Moore n.d.)

Importantly, Moore argues that guerrilla attacks and terrorism comprise only one element of insurgencies, and sometimes not the primary one. The argument is that more important than the violence of insurgency are:

> [its] political, economic, and social components. These are at the heart of the conflict, both its causes and its effects. Instead of defeating armies, insurgents slowly chip away at the authority and legitimacy of the ruling government … Thus subversion, social disruption, and political action become more important than violence, however spectacular or horrendous. (*ibid.*)

Viewing Boko Haram as an insurgency movement allows us, therefore, to not only consider the use of strategies of terror by the group, but also wider tactics that further help to explain the response elicited from the Nigerian state as well as the ensuing cycle of violence.

An insurgency requires two fundamental elements to ensure its long-term viability as a functioning organisation within a particular operating environment: support and fear. Support is required in the sense that an insurgent organisation requires a relatively consistent recruitment base and a reliable safe haven from which to plan and carry out operations. Support does not require majority portions of a population to be actively engaged, but enough to ensure that counter measures against the organisation remain relatively difficult. Alternatively, insurgent organisations can operate from bordering countries, but increased travel distances and required border crossings substantially add to the operational risks associated with any action. As such, the support of a local population is a vital requirement for the survival of an insurgent movement. It is for this reason that maintaining its base of operations in and around Maiduguri is essential to Boko Haram's long-term viability.

THE CYCLE OF ESCALATING VIOLENCE

Since the 2003 clashes between followers of firebrand leaders Mohammed Ali and Mohammed Yusuf—founders of the extremist albeit still abstruse sect—and Nigeria's security forces, there has been a non-stop cycle of brutal repression and violent revenge. The cost in human lives has been estimated at between one and three thousand victims, but accounts and specific details vary widely from source to source (Campbell 2011; Aghedo & Osumah 2012; Walker 2012; Murdock 2013; Chouin, Reinert & Apard: this volume). It should be noted that even if the high-end estimate of fatalities directly or indirectly attributed to the Boko Haram insurgency were accepted at face value, they would still represent a small percentage of the overall violent deaths that have occurred in Nigeria over that same period of time (Ajaegbu 2012; Ayuk et al. 2012). According to UNODC data, Nigeria had 18,422 intentional homicides in 2008, the year after the violently contested elections (UNODC 2013). Based on those numbers remaining relatively constant, Boko Haram would constitute approximately 5 percent of all violent deaths in Nigeria since their peak in fatalities in 2009. The question of who fired the first shot or what act precipitated a given response in the now nearly decade-long struggle is less important than the recurring pattern of violence and retaliation that has engulfed the northern region of Nigeria. This is especially true insofar as it pertains to examining the efficacy of the efforts to curb violence in northeastern Nigeria. A largely underreported and underexamined element of the crisis in the North is the number of fatalities associated with the state response to the insecurity associated with the emergence of Boko Haram.

Since the earliest clashes with Mohammed Ali, one of the original leaders along with Mohammed Yusuf, and his followers in Yobe State, there has been a cycle of retaliation and retribution that has exacerbated an already fraught situation. The initial settlement established by Yusuf's followers, dubbed "Afghanistan", appeared to be a largely non-violent albeit simultaneously socially antagonistic move, meant to mirror the actions of Islam's Prophet Mohammed during his *hijrah* (migration) from Mecca to Medina in 622 AD as a means of fleeing threats and persecution (Masud 1989). This action, as explained by other analysts, confirms the scripturally literalist inclination of Yusuf and his followers, a characteristic that can lend itself to creating deep social divisions with all other forms of religious and political interpretations of what constitutes a morally acceptable society (Onuoha 2012; Tanchum 2012: 77). According to available reporting, while the movement was not opposed to violence in defence of its social agenda, the initial clashes appeared to be localised communal violence, an occurrence that is widespread across Nigeria. This violence was accompanied by increasingly anti-government rhetoric as well as exclusionary practices on the part of the *Yusufiyya* followers, such as encouraging followers to tear up higher education degrees and establishing communal police and judicial systems to openly challenge existing state institutions (Onuoha 2012). Nevertheless, the state response between 2003 and 2004 to these initial occurrences of violence—which according to reports ultimately claimed the lives of a significant number of sect members—in comparison with similar forms of criminal deviance and insurrection elsewhere in Nigeria appeared to be quite disproportionate (Cook 2011; Onuoha 2012; Walker 2012).

The scale of the response has likely been influenced by the direct challenge to the legitimacy of the Nigerian federal government's right to rule over northern Muslims, especially Yusuf's followers. The military response, which was delayed following the initial small-scale clashes with police forces (Cook 2011), was possibly unavoidable in the long term given Yusuf's growing number of followers and staunch opposition to central government authority. However, the scale of this response can and should be scrutinized and further debated. The need for proportionality in effectively countering internal instability and uprooting localised insurgencies is a central element of widely accepted counter-insurgency doctrine (Moore n.d.). The ability of the Nigerian federal government to find the necessary balance in its early response to Yusuf and subsequent attempts to deal with a more violently inclined movement can and should be called into question.

In 2003, when followers of Yusuf assaulted locals near Kanama who challenged their rights to use fishing waters in lands not owned by the sect, it raised concerns with local authorities and eventually led to clashes with local police (Walker 2012). Police were then, and still are, largely unable to effectively deal with such situations across Nigeria at a local level, owing to a lack of investment, training, and capacity, which continues to plague them to this day (Okunola 2013); therefore, their failure to address the problems in Kanama village should have come as no surprise. The destruction of two local police stations and the looting of police armouries provided Yusuf's followers with improved weaponry and increased the urgency of the Nigerian security apparatus (Cook 2011; Onuoha 2012). Moreover, it provided the first in an increasing number of public humiliations for local security officials at the hands of determined militants and represented a sign of the escalating violence that would come. However, the event was not without precedent in Nigeria, where there is little regard for law enforcement officers, and numerous armed militias have attacked such institutions (Ikelegbe 2005; Alemika & Chukwuma 2012). In fact, police stations and police have routinely been assaulted throughout Nigeria by a number of different groups for a variety of reasons (Marenin 1987; Ikelegbe 2005; Udo 2013).

The one concerning and uniquely distinguishing factor about Yusuf and his followers, nevertheless, was the content of their vocal contempt and disregard for the legitimacy of the Nigerian state, a contempt which in some regards exceeded that of more financially, ethnically, or purely grievance-driven movements. This more overtly religious element, especially the social exclusion and public withdrawal aspects, possibly increased the stakes of the situation in the minds of the security officials tasked with resolving the problems in Yobe State (Adesoji 2011; Marchal 2012). While criminal organisations typically have little, if any, respect or regard for the central authority of rule of law, such inclinations do not necessarily constitute the primary motivators of membership or collective action and do not always supersede the desire for monetary gain or sense of increased security (Salaam 2011; Sharkey *et al.* 2011).

Such complexities in motivation and intent are likely also to be as present in the membership composition of outwardly religious groups like Boko Haram as they are in other criminal organisations. This is important because it was the overall criminal violence that initially prompted the Nigerian authorities to establish Operation Flush units, among other such operations, throughout the country to deal with near endemic crime rates (Joab-Peterside 2007). It was units established and intended for anti-crime operations, not properly trained or skilled in dealing with militant social movements, that first engaged Yusuf and his followers; and it was these units which, in combination with Yusuf, helped to initiate the cycle of violence and retribution that has ensnared the North-East.

The clashes in and around Kanama village in Yobe State played a significant role in the genesis from which the "Nigerian Taliban" movement began its gradual progression to increasingly more violent operational modes (Onuoha 2012; Walker 2012). The clash, as previously stated, was possibly inevitable since the movement had by this time already taken a position of absolute disregard for the legitimacy of the Nigerian state and afforded no respect or regard to security and law enforcement elements (Onuoha 2012; Walker 2012). According to various estimates, approximately seventy sect members were killed in the raids following the police station attacks (Cook 2011; Walker 2012). This number of fatalities, which by most accounts amounted to the majority of the sect members in Kanama, in addition to the arrests of others, almost decimated the nascent movement. The killings represented the first in a series of arguably disproportionate state responses.

The incident likely provided Yusuf with clearly visible current actions to substantiate his previous claims against the Nigerian state and probably aided in the recruitment of further disaffected youths to restore and bolster the movement's active membership. Eventually, the movement regrouped and was able to pose an even greater threat to the Nigerian state. At this time, Yusuf's movement had, according to some accounts, more than doubled (Cook 2011; Onuoha 2012; Walker 2012). Again, as was the case in Yobe State, it was a potentially avoidable violent incident between the JTF and Yusuf's followers which incited the deadly 2009 uprising across several Nigerian states. While details of the encounter vary depending on sources, what is clear is that sect members participating in a funeral procession had an altercation with the JTF in Maiduguri, which eventually led to several unarmed sect members being shot and dozens of others arrested (Cook 2011; Walker 2012). Yusuf wasted no time in capitalising upon this perceived assault on 'the faithful' by the 'illegitimate' Nigerian state, fomenting anger and a desire for revenge among his followers (Walker 2012). The ensuing uprising resulted in several hundred fatalities, of which approximately 200 were alleged to have been sect members, according to local media reports on JTF statements. In addition, this led to the widely condemned extrajudicial killings not only of Mohammed Yusuf but of dozens of other individuals in police custody, including prominent sect member Alhaji Buji Foi (Cook 2011; Onuoha 2012; Walker 2012).

Following the uprising and violent crackdown, the group once again dispersed, into remote areas of Nigeria and into neighbouring countries, until they were able to reorganise and again recruit (Onuoha 2012). This encounter ushered in a new evolution of the movement, one that embraced the far more violent tendencies of its new leader, Abubakar Shekau (Cook 2011; Onuoha 2012; Rodgers 2012). Following the 2009 crackdown, the group built on the charismatic anti-establishment preaching of Yusuf and was transformed into a full-blown insurgency, which has trapped the North in a seemingly never-ending cycle of violence and retaliation. The group not only changed in its willingness to initiate and instigate violence, but it began to adopt tactics and methods more akin to global terrorist organisations. This evolution dramatically altered the dynamic of the battle between the sect and the Nigerian security forces.

In the time between the 2009 crackdown and the group's re-emergence, according to local media reporting, Boko Haram members engaged in a series of targeted assassinations on individuals directly related to the crackdown or those suspected of having provided information or support to the crackdown. This series of violent attacks, largely carried out in areas considered to be sect strongholds, would later pale in comparison with the hit-and-run, mass-casualty attacks that became commonplace across northern Nigeria and into the Federal Capital Territory. In 2011, the group once again resurfaced, this time with Nigeria's first suicide attack—a type of action previously thought to be cultural anathema for Nigerians (Lee 2010; Oghre 2012)—on Police Headquarters in Abuja, and it was followed by a more daring suicide attack on the UN facility in Abuja (Onuoha 2012). The tactics employed by the security services, tactics that had previously worked in largely quelling the 1980s' Mahdi insurgency led by Mohammed Marwam known as the Maitatsine uprising (Danjibo 2010; Adesoji 2011), had served only to further spread the violence and seemingly stiffen the resolve of sect members.

This evolution represented the second time in which attempts by security forces to destroy Boko Haram had negligible or adverse effects. Shekau's ascension to power and the subsequent rapid escalation of persistent and sustained violence were largely unexpected in Nigeria (Cook 2011; Onuoha 2012). The failure of the Nigerian security and intelligence services to adequately understand and properly contextualise the problem Yusuf's movement presented, coupled with the failure to determine the best options for dealing with the security implications while ensuring the security and welfare of the citizens, are in part responsible for the course of events that followed (Marchal 2012; Kogbara 2013). Moreover, the widespread human rights abuses and indiscriminate crackdowns in the North, particularly in Borno and Yobe, further alienated an already sceptical north-eastern population and served to further complicate any attempts to deal with the problems posed by Boko Haram (Onuoha 2012; Nossiter 2013). This was made clear in a recent Human Rights Watch report, which claimed that "JTF abuses have created growing resentment in communities, making community members more unlikely to provide information that could help curtail Boko Haram" and that "abuses by the JTF have created more distance between the people and the government" (Human Rights Watch 2012: 59). This sentiment was echoed in the frustrations, expressed by the JTF, regarding the perceived lack of public support in Borno State for Operation Restore Order, designed to 'protect the people' (Idris 2013; Ugah 2013).

The latest security force attempt to once and for all dismantle Boko Haram has led to the third violent crackdown, primarily focusing on Borno and Yobe states. This crackdown led to the alleged killing of an even greater number of Boko Haram members but has yet to deal the decisive final blow to the organisation (Al Jazeera 2013; Nossiter 2013; Umar & Gambrell 2013). The JTF operations have included imposing rigid curfews, mass arrests, door-to-door searches, destruction of homes, and prolonged detentions and/or interrogations of anyone suspected of being associated with Boko Haram. These actions have contributed to the low levels of public support for the security forces and have led to public protests in Maiduguri as well as condemnation by opposition politicians (Olugbode 2013). Moreover, the crackdowns, while not only failing to deal with the insurgency, have potentially spurred yet another evolution in the group. This latest evolution presents an even more complex and potentially more dangerous problem than previously seen. This evolution has split the organisation into multiple loosely interconnected groups that now complicate analysis and accurate attribution of events (Zenn 2013). Furthermore, the various groups have adopted new tactics, in the form of kidnappings for ransom or political statement, which have increased the targets to include expatriate workers, foreign corporations, and regional business infrastructures (*Peoples Daily* 2013).

COUNTERINSURGENCY AND THE BODY COUNT

The raw data, while not optimal in terms of providing absolute certainty, tells a significant story in itself. In the case of the clashes between the JTF and Boko Haram, certain patterns emerge which provide a unique perspective. For example, the ratio of reported militants killed versus militants arrested in a given year shows a potentially significant indication of the willingness of JTF forces to resort to deadly force during counter-insurgency operations. The rate at which counter-insurgency operations lead to deaths rather than detentions is an important variable of analysis. This perspective is especially revealing when contrasted with numbers from similar historical case studies of military and paramilitary efforts to counter domestic militant groups. According to our compiled statistics, the approximate number of Boko Haram fatalities from 2007 to 2013, largely reported by the JTF, stands at approximately 620, which is admittedly at the low end of overall estimates for reasons of methodology. During the same period, according to our data, approximately 777 suspected Boko Haram members were arrested. Some commentators suggest approximately 1,000 Boko Haram followers were killed in the 2009 riots alone (Cook 2011; Human Rights Watch 2012; Zenn 2013), but we have thus far been unable to find reputable or reasonably verifiable reporting to substantiate such claims. Moreover, such numbers, while not impossible, are rather high; for example, the Pakistan military claimed to have killed similar numbers of militants during a 2008 offensive in the Federally Administered Tribal Areas, but those occurred over the course of a month-long sustained offensive (AFP 2008). Therefore, reports suggesting that those numbers were equalled over the course of an uprising that lasted less than a week in north-eastern Nigeria are dubious.

While reporting agencies have different approaches to calculating total fatalities and casualties during the ongoing Boko Haram conflict, the one consistent factor is the reliance to varying degrees on media reporting. As such, the assumption is that certain portions of the data should be somewhat stable across the board, based on seemingly consistent sourcing. There are, however, instances of significant disparity in reporting within the data that emerged from the 2009 militant uprising across the several northern states and the ensuing state of emergency, a fact that is likely the primary cause of discrepancies in fatality totals between various entities tracking such data. In particular, reports that emerged regarding the security forces' siege of Maiduguri from 27 to 29 July 2009 are especially problematic because the flow of information from the city was largely stifled. The greatest disparity in fatality numbers emerges in this reporting, with estimates upwards of 1,000 fatalities, including from 200 to 700 militants killed (Al Jazeera 2009; Mukairu & Muhammad 2009; *Telegraph* 2009). The actual events in Maiduguri are virtually impossible to accurately assess, given the media blackout and rigid civilian curfew in which non-combatants were forced to remain indoors for the majority of the fighting.

For the purposes of this analysis, we clarify our position on two accounts. First, given the lack of reliable census data in Nigeria to provide context to reports, we accept that the probable range of total fatalities, according to Nigerian media reports, in the 2009 uprising is somewhere between 600 and upwards of 1,000 (BBC 2009; *The Nation* 2009). We also accept that the security services are likely responsible for a significant share of that total as well as the militants. However, since we do not have reliable comparative data on prior Nigerian military raids and equally heavy-handed military crackdowns on organised populist insurgencies—for example, the Maitatsine riots—we are less inclined to accept that 600 to 1,000 "militants" were killed. This position is based on our particular data collection methodology to assess the most likely totals of militant and security force fatalities, which form the basis for analysis within this piece. We fully acknowledge that our data, as with all other datasets, is open to further discussion and debate.

Accurately assessing fatalities directly attributable to low-intensity conflicts, such as that of Boko Haram, while a worthwhile and necessary endeavour, is an imperfect science and immensely difficult even with good pre-existing population data, which Nigeria does not have; this therefore leaves the range between fatality estimates in a given conflict somewhere between the thousands and hundreds of thousands (Murray *et al.* 2002). As such, variations in estimates from reporting agency to reporting agency are to be expected, given the various sources of collection. The disparity in reported statistics can be attributed to a number of variables, and few estimates can be categorically dismissed as entirely inaccurate. Nevertheless, numbers alone say less than the patterns that emerge regarding the actions and reactions of both the JTF and

Boko Haram in their ongoing struggle. It is here that we wish to draw the focus of our analysis within this particular dataset.

For example, irrespective of the body count or damage inflicted on the militant movement, the typical response from the group to any violent crackdowns has been a reactionary wave of violent revenge attacks, thus continuing a seemingly endless cycle of violence that largely affects surrounding civilian populations. According to the collected data, the timing of such retaliatory attacks by Boko Haram can range from days to even a year, but they occur without fail. This calls into question whether the tactics employed by the security forces are dealing with the root problems causing the insurgency and instability in the north-eastern regions of Nigeria. Part of this question directly relates to the impact of civilian casualties attributable to security forces in a war among the people—as opposed to a strictly military combatant conflict—but we will address this issue only briefly. As already stated, this analysis will focus on the numbers of militant and security force fatalities and the patterns of militants killed or detained during the ongoing conflict, to contextualise the conflict.

The current JTF strategy neither embraces all-out brutal repression nor does it effectively implement a more holistic counter-insurgency model. Instead, the operational strategies are largely reactionary, and tactics like the routine demolition of properties of individuals even accused or suspected of tacitly supporting Boko Haram militants have placed the civilian population in a virtual no-win situation between the violence and destruction of both the militant and the security forces. In addition to alienated residents, the operating environment within which the security forces are attempting to carry out their counter-insurgency operations is made more complex by failures in other national institutions. Weak judicial and penal systems in the country, which also suffer from varying degrees of corruption, have made it so that there is only limited faith that insurgents will be properly prosecuted or effectively detained. Moreover, the series of daring prison breaks in northern prisons, along with the problems of poor funding and inadequate staffing and equipment, have created a situation where security officials and their families can become targets for reprisal, a reality that has played out repeatedly in the North.

In examining the fluctuating scale of violence in the course of the ongoing counter-insurgency or counter-terrorism operations (depending upon the particular agenda and perspective), the trends that emerge in the relationship between Boko Haram and the security forces tell a story in themselves. This story correlates directly with the relationship between the citizens in Nigeria and the state institutions tasked with providing their "safety and well-being" as outlined in the Nigerian Constitution. For comparison, the total numbers of security forces, militants, and civilians killed in other conflicts are shown in the table below.

	Militants Killed	Security Forces Killed	Ratio
IRA "Troubles" (35+ years)	350*	1,100*	1:3
FARC (50+ years)	13,197**	4,286**	4:1
2nd Chechen War (10 years)	14,113***	7,425***	2:1
Boko Haram (6 years)	620^	127^	5:1

*IRA totals (O'Brien 1999; Thorton et al. 2004; CAIN 2013); **FARC [Revolutionary Armed Forces of Colombia] totals (Cadavid n.d.; Human Rights Watch 2011); ***Chechen totals (Lee n.d.; Dunnigan 2002; Sapozhnikov 2003; REFRL 2005); Boko Haram totals based on media reporting from January 2007 through February 2013.

Table 8.1 Comparison of Militants and security forces killed in selected conflicts

This data highlights that the Nigerian security forces are by no means the most brutal in terms of total alleged counter-insurgent fatalities; however, the numbers are not particularly positive either, especially in terms of the ratio of militant to security force deaths, in which Nigeria ranks highest. It must be stated that security sector abuses in Nigeria are not isolated to counter-insurgency operations against Boko Haram and are responsible for fatalities on an almost daily basis throughout the country (Pérouse de Montclos 2011); however, such abuses are also common in the Caucasus and in Colombia, which further highlights this particular comparative data with Nigeria as it pertains to counter-insurgency operations. These problems occur when trying to resolve a largely law enforcement issue with primarily traditional military forces, a lesson learned by all the other case studies. There is no clear figure to distinguish the point at which fatalities caused by the security forces contribute to a growing sense of insecurity; however, given the fact that Boko Haram has continued and, at times, expanded operations, that point is probably not far off.

In addition, if one takes into account the rates at which militants are either killed or detained/arrested in a given year in Nigeria from the 2009 uprising to date, the data shows some interesting trends:

	BH Militants Killed	Security Forces Killed	BH Ratio
2013	99	4	82
2012	210	18	197
2011	20	47	119
2010	0	5	13
2009	251	21	373

*Totals based on media reporting from January 2009 through February 2013

Table 8.2 Comparison of arrests with kills

The arrest/kill data shows that the ratio between arrests and killings begins to shift increasingly towards killing over the last 18 months, especially in the last year of the conflict. This suggests that there is a possible growing preference amongst Nigerian security forces to kill. If the current ratio from the first months of 2013 remains consistent through the remainder of the year, it will represent a dramatic increase in already repressive tactics. In the end, such a shift will likely further distance the 'protectors' from the 'victims', thereby undermining security operations and perpetuating negative perceptions of the security forces by the public. This does not have to be the case. The security forces have, in other violent clashes, conducted themselves in a manner that has resolved the crisis without resorting to heavy-handed tactics (Ezeobi 2013).

CONCLUSION

Based on the regenerative nature of Boko Haram and the splintering of the violent movement into competing groups, there is nothing to suggest that the Nigerian security forces are in a position to kill their way to stability in the North. Even the historically heavy-handed Russian counter-insurgency units operating in the Caucasus region have adopted more even-handed tactics, which have led to increased security for local residents (Flintoff 2013). Such realisations have come to most successful counter-insurgency operations and are core elements of sound strategy to achieve sustained security (Moore n.d.). As such, to return to a reasonable sense of security, a serious shift away from the current reactionary strategies and the heavy-handed tactics currently employed by the Nigerian security forces is likely to be the only viable option. The fact that operating environments have improved and public support, even in counter-Boko Haram operations, has been greater in areas where the security forces have not so strictly adhered to such heavy-handedness is evidence to that end (Garba 2012).

In the relatively short history of security force operations against Boko Haram, there have been far too many incidents of inexcusable abuses of state power, from extrajudicial killings to indiscriminate retaliatory responses. Such events have continued to contribute to the ever-growing sense of insecurity amongst the people. The peaks and troughs in overall violence within the Nigerian security response speak to the reactionary nature of the strategy. In the war currently being waged amongst the people, the reactionary strategy being employed by the Nigerian security forces must be re-evaluated and altered to better address both the causes and results of the ongoing violence. With a more cohesive operational focus and tempo, knee-jerk retributions of uncontrolled violence can be better controlled. Until such time, the majority of the insecurity burden will continue to be shouldered by the public. The public are in no position to bear such a burden, and in such an environment there will almost certainly be no substantive security gains.

Note

1. See Section 14 (b) of the 1999 Nigerian Constitution.

References

Adesoji, A.O. (2011). "Between Maitatsine and Boko Haram: Islamic Fundamentalism and the Response of the Nigerian State", *Africa Today* 57(4): 99-119.

AFP (2008), "Pakistan says 1,000 militants killed near Afghan border", Associated Free Press, 26 September. http://afp.google.com/article/ALeqM5iGTgxqoTldD4lBtlbyfU5MSNowjg [Accessed 28 May 2013].

Aghedo, I. & O. Osumah (2012), "The Boko Haram Uprising: how should Nigeria respond?", *Third World Quarterly* 33(5): 853-869.

Ajaegbu, O. (2012), "Rising Youth Unemployment and Violent Crime in Nigeria", *American Journal of Social Issues and Humanities* 2(5): 315-321. http://

indianforester.co.in/index.php/ajsih/article/view/28970/25093 [Accessed 16 April 2013].

Al Jazeera (2009), "Nigeria hunts Islamist fighters", Al Jazeera, 29 July. www.aljazeera.com/news/africa/2009/07/20097294511346828.html [Accessed on 15 May 2013].

——— (2013), "Conflicting deaths tolls in Nigeria violence", Al Jazeera, 1 May. www.aljazeera.com/news/africa/2013/5/201351141539508118.html [Accessed 1 May 2013].

Alemika, E. & I. Chukwuma (2012), *Criminal Victimization and Public Safety in Nigeria*. Lagos: Malthouse & CLEEN Foundation.

Ayuk, A.A., E.J. Owan, O.C. Ekok & G.E. Odinka (2012), "Curbing Multi-Dimensional Violence in Nigeria Society: Causes, Solutions and Methods of Solving this Trend", *Journal of Emerging Trends in Educational Research and Policy Studies* (JETERAPS) 3(5): 616-623 http://jeteraps.scholarlinkresearch.org/articles/Curbing%20Multi%20Dimensional%20Violence%20in%20Nigeria%20Society.pdf [Accessed 29 March 2013].

BBC (2009), "Nigerian police find sect women", BBC Africa Service, 2 August. Available at: news.bbc.co.uk.

Cadavid, E.S. (n.d.) "Historia de la Guerrilla en Colombia", Universidade Federal de Juiz de Fora. http://www.ecsbdefesa.com.br/defesa/fts/HGC.pdf [Accessed 29 April 2013].

CAIN (2013), Draft List of Deaths Related to the Conflict from 2002 to the present. Ulster University, Conflict Archive on the Internet. http://cain.ulst.ac.uk/issues/violence/deathsfrom2002draft.htm [Accessed 29 April 2013].

Campbell, J. (2011[electronic resource]), *Nigeria: Dancing on the Brink*. Lanham: Rowman & Littlefield Publishing Group, Inc., 2010.

Colombant, N. (2012), "Terror Label for Boko Haram Debated", Voice of America. http://www.voanews.com/content/terror-label-for-boko-haram-debated-139892403/159640.html [Accessed 12 March 2013].

Cook, D. (2011), "Boko Haram: A Prognosis", James A. Baker III Institute for Public Policy. http://bakerinstitute.org/publications/REL-pub-CookBokoHaram-121611.pdf [Accessed 25 March 2013].

Danjibo, N.D. (2010), "Islamic Fundamentalism and Sectarian Violence: The 'Maitatsine' and 'Boko Haram' Crises in Northern Nigeria", Published online by the University of Ibadan, 2010. http://www.ifra-nigeria.org/IMG/pdf/N-_D-_DANJIBO_-_Islamic_Fundamentalism_and_Sectarian_Violence_The_Maitatsine_and_Boko_Haram_Crises_in_Northern_Nigeria.pdf [Accessed 4 November 2012].

Dunnigan, J. (2002), "Reported Casualties in Chechnya", Strategy Page, 25 December. http://www.strategypage.com/qnd/russia/articles/20021225.aspx [Accessed 29 April 2013].

Ezeobi, C. (2013), "A Community at War with its Ruler", *ThisDay*, 29 April. http://www.thisdaylive.com/articles/A-Community-at-War-With-its-Ruler/146194/ [Accessed 29 April 2013].

Flintoff, C. (2013), "Investigating the Bombing Suspects... In Southern Russia", National Public Radio, 1 May. http://www.npr.org/2013/05/01/180108357/investigating-the-boston-bombing-in-southern-russia [Accessed 1 May 2013].

Garba, I. (2012), Nigerian forces raid suspected Boko Haram bomb factory", Christian Science Monitor, (24 April). http://www.csmonitor.com/World/Africa/2012/0424/Nigerian-forces-raid-suspected-Boko-Haram-bomb-factory [Accessed 12 May 2013].

Hobbes, T. (1988), *Leviathan*. London: Penguin.

Idris, H. (2013), "Nigeria: JTF—Borno People Condoning Boko Haram", *Daily Trust*, 2 January. http://allafrica.com/stories/201301020836.html [Accessed 8 May 2013].

Human Rights Watch (2010), "Country Summary: Nigeria", Human Rights Watch, January. http://www.hrw.org/sites/default/files/related_material/nigeria_0.pdf [Accessed 15 May 2013].

——— (2011), "Country Summary: Colombia", Human Rights Watch, January. http://www.hrw.org/sites/default/files/related_material/Colombia_English%201-27.pdf [Accessed 29 April 2013].

——— (2012), "Spiraling Violence: Boko Haram Attacks and Security Force Abuses in Nigeria". http://www.hrw.org/sites/default/files/reports/nigeria1012webwcover_0.pdf [Accessed 15 May 2013]

Ikelegbe, A. (2005), "State, Ethnic Militias, and Conflict in Nigeria", *Canadian Journal of African Studies / Revue Canadienne des Études Africaines* 39(3): 490-516.

Joab-Peterside, S. (2007), "On the Militarization of Nigeria's Niger Delta: The Genesis of Ethnic Militia in Rivers State". Economies of Violence: Niger Delta, Working Papers No. 21. http://oldweb.geog.berkeley.edu/ProjectsResources/ND%20Website/NigerDelta/WP/21-Joab-Peterside.pdf [Accessed 16 April 2013].

Kogbara, D. (2013), "Nigeria underestimated Boko Haram's brutal power", *The Guardian*, 28 February. http://www.guardian.co.uk/commentisfree/2013/feb/28/nigeria-underestimated-boko-haram [Accessed 27 March 2013].

Lee, K. (2010), "Suicide Bombing is Not Nigerian", Naija Digest, 8 January. http://9jadigest.blogspot.com/2010/01/suicide-bombing-is-not-nigerian.html [Accessed 25 April 2013].

Lee, R.A. (n.d.) "The Second Chechen War", Historyguy.com. http://www.historyguy.com/chechen_war_two.html#.UYMv9KJOSa8 [Accessed 29 April 2013].

Marenin, O. (1987), "The Anini Saga: Armed Robbery and the Reproduction of Ideology in Nigeria", *The Journal of Modern African Studies* 25(2): 259-281.

Marchal, R. (2012), "Boko Haram and the resilience of militant Islam in northern Nigeria", Norwegian Peacebuilding Resource Center, June. http://nis-foundation.org/files/2913/5221/8297/boko_haram_and_the_resilience_of_militant_islam_in_northern_nigeria.pdf [Accessed 28 April 2013].

Masud, M. (1989), "Being Muslim in a non-Muslim polity: three alternate models", *Journal of the Institute of Muslim Minority Affairs* 10(1): 118-128.

Moore, R.S. (n.d.), "The Basics of Counterinsurgency", *Small Wars Journal* [online]. http://smallwarsjournal.com/documents/moorecoinpaper.pdf [Accessed 6 March 2013].

Mukairu, L. & A. Muhammad (2009), "Another 43 Islamic fanatics killed in Yobe", News Nigeria, 29 July. http://newsnigeria.onlinenigeria.com/templates/?a=6559 [Accessed 15 May 2013].

Murdock, H. (2013), "Nigeria Violence Escalates", Voice of America. http://www.voanews.com/content/nigerian-violence-escalates/1648704.html [Accessed 29 March 2013].

Murray, C., G. King, A. Lopez, N. Tomijima & E. Krug (2002), "Armed conflict as a public health problem", *BMJ* 324: 346-9. http://gking.harvard.edu/files/armedph.pdf [Accessed 24 May 2013].

Nossiter, A. (2013), "More Than 180 Dead After Nigerian Military and Insurgents Clash in Village", *New York Times*, 22 April. http://www.nytimes.com/2013/04/23/world/africa/in-nigeria-clash-with-militants-kills-scores.html [Accessed 29 April 2013].

——— (2013), "Massacre in Nigeria Spurs Outcry Over Military Tactics", *New York Times*, 29 April. http://www.nytimes.com/2013/04/30/world/africa/outcry-over-military-tactics-after-massacre-in-nigeria.html?pagewanted=all&_r=0 [Accessed 29 April 2013].

Oghre, G. (2012), "Boko Haram 're hired external militants—Muoboghare", *Vanguard*, 13 August. http://www.vanguardngr.com/2012/08/boko-haram-re-hired-external-militants-muoboghare/ [Accessed 24 April 2013].

Okunola, R.A. (2013), "The Gods are not to Blame: Youths, Growing Insecurity, and Crime Challenges in Rural Nigeria", University of Ibadan, Nineteenth Faculty Lecture, (28 February 2013).

Olugbode, M. (2013), "Women Protest Non-release of Husbands in Maiduguri", *ThisDay*, 8 February. http://www.thisdaylive.com/articles/women-protest-non-release-of-husbands-in-maiduguri/138859/ [Accessed 25 April 2013].

Onuoha, F.C. (2008), "US Africa Command (AFRICOM) and Nigeria's National Security", *Africa Insight* 38(1): 173-184.

―――― (2010), "The Islamist challenge: Nigeria's Boko Haram crisis explained", *African Security Review* 19(2): 54-67.

―――― (2012), "Boko Haram: Nigeria's Extremist Islamic Sect", Al Jazeera Centre for Studies. http://studies.aljazeera.net/ResourceGallery/media/Documents/2012/2/29/201229113341793734BOKO%20HARAM%20NIGERIAS%20EXTREMIST%20ISLAMIC%20SECT.pdf [Accessed 1 March 2013].

―――― (2012), "From Ahlulsunna war'jama'ah hijra to Jama'atu Ahlissunnah lidda'awati wal Jihad", *Africa Insight* 41(4): 159-175.

―――― (2012), "(Un)Willing to Die: Boko Haram and Suicide Terrorism in Nigeria", Al Jazeera Centre for Studies. http://studies.aljazeera.net/en/reports/2012/12/20121224914165953 37.htm [Accessed 10 January 2013].

Peoples Daily (2013), "Boko Haram to embark on kidnappings for ransom—JTF", *Peoples Daily* 10(56), 29 April. http://peoplesdailyng.com/boko-haram-to-embark-on-kidnappings-for-ransom-jtf/ [Accessed 29 April 2013].

Pérouse de Montclos, M. (2011), "Third Report on Violence in Nigeria 2006–2011", *Nigeria Watch*. http://www.nigeriawatch.org/media/html/NGA-Watch-Report11%281%29.pdf [Accessed 12 June 2013].

Press TV (2009), Red Cross finds 780 corpses in single Nigeria city. Press TV website, 3 August. Available at edition.presstv.ir.

REFRL (2005), "Russia: Chechen Officials Put War Death Toll at 160,000", Radio Free Europe Radio Liberty, 16 August. http://www.rferl.org/content/article/1060708.html [Accessed 29 April 2013].

Rodgers, P. (2012), "Nigeria: The Generic Context of the Boko Haram Violence", Oxford Research Group, Monthly Global Security Briefing, 30 April. http://reliefweb.int/sites/reliefweb.int/files/resources/AprEn12.pdf [Accessed 1 May 2013].

Salaam, A.O. (2011), "Motivations for Gang Membership in Lagos, Nigeria: Challenge and Resilience", *Journal of Adolescent Research* 26(6): 701-726.

Sapozhnikov, B. (2003), "Second Chechen Campaign Takes its Toll", *Gazeta*, 18 February. http://www.russialist.org/7067-8.php [Accessed 29 April 2013].

Sharkey, J.D., Z. Shekhtmeyster, L. Chavez-Lopez, E. Norris & L. Sass (2011), "The protective influence of gangs: Can schools compensate?", *Aggression and Violent Behavior* 16(1): 45-54. http://www.sciencedirect.com/science/article/pii/S1359178910000716.

Smith, H. (2008), "Defining Terrorism: It Shouldn't Be Confused With Terrorism", *American Diplomacy*, December. http://www.unc.edu/depts/diplomat/

item/2008/1012/comm/smith_defining.html [Accessed 2 March 2013].

Tanchbum, M. (2012), "Al-Qaida's West African Advance: Nigeria's Boko Haram, Mali's Touareg, and the Spread of Salafi Jihadism", *Israel Journal of Foreign Affairs* 6(2): 75-90.

Telegraph (2009), "Nigerian Army claims rout of Islamic rebels", *The Telegraph*, 30 July. http://www.telegraph.co.uk/news/worldnews/africaandindianocean/nigeria/5939065/Nigerian-Army-claims-rout-of-Islamic-rebels.html [Accessed 15 May 2013].

The Nation (2009), "Sect Leader Yusuf Killed", The Nation Newspaper Nigeria, 31 July. Available at thenationonline.ng.net/articles/12391/1/Sect-leader-Yusuf-dead/Page1/html.

Thorton, C., D. McKitrick, S. Kelters, D. McVea & B. Feeney (2004), *Lost Lives: The Stories of the Men, Women and Children Who Died as a Result of the Northern Ireland Troubles* (2nd rev. ed.). Edinburgh: Mainstream Publishing.

Tilly, C. (2004), "Terror, Terrorism, Terrorists," *Sociological Theory* 22: 5-13. Theories of Terrorism: A Symposium: 5-13.

Udo, B. (2013), "MEND claims it killed 15 police officers in Bayelsa boat attack", *Premium Times*, Nigeria, 7 April. http://premiumtimesng.com/news/128543-mend-claims-it-killed-15-police-officers-in-bayelsa-boat-attack.html [Accessed 29 April 2013].

Ugah, N. (2013), "Nigeria: JTF Kills Four Boko Haram Members, Recovers Weapons in Potiskum", *ThisDay*, 3 January. http://allafrica.com/stories/201301030280.html [Accessed 25 April 2013].

Umar, H. & J. Gambrell (2013), "Satellites, Witnesses Show Scope of Nigeria Attack", ABC News, 1 May. www.abcnews.go.com/International/wireStory/witnesses-describe-nigeria-assault-killed-187-19078297#.UYCAj6JOSa8 [Accessed 1 May 2013].

UNODC (2013), Intentional homicide, count and rate per 100,000 population (1995-2011). Available at unodc.org/documents/data-and-analysis/statistics/crime/Homicide_statistics2013.xls.

Walker, A. (2012), "What is Boko Haram?", United States Institute of Peace Special Report. http://reliefweb.int/sites/reliefweb.int/files/resources/SR308.pdf [Accessed 27 April 2013].

Zenn, J. (2013), "Cooperation or Competition: Boko Haram and Ansaru After the Mali Intervention", *CTC Sentinel* 6(13), Combating Terrorism Center at West Point, 27 March. http://www.ctc.usma.edu/posts/cooperation-or-competition-boko-haram-and-ansaru-after-the-mali-intervention [Accessed 1 May 2013].

9

BODY COUNT & RELIGION IN THE BOKO HARAM CRISIS

Evidence from the Nigeria
Watch Database

Gérard Chouin
College of William and Mary

Manuel Reinert and Elodie Apard
French Institute for Research in Africa (IFRA-Nigeria)

This chapter tackles the issue of victims and religion in the Boko Haram crisis through a quantitative, critical examination of the deaths it has resulted in among Christians and Muslims in the affected states of Nigeria. After a brief discussion of the sectarian movement's changing ideology towards Christians, 317 Boko Haram-related events, identified in the Nigeria Watch database from July 2009–December 2012 data, are analysed to provide the most reliable possible body count for the period. The study assesses the status—civilian, Boko Haram member, JTF member, etc.—and the religious affiliation of all reported individuals who died as a result of the conflict. As it proved impossible to determine the religion of more than 60 per cent of the fatalities (mostly civilians), available demographic data were used to provide estimates. Despite an obvious increase in deadly attacks against Christian civilians, the combined data suggest that approximately two civilian victims out of three were Muslims. This challenges the commonplace temptation to understand the crisis in terms of a religious confrontation between Muslims and Christians. It suggests that such a representation may be fed by an overreporting of Christian victims compared with Muslim victims, in both Nigerian newspapers and international reports.

INTRODUCTION

A small Islamic sect created in the early 2000s by Mohammed Yusuf with a few dozen followers in Borno and Yobe states has become, in less than ten years, a high-profile terrorist organisation known as *Boko Haram*, strong enough to challenge the Nigerian state and threaten the stability of bordering countries such as Niger, Chad, and Cameroon. The essence and goals of the radical group, as well as its methods, targets, and victims, have evolved over time and are not easily retraceable. In the Western narrative, the conflict is frequently presented as a religious war opposing Islamic extremists to Christian communities. Christian killings have indeed been widely reported, in both the Nigerian and international media, strengthening the idea that Christian communities are the primary victims of the crisis in terms of fatalities. In 2013, declarations by Nigerian President Goodluck Jonathan, however, stressed that Muslims are the most numerous victims of the ongoing struggle (*Daily Trust* 2013). The issue is undoubtedly sensitive as the Christian Association of Nigeria (CAN) immediately replied to the statement by accusing President Jonathan of "distorting facts", and recalling "the statistics" that "are there for everybody to see how Christians have been massacred by the terrorists" (*The Nation* 2013a). The debate is not meaningless; it gives the conflict a particular definition and chooses to analyse it exclusively in terms of religious confrontation. This perspective, which is undoubtedly an important characteristic of the current crisis, disregards a number of other factors. Nevertheless, even when tackling the issue of casualties in terms of religion, a major problem remains: statistics are not there. Indeed, data presented to support both President Jonathan's and CAN's affirmations are nonexistent at worst, and rather weak at best.

In this article, we use the Nigeria Watch database to build a statistical basis for a discussion on the religious affiliation of the fatalities in the conflict and the preferred targets of the radical group. The aim is to empirically examine the identity of the victims, through their religion (basically Islam and Christianity) and also their status (civilians, Boko Haram members, Nigerian security force members, other officials, etc.). The Nigeria Watch database provides material on violent deaths in Nigeria from 2006 onward, and our analysis covers the case of the Boko Haram crisis from July 2009 to December 2012. Religious affiliation as a category has been excluded from public censuses in Nigeria since 1962; but since this question is inherently linked to our study, we also tackle the issue of demographics and religion in the Nigerian states where Boko Haram has been active. Our results are used to better assess the reality of the ongoing violence and debunk some preconceived ideas.

First, we recall the ideological background of Boko Haram and attempt to provide an account of its public stance towards Christians. We then present the Nigeria Watch database, the nature of the data used, and the way it was extracted. Finally, we propose a step-by-step analysis of these data, leading to estimates of the numbers of Muslims and Christians who fell victim to the crisis during the period under consideration.

IDEOLOGICAL BACKGROUND AND ATTITUDE TOWARDS CHRISTIANS

Until the beginning of the 2000s, before becoming the spiritual leader of his own spiritual community, Mohammed Yusuf was a follower of Sheikh Ja'far Adam, a renowned and charismatic Islamic scholar in the Izala movement. The two men shared the same Salafi/Wahhabi religious ideal inspired by the Saudi model. The Izala doctrine, which appeared in Nigeria in the late-1970s, advocates for the establishment of an Islamic society that will correspond to the values and practices of the pious ancestors (*Salafs*) but has never prevented members from being active participants in the state system or attending public schools.[1] The movement is characterised by its active proselytism (*dawah*), and Yusuf, being an excellent preacher, subsequently became a significant Izala figure in Maiduguri (Brigaglia 2012a).

From 2003 onwards, Yusuf's ideology gradually moved away from the Izala ideal, radicalised, and developed into a discourse characterised by the systematic rejection of all secular aspects of Nigerian society ([Anon.] 2012).[2] He built his argumentation around the concept of *boko* (Higazi 2013), a Hausa word that brings together the notions of sham, fraud, deceit, and lack of authenticity, but also refers to Western education (Newman 2013). According to Yusuf, the federal state of Nigeria represents a *boko* model in which Muslims cannot participate. In his preaching, Yusuf used to repeat that *"Boko haram da aïki'n gomenati haram"*, which means that receiving a secular education, as well as working for the government, was forbidden for Muslims—hence the nickname *Boko Haram* given to the movement by outsiders.[3]

Such divergences led to an open conflict with Sheikh Ja'far and Yusuf's departure from the Izala movement. Secluded in Maiduguri, he was prevented from preaching in Izala mosques and was directly attacked in sermons given by his former mentor ([Anon.] 2012; Brigaglia 2012a). At about the same time, in 2002–2003, a group of presumed Yusuf students calling themselves *Al Sunna Wal Jamma* (Followers of the Prophet's Teaching) decided to create a distinct community near Kanama, a small town of Yobe State, in order to live outside of any secular framework. Members of this community were the first to engage in violent confrontations with state authorities. The process of Yusuf's ideological escalation is, in a way, consistent with the Izala philosophy, which was born out of the contestation of the traditional Muslim elite's authority. By refusing the supremacy of Tijanyyia scholars, the proponents of the Izala doctrine encouraged the acquisition of an individual religious knowledge that promotes a direct relation with God and facilitates a certain disconnection from Islamic clerics. Yusuf's dissidence also arose from a desire for emancipation from the control of Izala's scholars as he developed a radical discourse in his preaching for the rejection of the secular state. By stepping outside of the Izala doctrine conveyed by the great figures of the movement, Yusuf created his own school of thought. Likewise, members of the Kanama community wanted to literally break away from the federal secular state and consequently began a new experiment which was consistent with the message of Yusuf (Higazi 2013). The radicalisation process of the Kanama community may have encouraged Yusuf to further strengthen his own rhetoric.[4] It is worth noting that Yusuf's sect began committing violent acts against police stations and other symbols of the Nigerian state authority after the repression of the *Al Sunna Wal Jamma* in 2003, although such actions long remained sporadic.

A tipping point was reached in July 2009, after a week-long battle in north-eastern Nigeria between government forces (both police and army) and members of the sect. A series of attacks on police stations by Boko Haram members in Bauchi, Borno, and Yobe states—indicating that the group had prepared for an armed confrontation with the secular state (even in a rather amateurish way in several instances)—was followed by harsh military repression. The uprising resulted in hundreds of casualties and led to the extrajudicial assassination of the sect's leader.[5] The first deliberate attacks against

Christians were witnessed at this time (Ishaya 2013). Subsequently, after more than a year of restructuring, and seemingly under the subdued leadership of Yusuf's second-in-command, Abubakar Shekau, followers became true activists and diversified their actions in a more politically focused way, with improved weaponry, logistics, and organisation. Large-scale terrorist attacks began in December 2010, systematically targeting people—such as Christians—and institutions that had not been strategic targets for Boko Haram before then.[6]

Unlike most terrorist groups, which formulate a discourse and define political goals before striking, Boko Haram's ideology seems to have developed gradually alongside its violent actions. The official name of the movement also evolved. Originally known as *Ahl al-sunna wa'l jama'a ala minhaj al-salaf* (Association of the People of the *Sunnah* for the Implementation of the *Salafs' Model*), it was renamed around 2010 as *Jamā'atu ahl al-Sunna li'l-Da'wa wa'l-jihād* (Association of *Sunnah* People for Proselytisation and Armed Struggle) (Higazi 2013). The reference to *jihad* seems to have appeared after the repression of July 2009 and anchored the group in a warmongering logic. Despite the "*Ahl al-Sunna*" mention, which refers to the Wahhabi school of thought, the new name confirms the split from the Izala movement, which never encouraged the use of lethal violence. If the official name provides interesting information, it is rarely used by commentators. The nickname *Boko Haram*, catchy and easy to remember, is preferred. Unfortunately, it is also a simplistic ideological shortcut that fits some classical stereotypes about Muslims being fanatics opposed to modernity (Brigaglia 2012a). Yet, since 2009, the group has shown significant abilities to adapt, innovate, and develop sophisticated means of action and propaganda. Over the past few years, Boko Haram has become a serious security threat for the Nigerian state, acquired a transnational influence, and redefined itself in the broader regional framework by networking with Salafi groups in Mali, Niger, and possibly Algeria and Somalia (Higazi 2013).[7]

The evolving and opportunistic nature of Boko Haram's ideology must be taken into account as we are attempting to clarify the rhetoric of the sect towards Christians. When Boko Haram took advantage of inter-community conflicts in Plateau and Kaduna states to spread violence in new territories, they essentially highjacked the long-standing tensions that had built up more around land access than religious issues (*ibid.*). Also, the rise of a dissident group, Ansaru, which has blamed the leaders of Boko Haram for killing Muslims and has introduced new practices such as the kidnapping of Westerners, signals the existence of internal debates and confirms our impression of the group's rather fuzzy and constantly evolving ideological substance. At the sect's beginning, it seems there was no particular animosity vis-à-vis other religions in Yusuf's doctrine, while Islamic clerics were clearly targeted and many of them assassinated (Brigaglia 2012b).[8] This seems to have changed surreptitiously from 2009. Between 26 July and 31 July, approximately twenty churches were destroyed and more than fifty Christians killed in Maiduguri. It was also reported that Boko Haram's members forced people to convert to Islam under the threat of death (Ishaya 2013). For Christians living in Borno State, it was beyond dispute that the uprising was religiously motivated. According to a witness of these events, who made public a detailed daily account from 23 July to 30 July, the objectives of the sect were both "crippling the government and terrorizing Christians in Borno" (*ibid.*). Nevertheless, he was very surprised when Boko Haram began targeting Christians. On 27 July, he writes:

> news began filtering in that some churches had also been destroyed including the Eklessiyar Yan'uwa a Nigeria [...], which was the largest indigenous church in Borno State. 'Impossible!' was my first reaction. The sect had assured us that the fight was only against the government. (*ibid.*)

In fact, for the first time in the history of the radical group, a somewhat clearer anti-Christian rhetoric appeared in the discourse of Yusuf right in the middle of the crisis. Asked by the press about Muslim and non-Muslim peaceful co-existence during the time of the Prophet, he stated that the latter came to a miscreant land and gradually turned it into an Islamic state when, on the contrary, Borno "was an Islamic state before the colonial masters turned it to a kafir land" (*Daily Trust* 2009).[9] So, in Yusuf's vision, the restoration of an Islamic state in north-east Nigeria required the suppression of others religions, especially Christianity, which is clearly assimilated with colonialism and its avatar, the post-colonial Nigerian state. The troubled days of July 2009 somehow illustrate a vain attempt by the radical group to launch an Islamic *reconquista* of Maiduguri and Borno, and Christians began at this point to be visibly included among the 'enemy', along with the Nigerian security forces and the secular state as a whole. This vision has been put into practice over the past few years despite the fact that Abubakar Shekau seems not to have ever reiterated such an anti-Christian agenda in his public videos.

We believe that a statistical, comparative study of lethal violence perpetuated against both Christians and Muslims during the conflict can help us move away from the difficult analysis of an elusive ideology to a survey of the actual number of victims it generates in practice.

NOTE ON THE METHODOLOGY: USING NIGERIA WATCH TO IDENTIFY VICTIMS, TARGETS, AND RELIGIOUS IMPLICATIONS OF THE BOKO HARAM CRISIS

The Boko Haram crisis fits into the category of conflicts where the collection of accurate data is a fundamental problem, and the general lack of relevant information leaves considerable space for bias and speculation in the analysis. For a number of reasons, it has been impossible to determine the exact total number of victims resulting from the crisis and to precisely assess their characteristics: Muslims, Christians, civilians, officials, soldiers, Boko Haram members, etc. Furthermore, the clear identification of Boko Haram's targets, a necessary condition to apprehend the group's agenda, if any, has also been found to be problematic. Among the factors accounting for this situation, we can underline the following:

First, the blurred nature of Boko Haram itself: since the death of Mohammed Yusuf in July 2009, the group has had neither a uniform leadership (despite the progressive affirmation of Abubakar Shekau) nor an entirely coherent agenda. Most attacks reported by the government forces or the press incriminate "suspected" Boko Haram because no claim is made and the identity of the perpetrators remains uncertain. Sometimes, attacks are clearly claimed by Boko Haram's 'original' leadership, or are consistent with its ideological line, or answer to obvious practical needs (such as assaults on prisons detaining Boko Haram members). In many cases, however, the perpetrators could just as well be common criminals using the name of Boko Haram or could be conveniently designated as such by the police as an easy answer to complex investigations. These 'usurping' practices have developed to the point that, in some instances, Boko Haram members have led punitive raids against their 'fake' counterparts (*Daily Post* 2012).

Second, the ideological and media war: the fight between government forces and Boko Haram can be described in terms of control of the truth and manipulation of public opinion. For example, the Joint Task Force (JTF)—composed of the Nigerian army for the most part, and also the police and the State Security Service (SSS)—seems to be extremely reluctant to release figures for the number of victims among its ranks and, as a result, the military personnel reported killed in action, even after major crises, may appear low compared with the level of violence reported. Furthermore, government forces rarely admit killing civilians, even after clear evidence,[10] and tend to report civilians as Boko Haram members. A similar strategy is undertaken by Boko Haram, which often denies figures given by the government and claims more deaths from the JTF than official reports do. Nevertheless, the media power is clearly on the government's side in this case, and it is significant that Boko Haram started targeting what it considers to be "biased" media, as shown by the attacks on the newspaper *ThisDay* in Abuja and Kaduna.[11]

Third, the technical difficulty of reporting deaths: there is no well-tested mechanism of covering all the deaths related to the violence of the Boko Haram crisis. Government reports, press coverage, and individual testimonies are incomplete, selective, and potentially biased. Especially in the states where the level of violence has been particularly high, such as Borno and Yobe, it can be assumed that the breakdown of deaths entails severe distortions.

It is thus striking to observe how NGO reports and press and academic articles, which aim to provide accounts of casualties, are characterised by an undeniable vagueness in their sources and methodology and a lack of critical analysis in their breakdowns. In this regard, the manner in which data were collected for this article, using the Nigeria Watch database, has the merit of being transparent and of admitting limitations.

The Nigeria Watch database

The database[12] monitors and compiles violent deaths occurring in Nigeria since 1 June 2006. It relies principally on ten Nigerian daily newspapers (*Daily Champion, Guardian, Punch, ThisDay, Vanguard, Independent, Daily Trust, The Nation, PM News,* and *New Nigerian*—the last two were replaced by *Leadership* and *Nigerian Tribune* in 2013), which are analysed by information retrieval specialists on a daily basis. All events reported in these newspapers and involving at least one violent death are listed and described in the database. Furthermore, other sources of information, such as the police, the judiciary, hospitals, human rights organisations (mainly Human Rights Watch and Amnesty International), as well as private security firms, companies, and embassies, are used to cross-check data and mitigate methodological biases. As stated on Nigeria Watch's website:

> [The database] deals with fatalities resulting directly from intentional or unintentional violence. In a country where civil registration hardly exists, estimates on the number of deaths are not very reliable and can vary a lot from one source to another, especially during violent events. The press in Nigeria is one of the most developed in Africa [...]. Yet journalists

often tend to overestimate casualties and do not always cross-check their information. Moreover, the press is mainly based in the Christian South, especially Lagos, and does not cover properly the Middle Belt and the predominantly Muslim North. As for the Nigeria Police, it underreports crime. It does not publish detailed crime statistics, while people do not trust the police and avoid reporting violence [...]. Such discrepancies are the reason why this database includes as many sources as possible, in order to cross-check information and compute averages.

An event is defined as one or more violent deaths happening in one or more contiguous local government areas (LGAs) and ends after at least seven continuous days with no death reported. Events are described briefly and recorded by date (start date / end date), location (state, LGA, city, town, neighbourhood), protagonists, type of conflict, cause of violence, and number of deaths. The database provides scanned copies of each source used, and several documents can be scanned for the same event if they bring additional or contradictory information.

Obviously, the Nigeria Watch project does not assert it can cover all violent deaths in Nigeria, but it has proved to be a useful and consistent tool to measure trends in violence in a systematic manner. In regard to a study on the casualties of the Boko Haram crisis, the database enables one to work with concrete and verified numbers, and helps show the inherent limitations of this type of research.

The collection of data on victims and targets

This study looks at all the deadly events related to the Boko Haram crisis, from 24 July 2009 (beginning of the so-called Boko Haram insurgency) to 31 December 2012.[13] The term "crisis" is used in order to obtain as comprehensive a spectrum of the victims as possible. We have considered any death related to the phenomenon: Boko Haram activities (suspected and confirmed), government forces' response and repression measures, and other connected events that do not belong to the first two categories. Included, for instance, is the killing of two suspected Boko Haram members by an angry mob in Maiduguri on 6 October 2011 (*ThisDay* 2011). Each event was therefore considered relevant or not on a case-by-case basis.

The first set of data was gathered through a search of the words "boko" and "haram" in the database. Approximately 360 events comprising about 650 scanned documents were screened as a result, and 317 remained after the screening process; indeed, several events had no connection with the crisis even if the description bore the name Boko Haram or the acronym "BH". In some cases, especially those involving a large number of deaths, further research was conducted beyond the scanned documents (online or in newspaper archives). The events were then classified according to the date, location, total number of deaths, perpetrators, security involvement, number of deaths per category, and targeted location if any. The perpetrators are divided into 4 basic groups: Boko Haram, suspected Boko Haram, government forces (JTF, police, SSS, etc.), and others (e.g. mob). Security involvement, either 0 or 1, indicates whether or not government forces killed at least one person during the event. The categories of victims are comprised of the following: Christians (total), Muslims (total), civilians of unknown faith, Boko Haram members, JTF, police, SSS, other official personnel (prison wardens for the most part), Christian civilians, Christian clerics, Muslim civilians, Muslim clerics, traditional leaders, politicians, media workers, and expatriates. The categories of targets encompass the following: churches, mosques, police stations, army barracks, JTF convoys, JTF checkpoints, beer gardens and other recreational places where alcohol is sold, markets, banks, schools, prisons, personal residences, immigration and customs offices, SSS buildings, and other official buildings. The categories were decided on the sample of the first 30 events and adjusted along the way.

In regard to the categories of victims, several obviously overlap. When it was possible to determine, we included both status and religion—in the case of a policeman explicitly presented as Christian, for instance. The faith of the victims, if not stated clearly, was derived from obvious Christian and Muslims names or titles reported in the source of information. Furthermore, people killed in a mosque were classified as Muslims while people who died in a church were assumed to be Christians. Boko Haram militants were obviously considered Muslims, although we created a distinct category comprising the total number of Muslims minus the number of Boko Haram militants. We attempted to distinguish as much as possible between civilians and fighters on each side of the conflict. In addition, any time there was a doubt about religious affiliation, victims systematically entered the category "faith unknown" in the final calculation. From our breakdown, we found a total of 2,993 deaths (including 766 Boko Haram militants) from July 2009 to December 2012, which is comparable with, but slightly lower than, numbers generally found in the literature about the crisis.

Methodological challenges

Our approach faces a number of obvious challenges. As previously stated, the search on the database was conducted through the words "boko" and "haram". This term, increasingly given by the national and international media and used by the Nigerian federal government, has become the generic appellation of the group, although it has never called itself so.[14] A first question is whether the search may have missed some events where Boko Haram militants were involved but not yet designated as such. In most of the 2000s, articles involving suspected followers of Mohammed Yusuf refer to "Nigerian Talibans". For instance, in the reporting of the confusing events of April 2007 that led to the deaths of Sheikh Ja'afar Mahmud Adam as well as civilians, militants, and policemen, connections are made with the group of Yusuf's students responsible for several attacks in Yobe in 2003: the protagonists are, most of the time, called "Talibans" in the diverse reports (*ThisDay* 2007; *Vanguard* 2007). Since our study begins with July 2009, this issue may have been mitigated. It seems indeed that from the 2009 insurgency onwards, the name Boko Haram has been recurring in the press and only a few articles may have avoided using the name. This leads to another problem: the identification of what is Boko Haram and what is not.

As previously underlined, many articles and reports talk about "suspected" Boko Haram. As a result, we classified events and dismissed those that were very unlikely to be among Boko Haram activities, although we kept several over which there was a legitimate doubt. The frontal attacks against the police, the JTF, prisons, and other state institutions, when not claimed by Boko Haram, are obviously likely to be part of the group's activities. Attacks against Christians, as well as targeted assassinations of divergent Muslim clerics, are also very plausible and common in the Boko Haram agenda. Offensives on bars and other places dispensing alcohol also fall into a coherent strategy. Robberies and attacks on banks can be perpetrated by the radical group for understandable economic reasons but are of course also conducted by common criminals, and the distinction between the two can be difficult. Finally, some assassinations imputed to Boko Haram do not appear to belong to any logical strategic framework and are therefore particularly difficult to classify.

Furthermore, another difficulty arose from the sometimes contradictory breakdown of deaths from one newspaper to another. When sources gave different numbers, we generally used the highest figure, considering that deaths are likely to have been underreported in the states where the crisis has been the most violent. However, we always gave weight to the most specific source—for instance, a source citing a witness who stated having seen a certain number of bodies—over more approximate sources.

Focusing now on a few case studies will illustrate better our methodological approach.

Case studies

One instance of crime vaguely imputed to Boko Haram and that we decided not to retain in our breakdown is the slaughter of two teenagers in Damaturu, Yobe State, in July 2012 (*Vanguard* 2012). The only source reporting the event was the Lagos-based *Vanguard* newspaper. The article states that "the state Commissioner of Police, Patrick Egbuniwe, who confirmed the incidence, said the command was suspecting members of the Boko Haram Islamic sect" but does not give any information justifying this suspicion, and it later adds: "the Commissioner, who wondered why the attackers will slaughter 15-year-old set of twins said the incident occurred on Saturday". The article also asserts that a primary school was burnt down in the same city—which fits into Boko Haram activities—but does not relate the two events. The religion of the twins is not mentioned. Given the extreme vagueness of the assumption, reported in a South-based newspaper, about a crime which does not make sense in terms of the Boko Haram agenda—at least from the information provided—the event was not counted as part of the Boko Haram crisis. We do not imply that such crimes cannot be committed by Boko Haram members. Some instances show they can; they are not numerous, however, and at least one source of motive can usually be roughly identified.

On the other hand, we retained cases where the involvement of Boko Haram is definitely not stated or not even clearly assumed in the source but makes sense in the broader context: for example, the killing of an Islamic cleric in a mosque in Biu, Borno State, in August 2012 (*The Nation* 2013b). The relevant report explains that, on the same day the JTF was distributing "thousands of audio tapes of Islamic messages criticising the Boko Haram", one Muslim cleric and one worshipper were shot during prayers at two different mosques in Biu by unidentified gunmen. The article mentions that "the distributed materials were mainly from the preaching of the slain Muslim cleric, Sheik Mahmud Ja'afar", previously mentioned. It specifies that Boko Haram's activities have been deadly in Borno State, but it does not clearly state that the gunmen are suspected to be Boko Haram members nor does it cite any officials suggesting this. However, we considered this event as part of the Boko Haram crisis because attacks against Muslim clerics and communities professing a different vision of Islam and condemning Boko Haram have been a recurrent feature in the sectarian group's strategy. Furthermore, the fact that the JTF was propagandising against Boko Haram through Islamic messages the same day as the murders occurred can hardly be a coincidence.

The choices that we had to make in reviewing the violent events encompassing the Boko Haram crisis led inevitably to some level of subjectivity in our methodology. Nevertheless, as a meticulous work, our breakdown is available for scholars to assess,[15] and every source used in the process can be checked in the Nigeria Watch database and the bibliography.

GENERATING AND INTERPRETING STATISTICAL DATA ON BODY COUNT AND RELIGION

Figures collated from our use of the database show that the faith of victims of the crisis is inconsistently reported by journalists and other sources, probably because they do not have this information or because it does not strike them as worth mentioning. As we processed the press cuttings and complementary sources related to 317 Boko Haram-related events that occurred from July 2009 to December 2012, we attempted to identify the religious affiliation of all the fatalities. The results of this investigation are presented in Table 9.1, which shows the total number of victims reported in our breakdown, including Boko Haram militants (who appear among Muslims).[16]

Different facts emerge from this table. Firstly, the faith of a majority of the victims remains unknown. More precisely, we do not have religious indications for about 61 percent of the victims, representing 1,527 alleged civilians and 309 members of the Nigerian armed forces or other officials. Clearly, in this case, the civilian category may include unidentified members of Boko Haram and government agents, for in several instances available data did not make it possible to differentiate them from civilians. Such is the case with the July 2009 crackdown on the sect in Maiduguri. Although gross estimates of the number of casualties circulate, the conditions in which the massive repression of the sect's uprising was conducted, the difficulty of differentiating civilians from Boko Haram fighters among the many corpses recovered in neutral clothing, disturbing videos showing members of the federal forces assassinating disabled young men who could not seriously be considered as combatants, and the expedient way victims were buried in mass or individual graves by a variety of actors, prevent the determination of precise figures. We shall see below how we propose to overcome such a difficulty and establish facts about the numbers of Muslim and Christian victims recorded in this conflict.

Recorded Victims According to faith	n=	Sub-categories of Victims	n=
All Muslims	897	Muslim Civilians	56
		Muslim Clerics	21
		Boko Haram Militants	766
		Nigerians forces/officials	54
Muslim minus Boko Haram Militants	131		
Christians	260	Christian Civilians	245
		Christian Clerics	6
		Nigerian forces/officials	9
Faith Unknown	1,836	Civilians	1,527
		Nigerian forces/officials	309
Total	2,993		

Table 9.1 Faith affiliation of deceased victims in the Boko Haram crisis (2009–2012)

Secondly, the table shows a clear difference between the established numbers of Muslim and Christian civilians killed. At first glance, this could lead us to think that for each Muslim civilian killed, five Christian civilians fell victim to the conflict. This interpretation, however, may not reflect the reality, as two factors need to be taken into account: 1) the relative disparity with which Christian and Muslim deaths are reported by the media; and 2) the relative size of the statistical populations. In fact, Christian victims are probably more likely to be reported in national newspapers because this type of information coincides with the interests—or anxieties—of the bulk of their readers, who are located, in the main, in the southern part of the country, the stronghold of most of the large Christian communities. In a way, we can say that an event involving a Christian civilian who fell victim in northern Nigeria to the Boko Haram crisis is far more likely to find its way into the columns of the Nigerian (and, for that matter, international) printed media than a similar event involving a Muslim civilian. The death of a Christian in northern Nigeria or the Middle Belt resonates with the well-established underlying fear among many Nigerians of seeing their country getting gradually engulfed in another civil war motivated by an explosive combination of ethnic and religious strife. This general statement, however, is not always verified in practice, and there are some cases where violence directed against Christian targets, although reported by the press, did not allow for a comprehensive breakdown of victims, and the number of Christians killed is likely to have been underestimated. This is, for instance, the case with the uprising of July 2009 in Borno as well as the series of bomb attacks claimed by Boko Haram at Jos on Christmas Eve 2010, both events being particularly deadly. Finally, we need to recognise that the statistical samples of Christian and Muslim civilians are small, respectively 13.4 percent and 3.1 percent of the entire population of alleged civilians documented in our database (n=1,828).[17] Basically, we cannot derive strong conclusions from a sample that does not take into account 83.5 percent of the civilian victims of the crisis who themselves represent over 51 percent of the total number of recorded victims.

On the other hand, the strong predominance of Muslim over Christian non-civilians killed during the conflict, at the rate of six to one, may well be representative of the fact that the Nigerian military and police forces fighting Boko Haram predominantly comprise Muslims, although no statistical data exist to support such a statement—and questions surrounding the reality of the Islamisation of the security forces remain an extremely touchy topic in Nigeria.[18] Once again, our statistical sample does not allow us to argue beyond conjecture.

Similarly, the fact that Muslim clerics seem to have paid a higher price than pastors and other Christian clerics mirrors the reality of the campaign of terror led by Boko Haram against strongly discordant voices among the Islamic scholarly community, through planned assassinations typically conducted by two men on a motorcycle firing an automatic weapon at close range at their targeted victim in the street.

Table 9.1 suggests that the key to a discussion of the religious factor in the death of thousands as a result of the crisis lies in our capacity to speculate in an informed way on the faith of the 1,836 unknown faith victims. Without resolving the question of the religious affiliation of unknown faith civilian and non-civilian victims, representing, respectively, approximately 51 percent and 10.3 percent of the total number of casualties, one wonders how analysts could discuss the Muslim-versus-Christian nature of the conflict.

Clearly, there is no satisfactory and indisputable way of attributing a religious affiliation to these 1,836 victims. Whatever strategy is used to do so, we need to acknowledge its experimental nature, expose clearly how figures have been reached, and remain open to criticism. In this paper, we have opted for a method based on available demographic data. Although the latter remain fragile, disputed, and scarce, they seem to be the only quantitative sources that can assist us in building a case. Our core hypothesis is simple: on a state-by-state basis, to correlate our data on civilian[19] victims of unknown faith affiliation with existing information about the relative demographic weight of Muslims and Christians across the area affected by the Boko Haram crisis. However, simple concepts are seldom translated into practice with ease, and the following paragraphs will expose choices that were made to circumvent a number of methodological obstacles. In any case, we understand that our assumption that all civilian victims are random collateral damage of actions by Boko Haram and Nigerian security forces—and therefore equivalent to random demographic data—is a mere theoretical position in which we are constrained by the limitations of our data.

First, what demographic data are we talking about? Nigeria is well-known for generating contested or even 'made-up' census data. This is attested by a vast literature that criticises its alteration and falsification for political reasons (Bamgbose 2009). Added to this general concern about the value of the census data, we must also deal with the fact that religion—as a discrete category on questionnaires used by enumerators—was excluded from all recent national surveys for being too sensitive. As a result, it is impossible today to reliably assert the relative percentage of Muslims and Christians who live in the different states of Nigeria. As we go back in time, however, we find that the first and last censuses incorporating 'religion' as a category were conducted in 1952 and 1963. Despite many controversies, these two censuses—especially the one conducted in 1952—seem to be considered much more genuine (*ibid.*) than all those that followed, including the last one conducted in 2006. The downside of this is that they provide a snapshot that reflects a fifty-year old reality far from that of present-day Nigeria. Furthermore, fifty years ago the administrative divisions of Nigeria were quite different from now, and it takes considerable patience and a pinch of boldness to attempt a projection of the figures recorded then onto the new administrative framework made up of 36 states and the Federal Capital Territory (FCT). Such an approach was adopted by Philip Ostien, a former lecturer in law at the University of Jos in Plateau

State and an independent scholar since 2008. His projections were published in different forms in 2007 and 2012 (Ostien 2007; 2012a; 2012b). In Table 9.2, we reproduce the results obtained by Ostien for the 13 states where we recorded at least one victim of the Boko Haram crisis without a recognised religious affiliation.

States	% Muslim Census 1952 (Ostien 2007)	% Christians Census 1952 (Ostien 2012b)	% Muslims Census 1952 (Ostien 2012b)	% Christians Census 1952 (Ostien 2012b)	% Muslims Census 1952 (Ostien 2012b)
Adamawa	N/A	3.8	32.9	16.0	34.6
Bauchi	74	1.1	76.3	1.6	83.4
Borno	84	0.6	80.9	2.7	88.3
FCT	N/A	N/A	N/A	N/A	N/A
Gombe	74	2.5	70.1	6.2	75.0
Jigawa	98	0.4	98.4	0.8	98.0
Kaduna	61	10.2	57.3	25.1	55.7
Kano	98	0.5	97.8	1.1	97.0
Katsina	95	0.3	95.2	0.4	94.6
Niger	44	3.5	46.8	4.0	62.4
Plateau	N/A	11.4	25.5	23.2	26.1
Sokoto	94	0.5	96.3	0.4	98.9
Yobe	84	0.5	87.3	1.0	94.8

Table 9.2 Relative proportion of Muslims and Christians recorded during the 1952 and 1963 censuses and projected onto the 2013 administrative map of Nigeria

Figures computed by Ostien differ slightly in his 2007 and 2012 studies, as the author refined his methodology. In addition, his 2007 work focused on Shariah states only, which left out Adamawa and Plateau on our list as well as the FCT. Interestingly, in 2007 he was able to obtain and publish comparative estimates of the relative percentage of Muslims per state from the World Christian Database (WCD), dating to 2002. Aware of potential biases, and "assuming the truth lies somewhere in between [the 1952 census and the WCD data]" (Ostien 2007), he proposed averaging the two percentages to produce a new estimate. Table 9.3 reproduces these data and proposes an update of Ostien's estimate on the basis of his revised 2012 interpretation of the 1952 census. The result, in column 5, is a theoretical percentage of Muslims per state, which we will consider to be our low-end estimate, as we are averaging the

1952 census—giving a lower percentage of Muslims than the 1963 census—with a Christian-affiliated source which provides the lowest estimates known. Following Ostien, we can agree that "there are many pitfalls here, but for many reasons, it is not easy to do better" (*ibid.*).

States	1 % Muslim Census 1952 (Ostien 2007)	2 % Muslims WCD estimate 2002 (Ostien 2007)	3 % Muslims Average of 1 and 2 (Ostien 2007)	4 % Muslims Census 1952 (revised by Ostien 2012b)	5 % Muslims Average of 2 and 4
Adamawa	N/A	N/A	N/A	32.9	N/A
Bauchi	74	61	68	76.3	68.7
Borno	84	49	67	80.9	65.0
FCT	N/A	N/A	N/A	N/A	N/A
Gombe	74	49	62	70.1	59.6
Jigawa	98	70	84	98.4	84.2
Kaduna	61	51	56	57.3	54.2
Kano	98	69	84	97.8	83.4
Katsina	95	74	85	95.2	84.6
Niger	44	52	48	46.8	49.4
Plateau	N/A	N/A	N/A	25.5	N/A
Sokoto	94	74	84	96.3	85.2
Yobe	84	49	67	87.3	68.2

Table 9.3 Low-end estimate of percentage of Muslims in selected states

To provide low-end estimates for Adamawa, Plateau, and the FCT, we needed to resort to other data, as no WCD estimates were available for them. For FCT, the only recent estimate in the literature is the informed opinion of Medugu (2012), who suggests that there should be roughly as many Muslims as Christians. This is not really satisfactory, but for lack of a better assessment, we shall adopt it in this study. For Adamawa, we decided to adopt the percentage of Muslims obtained during the 1963 census (34.6 percent, after Ostien) (Ostien 2012b), which is slightly higher than the one obtained in 1952 (32.9 percent, after Ostien) (*ibid.*) and therefore probably more credible. Finally, in the case of Plateau, we retained the percentage proposed by the Ostien in his 2012 study of Plateau State (2012a), which we found to be the lowest figure available (16 percent). All final estimates are listed in Table 9.4.

States	Estimate % Muslims Min.	Estimate % Muslims Max.
Adamawa	34.6	65.0
Bauchi	68.7	97.0
Borno	65.0	97.0
FCT	50.0	50.0
Gombe	59.6	73.0
Jigawa	84.2	98.0
Kaduna	54.2	55.7
Kano	83.4	97.0
Katsina	84.6	94.6
Niger	49.4	91.0
Plateau	16.0	26.1
Sokoto	85.2	98.9
Yobe	68.2	94.8

Table 9.4   Minimum and maximum estimated % of Muslims in states affected by the Boko Haram crisis

On the other hand, to obtain high-end estimates, we relied on recent scholarship when available. For instance, several recent studies developed within the framework of the Nigerian Research Network and commissioned by the Oxford Department of International Development suggest a link between the overall percentage of Muslim population and the percentage of elected Muslim politicians (Alkali 2012). Figures provided by these authors were adopted in the case of Adamawa, Bauchi, Borno, and Gombe because no other data was available. For all remaining states, we adopted results obtained from the 1963 census, which were the highest available. Although 100 percent of elected politicians in Yobe State are Muslims (Alkali 2012), Christians are present in this state, and we therefore preferred to rely on the percentage obtained from the 1963 census (94.8 percent, after Ostien) (Ostien 2012b). Table 9.4 presents low-end and high-end estimates of the relative percentage of Muslims in all the states selected in this study.

Based on these figures, we can now extrapolate how many of the 1,527 civilian victims recorded as "faith unknown" may actually have been Muslims. Results are presented in Table 9.5. Overall, we estimate that between 64 and 90 percent of the 1,527 civilian victims were Muslims, while between 10 and 36 percent of them professed another religion, most probably Christianity.

Clearly, the religious landscape of northern Nigeria is not as dualistic as we tend to believe, and other forms of worship and belief coexist with Islam and Christianity. However, social pressure has taken its toll on such belief systems to the extent that they tend not to be publicly and explicitly acknowledged by actors. For the purpose of this study, we therefore simplified the reality and considered that Islam and Christianity were the two main acknowledged religions in the area under scrutiny.

States	Number of Victims Recorded as "Faith Unknown"	Number of assumed Muslims (Min.)	Number of assumed Muslims (Max.)	Number of assumed Muslims (Mean)	Estimate % Muslims (Min.)	Estimate % Muslims (Max.)
Adamawa	62	21	40	31	34.6	65.0
Bauchi	15	10	15	12	68.7	97.0
Borno	837	544	812	678	65.0	97.0
FCT	41	21	21	21	50.0	50.0
Gombe	15	9	11	10	59.6	73.0
Jigawa	1	1	1	1	84.2	98.0
Kaduna	53	29	30	29	54.2	55.7
Kano	183	153	178	165	83.4	97.0
Katsina	1	1	1	1	84.6	94.6
Niger	16	8	15	11	49.4	9.0
Plateau	53	8	14	11	16.0	26.1
Sokoto	2	2	2	2	85.2	98.9
Yobe	248	169	235	202	68.2	94.8
Total	1,527	976	1,373	1,174		
Total %	100	63.9	89.9	76.9		
Estimated total % of Christians		36.1 (min)	10.1 (max)	23.1 (mean)		

Table 9.5 Estimation of the percentage of Muslim and Christian believers among the civilian victims labelled as "faith unknown" in the Boko Haram conflict

For the 309 members of the Nigerian armed forces and officials killed in the same conflict and labelled as "faith unknown", we decided not to apply the same methodology because soldiers, policemen, SSS operatives, and other categories of personnel can be drawn from many different parts of the country. There are no available data on the "state of origin" of these victims, nor do we have general statistical data on the religious affiliation of the different components of the armed forces, police, etc. On this basis, we decided to consider hypothetically significant the ratio we recorded in Table 9.1 between identified "Muslims" (n=54) and "Christians" (n=9) in the category "Nigerian forces/officials". On this basis, we propose that 85.7 percent of our group of 309 victims could have been Muslims (n=257), while the remaining victims could have been Christians (n=52). Due to the lack of comparative data, we tentatively adopted this percentage as our high-end hypothesis, and introduced a ratio of circa 50:50 as a low-end hypothesis, giving an estimate of 155 Muslims and 154 Christians.

Using the methodology presented above, we are finally able to provide estimates of the alleged total number of Christians and Muslims killed during the Boko Haram crisis between 2009 and 2012 (Table 9.6). This table clearly indicates that whatever configuration is used (low-end or high-end estimate), the number of Muslim victims is always higher than the number of Christian victims. Boko Haram members aside, the number of Muslim victims is expected to be two to three times higher than that of Christian victims.

Returning to Table 9.1, it is striking to realise that figures derived from our database and showing known religious affiliation of victims provide us with a reversed perspective, with 260 Christian against 131 Muslims casualties, i.e. two times more Christians than Muslims. Clearly, as we discussed above, this is an artefact of the much stronger visibility of Christian casualties in the media and in other open sources. Such a visibility sustains the popular idea in some circles that Christians are the primary victims of the Boko Haram insurgency. However, such a view needs to be challenged, as we know that most of the terrorist and counter-terrorist attacks that resulted in massive casualties produced a large number of collateral victims among civilians, whose faith is usually not reported. Our methodology helps us to reframe the debate by including the large majority of the anonymous, collateral victims whose voice is ordinarily suppressed from scholarly and non-scholarly discussions alike. There is no reason to believe that the bulk of these collateral victims are not demographically representative of faith distribution in north-eastern Nigeria, and, if this hypothesis is correct, we should therefore accept the idea that the conflict has resulted in the majority of its victims being among civilian Muslims populations.

Recorded Victims According to faith	n=	%	Sub-categories of Victims	n=	%
Muslims			Muslim Civilians		
(Minimum)[a]	2,028	67.8	(Minimum)[b]	1,032	56.5
(Maximum)[c]	2,527	84.4	(Maximum)[d]	1,429	78.2
Muslims minus Boko Haram militants:			Muslim Clerics	21	
			Boko Haram Militants	766	
(Minimum)	1,262	42.2	Nigerian Forces/Officials		
(Maximum)	1,761	58.8	(Minimum)	209	
			(Maximum)	311	
Christians			Christian Civilians		
(Minimum)[e]	466	15.6	(Minimum)[i]	399	21.8
(Maximum)[g]	965	32.2	(Maximum)[b]	796	43.5
				6	
			Christian Clerics		
			Nigerian Forces/Officials	61	
			(Minimum)	163	
			(Maximum)		
Total	2,993				

Table 9.6 Estimated faith affiliation of deceased victims in the Boko Haram crisis (2009–2012)

Notes:

a) *This figure was obtained by adding the total number of known Muslims (n=897, see Table 9.1), the estimated minimum number of Muslims among civilians labelled as "faith unknown" in Table 9.1 (n=976, see Table 9.5), and the estimated minimum number of Muslim victims who were either members of the armed forces or officials (n=155).*

b) *This represents the minimum % of Muslims among civilian victims only.*

c) *This figure was obtained by adding the total number of known Muslims (n=897, see Table 9.1), the estimated maximum number of Muslims among civilians labelled as "faith unknown" in Table 9.1 (n=1373, see Table 9.5), and the estimated maximum number of Muslim victims who were either members of the armed forces or officials (n=257).*

d) *This represents the maximum % of Muslims among civilian victims only.*

e) *This figure was obtained by adding the total number of known Christians (n=260, see Table 9.1), the estimated minimum number of Christians among civilians labelled as "faith unknown" in Table 9.1 (n=154, see Table 9.5), and the estimated minimum number of Christian victims* who were either members of the armed forces or officials (n=52).

f) This represents the minimum % of Christians among civilian victims only.

g) This figure was obtained by adding the total number of known Christians (n=260, see Table 9.1), the estimated maximum number of Christians among civilians labelled as "faith unknown" in Table 9.1 (n=551, see Table 9.5), and the estimated maximum number of Christian victims who were either members of the armed forces or officials (n=154).

h) This represents the maximum % of Christians among civilian victims only.

CONCLUSION

Establishing a precise number of victims in this crisis, as well as identifying both their religion and status, has proven a perilous enterprise. Our breakdown—which stops on 31 December 2012, although Boko Haram-related violence has continued since—has inevitable flaws, and it is assumed that even within the time-frame studied, some important events may have been missed. Nevertheless, the data presented here, made available to the academic community, is the result of a transparent approach. What is most significant in our contribution is probably not the number of casualties we arrive at, but the percentages resulting from the data analysis. Indeed, beyond the religious divide, one striking conclusion is that 62 percent of the victims of the Boko Haram crisis are civilians (inclusive of clerics), reinforcing the idea that modern conflicts mainly affect non-combatant populations (Ramsbotham, Woodhouse & Miall 2007). Our data suggest that roughly 25 percent of the victims are Boko Haram activists and 13 percent are Nigerian security force members and other state officials. It should not been forgotten that, as discussed above, a number of civilians may have been presented as Boko Haram members in government reports and that the army has been very careful not to disclose too many of its casualties.

As for the religious affiliation, we estimate that a minimum of 42.2 percent and a maximum of 58.8 percent of the victims are Muslims (excluding Boko Haram members). The proportions in regard to the Christian populations are respectively 15.6 percent and 32.2 percent (Table 9.6). Therefore, and most likely, Muslims are particularly hit by the ongoing crisis. However, our data also show that attacks against Christians have been continually increasing, both in scale and frequency, from Christmas Day 2010 and the bombings in Jos. Yet, we need to warn against engaging carelessly in a debate over which community suffers the most, as it may serve the strategy of Boko Haram's leadership aimed at fomenting antagonism between Christians and Muslims.

By targeting Christians, the sect tugs at Nigerian identity's heart-strings and deeply challenges the fragile basis of the nation's unity. Boko Haram sees the secular state as a colonialist reminiscence, and Christians are fully integrated in this colonial picture. Nevertheless, the state and its security prerogatives remain a privileged target, as our data accounts for more than 100 official buildings (police stations, army barracks, prisons, etc.) attacked, with subsequent fatalities, over the period examined. The Nigerian state itself is greatly accountable for the aggravation of the situation. The long-lasting flaws in public administration, the fluctuating strategies, and the blind and deadly repression that reminds us of the darkest pages of the colonial wars have left civilians from both faiths with very little means of protection.

Our paper aims to trigger debate on the issue of casualties and religion in the Boko Haram crisis. How should data be collected and presented? How should such data be interpreted? To what extent is the religious approach pertinent in identifying the victims? Our initiative is thus far unique in regard to the Boko Haram phenomenon, even if it also demonstrates clearly the limitations and difficulties of such a task. The Nigeria Watch database, moreover, is a pertinent tool in analysing the current crisis.

Notes

1. In their sermons, the Izala *mallam*s such as Sheikh Mahmoud Ja'far, Sheikh Abubakar Giro, Sheikh Kabiru Gombe, and Sheikh Albani Zaria attach considerable importance to education. The deep social and religious reform they advocate for requires the involvement of their followers at every level of the state. These speeches, made in Hausa and recorded on DVDs manufactured by small local production companies (such as *An-Noor Islamic Production, Sawtul-Hikmah, Sautu Rijaalis Sunnah, Darul Islam Production*), are on sale in street shops and markets all over northern Nigeria.

2. In support of his argument, Yusuf referred to Abu Zayd, a Saudi Islamic scholar who claimed that modern secular education was "totally lacking any Islamic legitimacy".

3. From 2005 onwards, the popularity of Mohammed Yusuf began to grow in the Republic of Niger, where his sermons recorded on DVDs were widely disseminated. The Nigerian version of his name was Mahamadou Issoufou, and he was known for the numerous references to the concept of *boko* in his preaching; thus, people began to call him Mahamadou Issoufou "Boko Haram" (interviews with DVDs sellers in Niamey, Maradi, and Zinder, 2012–2013).

4. Although most of them are thought to be former students of Mohammed Yusuf, the nature of the relation between members of the Kanama community and the Boko Haram leader have not been fully clarified. It seems, however, that most of the survivors integrated into Yusuf's group after the government repression in 2004.

5. Borno in general and Maiduguri in particular were by far the two places most affected in terms of casualties. Our breakdown accounts for about 900 victims. However, other estimates propose more than a thousand people killed. See Brigaglia (2012a: 35) and Higazi (2013: 4). The latter cites the *Report of the Administrative Committee of Inquiry into the Boko Haram Insurgency in Borno State. Main Report* (5 volumes), October 2009. This report has never been made public and records 1,387 victims.

6. Including the bomb attack on the UN building in August 2011 and the series of attacks on Christian targets at Christmas 2010 and 2011, the coordinated attacks in Kano in January 2012, the bombing of *ThisDay* newspaper headquarters in April 2012, and the destruction of several telecommunication facilities.

7. Boko Haram's connections with Niger Republic are particularly strong, since victims of the repression of the Nigerian government in northern Nigeria have been crossing the border. These connections are also grounded in very dynamic trans-border trade and kinship-based relationships among groups on both sides of the border with shared ethnicity, language, and long-term history. In Niger, groups based on a similar ideology are known to have been formed, such as *Sake gueme Haram* (Hausa: "shaving the beard is forbidden"), which appeared in 2007 in the region of Diffa.

8. The most symbolic assassination was the murder of Sheikh Ja'far, perpetrated in April 2007 at the Juma'at Mosque of Kano, when he was leading the morning prayer.

9. *Kafir* is an Arabic term which means "miscreant" or "infidel".

10. See for instance the controversy involving government forces during the 2009 uprising, when the Nigerian police were filmed perpetrating extrajudicial killings on civilians: "Nigeria killings caught on video", Al Jazeera, 10 February 2010. http://www.aljazeera.com/news/africa/2010/02/20102102505798741.html [Accessed July 2013].

11. "Nigeria's *ThisDay* newspaper hit by Abuja and Kaduna blasts", BBC World News, 26 April 2012, http://www.bbc.co.uk/news/world-africa-17856362 [Accessed August 2013].

12. The project was created in 2006 by Dr. Marc-Antoine Pérouse de Montclos, researcher at the Institut de Recherche pour le Développement (France), with the support of private firms. The database and more information are accessible online

at: http://www.nigeriawatch.org/. Since 2013, the analysis of newspapers has been conducted from the French Institute for Research in Africa (IFRA-Nigeria), on the University of Ibadan's campus, with funding from DFID through the Nigerian Stability and Reconciliation Programme (NSRP) and the British Council.

13. We began our analysis from this date because, aside from the death of Sheikh Ja'afar in 2007 and the subsequent deadly events (whose perpetrators remain unconfirmed), no data was available prior to July 2009.

14. As previously stated, the proper name is *Jamā'a Ahl al-sunnah li-da'wa wa al-jihād*. See also the interesting discussion on the meaning of *boko*, in Newman (2013).

15. The final spreadsheet can be accessed at: http://ifra-nigeria.org/IMG/xls/table-boko-haram-conflict.xls.

16. As explained in this chapter, there are legitimate doubts over certain official reports, which may have amalgamated civilians and Boko Haram members.

17. This figure was obtained by adding Muslim civilians, Christian civilians, and civilians of unknown faith.

18. A recent petition circulated by a Nigerian NGO was widely debated over the Internet. See for instance "Group drags IGP Abubakar to President Jonathan over 'Hausanisation & Islamisation' of Nigeria Police", *News Express*, 6 May 2013. http://www.newsexpressngr.com [Accessed October 2013].

19. Members of the Nigerian government forces and officials are treated separately, using a different method. See later discussion.

References

Alkali, Muhammad Nur *et al.* (2012), "Overview of Islamic Actors in Northeastern Nigeria", Working Paper No. 2, *Nigeria Research Network*, University of Oxford.

Amaza, I.P. (2013), "The Boko Haram tragedy", published on Christian Solidarity Worldwide. http://cswng.org/the-boko-haram-tragedy/#comment-922 [Accessed July 2013].

[Anonymous] (2012), "The Popular Discourses of Salafi Radicalism and Salafi Counter-radicalism in Nigeria: A Case Study of Boko Haram", *Journal of Religion in Africa* 42(2): 118-144.

Bamgbose, J.A. (2009), "Falsification of population census data in a heterogeneous Nigerian state: The fourth republic example", *African Journal of Political Science and International Relations* 3(8): 311-319.

Brigaglia, A. (2012a), "Ja☐far Mahmoud Adam, Mohammed Yusuf and Al-Muntada Islamic Trust: Reflections on the Genesis of the *Boko Haram* phenomenon in

Nigeria", *Annual Review of Islam in Africa* 11: 35-44.

––––– (2012b), "A Contribution to the History of the Wahhabi Da'wa in West Africa: the Carrer and the Murder of Shykh Ja'far Mahmoud Adam (Daura, ca. 1961/1962-Kano 207)", *Islamic Africa* 3(1): 1-23.

Daily Post (2012), Abiodun Badejo, "Nine killed, as Boko Haram fights Fake Members in Damaturu", 29 August.

Daily Trust (2009), Ahmad Salkida, "Muhammad Yusuf interview", 27 July.

––––– (2013), Wakili, Isiaka, "Insurgents killed more Muslims than Christians— Jonathan", 21 June, p. 4.

Higazi, A. (2013) "Les origines et la transformation de l'insurrection de Boko Haram dans le nord du Nigeria", *Politique Africaine* 130: 137-164.

Medugu, Nasiru Idris, (2012), "Muslims of the Federal Capital Territory: a Survey", Background Paper No. 5, *Nigeria Research Network*, University of Oxford.

Newman, P. (2013), "The Etymology of Hausa *Boko*", Mega-Chad Research Network. http://lah.soas.ac.uk/projects/megachad/publications/Newman-2013-Etymology-of-Hausa-boko.pdf.

Ostien, P. (2007), *Sharia Implementation in Northern Nigeria 1999-2006: A Sourcebook*, vol. I-V. Ibadan: Spectrum Books.

––––– (2012a), "A Survey of the Muslims of Nigeria's North Central Geo-political Zone", Working Paper No.1, *Nigeria Research Network*, University of Oxford.

––––– (2012b) "Percentage by Religion of the 1952 and 1963 Populations of Nigeria's present 36 States", Background Paper No.1, *Nigeria Research Network*, University of Oxford.

Ramsbotham, O., T. Woodhouse & H. Miall (2007), *Contemporary conflict Resolution* (2nd ed.). Cambridge: Polity Press.

The Nation (2013a), Akowe, Tony, "Jonathan distorting facts on Boko Haram victims- Northern CAN", 23 June. http://thenationonlineng.net/new/jonathan-distorting-facts-on-boko-haram-victims-northern-can/ [Accessed September 2013]

––––– (2013b), Joseph Abiodun, "Gunmen kill two in Borno mosques as JTF distributes anti-Boko Haram tapes", 22 August.

ThisDay (2007), Ibrahim Shuaibu, "Talibans Kill 13 Policemen in Kano", 18 April.

––––– (2011), Michael Olugbode, "Mob Kills 2 Suspected Boko Haram Members", 8 October.

Vanguard (2007), Tina Anthony, "Soldiers kill 25 fundamentalists in Kano", 19 April.

––––– (2012), "15 years old twins slaughtered in Yobe", 23 July.

A CHRONOLOGY

Manuel Reinert and Lou Garçon
African Studies, SOAS University

1995: Creation of the Sahaba group ("The Prophet's Companions"), under the leadership of Mallam Abubakar Lawal. Mohammed Yusuf, born in 1970 in Yobe State, is thought to be among the followers.

2000–2003: In Borno State, rivalry increases between Governor Mala Kashalla and Senator Ali Modu Sheriff. The latter, running for governor, criticises the flawed implementation of Shariah in the state and rallies a group of political thugs. Many of the recruits are students of *imam* Mohammed Yusuf. Subsequently, Sheriff and Yusuf strengthen ties.

2002: Mohammed Yusuf, who has been expelled from two mosques in Maiduguri because of fundamentalist preaching, becomes the head of the Sahaba. Yusuf detaches himself from his mentor Ja'afar Mahmud Adam, an influential Salafi cleric from Kano, because of doctrinal disagreements. He gradually removes the older Sahaba clerics and radicalises the group's ideology, giving birth to the organisation later known as *Jama'atu Ahlis-Sunnah Lidda'awati Wal Jihad* (People Committed to the Propagation of the Prophet's Teachings and Jihad) or, more commonly, Boko Haram.

April 2003: Ali Modu Sheriff is elected Governor of Borno. An intimate of Mohammed Yusuf, Alhaji Buji Foi, is nominated Commissioner for Religious Affairs. Yusuf is permitted to develop a compound with a mosque and a Quranic school in Maiduguri.

2003: In mid-2003, a group of 200 young men, composed of Mohammed Yusuf's students for the most part, decide to break away from the secular state and found a religious community in the Yobe countryside, calling themselves *Al Sunna Wal Jamma* (Followers of the Prophet's Teaching). Following conflicts with local communities and authorities, the congregation relocates to Kanama, near the border with Niger. From 23 to 31 December 2003, the group launches a series of deadly attacks on police stations and government buildings in Kanama and four other cities of the North. Military troops are deployed to contain the insurrection and they kill several militants. A majority of the surviving members return to Maiduguri, where they reintegrate into Mohammed Yusuf's community. Yusuf is blamed by the authorities and has to leave Nigeria; after a long stay in Saudi Arabia, he is eventually permitted to return.

June 2004: Four members of Boko Haram are killed by prison guards in a foiled jail break in Yobe State capital, Damaturu.

23 September 2004: Suspected Boko Haram members launch a militia attack on police stations in the towns of Gwoza and Bama in Borno State, killing several policemen and civilians. They move to the Mandara Mountains along the Nigeria–Cameroon border. Soldiers are deployed and kill an estimated 27 sect members.

10 October 2004: An affiliate group of Boko Haram attacks a police convoy in Kala-Balge near the Chadian border. The militants kidnap 12 policemen and all attempts to trace them fail.

2005–2007: Boko Haram focuses on recruiting new members and shoring up its resources. Little is known about Boko Haram's activities during this period of time. Yusuf is arrested on numerous occasions, but seems to be protected by some powerful men as he is systematically released and permitted to return to his stronghold in Maiduguri.

April 2007: The doctrinal conflict between Mohammed Yusuf and Ja'afar Mahmud Adam reaches a peak when the latter is murdered in his mosque in Kano. This event is seen as a violent resurgence of Boko Haram after three years of apparent inactivity.

11–12 June 2009: Following the shooting of 14 of his followers in a joint military and police operation in Borno State, Mohammed Yusuf threatens the federal state with reprisals, in a video addressed to the president. The incident follows a disagreement over Boko Haram members' alleged refusal to wear crash helmets during a funeral procession to bury some of its members.

26–31 July 2009: Boko Haram launches a short-lived uprising in Borno, Bauchi, Yobe, Gombe, Kano, and Katsina, which is quelled by a military crackdown that allegedly leaves more than 800 dead—mostly sect members and civilians. The mosque in Maiduguri used as the sect's headquarters and Yusuf's compound are destroyed. Approximately forty Christians are executed by members of the sect and twenty churches are burnt down. Hundreds of Boko Haram members are arrested, including Mohammed Yusuf. Handed over to the police by the army who arrested and interrogated him, Yusuf is summarily executed while in custody on 30 July. **Alhaji Buji Foi**, the former Commissioner of Religious Affairs and a financier of Boko Haram, is also captured and later killed at the police headquarters in Maiduguri.

June 2010: Abubakar Shekau, Yusuf's second-in-command, announces in a video that he has taken over as leader of the sect. Authorities announce his death after the crackdown on the sect in Maiduguri in July 2009.

7 September 2010: Boko Haram raids a prison in the city of Bauchi, freeing more than 700 prisoners—including at least 100 members of the sect. This attack is followed by many others on prison facilities in northern Nigeria.

24 December 2010: Approximately ninety people are killed during attacks in Jos and Maiduguri. A series of explosions claimed by Boko Haram in nine Christian neighbourhoods of Jos result in the deaths of 32 people, while immediate reprisals kill about fifty. The same day, Boko Haram members open fire on two churches in Maiduguri, killing six. The bomb blasts in Jos spark a month of sectarian violence, claiming more than 200 victims among Christians and Muslims alike.

29 December 2010: Suspected Boko Haram gunmen shoot dead eight people in Maiduguri, including the governorship candidate of the ruling All Nigeria Peoples Party (ANPP) in Borno State.

8 April 2011: Goodluck Jonathan is declared winner of the presidential elections with 59 percent of the votes. This announcement sparks a series of post-electoral violence in parts of northern Nigeria.

29 May 2011: Three bombs rip through a beer garden situated inside military barracks in the northern city of Bauchi, killing 13 and wounding 33. Boko Haram claims responsibility. (More than 25 beer gardens and markets associated with barracks have been targeted by Boko Haram militants since 2009.)

6 June 2011: Muslim cleric Ibrahim Birkuti, an outspoken critic of Boko Haram, is shot dead by two motorcycle-riding gunmen outside his house in Biu, 200 km from Maiduguri. (More than twenty Muslim clerics opposed to the sect were assassinated between 2009 and the end of 2012.)

7 June 2011: Alleged attacks by the sect on a church and two police posts in Maiduguri leave at least 14 people dead.

16 June 2011: A Boko Haram suspect detonates a car bomb in the car park of the police headquarters in Abuja, leaving at least two people dead in the first reported suicide bombing in Nigeria.

20 June 2011: Seven people, including five policemen, are killed in a gun and bomb attack on a police station and a bank in Kankara, Katsina State. Multiple attacks on banks are attributed to Boko Haram, which allegedly serve to refinance the sect.

27 June 2011: Boko Haram's gun and bomb attack on a beer garden in Maiduguri leaves at least 25 dead and dozens injured.

July 2011: The government announces that it will set up a panel of experts to initiate negotiations with the sect. Five police officers held responsible for Mohammed Yusuf's murder are charged by a federal high court in Abuja.

3 August 2011: Government says it rejects negotiations with Boko Haram.

25 August 2011: The sect storms two banks and two police stations in Gombi, killing at least 16 people. This is the first reported attack in Adamawa State.

26 August 2011: A Boko Haram suicide bomber drives his vehicle into the United Nations building in Abuja, killing 25 people and injuring more than 100. This is the first time the sect targets the international community.

17 September 2011: Babakura Fugu, brother-in-law of Mohammed Yusuf, is shot dead outside his house in Maiduguri two days after acting as an intermediary in a peace meeting between Nigeria's ex-president Olusegun Obasanjo and Boko Haram. The sect denies any involvement in his murder.

22 October 2011: Boko Haram claims responsibility for the murder of a cameraman working with the government-owned National Television Authority (NTA) in Maiduguri. The sect says the cameraman was spying on the militants.

November 2011: Boko Haram announces there will be no dialogue with the government until all of its members are released from jail.

4 November 2011: Boko Haram carries out a series of attacks on security facilities, banks, and churches in Damaturu and Potiskum, Yobe State, leaving approximately 150 people dead. Two Boko Haram suicide bombers fail to detonate their bombs inside the headquarters of the Joint Task Force (JTF) and blow themselves up outside the military compound. The Borno governor's convoy is targeted on its way from the airport to the governor's mansion.

7 December 2011: A bomb attributed to Boko Haram kills eight in the Oriyapata district of Kaduna city.

17 December 2011: A shootout between sect members and policemen following a raid on the hideout of a Boko Haram sect leader in the Darmanawa area of Kano State kills seven, including three police officers.

22 December 2011: Boko Haram places bombs in various parts of Maiduguri, killing twenty people. Meanwhile, four policemen and a civilian are killed in another gun and bomb attack on a police building in Potiskum, Yobe State. Approximately 100 people are also killed following multiple bomb and AK47 attacks by Boko Haram and ensuing gun battles with military troops in the Pompomari outskirts of Damaturu, Yobe State.

25 December 2011: A man driving a vehicle laden with bombs blows himself up outside Saint Theresa Catholic Church in Medulla, Niger State, killing 26 worshipers and 17 bystanders. Three secret police (SSS) operatives and a Boko Haram bomber are killed in another suicide attack on a military convoy at the gates of the SSS headquarters in Damaturu. A policeman is killed in a botched Boko Haram bomb attack on a church in the Ray Field area of Jos.

30 December 2011: Four Muslims are killed in a Boko Haram bomb and shooting attack targeting a military checkpoint in Maiduguri as worshippers are leaving a mosque after attending Friday prayers.

31 December 2011: President Jonathan declares a state of emergency in parts of Borno, Niger, Plateau, and Yobe states and announces the closing of all northern borders.

2-11 January 2012: Boko Haram issues a three-day ultimatum to southern Nigerians to depart from the North.

6 January 2012: Eight worshippers are killed in a shooting attack on a church in Yola. Boko Haram gunmen also shoot dead 17 Christian mourners in the town of Mubi in the north-eastern state of Adamawa.

9 January 2012: Boko Haram gunmen shoot dead a secret police operative along with his civilian friend as they leave a mosque in Biu, Borno State. Nigeria's President Goodluck Jonathan says Boko Haram has infiltrated the executive, parliamentary, and judicial wings of government.

18 January 2012: A key suspect in the 2011 Christmas Day bombing in Abuja, which left more than forty people dead, escapes police custody. The scandal forces the Inspector General of Police, Hafiz Ringim, to resign.

20 January 2012: Boko Haram launches coordinated attacks on police facilities in the city of Kano, leaving an estimated 250 people dead, most of them civilians—the highest death toll in a single attack since 2009. Among the victims is Enenche Akogwu, a journalist working for Channels Television, as well as three Indian nationals. Boko Haram gunmen also free between 50 and 100 jailed members in Kano.

24 January 2012: In Kano, security forces kill Uzairu Abba Abdullahi, a textile seller and member of the sect, who is suspected of having planned the attacks that took place in Kano on 20 January.

2 February 2012: Six people suspected to be dissident members of the sect are shot dead in Maiduguri by Boko Haram. A sect spokesman declares to journalists that the sect will execute any of its members who take the side of the government.

7–9 March 2012: The Nigerian army arrests Abu Muhammad, a leader of a group close to Al-Qaeda and suspected to have kidnapped the British and Italian engineers Chris McManus and Franco Lamolina on 12 May 2011 at Birnin

Kebbi in north-western Nigeria. On the basis of the information given by Muhammad, security forces raid a hideout in Sokoto. The hostages are killed by their abductors during the operation. Although Boko Haram is suspected, there is no clear evidence that the sect is actually involved in the abduction and killing of the two foreigners.

8 April 2012: A suicide car bomber fails to reach the church he was targeting and detonates his bomb on a busy street in Kaduna on Easter Sunday, killing at least 41 people. The army claims that Boko Haram has executed its own spokesman, Abul Qaqa II, and that the sect is riven by internal divisions. (In January 2012, the SSS said it had captured Boko Haram's previous spokesman, Abul Qaqa I.)

26 April 2012: Boko Haram bombs the offices of the newspaper *ThisDay* in Abuja and a building that houses several media outlets, including *ThisDay*, in Kaduna, killing four people in Abuja and three in Kaduna. The sect claims the newspaper has been reporting "lies" about the militants and condemns an article dishonouring the Prophet, published in 2002.

29 April 2012: Suspected Boko Haram gunmen attack two Christian services at Bayero University in Kano and kill 19 people, including two university lecturers.

10 May 2012: Muhammad Ali, the branch leader of the Shiite Islamic sect in Kano city, is killed by armed men suspected to be Boko Haram members. Authorities fear a conflict between Boko Haram and other northern Nigerian sects.

17–19 June 2012: 100 people are killed and more than 300 injured during attacks by Boko Haram on churches in Kaduna and Zaria. In reprisal, Christian youth mobs kill about twenty people they suspect to be Hausa-Fulani in Kaduna.

21 June 2012: The US State Department lists three Boko Haram commanders—Abubakar Shekau, Abubakar Adam Kambar, and Khalid al-Barnawi—as "Specially Designated Global Terrorists".

6 August 2012: Seven policemen die in a Boko Haram suicide attack against a police station in Sokoto. The station is situated a few metres from the house of former Nigerian president Shehu Shagari.

21 August 2012: A Muslim religious leader and one of his followers are executed in a mosque in Biu by suspected Boko Haram militants. In Maiduguri, men of the Joint Task Force (JTF) begin to distribute anti-Boko Haram video tapes to locals.

5–6 September 2012: The sect destroys more than two dozen mobile telephone towers across northern Nigeria. Boko Haram states that the attacks are meant to avenge the mobile phone companies' cooperation with Nigerian intelligence services.

23 September 2012: The JTF says it has killed 35 Boko Haram militants in Damaturu and arrested sixty others.

24 September 2012: The army and the police announce the death of a commander of Boko Haram—Abubakar Yola—and the arrest of 156 militants by troops of the Restore Sanity Operation in Mubi, Adamawa State.

6 October 2012: Three Chinese nationals working as cooks are executed as they are leaving a market at Gubio, not far from Maiduguri. Some media reports also mention the assassination of a Ghanaian and two Indians in Maiduguri.

7 October 2012: Soldiers of the JTF declare that they have killed thirty members of Boko Haram in Damaturu, including its leader Abubakar Shekau, and arrested ten others in Kandahar.

8 October 2012: An officer of the JTF is killed in Maiduguri when Boko Haram members hit his convoy with an IED. In reprisal, soldiers attack civilians suspected of supporting the sect in the Gwange area of Maiduguri, setting on fire at least fifty houses, stores, and vehicles, and killing thirty people.

12 October 2012: United Nations Security Council passes a French resolution approving an African-led force to assist the army of Mali in combating secessionist and Islamist groups in the northern part of Mali.

28 October 2012: At least eight people die and 145 are wounded in an attack by alleged Boko Haram members against St. Rita's church in Kaduna. In reprisal, groups of Christian youth attack Muslims in the area.

1 November 2012: Amnesty International releases a report denouncing grave human rights violations by both Boko Haram and the Nigerian security forces in northern Nigeria. The same day, Abu Muhammad Ibn Abdulazeez, presenting himself as a spokesman of the sect, declares that Boko Haram is ready to negotiate with the government.

20 December 2012: Gunmen seize French engineer Francis Collomp in his compound in Katsina. In a statement sent to journalists four days later, Boko Haram splinter group Ansaru claims responsibility for the kidnapping.

11 January 2013: France launches the military intervention "Opération Serval", officially aiming to uproot Islamist groups in control of northern Mali and to restore Mali's territorial integrity. The groups include Ansar Dine, MOJWA, and AQIM, with the alleged cooperation of Boko Haram.

19 January 2013: Gunmen attack the convoy of the Emir of Kano. The emir survives but his driver and two guards are killed in the attack.

8-11 February 2013: Nine female polio vaccinators are killed in two separate shootings in health centres of Kano. Three days later, three North Korean doctors are hacked to death in Potiskum. Boko Haram is suspected of both attacks.

11 February 2013: Nigerian President Goodluck Jonathan pays an official visit to France. The discussions with French President François Hollande focus on the situation in Mali and the rise of Islamist militancy in the region.

16 February 2013: Ansaru, a splinter group of Boko Haram, kidnaps seven foreign expatriates from a Lebanese construction company, Setraco, at Jama'are in Bauchi. It is the largest kidnapping in northern Nigeria in recent times.

19 February 2013: Four children and three adult members of the French Moulin-Fournier family are kidnapped by gunmen in northern Cameroon while visiting the Waza National Park, near the border with Nigeria. After contradictory statements, Boko Haram finally claims responsibility.

7 March 2013: During his first official visit to Maiduguri, Nigerian President Goodluck Jonathan rejects the amnesty programme for Boko Haram members, suggested by the Sultan of Sokoto.

10 March 2013: Ansaru executes the seven abducted construction company expatriates in response to troop movements perceived as signs of a rescue mission by the British forces in Bauchi.

18 March 2013: More than seventy people are killed in the bombing of luxury buses at a station in the Sabon Gari district of Kano—home to many Christians from southern Nigeria. Boko Haram is suspected.

4 April 2013: Nigeria's President Goodluck Jonathan sets a committee of experts to work on an amnesty programme for Boko Haram militants.

11 April 2013: Boko Haram rejects the idea of an amnesty.

19 April 2013: Cameroon's President Paul Biya announces the release of the French Moulin-Fournier family being held by Boko Haram, after the family spent two months in captivity.

22 April 2013: Fighting between military forces and Boko Haram militants leaves more than 185 people dead at Baga in Borno State, near the border with Chad. Violence began when gunmen opened fire in a video-viewing centre.

14 May 2013: President Goodluck Jonathan declares a state of emergency in the states of Borno, Yobe, and Adamawa in an attempt to combat the activities of Boko Haram head-on. This involves the largest contingent of military personnel mobilised in Nigeria since the Civil War.

June–October 2013: Multiple confrontations between Boko Haram members and the JTF in Borno (along the Cameroon border and many other parts of the state), in Yobe, and to a lesser extent in Adamawa, result in hundreds of deaths. The "Mechanised Division's Operation BOYONA" makes use of the air force and heavy artillery to bomb suspected Boko Haram camps and hide-outs.

19 August 2013: Lieutenant-Colonel Sagir Musa releases a statement claiming that Abubakar Shekau is likely to have died between 25 July and 3 August 2013 from gunshot wounds following a clash with the JTF in the Sambisa forest near Cameroon. The statement creates confusion among top army officers.

25 September 2013: Abubakar Shekau appears in a video sent to news agencies. He mentions some recent developments of the conflict, such as the attacks in Benisheik on 17 September, which resulted in about ninety deaths, and mocks the military for claiming him dead. The JTF states the authenticity of the video is doubtful.

29 September 2013: An attack on the College of Agriculture in Gujba, Yobe by suspected Boko Haram members kills forty students.

4 October 2013: Newspapers cite sources reporting that the retaliation operations following the events in Gujba have resulted in the deaths of more than 180 Boko Haram members and a few soldiers. Since the state of emergency was declared, the press has reported six events, mentioning between 50 and 190 fatalities.

13 November 2013: Boko Haram and Ansaru are formally designated "Foreign Terrorist Organizations" by the US Department of State.

28 November 2013: In Bita village, in Borno State, some 40 suspected Boko Haram members were killed by the military on a raid of hideouts in the area.

1 January 2014: As of 1 January 2014, the UN's humanitarian office says that a total of about 290,000 people have been internally displaced in Adamawa, Borno, and Yobe due to violence caused by Boko Haram.

13 February 2014: 39 people are killed and 2,000 houses and buildings (health clinics, maternity homes, the Konduga Central Mosque, and hospitals) are burnt down or bombed. Some citizens have warning of the attack, allowing some residents to flee into the surrounding areas before the attack. Governor Kashim Shettima of Borno State says that the Nigerian security agents are trying to help, but the members of Boko Haram are more motivated to wreak havoc.

14 April 2014: Boko Haram militants kidnap more than 200 schoolgirls from Chibok, Borno State.

19 April 2014: Boko Haram's leader, Abubakar Shekau, claims responsibility for the Abuja bombing that killed at least 75 people. The target was a bus station, crowded with morning commuters.

7 May 2014: Boko Haram mislead security forces in Gamborou Ngala, sending them to the Lake Chad axis where they think gunmen have been sighted with the abducted schoolgirls. Soon after the security forces left the city, Boko Haram gunmen with armored vehicles enter Gamborou Ngala and proceed to spend about twelve hours burning shops and homes, and killing civilians. Around 300 people are killed in the attack.

12 May 2014: Boko Haram releases a video that shows the kidnapped Nigerian schoolgirls, claiming that some of the girls had been converted to Islam and would be released only if all the militant prisoners of Boko Haram are freed.

27 May 2014: Olusegun Obasanjo, Nigeria's ex-president, meets with relatives of senior Boko Haram fighters and intermediaries to attempt to organize the release of the more than 200 kidnapped schoolgirls from Chibok, Borno state, through negotiation.

16 June 2014: Christian Association of Nigeria (CAN) calls on all Christians to undertake fasting and prayers to fight the terrorism of Boko Haram spiritually.

13 July 2014: Abubakar Shekau claims responsibility for an explosion in the port of Apapa, in Lagos, on 25 June 2014. This is the first attack from Boko Haram in the south. From a strategic point of view, such attacks before the general elections of February 2015 are likely to provoke retaliatory attacks against Muslim minorities in the South, risking a cycle of escalating retaliatory attacks.

28 July 2014: Boko Haram fighters make an attack in Cameroon on the home of Cameroon's vice Prime Minister, Amadou Ali, whose wife is abducted. Six others are killed in the process, local religious leader Seini Boukar Lamine is kidnapped from his home, and according to a source close to the sultan's family, the younger brother of the sultan is killed and his spouse and children are kidnapped. This occurs a week after an enormous assault by Boko Haram in the Nigerian town of Damboa, which displaced around 15,000 people.

23 July 2014: Former chief of state Muhammadu Buhari narrowly escapes assassination. Boko Haram does not claim responsibility, but is suspected.

30 July 2014: Fourth female suicide attack, this time, in Kano.

24 August 2014: In a video, Abubakar Shekau claims to control the city of Gwoza and to have established a caliphate following the model of the Islamic State in Iraq.

ANNEXES

ANNEX 1

The Charter of Jama'at Ansar Al Muslimin Fi Bilad al-Sudan

(a.k.a. Ansaru)

Broadcast on Internet on 18 January 2012

Translated from Arabic by Mathieu Guidère

The Name of the the Group
Jama'at Ansar Al Muslimin Fi Bilad al-Sudan
["The Supporters of Muslims in the Land of the Blacks"]

The Motto of the Group
Fighting in the Name of Allah

The Logo of the Group
The Holy Quran is between two machine guns and on top of each machine gun, and there is a banner that reads "There is only one God and Mohammed is His Prophet". It signifies that the implementation of the religion can be achieved only through the Holy Book of the Quran and steel (weapons).

The Methodology of the Group and its Beliefs
- We are in this religion with all who entered it before us, including brothers and others who followed the Prophet with faith.
- The basics of faith and the details of religious matters are clear from the words of Allah and the words of His Prophet. This is why these words have to be followed to the letter, and one should never follow anything else that contradicts them.

- Our allegiance is to Allah, His Prophet, and all of the believers in Him.
- Those who pray the five prayers and pray in the direction of the Qibla and show their Islam are Muslims. They have the same responsibilities and obligations as us, and they have the same rights as us. We will not hurt them, and they will not suffer any injustice at our hands.
- We will not call any Muslim an infidel or accuse him of blasphemy unless there is proof and unless all of the conditions of such a case exist. We will be fair and we will be just. We will judge Muslims according to their Islam and religion, and we will make jihad and fight against criminals according to their crimes.
- This jihad is a duty for all of us Muslims. The world and the religion will not be good without it.

> He said, 'O my people! Have you considered, should I stand on a manifest proof from my Lord, who has provided me a good provision from Himself? I do not wish to oppose you by what I forbid you. I only desire to put things in order, as far as I can, and my success lies only with Allah: in Him I have put my trust, and to Him I turn penitently. (Quran, Hud: 88)

And this is why our beloved Prophet decided to take up arms and engage in jihad.

- The meaning of jihad in the Book and the Sunnah has many forms and methods.
- In the end, our methodology depends on the words of Allah and His Prophet and according to the guidance of the Prophet and the basics of religion. If we have different opinions, we will always go back to the Holy Book of the Quran to settle these differences.

The Targets of the Group

Our goals and targets are noble, fair, and supreme. These goals include defending those who believe and fight against the infidels so there is no disorder, and for all religion to be for Allah.

These goals will be clearer if we say that we follow all the goals of the Shariah, which are known as the five or six necessities. These necessities are defending and saving religion, human life, money, mind, fidelity, and honour.

This comes straight from the Godly covenant, which brings only the truth. It is what balances everything in life, and it lowers the words of infidels and raises the words of Allah.

The Means

Our way is to engage in jihad in the name of Allah. Everything that helps us reach our superior and noble targets and goals in science, religion, education, the calling, guidance, and spiritual and material readiness are all found in jihad, which is the pinnacle of Islam. Through it, injustice is lifted from Muslims and through it we fight tyrants and save the weak and battle the infidels. It heals the hearts of the believers and helps them be calm and peaceful inside.

> Thus they routed them with Allah's will, and David killed Goliath, and Allah gave him the kingdom and wisdom, and taught him whatever He liked. Were it not for Allah's repelling the people by means of one another, the earth would surely have been corrupted; but Allah is gracious to the world's creatures. (Quran, Al-Baqarah: 251)

> Why should you not fight in the way of Allah and the abased men, women, and children, who say, 'Our Lord, bring us out of this town whose people are wrongdoers, and appoint for us a guardian from You, and appoint for us a helper from You'? (Quran, Al-Nisâ': 75)

Make war on them so that Allah may punish them by your hands and humiliate them, and help you against them, and heal the hearts of a faithful folk, and remove rage from their hearts, and Allah turns clemently to whomever He wishes, and Allah is all-knowing, all-wise. Do you suppose that you will be let off while Allah has not yet ascertained those of you who wage *jihād* and those who do not take, besides Allah and His Apostle and the faithful, anyone as [their] confidant? Allah is well aware of what you do. (Quran, Al-Tawbah: 14-16)

As for other methodologies in other policies and systems, such as Democracy and other ignorant systems, they have all proven to be failures. We do not see any one following and abiding by these ignorant ways unless he is wrong, and he should be guided and should repent from these devious ways and return to the one righteous path.

Membership

Any Muslim male or female has the right to be a member in order to be able to support and help their brothers who are suffering from injustice.

Anyone can be a member who loves jihad and wants to join it to fight the infidels and to help the word of Allah be the prevalent one.

As for people who want to work in the name of the group and to be a part of its operations: they will have to abide by some legitimate rules and considerations, and they will have to be able to help; they have to be clean from any disabilities, and they have to have complete faith in and allegiance to the group and its leadership.

This allegiance is not obligatory for any person who is not a part or a member of the group.

An official member who pays allegiance to the group has responsibilities and rights that are not applicable to people who are not members. Any person, whether a member or not, will not be faced with injustice; and if any differences occur, the problem will be settled by a committee of judges. Know that we will never do anything that is against the Shariah, the *Sunnah*, and the Holy Book of the Quran:

> **O mankind!** Indeed We created you from a male and a female, and made you nations and tribes that you may identify yourselves with one another. Indeed the noblest of you in the sight of Allah is the most Godwary among you. Indeed Allah is all-knowing, all-aware. (Quran, Al-Hujurât: 13)

Empowerment and Support Group

They are tasked with helping and supporting the group on all levels. It depends on the abilities and the needs of the group. They are trusted and protected by the group, and their wives and children and secrets have to be protected. When dealing with them, there has to be:

- A benefit from such dealing
- Safety from harm
- The existence of a documented permission

General Command

The general command of the group consists of its Amir and the princes of different areas, the leaders of the committees who represent the Consultative Council of the group. They all work as one cooperative and complete unit, as Allah has said: "and their affairs are by counsel among themselves" (Quran, Al-Shurâ: 38).

First: Its judgment: Binding[i]

Second: Its type: It is a necessary private emirate, and it can expand to include some of the characteristics of a general emirate. This depends on the abilities and the specific needs of the group, which are decided by the Consultative Council of the group.

Third: The conditions of leading the emirate
- To be a true Muslim
- Maturity and puberty
- Sanity
- Maleness
- Freedom
- Justice
- Shariah science
- Wisdom
- Freedom from any disability

Fourth: The things that would prevent someone from leading the emirate
- Death
- Lack of faith in God / being an unbeliever
- The emergence of any disabilities or obstacles
- Straying away from religion and the true path, which can harm the calling and the group
- Any treason against the group and its principles and basics; for example, executing things in ways other than the group stated
- Captivity, depending on the decision of the Consultative Council of the group

Fifth: The rights of the Amir over the members of his group
- They must obey him in doing good
- Help and support him to do right
- Advise him
- Think well of him
- Respect him
- Stop people from talking badly about him

---

i   Translator's note: According to Islamic jurisprudence, the judgments of an amir and general command are binding on all members of the related group.

Sixth: The duties of the Amir
- Being fair and just in his duties and rights
- Thinking well of the members and being kind to them
- Advising Muslims
- Making sure that the wives, children, and safety of Muslims are protected
- Preparing for jihad mentally and financially
- Keeping secrets
- Being a good role model for Muslims in general and jihadists in particular
- Working to maintain the unity of the group
- Working to reunite Muslims
- Handling and managing the affairs of the group
- Protecting the women
- Taking care to achieve the interests of the group
- Gathering and raising money according to the Shariah and spending it also in accordance with the Shariah
- Settling differences between the brothers
- Coordinating work with the Consultative Council of the group
- Heading the consultative sessions and choosing the best opinions after consulting with others

Seventh: The powers of the Amir
- Managing the affairs of the group completely
- Obligating the members of the group to follow the decisions and the instructions that the group issues
- Choosing the princes of the committees for the different areas and districts
- Choosing the persons responsible for special and temporary missions
- Choosing the person who will replace him if he is not there
- Issuing decisions, guidelines, and instruction for the group, with the exception of crucial decisions, which have to be taken with the presence of the Consultative Council of the group, such as:
- Changing any of the basics and principles mentioned in the covenant of the group
- Opening a new battlefront
- Making peace or truces with enemies
- Deposing himself from leadership
- Deposing any member of the council or any judge of the group
- Dealing with any foreigner organisations
- Deposing any of the district princes

Consultative Council (Leadership Council)
First: The judgment of the Consultative Council: Binding

Second: Identifying the Consultative Council (Leadership Council)
The Consultative Council of the group consists of its general leadership and management. It consists of its prince, the princes of the districts, the heads of the committees, and others from the best men of the group who are wise and are known for their rightful decisions and opinions as well as experienced and specialised personnel.

Third: The mission and duties of the Leadership Council (the Consultative Council)
- Helping the Amir manage the affairs of the group and its policies
- Taking care to achieve the interests of the group
- Appointing the Amir or deposing him when necessary
- Watching and monitoring the Amir and holding him accountable for his actions
- Every member has the right to call for the assembly of the council with the leadership of the Amir in cases of any urgent and crucial matter. If the urgent matter is related to a quarrel with the Amir, he has the right to call for the assembly. In this case, the council is tasked with choosing someone to settle the quarrel without having the Amir present.
- Picking a judge other than the judge of the group when necessary
- Picking the members of the Consultative Council or deposing them
- Paying allegiance to the Amir—and their allegiance is obligatory for the members of the group, as they will have to follow it

Leading the Districts
First: Identifying the Amir (Leader) of a District
He has the same respect and position as the Amir but in his own area and district. Upon choosing him, there are some local considerations to be borne in mind.

Second: The conditions
It is essential for the leader of each district or area to meet all of the conditions of the group leader (Amir).

Third: His rights
He has the same rights in his district as the group leader or Amir.

Fourth: His duties
He has the same duties as the group Amir towards the people in his district. He also has to report to the Amir of the group everything that happens after consulting with his men in order to guarantee the unity of the group. He also has to consult his men concerning how to execute the decisions of the Consultative Council.

The Local Consultative Council of the District's duties are: to investigate how to execute what the Consultative Council has decided and investigate everything that is related to their district after the district leader reports it to the group leader.

Fifth: The powers of the District Amir
Choosing the best men from his district to consult with them about the affairs of the district

Choosing the people who will carry out the special operations and the temporary operations in his district

He has the right to look into and manage the affairs of his district, but he will have to present it and confirm it with the leadership first to maintain the chain of command

Committees and Organisations
- The Shariah Committee
- The Military Committee (includes the Medical Committee)
- The Economy Committee
- The Media and Foreign Affairs Committee
- The Social Affairs Committee
- The Judicial Committee
- The Security Committee

The Calling and Guidance Committee
This includes a group of qualified people who have qualifications in religious sciences / theology and Shariah-related qualifications.

Their mission: to guide the group in a way that pleases Allah and to investigate any ignorance that could misguide or make the brothers stray from the one true path.

This committee consists of its head and three branches
- The Calling and Guidance Branch
- The Composition Branch
- Printing and Distribution Branch

Third: The powers and permissions of the head of the committee
- Organising a practical working program for the committee and presenting it to the Amir
- Working hard to implement the proposed program
- Establishing legitimate Shariah schools
- Picking the correct and suitable people for teaching and dispatching them to do the job after consulting the Amir
- Revising and enhancing everything that the committee issues before it is printed
- He has the right to cancel or revise any research topics that are proposed by the members
- He has the right to research and expand that research in order to fix any issues
- He is tasked with researching the religious/theological issues that are presented to the committee

The Calling and Guidance Branch
The mission of this branch is to call people to Islam and then to guide those who enter the religion and help them understand Islam and follow its guidelines and the words of the Quran and the Sunnah. They are also tasked with spreading Shariah science in the ummah and warning Muslims against the treacherous traps that are laid by their enemies to make them stray from Islam.

Printing and Distribution Branch
This branch is tasked with printing and distributing everything that the committee issues, by any means and any ways possible

The Composition Branch
The duty of this branch is to pick a group of suitable people and qualified personnel to head the scientific department. They will do this by using any means necessary. This is done in order to fight the upcoming theological challenges in the future.

The Military Committee

First: Identifying it: This committee is considered one of the main supporting pillars of the group. It represents the protective fortress that protects Muslims from the attacks of their enemies. It is also the way to strike terror into the hearts of the enemies.

The task of this committee: Supervising and dealing with and managing everything that is related to the military affairs of the group. This has to be done in coordination with the other committees to guarantee the safety of the affairs of the group.

Second: Its composition: It consists of its leader (the general commander) and seven branches, namely:
1. Recruitment and Training Branch
2. Funding and Supply Branch
3. Industrial Branch
4. Recon Branch
5. Military Engineering Branch
6. Military Planning and Studies Branch
7. Medical and Nursing Branch

The powers of the Military Committee leader
8. He is appointed and can be removed by the Amir
9. Determining the practical program of the committee and presenting it to the Amir
10. Doing his best in order to implement the program
11. He has the right to issue military decisions with the approval of the Amir
12. Supervising the implementation of the military instructions
13. He is tasked with building training camps for the entire group
14. Supervising the general military actions
15. Supervising the utilisation of all of the means necessary to satisfy the military needs of the branch, including weapons and materials
16. He has the right to handle and manage the foreign ammunition according to the terms of the agreement
17. He has the right to hold all of the committee members accountable

Recruitment and Training Branch

The duties of this branch of this committee are the following:
1. Determining a training program for the soldiers

2. Supervising the implementation of such a program
3. Studying the characteristics of the newly recruited soldiers and then dispatching them to the locations that are suitable for them, with the help of the Social Affairs Committee

Funding and Supply Branch
The duty of this branch is to supervise the spending of money on the jihadists in order to fulfil their military needs.

ANNEX 2

One of the first videos of Ansaru

available on 1 June 2012

Translated from Hausa by Nathaniel Danjibo

The Enlightenment/Information Committee presents an important message from Jama'a Atu Ansaril Muslimina Fi Biladis-Sudan

In the name of Allah, the Beneficent, the Merciful.

We reject the reports and explanations that some newspapers and other channels of information propagated and fashioned with regards to this blessed group, Jama'a atu Ansaril Muslimina fi Biladis-Sudan, which wishes the people well.

Without any cogent reason or reliable source, they have spread the news that Muhammed Nuhu is our leader and that we came out to fight the Jama'a atul Alul Sunna Lid Da'awatis Jihadi. At the same time, some of them [the media] thought that we connived with the Jama'a atul Alul Sunna Lid Da'awatis Jihadi in order to confuse the people, and they have spread other rumours.

In order to set the record straight and enlighten the people concerning the various lies, we have decided to provide a full explanation with regards to this group. This had already been provided by our leader, Abu Osama, who explained that the reason we took these steps is because of the occurrence of evil and terrorist acts in Nigeria, which the infidels are carrying out against Muslims. He explained our [...] clear intentions, calling on the real religion to enlighten the people.

Assisting Muslims and defending them from terrorism and evil acts inflicted upon them, taking revenge on anybody who inflicts evil on Muslims, restoring right values for Islam and for Muslims [...] —these were what led to our emergence. These are our crystal-clear intentions and the reasons for our emergence. There is no connivance or its like with the Jama'a atul Alul Sunna Lid Da'awatis Jihadi, save the fact that they are our brethren in Islam. We accept them as we do every Muslim. Sometimes they are on the right path, and sometimes they commit error. We are together with them when they are on the right path, and we strengthen and support them. However, we do not support them when they commit error.

However, in our understanding, the leader of the Jama'a atul Alul Sunna Lid Da'awatis Jihadi has gone slightly beyond his bounds by refusing to admonish his followers. In our understanding, he has erred with the kind of position he bestows on himself, referring to himself as the *imam*, and the teachings he bequeaths to his followers on the problems confronting the country. Furthermore, we do not support his teachings concerning these problems. This is, however, a different issue altogether.

The issues that the media are projecting, that there is absolute enmity and disagreement between us and the leader of the group [Boko Haram], are further perpetrated lies. Allah the Eternal knows better. However, the deeds of the Jama'a atul Alul Sunna Lid Da'awatis Jihadi continue to perplex and worry us.

On the 10th of April of this year [2012], that is of the Western calendar—which is the same as the 18th of the month of Jumadal Ulla in the year 1433 of the pilgrimage of the Messenger of Allah (peace be upon him)—some among the followers under the leadership of Jama'a atul Alul Sunna Lid Da'awatis Jihadi were trying to murder a servant of Allah, their fellow Muslim brother and a leading Islamic scholar without committing any offence, save that he is among those that would not continue to obey what is contrary to Allah's injunction; those that are now with Ja'ama tul Ansaru Muslimina Fibiladis-Sudan.

They carried out these attacks at about 7:30 pm. Before then, another brother, at a location the targeted brother used to visit, confirmed that they had come armed to this location in search of the targeted servant of Allah. They intensified their search for him until Allah the Eternal made it possible for them to find him at a particular time on a given day at the place of another brother, who confronted them and tried to escape. Then they took out their weapons in broad daylight and opened fire on him and those with him in the car. However, Allah the Eternal and Knowing thwarted their mission.

The beginning of these attacks took different forms, like when they were seen carrying out the attacks and in the presence of many witnesses. In fact, some among the leaders have also confirmed this. They chided them and condemned these attacks. Still, some amongst them have tried to say that the group was not aware of the attacks. We, however, know that if the group carried out the attacks, it would not come out to accept responsibility. And in fact, more than one year ago, this is the same group that issued an assassination verdict in various write-ups of their leader, such as [in Mohammed Yusuf's] book, where they tried to justify the execution of anybody who disobeys the *imam*. And in other sections of that book, they have conveyed this same message [...]. According to what he [their leader] said on one of the cassettes, either a person is repentant and joins the group or he will have himself to blame.

Because of these kinds of statements that the group issues, and indoctrinating the people who obey them, for a long time now some members of the group [Boko Haram] have boasted that they will phase out our group. Now they have started. Why does the group not learn from the Messenger of Allah when he was confronted with such situations? Take for example the *Hadith* of Abdullahi the son of Umar in the Sahih Buhari, when they went to a certain war. Then Khalihu Ibn Walid killed some Muslims by mistake. When they returned from war and the issue was reported to the Messenger of Allah, then the Messenger of Allah raised his hand up to Allah and said [...]: In the multitude, everybody is a witness and it is written and read until this date. Even the knowledgeable scholars, such as Abdullahi Ibn Umar, dissociated themselves from such acts, and they refused to revere Khalihu even though he was appointed the commander of the war by the Messenger of Allah for the expected jihad.

The second example is the killing of Osamatu Ibn Zayed, in Sahil Buhari and Sahil Muslim and several books of the *Hadith*, when he killed a Muslim in error. The Messenger of Allah was very hard on him, to the point that Sahid Ibn Osama was gravely troubled. He said: "I wished that this had happened before I became a Muslim"—because of the way the Messenger of Allah kept reminding him. In *Fat-hil Bari*, Alhaju Ibn Haja brought another example [...] about the son of Umar when a report came that a certain non-believer was killed before Istitaba, when Shariah had said such should be executed after Istitaba. There and then Umar dissociated himself in the presence of the gathering and said, "Oh Allah, I did not carry out the act and I am not in support of it; and when the report came to me, I did not rejoice. I expressed my sadness."

It then behoves us that, if we are following in the footsteps of real leaders before us, it is expected that if such happens, the Jaa'matu Alul Sunna Lid Da'awatis Jihadi group—if it did not sanction the attacks and is not in support of the attacks and is not happy with the attacks—it is expected that the group should come out into the open to exonerate itself. It is the tradition of the Messenger of Allah; it is the tradition of the Rightly Guided Caliphs. And if these kinds of attacks happened without the knowledge of the group, then we would say that it is incumbent upon all of us to be on the right path. We should refrain from blood shedding and the destruction of people's wealth without any reason derived from either the Koran or the *Hadith*. We are saying this because these attacks are not the first nor are they the second. In fact, apart from that, we doubt their true intention.

Last year, they murdered Mallam Tuja, the father of Abba Jinel, at Bama Park in Maiduguri, without any cogent, acceptable reason embedded in Shariah. Not long after that, recently, they have killed Babagana Zarami, the older brother of Bashir Abulabule, without any cogent reason acceptable to Shariah. And if we had to give an explanation of these attacks, carried out on the blood and wealth of Muslims without any acceptable reasons derived from Shariah, these types of attacks would not have taken place. Yet they have boasted that they are responsible for carrying out the attacks.

Oh brethren, we should know that apart from *shirk*,[1] the gravest sin before Allah Eternal is the taking of a life, without a basic reason from His verses or the *Hadith* of His Messenger. Another offence that may be greater than this, an offence that may be greater than murder, is reverence and obedience to, or an invitation to join, leaders who have chosen the wrong path by carrying out evil deeds—regardless of whether a person is knowledgeable or ignorant about what these leaders do.

Taking instruction from any leader or champion or any teacher or *imam* for the purpose of carrying out evil acts without any reason is contrary to Shariah. It is amongst what leading Tawhid scholars would classify as *shirqup da'a* [wrong predication]. It is for this reason that Ibn Kaiyul, when he was explaining, asked [...]: What is reverence beyond expectation? Allah's Messenger said [...]: Reverence is accorded based on what Shariah has approved, and be mindful of what the Messenger of Allah has termed *ma'aruf* [accepted]. There is something you know that Shariah approves of; there is something you know that Shariah does not approve of; there is also that which you are doubtful concerning whether or not Shariah has approved of it. You should know then that only the first is considered *al-ma'aruf* [acceptable].

Whatever you know that Shariah approves of is *ma'aruf*, but whatever Shariah does not approve of is forbidden. If, in the latter case, you decide to revere your parent, a leader, an *imam* or a champion, you will be guilty of *shirqa*, *shirqu* [the wrong] type of reverence. Allah said [...], let us excel in our spiritual deeds [...]. And even if it is the Maliki school of thought, or hanifiya Hanafi, or hambaliya Hanbali, or shfi'iya Shafi'i, that you tend to break in order to abide by the word of Imam Malik or Abu Hanifa or Imam Shafi'i or Imam Ahmed, teachers have said you will be guilty of *shirqut* type of reverence [...]. Then what if the one you are according reverence to without investigation is not as knowledgeable as the pious forebears?

Some love their parents or their teachers or their leaders, hoping that they will not instruct them on things that are not of Allah. If someone finds himself in this situation of reverence, he will be guilty of *shirqul muhabba*, which is an offshoot of *shirqut da'a*. If you have not forgotten the explanation of Ibn Khailil, he stated that [...] is when someone is worshipped or followed ignorantly. According to the explanation of Ibn Khailil, if you do wrong things ignorantly you are guilty of *shirqa* and not just offending Allah the Eternal. Therefore, brethren, it is important that we become mindful; we should know that for all our actions and whatever we say, we shall stand before Allah the Eternal, who will judge us.

My brethren, we should continue to exercise patience with regards to the troubles we receive from our brothers. We should not let that make us deviate from our noble intention; we should not be lackadaisical and embrace evil deeds. It is incumbent upon those who support wrongdoing to wake up; they must know that Allah the Eternal forbids any wrongdoing, even in the slightest way, by those who offend him, or the wicked and oppressive or those who commit *bidi'a* [forbidden innovation]. [...] Let us refer to the Tafsiri [lesson] of Qurbal [...] that forbids wrongdoing by a group or belonging to a group that is notorious for evil deeds. Does the magnitude of the *bidi'a* extend to unbelief or not? If you go against Allah's wish [...], you should not expect mercy [...]. It is under this verse that teachers make reference to [...] Izfuyanu Sarhi. Someone that associated with an evil king came to seek clarification from Izfuyanu Sarhi. The person said he was only a tailor to the evil king, and asked if he himself was guilty of committing evil against others. Izfuyanu Sarhi said to him: "You, in fact, are among the wicked ones from the beginning."

Then my brother, why should you be the one that will be instructed to kill your brother or provide a clue to how he will be targeted or something similar to that? In fact, even if you are instructed to destroy your brother, the Messenger of Allah said [...]: Do not hate one another; do not turn your back on others; do not be angry with one another; and do not allow an unbeliever to cheat your brother Muslim. He is your Muslim brother and the Messenger of Allah said you should not oppress your fellow Muslim [...]. You must not oppress him; you must not dismiss him so that an oppressor will oppress him; you must not ignore him when he is in most need of your help. [...] The Messenger of Allah said all of this. But you stay put and are instructed that you do not have any business with anybody; you should not speak to him even though he is your Muslim brother. The Messenger of Allah said you must not stop speaking to him; yet the *imam* said you must not speak to him. Then you accept the words of the *imam* and reject the words of the Messenger of Allah. The Messenger of Allah says do not hate him because he is your fellow Muslim brother, but your champion says you should hate him because he is not your brother. Then you decide to follow the words of your champion and reject the words of the Messenger of Allah. It is important for us to know that this is a grievous offence, which will make us dread what will befall us if we do not desist.

We should learn from real and reliable scholars, such as Abdullahi the son of Umar and Sa'ad the son of Abu Wakkas, when they aver that Allah says war should only be executed in order to avert trouble. But you prefer war so that there will be trouble. Because if you kill your fellow Muslim brother, do you avert trouble or do you invite trouble? Remember Abubakar among the Companions of the Messenger of Allah, the one that shows us mercy with the *Hadith* he wrote derived from the Messenger of Allah, where he says that if a Muslim and a fellow Muslim confront each other with weapons with the intention to kill each other, the one that is killed and the one that kills will both go to Hell. The Companions of the Prophet said: "We understand the fact that the one who killed enters Hell; but the one that is killed, what is his offence?" "The Messenger of Allah said he too came with the intention to kill."

In this era, reliable *mujahideen* are those like Abu mis Abin Zarkhawi, who said: "It is better for me to be beheaded in public rather than kill a Muslim without any reason." Shariah has confirmed that it is not right for you to allow anybody to oppress you, to shed your blood or confiscate your property while you fold your arms and watch him. So several *Hadith*, also in Sahih Muslim, have taught, but especially that of Abdulrazak and the others. An example among the Companions of the Prophet is Abdullahi son of Umar, son of Ahs, as recorded in Aqbul and Sahih Muslim. He was to be oppressed by someone, a commander of Islam who wanted to confiscate his farm. He did not understand why and therefore refused. He and his people took up arms like [...] Sahid Abu Zayd, one amongst the Companions of the Prophet [...]. Indeed, Shariah said you are not expected to remain idle and allow others to come and kill you or confiscate your property. This means that if anybody seeks to oppress you, Shariah has authorised you to defend yourself. However, we must not go beyond what Shariah has approved and say we will imitate what they do. This would make us deviate from our noble intention; it would send us to perdition. Our real enemies, atheists and Christians, will rejoice when they see us fighting amongst ourselves, and our enemies will be laughing at us. This will make the Lord Almighty angry with us.

Oh Allah, may you increase in us the knowledge of Shariah, give us the perseverance, and confirm us in the tradition of your Messenger [...]. It is better to do the kind of thing that Abu the son of Adam did when he said to his bother: "If you want to stretch out your hand to kill me, I will not stretch out my hand to kill you, because I am afraid of Allah the Almighty and Everlasting." When his brother killed him, what was his life like? Allah said [...]: Brethren, let us know that oppression and wickedness towards Muslims is one of things that will not make us succeed [...].

Note

1. Associating others with Allah.

ANNEX 3

Islam and Western education in Nigeria
between accommodation and confrontation

Marc-Antoine Pérouse de Montclos

Boko Haram violently rejects the Western model of education, but its position does not reflect the general feelings of the population. On the contrary, many Nigerian Muslims have adopted and invested in modern education, especially the Yoruba. From a historical point of view, it is quite interesting in this regard to compare their process of accommodation with the confrontational attitude of Boko Haram. In the South-West, in particular, the way the colonial authorities attempted to appease local apathy, opposition, and resistance to British education is also instructive. In the beginning, indeed, many Yoruba Muslims ignored or boycotted missionary schools because they feared their children would be converted to Christianity. As a result, the Lagos-based colonial authorities decided in 1889 to fund Arabic courses in Christian schools. In the same vein, the British paid Muslim teachers and established government Muslim schools, first in Lagos in 1896, then in Epe in 1898, and Badagry in 1899.

Meanwhile, Yoruba Muslims set up their own organisations to encourage literacy and disseminate the message of Islam. Generally restricted to the educated urban elite, especially in Lagos, these groups clearly opted for adapting the Western model to Islamic requirements, unlike Boko Haram. Interestingly enough, some of these groups were and are still considered sects. A quick review of the Ahmadiyyah, the Islamic Society of Nigeria, and the Young Ansar-ud-Deen shows how Islamic reform could cope with the challenges of modernity without resorting to violence.

The Ahmadiyyah Brotherhood, to begin with, was created by an Indian prophet, Mirza Ghullam Ahmad, and imported to Nigeria around 1913 through publications found in London. It mainly reached the Muslim educated elites in Lagos, where a Moslem Literary Society and a Juvenile Moslem Society were set up. The Ahmadiyyah did not reject modern education and aimed to benefit from both Western and Islamic training. In Nigeria, it was the first Muslim organisation to establish its own denominational primary school, opened in Lagos in 1922 and followed by a secondary school in 1948. It was also the first to translate the Quran into Yoruba in 1976. In the same vein, it did not reject the Nigerian secular state. Some of its members or sympathisers were high-ranking officials, such as Kafaru Oluwole Tinubu, a senior police officer, and Musliu Adeola Kunbi Smith, an Inspector General of Police who was a "crescent bearer". But the Ahmadiyyah always remained an elitist organisation. In 1939, for instance, it participated in the formation of the "Crescent Bearers" to promote Western literacy amongst the Muslim community. This offshoot was self-restricted to a maximum of thirty members, who had to be between forty and sixty years of age. Moreover, the Ahmadiyyah was always considered a heterodox sect, and some clerics even declared that it was not Muslim at all. Saudi Arabia finally refused its members entry to perform the *hajj* and, in 1973, the Ahmadiyyah was banned by Pakistan, Syria, Jordan, Egypt, and the World Muslim League. In 1974, it eventually had to change its name to Anwar ul-Islam.

The Islamic Society of Nigeria was launched in 1924 by Lawal Basil Augusto, a founder of the Nigerian Ahmadiyyah who renounced Mirza Ghullam Ahmad as prophet. Like its predecessor, it touched Muslim urban educated elites. Before seceding from Ahmadiyyah, Lawal Basil Augusto had actually established the first Muslim grammar school in 1916, and in 1924 he was to become the first Muslim lawyer in West Africa. The Islamic Society of Nigeria championed education for girls and aimed to acquire land to build schools, publish books, produce Islamic literature, and fund libraries—the same fundamental objectives as its successor in 1964, Jamaatul Islamiyya. Unlike Boko Haram, it did not reject Western modernity and the secularity of the state. Amongst its members were, for instance, Hamzat Adisa Subair, a co-founder of the National Bank of Nigeria and the first Nigerian Muslim to qualify as a professional chartered accountant, and Professor Aliu Babatunde Fafunwa, a federal minister of education and the president of Jamaatul Islamiyya from 1995.

Young Ansar-ud-Deen (The Followers of the Religion) was created in 1923 to disseminate the message of Islam, translate the Quran into local languages, encourage literacy, compete with mission schools, and provide quality Western education free of Christian indoctrination. Like the

Ahmadiyyah and the Islamic Society of Nigeria, it was initially based in Lagos only, where it opened its first primary school in 1931. It then extended into the hinterland and was quickly recognised as a pioneer in education. In 1939, for instance, it inspired the formation of the Young Nawair-ud-Deen in Abeokuta, which built many schools and became the Nawair-ud-Deen Society of Nigeria in 1966. In 1942, Ansar-ud-Deen opened another primary school, in Okepopo, and in 1946 it established a training college in Otta to solve the problem of shortage of Muslim teachers. It also gave scholarship awards to study abroad. With eighty schools all over Yorubaland in 1955, it was formally registered as the Ansar-ud-Deen Society in 1961. However, religious mission schools were later on nationalised by the military regime in the 1970s. Moreover, Ansar-ud-Deen never succeeded in establishing an Islamic university, unlike NASFAT (Nasrul-Lahi-il-Fathi), a newer organisation. The Ansar-ud-Deen Society is still active today and has no relationship whatsoever with the homonymous terrorist group Ansar Dine in northern Mali. The Nigerian Ansar-ud-Deen has always believed that a reformist Islam could co-exist with Western innovations. It permitted women to pray in the mosque and rejected Salafism. According to Sheikh Abdur-Rahman Olanrewaju Ahmad, its leader since 2002, Boko Haram is thus a social deviance, which does not represent the message of Islam because the Quran emphasises the need for education and study.

Bibliography

Fisher, H. (1961), "The Ahmadiyya Movement in Nigeria". In: K. Kirkwood, ed., *African Affairs*. Carbondale: Southern Illinois University Press, pp. 60-88.

Gbadamosi, T. (1978), *The Growth of Islam Among the Yoruba, 1841–1908*. London: Longmans.

Imam, Y.O. (2004), "Religious Organisations as Progressive Social Change: A Case Study of Ansar-ud-Deen Society of Nigeria", *Islamic Studies* 43(4): 631-51.

Oyeweso, S. & M. Raheemson, eds (2013), *Actors and Institutions in the Development of Islam in Lagos State*. Ibadan: Matrixcy Books.

Reichmuth, S. (1996), "Education and the Growth of Religious Associations Among Yoruba Muslims", *Journal of Religion in Africa* 26(4): 365-405.

ANNEX 4

Marc-Antoine Pérouse de Montclos

Religious Organization	Political party	Period in power	Main leaders
Ansar / Mahdists	Umma Party (UP)	Coalition with the PDP from Independence in January 1956 until the first military coup of November 1958. Following the return of civilians to power and elections in June 1965, it formed a coalition government with the National Unionist Party (NUP) under the Premiership of a UP stalwart, Muhammad Ahmad Mahgoub. After the elections of April 1968, it joined another coalition government with the Democratic Unionist Party (DUP), but was banned by Jaafar Muhammad Nimeiri in May 1969. After the fall of the military junta, it won elections in April 1986 and came back to power under the premiership of Sadiq al-Mahdi, first with the DUP, then in a larger government of national unity with the NIF following a second round of elections in April 1988. Following the Islamist coup of June 1989, the UP joined the opposition in exile in Eritrea under the umbrella of the National Democratic Alliance (NDA). However, it left this coalition in March 2000, when political parties were legalised without requiring a special authorisation from the government, except for elections.	Sadiq al-Mahdi, who replaced his father Said Abd al-Rahman al-Mahdi after the latter's death on 24 March 1959. Within the UP, he was contested by Prime Minister Abdallah Khalil because he tried to negotiate an agreement with the NUP after the elections of February 1958. When Sadiq al-Mahdi died in September 1961, his homonymous son replaced him and was briefly Prime Minister between July 1966 and May 1967. After the military coup of June 1989, Sadiq al-Mahdi Junior stayed for a period in Khartoum and eventually fled to Asmara in Eritrea, where he joined the opposition in exile (both the UP and the DUP) under the umbrella of the National Democratic Alliance (NDA) in November 1996. He returned to the Sudan in November 2000 to reorganise the UP and participate in a government of national unity, following the signature of a comprehensive peace agreement in Nairobi (Kenya) in January 2005.

Annex 4 Islam and political parties in the Sudan (continued)

Religious Organization	Political Party	Period in Power	Main Leaders
Khatmiyya	People's Democratic Party (PDP)	From January 1956, coalition with the UP to succeed the NUP government of Ahmed Ismail el Azhari, in power since January 1954. Led by Said Ali al-Mirghani, the Khatmiyya initially supported Ahmed Ismail el Azhari to form a political body, the Ashigga, in 1944 and opposed the UP by participating in 1950 in the launch of a National Front, the predecessor of the National Unionist Party (NUP).	Said Ali al-Mirghani. Unlike his arch-rival Said Abd al-Rahman al-Mahdi, who preferred to cooperate with the British coloniser to avoid the domination of Cairo, he favoured Egypt. But he was weakened by the military coup of Gamal Abdel Nasser in 1952 and the fall of General Muhammad Naguib in 1954, who was quite popular in Khartoum because of his Sudanese origin.
Khatmiyya	Democratic Unionist Party (DUP), a merger of the PDP and the NUP	Coalition with the UP under the Premiership of Muhammad Ahmad Mahgoub after winning the elections of April 1968 and until the coup of Jaafar Muhammad Nimeiri in May 1969. After the fall of the military junta, the DUP won elections in April 1986 and came back to power, first with the UP, then in a larger government of national unity with the NIF in April 1988. However, the DUP left the government when the UP and the NIF refused to acknowledge the peace agreement it had signed with the SPLA (Sudan People's Liberation Army) in Addis-Ababa in November 1988. Pressed by the Army to give more funds to fight in the south, it then formed a last coalition government with the UP and without the NIF in March 1989, just before the coup of General Omar Hassan Ahmad al Bashir.	Mohammed Osman al-Mirghani, who succeeded Said Ali al-Mirghani after the latter's death in February 1968. Another member of the family and the party, Ahmed Ali al-Mirghani, was President of Sudan from May 1986 until the military coup of June 1989. He then went into exile in Egypt, where he died on November 2008 after a brief return to Khartoum on November 2001.

Annex 4 *Islam and political parties in the Sudan (continued)*

Religious Organization	Political Party	Period in Power	Main Leaders
Muslim Brothers	Islamic Charter Front (al-Jabhah al-Islamiyah al-Qawmiyah)	Established in the mid-1960s and briefly in power when its leader, Dr. Hassan al-Turabi, entered a coalition government in August 1979. The organisation was often called the Muslim Brotherhood (al Hizb al-Akhwan al Muslimin) after its Egyptian model.	Hassan al-Turabi, until he launched his own NIF in 1985 against the old guard of the Muslim Brothers, who grew closer to the Ansar and denounced the speculation of Islamic banks.

Religious Organization	Political Party	Period in Power	Main Leaders
Muslim Brothers	National Islamic Front (NIF)	From April 1988, government of national unity with the UP, the DUP and a few southerners. After the coup of June 1989, which banned political parties, a transitional parliament was established in January 1992, and Hassan al-Turabi grew closer to General Omar Hassan Ahmad al Bashir, who officially dissolved the military junta and put in place a civilian regime in October 1993. In October 1992, the NIF thus participated in local elections conducted according to the Islamic principles of consultation (shura) and consensus (ijma). However, it lost in Khartoum, where it circumvented the results by placing clients as heads of districts. Likewise, during the general elections of March 1996, which were boycotted by the democratic opposition, only 53 per cent of the seats in the parliament were contested; the rest were allocated through a process of "silent consensus" (ijma al-sikouti). The turnout varied between 72 per cent, according to the government, and 5 per cent, according to the opposition. More probably the figure was 45 per cent of registered voters, as against 80 per cent in 1986. Bashir was declared the winner with 75.7 per cent of the votes.	Hassan al-Turabi, who had refused to join the military junta when Jaafar Muhammad Nimeiri imposed Shariah in September 1983, remained in the opposition when the NIF became the third-largest party in the Sudan at the elections of April 1986. From April 1988, he then participated in a government of national unity with his brother-in-law Sadiq al-Mahdi (UP) and even became Vice-Prime Minister in December 1988. But he was dismissed in March 1989 and briefly jailed as Foreign Affairs Minister of Sadiq al-Mahdi, when General Omar Hassan Ahmad al Bashir took power three months later. Hassan al-Turabi was later to be a key element in the Islamist junta throughout the 1990s.

Annex 4 Islam and political parties in the Sudan *(continued)*

Religious Organization	Political Party	Period in Power	Main Leaders
Muslim Brothers	National Congress (Mutammar al Watani)	Succeeding to the NIF when a new constitution re-introduced a multiparty system in June 1998, it remained in power until the dissolution of the parliament (December 1999) and the proclamation of a state of emergency by General Bashir to get rid of Hassan al-Turabi.	Hassan al-Turabi, who began secret negotiations with Sadiq al-Mahdi and the opposition to establish a prime minister and elect-governors in order to counterbalance the absolute powers of General Bashir. He was then suspended and deposed from his post of General Secretary of the National Congress in May–June 2000
Muslim Brothers	People's National Congress	Officially in power from June 2000, as a continuation of the National Congress without Hassan al-Turabi. However, the latter still had some supporters within the party. He was arrested on 21 February 2001 because he had just negotiated in Geneva an unusual alliance with the SPLA. Released on 13 October 2003, he was again placed under arrest on 30 March 2004, jailed in the prison of Kober, and accused of plotting a coup.	General Omar Hassan Ahmad al Bashir: he got 86 per cent of the votes during the presidential elections of December 2000, which were contested by Jaafar Muhammad Nimeiri (just back from exile) but boycotted by the democratic opposition (DUP, UP) and Hassan al Tourabi's faction of the People's National Congress.

Source: Hunwick (1992); Warburg (2003); Fluehr-Lobban (1987); Pérouse de Montclos (2003).

CONTRIBUTORS BIOS

Kyari Mohammed (PhD) is Professor of History and Director of the Centre for Peace and Security Studies at the Modibbo Adama University of Technology, Yola, Adamawa State in north-eastern Nigeria. He has written extensively on the history of inter-group relations, radical Islamic groups, and communal and ethno-religious conflicts and violence in northern Nigeria.

Johannes Harnischfeger (PhD) studied Social Anthropology, Political Science, Philosophy and Literature. He has taught at universities in Kenya, Nigeria, and South Africa. He is a specialist on ethnic and religious conflicts, African folktales, and traditional religion.

Henry Gyang Mang is an assistant lecturer and member of the research staff at the Centre for Conflict Management and Peace Studies, University of Jos, Nigeria. He has a Bachelor's Degree in History from the University of Jos, a Master's of Science in African Studies from the University of Oxford, and a Master's of Arts in History from the Nigerian Defence Academy, Kaduna, Nigeria.

Hannah Hoechner studied International Relations and Development in Dresden and Oxford. Since 2010 she has been pursuing her doctorate at Oxford. She is researching traditional Quranic schools and has conducted over a year of field research in Kano in northern Nigeria.

Portia Roelofs is studying for a PhD in Politics at the Department of Political Economy, King's College London. She has a Bachelor's Degree in Politics, Philosophy and Economics from The Queen's College, Oxford and a Master's in African Politics from the School of Oriental and African Studies, University of London.

Marc-Antoine Pérouse de Montclos is a Doctor in Political Science and a Professor at the French Institute of Geopolitics in the University of Paris 8. A specialist on armed conflicts in Africa south of the Sahara, he graduated from the Institut d'études politiques de Paris (IEP), where he teaches, and is a researcher at the Institut de recherche pour le développement (IRD). He lived for several years in Nigeria, South Africa, and Kenya. He has published some eighty articles and books, including *Le Nigeria* (1994), *Violence et sécurité urbaines* (1997), *L'aide humanitaire, aide à la guerre?* (2001), *Villes et violences en Afrique subsaharienne* (2002), *Diaspora et terrorisme* (2003), *Guerres d'aujourd'hui* (2007), *Etats faibles et sécurité privée en Afrique noire* (2008), *Les humanitaires dans la guerre* (2013), and *La tragédie malienne* (2013).

Freedom Onuoha is a Research Fellow at the Centre for Strategic Research and Studies of the National Defence College, Abuja, Nigeria. With several publications to his credit, Onuoha has been interviewed by many radio and television journalists and is regularly invited to give speeches and lectures in the US and other countries on violent extremist movements.

Rafael Serrano is a research analyst at the Citizenship Initiative (University of South Florida) and graduate student at the Security and Strategy Institute at the University of Exeter. Rafael has researched terrorism, insurgency, militancy, and radicalisation for the last decade in a variety of professional and academic roles.

Zacharias Pieri is a political sociologist and Postdoctoral Research Fellow with the Citizenship Initiative (University of South Florida). Dr. Pieri has extensive ethnographic research experience with Muslim communities and is especially interested in the interactions between religion, politics, and violence.

Gérard Chouin is Assistant Professor of African History at the College of William and Mary, VA, USA, and former Director of the French Institute for Research in Africa (IFRA-Nigeria). He is the series editor of the WAPOSO collection, co-published by IFRA-Nigeria and the African Studies Centre, Leiden.

Manuel Reinert is a researcher and research administrator at the French Institute for Research in Africa (IFRA-Nigeria). He specialises in international relations and conflict analysis. His current project focuses on the rationale behind the designation process of terrorist organisations and uses Boko Haram as a central case study.

Elodie Apard is a specialist in the contemporary history of the Sahel. She holds a PhD from the University of Paris 1 Panthéon-Sorbonne. She is currently Deputy Director and a senior researcher at the French Institute for Research in Africa (IFRA-Nigeria).

Lou Garçon holds a MA in African Studies from SOAS University in London and is currently studying for a PhD in anthropology at EHESS in Paris.

Mathieu Guidère is Professor of Islamic and Middle-Eastern Studies at the University of Toulouse (since 2011). He has held other professorships, at the University of Geneva, Switzerland (2007–2011) and at the French Military Academy of Saint-Cyr, France (2003–2007), where he also chaired the "Strategic Information Analysis Laboratory". Dr. Guidère is co-founder of the "Radicalization Watch Project" and was awarded a Fulbright Grant in 2006 to advance his research on radical Islamism and terrorism. He is fluent in several languages, including a dozen Arabic dialects. Dr. Guidère has published books on the Al-Qaeda organisation and its activities in North Africa and the Middle East. His most recent book published in English is the *Historical Dictionary of Islamic Fundamentalism* (Scarecrow Press, 2012).

Nathaniel Danjibo, PhD, is a fellow of the Peace and Conflict Studies Programme of the Institute of African Studies, University of Ibadan. He holds a PhD in Political Science from the University of Ibadan. He currently teaches in the field of Ethnic Violence and Conflict Resolution, and Religious Conflicts. His major research interest is on ethnicity, religion, democratic governance and human security. He is a consultant with the Nigerian Army School of Education, the UNDP in Nigeria, Kofi Annan International Peacekeeping and Training Centre (KAIPTC), the West African Civil Society Institute (WACSI), the West African Network for Peacebuilding (WANEP), and the West African Peace Institute (WAPI).

INDEX

A

Abacha, General Sani 37, 53, 169
Abuja xv, xix, 5, 28, 40–41, 57, 74, 91–92, 94, 96, 116, 124, 137, 158, 161, 165, 169, 175, 177, 183, 190–91, 196, 198, 200, 207, 218–19, 234, 254, 271, 277–80, 283, 312
Afghanistan 4, 19, 26, 152, 162, 194, 231
al-Barnawi, Khalid 160, 176, 211–12, 280
Ali, Muhammad 4, 7, 280
All Nigeria Peoples Party (ANPP) 5, 21, 40, 41, 49, 138, 169–70, 174, 198, 277
almajirai (itinerant students) vii, xviii, 19, 26, 46, 71–91, 93, 95, 187–89, 217
Al-Qaeda xv, 4, 26, 47, 63, 139, 161, 176–77, 190, 201, 205–207, 210, 219, 279, 312
Anglican 104, 112, 115, 118, 122
Ansaru viii, xvii–xviii, 25–26, 176, 210–212, 220, 222, 225, 246, 251, 281, 282–283, 285, 296–297
Al-Qaeda in Islamic Maghreb (AQIM) xv, xvii, xx, 161–62, 176–77, 184, 199, 205–209, 211–12, 221, 281
army xxi, 21, 27, 49, 51, 59, 133, 151, 158, 172, 175–76, 196, 209, 218, 246, 250, 253, 256, 269–70, 276, 279, 280–81, 283, 307, 313

B

Bauchi 4, 8, 12, 15–16, 25–26, 31, 132, 134, 170–71, 187, 192–93, 196–97, 211, 216, 250, 263–64, 265–66, 276–77, 282
bin Laden, Osama 10, 47, 63, 68, 157, 161, 190

Borno, Bornu xi, xv, xvii, 3–8, 10, 14–15, 19, 21–23, 25, 27, 29, 31, 33, 39–40, 43, 48, 55, 59, 62–63, 65–68, 126, 132, 133–34, 136, 150, 152, 156–59, 161, 168–73, 176, 178, 185, 187, 189–93, 195–98, 200–201, 215, 218–19, 221, 224, 235, 243, 248, 250, 252, 254, 258, 261, 263–66, 271, 273, 275–79, 282–84
Buhari, Muhammadu 35, 48–49, 65, 86, 169–70, 284, 298

C

caliphate xix, 5–6, 17, 30–31, 34, 51, 55, 65, 68, 157, 159, 163, 165, 173, 177, 284
Christian Association of Nigeria (CAN) ix, 15–16, 28, 112, 115–17, 119–20, 122–24, 140, 156–57, 178, 248, 273, 284
Catholic 16, 28, 59, 64, 103–104, 112, 115–20, 123, 222, 278
Church of Christ in Nigeria (COCIN) 16, 122

D

Daily Trust 28–29, 56, 61–66, 92, 122–23, 125, 135, 142–43, 145–46, 148–51, 161, 190, 216, 218–20, 226, 243, 248, 252, 254, 273
Damaturu 7, 22, 29, 42, 133–34, 258, 273, 276, 278–79, 281
dawah (proselytisation) 3–4, 7–10, 19–20, 249
Diffa 162, 271

E

emergency rule, state of emergency 23, 50, 62, 175, 237, 279, 282–83, 309
extrajudicial killing 20, 22–23, 158, 160, 171, 210, 234, 241, 271

F

Fodio, Sheikh Usman dan 51, 55–56, 159, 163, 176
Foi, Buji 169, 189, 193, 234, 275–76
Fulani 16, 22, 34, 44, 50–51, 53, 55–56, 64, 104, 108, 119, 159, 280

G

Gumi, Sheikh Mahmud Abubakar (Izala) 18

H

Hausa xvi–xvii, xxi, 12, 27, 31, 34, 44, 50, 56, 75, 82, 84, 87, 92, 95, 101, 104, 107–108, 110, 119, 121, 135, 159, 163–64, 170, 172, 177, 180, 185, 209, 212, 249, 270–71, 273, 280, 296
hisbah (islamic vigilantes) 43, 166, 172
hostage 3–4, 7, 24, 29, 211, 216, 280

I

improvised explosive devices (IED) 4, 22, 28, 184, 198, 199–201, 207, 213, 221, 281
Iran, Iranian 18, 38, 57, 162
Izala xii, 6, 10–15, 18–20, 34, 38–39, 44–48, 52–53, 56–57, 61, 64, 67, 157–59, 161–162, 168, 172–74, 176, 178, 181, 209, 213, 249–51, 270
Izalatul Bidi'a wa Ikhamatis Sunnah (People Committed to the Removal of Innovations in Islam) 6. *See* Izala

J

Ja'afar, Sheikh Mahmud Adam 7–8, 27–28, 257, 275–76
Jama'at Ansar Al Muslimin Fi Bilad al-Sudan (Vangaurd for the Protection of Muslims in Black Africa) viii, xvii, 285. *See* Ansaru
Jama'atu Ahlis-Sunnah Lidda'awati Wal Jihad (People Committed to the Propagation of the Prophet's Teachings and Jihad) xvi, 155, 157, 164, 186, 275. *See* Boko Haram
Jihad xvi, xxi, 8, 27, 61, 65, 155, 157, 164, 185–86, 208, 221, 245, 275
Joint Task Force (JTF) xix, 21–24, 29, 200, 202, 220, 224–25, 227–28, 233–38, 243, 245–47, 253–54, 256–59, 273, 278, 280–83
Jonathan, Goodluck xv, 80, 156, 160, 170, 209, 248, 277, 279, 282
Jos vii, 29, 61, 63, 97–98, 108, 110, 121–26, 137–38, 158, 160, 177, 179, 261–62, 269, 277, 279, 311

K

Kaduna 27, 30, 34, 57, 61, 63, 95, 109, 118, 121–23, 125, 148, 158–59, 174, 177–80, 187, 197, 216, 251, 254, 263–66, 271, 278, 280–81, 311
Kambar, Abubakar Adam 160, 169, 176, 206, 211, 280
Kanama 4, 6–8, 18, 27, 133, 194, 232–33, 250, 271, 275
Kano xviii, xx, 22, 25, 27, 30, 36, 62–63, 67–68, 74–75, 77, 80–81, 84–85, 91, 93–96, 104, 134, 138, 159–63, 165–166, 170, 172–73, 176, 178–80, 187, 193, 196–97, 210–11, 213, 217, 263–66, 271, 273, 275–76, 278–82, 284, 311
Kharijism, Kharijite 10, 13–15
kidnapping 4, 5, 24–26, 29, 176, 191, 209, 211, 236, 245, 251, 281–82
Kukah, Bishop Matthew Hassan 16, 121

M

Maiduguri xi, xv, xxii, 4, 6, 8, 13, 20, 22, 23–24, 27–29, 31, 36, 40, 62, 66,

132–34, 137–38, 145, 150, 158–60, 165, 171–72, 176–77, 181, 185, 187, 195–98, 200–201, 222, 230, 233, 235, 237, 244, 249–50, 252, 255, 259, 271, 275–82, 299
Maitatsine 47, 52, 81, 91, 148–49, 162, 179, 214, 217, 219, 234, 237, 241–42
Mali xv, xvii, xx, 3–4, 26, 161, 176–77, 181, 202, 208–209, 212, 220–22, 246, 251, 281–82, 305
Mandara Mountains 7, 162, 276
Mecca 8, 17, 57–58, 161, 173, 207, 231
Middle Belt xx, 107, 119, 124, 126, 160, 206, 213, 255, 261
Muslim Brothers 155, 174, 308–309

N

National Party of Nigeria (NPN) 174
Niger Delta xv, 42, 114, 137, 148, 156, 193, 243
Niger Republic 7, 271
Northern Elements Progressive Union (NEPU) 170, 173–74
Northern People's Congress (NPC) 107, 111, 173

O

Obasanjo, Olusegun 34, 40, 50, 63, 116, 160, 215, 278, 284
Operation Flush 20, 195, 215, 233
Oritsejafor, Pastor Ayo (CAN President) 115, 117, 157

P

Pentecostal 101, 103, 115–17, 121, 125
People's Democratic Party (PDP) 41, 169–70, 174, 306, 307
People's Redemption Party (PRP) 174
police xvii, 5, 7, 23–24, 28, 55, 93, 128, 133–34, 138, 140–43, 145, 149, 158–59, 166, 171, 178–80, 184, 187, 190–91, 194–96, 200, 207, 209, 215–18, 224, 227, 231–34, 242, 246, 250, 253–58, 261, 267, 270–71, 275–81, 304
prison 4, 7–8, 20–21, 28, 49, 166, 189, 238, 256, 276–77, 309

Q

Qadiriyya xv, 6, 39, 53, 159, 172–73
Qaqa, Abul 24, 56, 63–65, 190, 280

S

Salafist xii, 4, 25, 34, 38, 45, 186, 204, 210
Saudi Arabia 3–4, 7–8, 27, 38, 47, 63, 162, 190, 192, 209, 276, 304
school 5–6, 24, 38, 46, 53–54, 56, 63, 76–78, 80–84, 87–91, 95–96, 133, 147, 150, 171, 177, 189, 195, 250–51, 258, 275, 300, 304–305, 311, 313
Shagari, Shehu 35, 174, 178, 280
Shariah xiv, xvi, xix, 9–11, 14–15, 18, 30, 33–38, 40, 42–43, 45, 48–51, 54–63, 65, 68–69, 100, 102, 105–106, 119–20, 137, 155, 157–58, 160, 162–63, 166–67, 169, 172–73, 175, 177–78, 186, 193, 210, 263, 275, 286, 288–90, 292–93, 298–302, 308
Shekau, Abubakar ix, xvii, 20, 33, 46–47, 52, 54, 61, 64, 69, 92, 123, 155, 160–61, 176, 187–88, 190, 196, 206–207, 211–12, 234–35, 251–53, 277, 280–81, 283–84
Sherriff, Ali Modu 136
Sokoto 5–6, 17, 24, 30–31, 37, 51, 55, 59, 63, 65–66, 68, 78, 95, 107, 110, 114, 116, 119, 121, 159–60, 165, 173–74, 177–78, 191, 211, 216, 221, 263–66, 280, 282
Sudan viii, xvii, 25, 55, 104, 155, 160, 173–75, 179–81, 187, 209–210, 220, 285, 296–97, 306–309
Sufi 6, 39, 47, 56, 93, 158–59, 162, 172, 174, 176, 213
suicide attack 165, 199, 207, 234, 279–80, 284

T

taghut (idolatry) 10–11, 14, 168
Taleban, Taliban xv, 6, 38, 132, 148, 151, 158, 159, 161–62, 185, 190, 194, 233
Taymiyyah, Ahmad Ibn 9–10, 17, 20, 28
Tijaniyya xv, 6, 34, 38–39, 43, 45–47, 56, 159, 172–74, 213
Timbuktu 161, 209, 220

U

ulama (islamic cleric) 4, 10, 14–15, 24, 51, 63, 93, 110–11, 165, 172, 180
ummah xix, 37, 53, 55, 110–11, 167, 175, 211, 293
United Nations (UN) xx, 5, 91, 95, 126, 158, 165, 196, 200, 203, 207–208, 216, 220, 234, 271, 278, 281, 283

W

Wahhabi 8, 10, 18, 27, 44, 161, 172, 213, 249, 251, 273

Y

yan daba 90, 170, 172, 193
Yar'Adua, Umar 143–145, 148, 152
Yobe vii, xv, xvii, xviii, xx, 6–7, 25, 27, 29, 33, 35, 39–40, 42–43, 47–48, 54, 58, 60, 62, 132–34, 158–59, 161, 170–71, 187, 192–97, 200, 219, 224, 227, 231–35, 244, 248, 250, 254, 257–58, 263–66, 273, 275–76, 278–79, 282–83

Yusuf, Mohammed xv–xviii, xxi, 3–4, 6–16, 18–20, 27–28, 33, 40, 52, 109, 155–62, 164–71, 176–78, 184–85, 187, 189–90, 193–96, 210, 230–31, 234, 248–49, 253, 257, 270–72, 275–76, 278, 298
Yusufiyya 7–10, 66, 132–33, 185, 192–93, 231. *See* Boko Haram

Z

Zaid, Sheikh Bakr Ibn Abdallah Abu 9, 11–12
Zakzaky, Ibrahim 18, 57, 162, 166
Zamfara 18, 34–35, 50, 57, 61, 65, 69, 169
Zaria iv, 30–31, 63, 101, 104, 123, 149, 172, 187, 216, 270, 280

www.ingramcontent.com/pod-product-compliance
Lightning Source LLC
Chambersburg PA
CBHW030734250426
43671CB00035B/314